In the name of God,

Sayyid Quṭb

IN THE SHADE OF THE QUR'ĀN

Fī Ẓilāl al-Qur'ān

VOLUME XII

SŪRAHS 21–25

Al-Anbiyā' – Al-Furqān

Translated and Edited by
Adil Salahi

THE ISLAMIC FOUNDATION
AND
ISLAMONLINE.NET

Published by

THE ISLAMIC FOUNDATION,

Markfield Conference Centre,
Ratby Lane, Markfield, Leicestershire LE67 9SY, United Kingdom
Tel: (01530) 244944, Fax: (01530) 244946
E-mail: i.foundation@islamic-foundation.org.uk
Website: www.islamic-foundation.org.uk

Quran House, PO Box 30611, Nairobi, Kenya

PMB 3193, Kano, Nigeria

ISLAMONLINE.NET,
PO Box 22212, Doha, Qatar
E-mail: webmaster@islam-online.net
Website: www.islamonline.net

British Library Cataloguing-in-Publication Data
Qutb, Sayyid, 1903–1966
In the shade of the Qur'an, Vol. 12: Surahs 21–25
1. Koran – Commentaries
I. Title
II. Salahi, M.A.
III. Islamic Foundation (Great Britain)
297.1'229

ISBN 0 86037 505 6
ISBN 0 86037 500 5 pbk

Typeset by: N.A.Qaddoura
Cover design by: Imtiaze A. Manjra
Printed and bound in England by: Antony Rowe Ltd, Chippenham, Wiltshire

Contents

Transliteration Table

Arabic Consonants

Initial, unexpressed medial and final:

ء	ʾ	د	d	ض	ḍ	ك	k
ب	b	ذ	dh	ط	ṭ	ل	l
ت	t	ر	r	ظ	ẓ	م	m
ث	th	ز	z	ع	ʿ	ن	n
ج	j	س	s	غ	gh	هـ	h
ح	ḥ	ش	sh	ف	f	و	w
خ	kh	ص	ṣ	ق	q	ي	y

Vowels, diphthongs, etc.

Short:	ـَ a	ـِ i	ـُ u
Long:	ـَا ā	ـِي ī	ـُو ū
Diphthongs:		ـَوْ aw	
		ـَىْ ay	

Sayyid Quṭb and the Islamic Revival

"At the end of the nineteenth century, a call for Muslims to unite was heard throughout the Muslim world. This was the start of Islamic revival in the modern era. That call was launched by Jamāl al-Dīn al-Afghānī." Thus did Sayyid Quṭb explain to me the different stages of the advocacy of Islamic revival. This occurred during my two visits with him in his summer apartment in Ras al-Barr in September 1964. "Al-Afghānī hoped to start a campaign of mass awareness among all Muslim peoples so that they would realize that the only way for them to preserve their identity and regain their status as a force on the world stage was through their unity. The only bond that could unite them, despite being of many races speaking a wide variety of languages, was their faith.

"Soon it was clear that such a call could not achieve the desired results. The Muslim masses throughout the world might dearly wish to unite, but their unity could not be brought about by writings and speeches alone. They needed a leadership committed to regaining the Islamic identity and power. It was left to al-Afghānī's friend and successor, Imām Muḥammad 'Abdū, to try to meet this requirement. He started a group of leading figures in society, some of whom were politicians while others belonged to all manner of professions. They all thought very highly of him and what he advocated. To them he was a great teacher for whom they had much respect, and they loved the ideals he presented.

"A different flaw was soon apparent in this attempt at Islamic revival. The élite cannot achieve real social change, even though they may be able to formulate a programme for such change, unless they are supported by a large section of the people whom are committed to the same goals. Hence, it was necessary to initiate revivalist advocacy at the popular level in order to form a nucleus of mass support for the return of Islam into people's lives after it had been marginalized by occupying powers. It was to recruit such public support and ensure such mass following that the Muslim Brotherhood was started by Ḥasan al-Bannā.

"Now we realize that even with such mass support, there remains a flaw in our strategy. It is not enough to raise popular support on the basis of an emotional commitment to Islam. Once the emotions subside, the commitment evaporates. Therefore, commitment must be based on a proper understanding of Islam, its beliefs, concepts, aims, and what it requires of its followers. This is what we are now aiming for through a comprehensive programme of study."

Such was Sayyid Quṭb's analysis of the strategy adopted by the Islamic revivalist movement and the stages it went through. He did not blame any of the early advocates for not having recognized the flaws that delayed a full revival. On the contrary he praised them for their sincerity and effort. It was not possible for them to anticipate what was to come about through active involvement.

We talked at length on the study programme that he wanted to be pursued by all members of the Muslim Brotherhood throughout the world. It was indeed a programme for all who were ready to commit themselves to Islamic revival, wherever they might happen to be. The programme, which would take an average member two years to complete, concentrated on understanding the basic principles of the Islamic faith and how they are to be implemented in life. A main focal point was the concept of God's Oneness and how this can remain pure in a person's understanding so as to shine through his daily actions and colour all his activities. This did not mean going into theology or philosophical debate; rather, it meant focusing on how Muslims should conduct their lives guided by their belief in God's Oneness.

A correlative of this was a proper approach to the Qur'ān. He wondered: "If Muslims' approach to the Qur'ān today was the same as that of the Prophet's Companions, would Arabic radio broadcasts coming out of Tel Aviv, London and Washington start every day with a Qur'ānic recitation? The fact that they do is clear evidence that the Qur'ān does not give us the same message it gave to early Muslims. This is not the fault of the Qur'ān, because its message is clear for all to understand. The fault is with us, because we now look at the Qur'ān as something beautiful, to be recited by those who have melodious voices and who deliver their recitation enchantingly and tunefully. The Qur'ān is God's message which He bestowed from on high so that it regulates human life and produces a better and superior human society in which the top values are those of freedom, justice, right, equality and belief in God."

Muslims in the twentieth century were certainly backward but only because they did not properly understand the Qur'ān. They were weak because they were oblivious of their main source of strength, namely, the Qur'ān. The only way for Muslims to rid themselves of their ignorance, weakness and backwardness was to adopt a proper approach to the Qur'ān which sought to implement it, rather than to enjoy the beauty of its style or the enchantments of its reciters. This was Sayyid Quṭb's purpose behind writing *In the Shade of the Qur'ān*. He wanted to give modern readers a glimpse of how the Prophet's Companions understood the Qur'ān, so that they would understand why the Qur'ān transformed them into a great nation that gave light and guidance to the whole world for many generations, and why it was not currently doing the same. It is the present generation of Muslims that should take clear steps to bring its approach to the Qur'ān in line with that of the Prophet's Companions so that we enjoy the same results they did.

Sayyid Quṭb hammers on this point throughout his monumental work, *In the Shade of the Qur'ān*. He never tires of stressing it when he discusses Makkan *sūrahs* which are principally devoted to issues of faith. He might be accused of repetitiveness at times, but he was aware that few readers would methodically go through these many volumes. Rather, readers might read separate *sūrahs* at different times, and since the main issues are discussed throughout the Qur'ān in different ways, he explained these issues each time they occurred.

Thus the Qur'ān represents the most important component of the comprehensive programme of study Sayyid Quṭb wanted to see pursued. Needless to say, such study of the Qur'ān would strengthen and enhance people's understanding of the basic Islamic beliefs and what they mean in practical life. A proper approach to the Qur'ān and a good understanding of it are essential to everyone who wishes to join the ranks of advocates of Islam. By contrast, the details of Islamic law, or *Fiqh*, were not of paramount importance. A short manual that outlines the basic rules pertaining to worship and conduct should be enough for most people. There should however be scholars who undertake such studies in depth, but the majority of advocates do not require such insight.

Yet to what would such a programme of study lead? Are we looking at a preparatory period that would usher in a different strategy that aimed to take power, oust governments and replace regimes? Would it bring about the transformation that all Islamic movements and groups aspire to, viz. the entire set-up in society and state being in line with Islam?

To start with, taking power was far removed from Sayyid Quṭb's short and medium term aspirations. This is clear throughout his writings. Advocates of Islam, he wrote, must free themselves of any personal interest or gain that they could achieve through their work for Islam. They must look for no prizes whatsoever, not even the victory of Islam through their own work. It would be enough for them that they had been chosen by God to be the advocates of the Islamic message, an honour so great that it ensured a happiness they could not otherwise achieve. Their task was to work tirelessly for Islam, and leave matters to God. He would determine what to do with them and their mission. He would decide to bring about the victory of Islam at a time He, in His infinite wisdom, knew to be right.

To Sayyid Quṭb, advocating the Islamic message transcended generations. When we work for Islam, we are unlike a political party that measures success and failure in terms of being in government or opposition. Our ultimate success is to make society fully understand the Islamic message and be willing to implement it. The absence of such a full understanding of Islam has been the main cause of all the social ills that Muslim countries have suffered from. Hence, our efforts should aim at regaining such an understanding of Islam.

This is something that cannot be achieved in the short term. There can be no set programme with steps and stages marked out in advance. All we can say is that our target is clear and that our method has been outlined for us by the Prophet who never deviated from his task of delivering God's message and explaining it to all people. He went through a very difficult thirteen years in Makkah before establishing his state in Madinah. Our task could take us any number of years until we establish a critical mass of Islamic advocates, with full understanding and commitment. When they demonstrate to God that they are worthy of the trust, He will give them power in the land to implement Islam. This is the meaning of His promise: "*God has promised those of you who believe and do good deeds that, of a certainty, He will cause them to accede to power on earth, in the same way as He caused those who lived before them to accede to it; and that, of a certainty, He will firmly establish for them the religion which He has chosen for them; and that, of a certainty, He will cause their erstwhile state of fear to be replaced by a state of security. They will thus worship Me alone and associate with Me no partners whatsoever. Those who, after this, choose to disbelieve are indeed wicked.*" (24: 55)

Sayyid Quṭb repeatedly stressed that advocates of Islam must never hasten the results of their efforts. It may be easy to take power in a certain country and declare an Islamic government, but if those who come into power under the name of Islam do not have a clear and accurate understanding of it, and do not have a solid base of Muslims equipped with such understanding who will ensure that such government continues to abide by Islam, implement its principles, uphold its values and never deviate from its requirements to ensure justice, right, equality and freedom for all people, taking power will not serve the interests of Islam or Muslims. They may mean well, but their lack of understanding will cause them to err, and their errors will be committed in the name of Islam. Thus, Islam will be seen through their errors, which may be monumental.

At the time when Sayyid Quṭb was writing *In the Shade of the Qur'ān* Egypt was going through a process called the Socialist

Transformation. It allied itself very closely with the Soviet Union. Indeed, the communists were given a considerable measure of freedom to operate in the country. Yet during our discussion, he said to me: "I have no fear that Egypt will become communist. The US will ensure that this will not happen. What I fear for Egypt is something much more serious. My worst fear is that when this regime goes, as it certainly will, it will be replaced by a weak government that raises Islamic slogans devoid of real substance. Its weakness will make it commit serious errors of policy and strategy that will lead to much suffering, and the blame for all this will be laid at Islam's doorstep. This could lead to a serious setback for revivalist efforts."

Things did not develop in that fashion, but blaming Islam and its advocates for the social ills that result from un-Islamic policies takes place all the time. Many Muslim countries have suffered under dictatorial regimes once they emerged from colonial rule. Both colonial and dictatorial rule are hostile to Islam, because Islam stands for the freedom of all mankind. Yet under both types Islam has been consistently blamed for practically every ill in society and advocates of Islamic revival have been suppressed under every tyrannical regime. Regimes which tried to appear in an Islamic guise have not differed much from their secular counterparts. Little did they realize that dictatorship is diametrically opposed to Islam.

In addition there has been a long and sustained campaign to paint Islam as extremist, unwilling to tolerate others, and as being dictatorial in its approach. This is manifested in what is now termed Islamophobia, a phenomenon that paints Islam as actively hostile to all that differs with its beliefs, values and practices. Similarly absurd is the attempt to trace such extremism to Sayyid Quṭb and his writings. Both assertions are false. God describes the Muslim community as a 'middle-of-the-road' community. (2: 143) Indeed it is God who declares that no compulsion is admissible in religion. (2: 256)

Sayyid Quṭb never espoused extremism. How could he when he enjoyed such a long and close relationship with the Qur'ān? It is certainly true that Sayyid Quṭb was profoundly committed to Islam; he made no secret of this, and was justly proud of it. His commitment was total. He declared in his last book *Milestones*: "There is nothing in Islam that will cause us any shame or embarrassment. There is nothing that we may feel any need to present to others in a roundabout way."

Sayyid Quṭb wrote at a time when most Muslim countries were still searching for their identity. Many were just emerging from colonial rule; many were starting life as new entities that had never had an independent existence before. He felt that the only identity they should have was Islamic. Hence, he wrote powerfully, drumming up the Islamic sense. His writings gave the advocates of Islamic revival a vision of a future in which Islam regains its leading role on the world stage. But nothing of this was based on any fanatical ideas. He dwelt at length on the role of Muslim advocates. They were to present Islam to all people as God's final message, the faith He has chosen for mankind, the constitution that should regulate their life, the code that must set their moral values and ensure their total happiness. When they had done this, even though they might have had to withstand a determined onslaught from hostile forces, their task was complete and they stood to receive their reward. Such reward would not entail political power, or amassing material wealth of any sort. Instead, their reward would be given to them by God on the Day of Judgement. They were not to look for any other reward, no matter how great the sacrifices they were called on to make in this life. To make this point clear, Sayyid Quṭb often cited the example of the *Anṣār* when they gave their pledges of support to the Prophet. On that occasion they were made aware that such pledges committed them to fight against superior forces, suffer much brutality, and render enormous sacrifices in terms of their lives and property. Expressing their awareness of all this, they asked the Prophet: "What will be our reward if we fulfil our commitment?" His answer was one word: "Paradise." They offered the Prophet their pledges, declaring that they would never renege on this bargain.

He presented this as a deal into which the advocates of Islam enter with God. In fact, this is how the Qur'ān describes it: a deal with all those who accepted the divine faith throughout all stages of history. It applied to Jews, Christians and the followers of other prophets in the past, and it applies to Muslims in the present and future: "*God has bought of the believers their lives and their property, promising them heaven in return: they fight for the cause of God, kill and be killed. This is a true promise which He has made binding on Himself in the Torah, the Gospel and the Qur'ān. Who is more true to his promise than God? Rejoice, then, in the bargain you have made with Him. That is the supreme triumph.*" (9: 111)

To Sayyid Quṭb, winning power and being in government was not a priority for advocates of Islam. It was welcome when it came about, but it should never be sought. It would be useful when those who assume power are worthy of the trust of Islamic advocacy, but they can still function and fulfil their task without it. Their bargain with God continues to be valid either way. Hence, they must never precipitate events. He repeatedly stated that once Islamic advocates have fulfilled their task of advocacy to the best of their ability their mission is over. God will do with them and with their message whatever He wills. It is not for them to determine what this should be.

Thus, his whole vision was based on the need to have a complete and accurate understanding of Islam, advocating its message and calling on people to adopt it. And the reason for such advocacy is clearly spelled out in *Milestones* as: "We only call on people to accept Islam because we love them and wish them well, no matter how they try to cause us harm. Such is the attitude of a Muslim advocate and such are his motives." He was under no illusion that people would readily accept Islam's message. Never in history was the divine faith accepted by any community without a struggle. But the struggle was always against aggression by the unbelievers who sought to suppress the call of faith in God's Oneness. Qur'ānic accounts of earlier prophets confirmed this, as did the Prophet's history with his own people, as also the experience of the modern revivalist movement, of which his own experience was a part. Yet such a struggle, and the sacrifices involved, are part of what an advocate of Islam is called upon to give. He expects nothing in this world in return. His reward is in the hereafter.

Can this be classified as extremism? Even Sayyid Quṭb's jailers, torturers and executioners did not accuse him of this. They accused him of trying to overthrow the Egyptian government, but that charge was absurd. They could not produce one single plausible piece of evidence to prove it. They concocted the charges, wrote the confessions, and presented them in a special military tribunal that was nothing short of a travesty of justice.

Today, he is blamed by some writers for the excesses of some fringe groups, some of which do not even mention him in their discourse. Others pay homage to Sayyid Quṭb and may present themselves as following his line. Their claims, do not, however, stand up to any careful scrutiny. When he was approached to assume the leadership of the new generation of Muslim Brotherhood followers, after his release from ten years imprisonment, he only accepted after they agreed to his ideas. These required them to abandon any thought of seeking revenge for the years of persecution suffered by the organization, as well as any scheme to overthrow the government. Instead, they were to concentrate on pursuing his study programme to acquire an accurate understanding of Islam, and to advocate Islam to the best of their ability.

If the world today is really serious about combating extremism, it should first of all undertake a thorough study of its causes. These will not take long to identify. The Muslim world has suffered a long period of injustice at the hands of Western imperialists, Israeli Zionists, tyrannical regimes, and more recently, US hegemony and neo-colonialism. It is injustice that breeds the seeds of extremism as the victims look for ways to redress the wrongs they suffer. In their weakness, such victims try to level some blows against their persecutors. This opens the way to an ill-balanced confrontation in which the perpetrators of injustice use their superior firepower to smash those who rise against their injustice. This leads to the vicious circle the world witnesses today. There are only two ways out: the first is to compound the injustice by annihilating its opponents. If such victory is achieved, it will only be temporary until a new generation of victims begin to group and rebel again.

The other way out is to restore justice. Unfortunately, it is not in the nature of things that the perpetrators of injustice would ever do so, not even under Western democracies. We need only consider the attitude of such democracies to the problem of Palestine, and their continued support of the aggression of the Zionist state. Hence, the restoration of justice in our world will only be accomplished under Islam. This may take many years to come about, but, according to Sayyid Quṭb, it certainly will. However, it needs a generation of advocates who are equipped with a clear, accurate and thorough understanding of Islam and its role in human life.

London **Adil Salahi**
Jumādā al-Ūlā 1425 H
June 2005

SŪRAH 21

Al-Anbiyā'

(The Prophets)

Prologue

Revealed in Makkah, this *sūrah*, as with all other parts of the Qur'ān revealed in that period, deals with the issue of faith. It does so under three main headings: namely, God's oneness, His message, and mankind's resurrection.

The flow of the *sūrah* deals with its subject matter, referring to a number of great universal phenomena and linking them with faith. The point of this is that faith is part of the universal structure, and the same phenomena apply to it. It illustrates the truth which is at the heart of the heavens and the earth and their constitution. It reflects the seriousness with which their affairs are conducted. It is neither a matter of play nor a question of falsehood, in the same way as the universe was not created for play, nor was any element of falsehood mixed with its creation: "*We have not created the heavens and the earth and all that is between them in mere idle play.*" (Verse 16)

The *sūrah* concentrates people's eyes, hearts and minds on the universe and its great phenomena: the heavens and the earth, mountains and valleys, night and day, sun and moon. It draws their attention to the unity of the laws that govern all these and conduct their affairs, and how this unity provides powerful evidence of the unity of the Creator who owns this vast universe. No partner has He in His kingdom, in the same way as He has no partner in its creation: "*Had there been in heaven or on earth any deities other than God, both would surely have fallen into ruin!*" (Verse 22)

The *sūrah* also draws our attention to the unity of the phenomena which govern life on earth and the unity of the source of life: "*We have made out of water every living thing.*" (Verse 30) All living things will face the same end: "*Every soul shall taste death.*" (Verse 35) They will then arrive at the same destiny: "*To Us you all must return.*" (Verse 35)

Faith is closely linked to these major universal phenomena. It is the same faith, even though many messengers have been sent to convey it to people: "*Before your time We never sent a messenger without having revealed to him that there is no deity other than Me. Therefore, you shall worship Me alone.*" (Verse 25) It is God's will that all messengers were human beings: "*Before your time, We never sent [as Our messengers] any but men whom We inspired.*" (Verse 7)

Just like faith is closely linked to major universal phenomena, the same applies to what the advocates of faith may encounter in this world. The rule that never fails is that the truth will ultimately triumph and falsehood will be wiped out, because the truth is a universal reality and its victory is a divine law: "*We hurl the truth against falsehood, and it crushes the latter, and behold, it withers away.*" (Verse 18) By the same token, the wrongdoers who deny the truth are bound to be destroyed, but God will save His messengers and the believers: "*We fulfilled Our promise to them, and We saved them and all whom We willed [to save], and We destroyed those who transgressed beyond bounds.*" (Verse 9) God's devoted servants are the eventual heirs of the earth: "*We wrote in the Psalms, after the Reminder [given to Moses] that 'the righteous among My servants shall inherit the earth'.*" (Verse 105)

The *sūrah* then presents a quick review of the single community that has followed God's messengers. It pauses long to reflect on the stories of Abraham, David and Solomon, but makes only brief references to Noah, Moses, Aaron, Lot, Ishmael, Idrīs, Dhu'l-Kifl, Jonah, Zachariah, John and Jesus, (peace be upon them all). Some of the issues, already tackled in the *sūrah* as general rules and phenomena, are reflected again in this review in the form of practical events encountered by God's messengers and their followers.

The flow of the *sūrah* also includes some scenes of the Day of Judgement in which we find the same meanings and concepts reflected again as part of the reality of that great day.

We see, then, how varying cadences employed in the *sūrah* serve the same purpose of alerting the human mind so that it recognizes the truth of the faith preached by the last of God's messengers. For people cannot receive the message while indulging in play, turning away and paying little heed to it, as they are described in the opening verses: "*Closer to people draws their reckoning, yet they continue to blithely turn away. Whenever there comes to them any new reminder from their Lord, they listen to it but take it in jest; their hearts set on pleasure.*" (Verses 1–3)

This message of Islam is both true and serious, in the same way as this universe is true and serious. Therefore, there may be no jest and play in receiving God's message, as in making demands for miraculous evidence. Evidence of a miraculous nature is available everywhere in the universe and its operative phenomena. It all confirms that God is the only creator who has power over all things, and that the message comes from Him alone.

As for its mode of expression and its rhythm, the *sūrah* employs factual statements which best suit its subject matter and ambience. This is clearly apparent when we compare its style with that employed in the preceding two *sūrahs*, *Maryam* and *Ṭā Hā*. In both these, the rhythm is soft, and hence more suited to their overall atmosphere. Here the rhythm is stronger, to fit its message. This is even clearer when we look at the way the story of the Prophet Abraham is related in *Maryam* and in this *sūrah*. In the former, the episode is given in the form of an expansive dialogue between Abraham and his father, whereas here we see Abraham's destruction of the idols worshipped by his people, and his subsequently being thrown in the fire. Thus, the subject matter, the style and the cadence achieve complete harmony in both instances.

This *sūrah* flows in four distinctive rounds. The first starts with a powerful opening that creates strong beats to shake people's hearts and alert them to the danger they will shortly face, while they remain oblivious to it: "*Closer to people draws their reckoning, yet they continue to blithely turn away.*" (Verse 1) This is followed by a scene of the fate suffered by earlier communities for turning their backs on God's messages, leading a life of wrongdoing: "*How many a community that persisted in evil-doing have We dashed into fragments, and raised another people in their stead?*" (Verse 11) Both the message of Islam and the system that governs the universe are based on truth and seriousness, which are here linked to the faith based on God's oneness and to the phenomena operating in the universe. The *sūrah* also links all this with the unity of the Creator who is in control of all things, the unity of the divine message and faith, and the unity of the source of life, its end and destiny.

The second round examines the unbelievers who hurled ridicule at God's Messenger while the matter he spoke to them about was very serious. Everything around them calls for close attention and alertness. They call for their punishment to be hastened, when it is close at hand. At this point the *sūrah* portrays a scene of the Day of Judgement, drawing their attention to what befell those before them who ridiculed God's messengers and their messages. It tells them very clearly that they enjoy no protection against God's punishment. It calls on them to reflect on God's power as He shrinks the earth from its edges, reducing its area. Should they so reflect, they may wake up to what awaits them after having long been oblivious to it.

This round concludes with a directive to the Prophet to outline his task: "*Say: I do but warn you on the strength of divine revelation!*" (Verse 45) He also alerts them to the danger to which they expose themselves by being so oblivious: "*But the deaf cannot hear this call, however often they are warned.*" (Verse 45) The result is that they will continue to pay no attention to what is presented to them until they are called to account on the Day of Judgement.

The third round provides a review of the single community of believers who followed God's prophets. This review reflects the unity of the message and the faith. It also portrays the grace God bestows on His righteous servants and His punishment of those who deny the truth.

In the fourth and final round, everyone's eventual destiny is described in an eventful scene of the Day of Judgement. The *sūrah* closes with a strong beat, a clear warning before leaving the unbelievers to their inevitable doom.

I

Clear Solid Evidence

Al-Anbiyā' (The Prophets)

In the Name of God, the Merciful, the Beneficent

Closer to people draws their reckoning, yet they continue to blithely turn away. (1)

Whenever there comes to them any new reminder from their Lord, they listen to it but take it in jest; (2)

their hearts set on pleasure. Yet, concealing their inner thoughts, the wrongdoers say to one another: 'Is this man anything but a human being like yourselves? Will you, then, follow his sorcery with your eyes open?' (3)

He says: 'My Lord knows whatever is spoken in heaven and earth. He is the One who hears all and knows all.' (4)

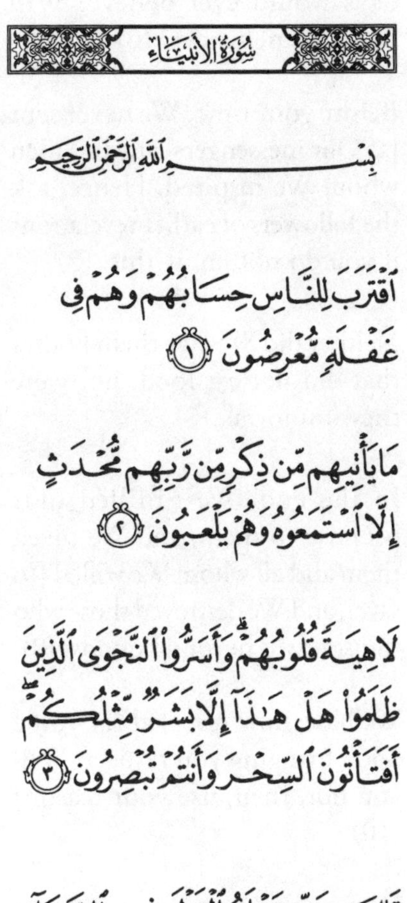
سورة الأنبياء

بسم الله الرحمن الرحيم

اقترب للناس حسابهم وهم في
غفلة معرضون ﴿١﴾

ما يأتيهم من ذكر من ربهم محدث
إلا استمعوه وهم يلعبون ﴿٢﴾

لاهية قلوبهم وأسروا النجوى الذين
ظلموا هل هذا إلا بشر مثلكم
أفتأتون السحر وأنتم تبصرون ﴿٣﴾

قال ربي يعلم القول في السماء
والأرض وهو السميع العليم ﴿٤﴾

بَلْ قَالُوٓا۟ أَضْغَٰثُ أَحْلَٰمٍۭ بَلِ ٱفْتَرَىٰهُ
بَلْ هُوَ شَاعِرٌ فَلْيَأْتِنَا بِـَٔايَةٍ كَمَآ أُرْسِلَ
ٱلْأَوَّلُونَ ﴿٥﴾

'Nay,' they say, 'it is but a medley of dreams!' – 'Nay, he has invented it himself!' – 'Nay, he is only a poet!' – 'Let him, then, bring us some sign, as the prophets of old were sent with.' (5)

مَآ ءَامَنَتْ قَبْلَهُم مِّن قَرْيَةٍ أَهْلَكْنَٰهَآ
أَفَهُمْ يُؤْمِنُونَ ﴿٦﴾

Not one of the communities whom We destroyed in bygone days would ever believe. Will these, then, believe? (6)

وَمَآ أَرْسَلْنَا قَبْلَكَ إِلَّا رِجَالًا نُّوحِىٓ
إِلَيْهِمْ فَسْـَٔلُوٓا۟ أَهْلَ ٱلذِّكْرِ إِن كُنتُمْ
لَا تَعْلَمُونَ ﴿٧﴾

Before your time, We never sent [as Our messengers] any but men whom We inspired. Hence, ask the followers of earlier revelations if you do not know this. (7)

وَمَا جَعَلْنَٰهُمْ جَسَدًا لَّا يَأْكُلُونَ
ٱلطَّعَامَ وَمَا كَانُوا۟ خَٰلِدِينَ ﴿٨﴾

Neither did We give them bodies that did not eat food, nor were they immortal. (8)

ثُمَّ صَدَقْنَٰهُمُ ٱلْوَعْدَ فَأَنجَيْنَٰهُمْ وَمَن
نَّشَآءُ وَأَهْلَكْنَا ٱلْمُسْرِفِينَ ﴿٩﴾

In the end, We fulfilled Our promise to them, and We saved them and all whom We willed [to save], and We destroyed those who transgressed beyond bounds. (9)

لَقَدْ أَنزَلْنَآ إِلَيْكُمْ كِتَٰبًا فِيهِ ذِكْرُكُمْ
أَفَلَا تَعْقِلُونَ ﴿١٠﴾

We have now revealed for you a book bringing you respect. Will you not, then, use your reason? (10)

وَكَمْ قَصَمْنَا مِن قَرْيَةٍ كَانَتْ ظَالِمَةً
وَأَنشَأْنَا بَعْدَهَا قَوْمًا ءَاخَرِينَ ﴿١١﴾

How many a community that persisted in evil-doing have We dashed into fragments, and raised another people in their stead? (11)

And as soon as they began to feel Our might they took to their heels and fled. (12)

فَلَمَّآ أَحَسُّواْ بَأۡسَنَآ إِذَا هُم مِّنۡهَا
يَرۡكُضُونَ ١٢

Do not run away. Return to all your comforts and to your dwellings, so that you might be called to account. (13)

لَا تَرۡكُضُواْ وَٱرۡجِعُوٓاْ إِلَىٰ مَآ أُتۡرِفۡتُمۡ فِيهِ
وَمَسَٰكِنِكُمۡ لَعَلَّكُمۡ تُسۡـَٔلُونَ ١٣

They said: 'Woe betide us! We were indeed wrongdoers!' (14)

قَالُواْ يَٰوَيۡلَنَآ إِنَّا كُنَّا ظَٰلِمِينَ ١٤

And that cry of theirs did not cease until We caused them to become like a field mown down, still and silent as ashes. (15)

فَمَا زَالَت تِّلۡكَ دَعۡوَىٰهُمۡ حَتَّىٰ
جَعَلۡنَٰهُمۡ حَصِيدًا خَٰمِدِينَ ١٥

We have not created the heavens and the earth and all that is between them in mere idle play. (16)

وَمَا خَلَقۡنَا ٱلسَّمَآءَ وَٱلۡأَرۡضَ
وَمَا بَيۡنَهُمَا لَٰعِبِينَ ١٦

Had We willed to indulge in a pastime, We would indeed have found one near at hand; if ever We were to do so! (17)

لَوۡ أَرَدۡنَآ أَن نَّتَّخِذَ لَهۡوٗا لَّٱتَّخَذۡنَٰهُ مِن
لَّدُنَّآ إِن كُنَّا فَٰعِلِينَ ١٧

Nay, but We hurl the truth against falsehood, and it crushes the latter, and behold, it withers away. But woe to you for all your false claims. (18)

بَلۡ نَقۡذِفُ بِٱلۡحَقِّ عَلَى ٱلۡبَٰطِلِ
فَيَدۡمَغُهُۥ فَإِذَا هُوَ زَاهِقٞۚ وَلَكُمُ
ٱلۡوَيۡلُ مِمَّا تَصِفُونَ ١٨

To Him belong all those who are in the heavens and on earth. Those that are with Him are never too proud to worship Him and never grow weary of that. (19)

وَلَهُۥ مَن فِى ٱلسَّمَٰوَٰتِ وَٱلْأَرْضِ ۚ وَمَنْ عِندَهُۥ لَا يَسْتَكْبِرُونَ عَنْ عِبَادَتِهِۦ وَلَا يَسْتَحْسِرُونَ ﴿١٩﴾

They extol His limitless glory by night and day, tirelessly. (20)

يُسَبِّحُونَ ٱلَّيْلَ وَٱلنَّهَارَ لَا يَفْتُرُونَ ﴿٢٠﴾

Or have they taken for worship some earthly deities who can restore the dead to life? (21)

أَمِ ٱتَّخَذُوٓا۟ ءَالِهَةً مِّنَ ٱلْأَرْضِ هُمْ يُنشِرُونَ ﴿٢١﴾

Had there been in heaven or on earth any deities other than God, both would surely have fallen into ruin! But limitless in His glory is God, Lord of the Throne, and exalted is He above all that they attribute to Him! (22)

لَوْ كَانَ فِيهِمَآ ءَالِهَةٌ إِلَّا ٱللَّهُ لَفَسَدَتَا ۚ فَسُبْحَٰنَ ٱللَّهِ رَبِّ ٱلْعَرْشِ عَمَّا يَصِفُونَ ﴿٢٢﴾

He cannot be questioned about whatever He does, whereas they shall be questioned. (23)

لَا يُسْـَٔلُ عَمَّا يَفْعَلُ وَهُمْ يُسْـَٔلُونَ ﴿٢٣﴾

Or have they taken for worship some deities besides Him? Say: 'Produce your convincing proof. This is the message of those who are with me and the message of those before me.' But nay, most of them do not know the truth, and so they stubbornly turn away. (24)

أَمِ ٱتَّخَذُوا۟ مِن دُونِهِۦٓ ءَالِهَةً ۖ قُلْ هَاتُوا۟ بُرْهَٰنَكُمْ ۖ هَٰذَا ذِكْرُ مَن مَّعِىَ وَذِكْرُ مَن قَبْلِى ۗ بَلْ أَكْثَرُهُمْ لَا يَعْلَمُونَ ٱلْحَقَّ ۖ فَهُم مُّعْرِضُونَ ﴿٢٤﴾

Before your time We never sent a messenger without having revealed to him that there is no deity other than Me. Therefore, you shall worship Me alone. (25)

وَمَآ أَرۡسَلۡنَا مِن قَبۡلِكَ مِن رَّسُولٍ
إِلَّا نُوحِيٓ إِلَيۡهِ أَنَّهُۥ لَآ إِلَٰهَ إِلَّآ أَنَا۠
فَٱعۡبُدُونِ ٢٥

They say: 'The Most Merciful has taken to Himself a son!' Limitless is He in His glory! No; they are but His honoured servants. (26)

وَقَالُواْ ٱتَّخَذَ ٱلرَّحۡمَٰنُ وَلَدٗاۗ سُبۡحَٰنَهُۥۚ
بَلۡ عِبَادٞ مُّكۡرَمُونَ ٢٦

They do not speak until He has spoken, and they act at His behest. (27)

لَا يَسۡبِقُونَهُۥ بِٱلۡقَوۡلِ وَهُم بِأَمۡرِهِۦ
يَعۡمَلُونَ ٢٧

He knows all that lies before them and all behind them. They do not intercede for any but those whom He has already graced with His goodly acceptance, since they themselves stand in reverent awe of Him. (28)

يَعۡلَمُ مَا بَيۡنَ أَيۡدِيهِمۡ وَمَا خَلۡفَهُمۡ
وَلَا يَشۡفَعُونَ إِلَّا لِمَنِ ٱرۡتَضَىٰ وَهُم
مِّنۡ خَشۡيَتِهِۦ مُشۡفِقُونَ ٢٨

If any of them were to say, 'I am a deity beside Him,' We shall requite him with hell. Thus do We reward the wrongdoers. (29)

وَمَن يَقُلۡ مِنۡهُمۡ إِنِّيٓ إِلَٰهٞ مِّن دُونِهِۦ
فَذَٰلِكَ نَجۡزِيهِ جَهَنَّمَۚ كَذَٰلِكَ
نَجۡزِي ٱلظَّٰلِمِينَ ٢٩

أَوَلَمْ يَرَ ٱلَّذِينَ كَفَرُوٓا۟ أَنَّ ٱلسَّمَٰوَٰتِ
وَٱلْأَرْضَ كَانَتَا رَتْقًا فَفَتَقْنَٰهُمَا ۖ
وَجَعَلْنَا مِنَ ٱلْمَآءِ كُلَّ شَىْءٍ حَىٍّ ۖ
أَفَلَا يُؤْمِنُونَ ﴿٣٠﴾

Are the unbelievers unaware that the heaven and the earth were once one single entity, which We then parted asunder? We have made out of water every living thing. Will they not, then, believe? (30)

وَجَعَلْنَا فِى ٱلْأَرْضِ رَوَٰسِىَ أَن تَمِيدَ
بِهِمْ وَجَعَلْنَا فِيهَا فِجَاجًا سُبُلًا
لَّعَلَّهُمْ يَهْتَدُونَ ﴿٣١﴾

We have also set firm mountains on earth, lest it sway with them, and We have cut out there broad paths, so that they might find their way, (31)

وَجَعَلْنَا ٱلسَّمَآءَ سَقْفًا مَّحْفُوظًا ۖ
وَهُمْ عَنْ ءَايَٰتِهَا مُعْرِضُونَ ﴿٣٢﴾

and We have set up the sky as a well-secured canopy. Yet they stubbornly turn away from all its signs. (32)

وَهُوَ ٱلَّذِى خَلَقَ ٱلَّيْلَ وَٱلنَّهَارَ وَٱلشَّمْسَ
وَٱلْقَمَرَ ۖ كُلٌّ فِى فَلَكٍ يَسْبَحُونَ ﴿٣٣﴾

It is He who has created the night and the day and the sun and the moon: each moves swiftly in its own orbit. (33)

وَمَا جَعَلْنَا لِبَشَرٍ مِّن قَبْلِكَ ٱلْخُلْدَ ۖ
أَفَإِي۟ن مِّتَّ فَهُمُ ٱلْخَٰلِدُونَ ﴿٣٤﴾

Never have We granted life everlasting to any man before you. Should you yourself die, do they, perchance, hope to live forever? (34)

كُلُّ نَفْسٍ ذَآئِقَةُ ٱلْمَوْتِ ۗ وَنَبْلُوكُم بِٱلشَّرِّ
وَٱلْخَيْرِ فِتْنَةً ۖ وَإِلَيْنَا تُرْجَعُونَ ﴿٣٥﴾

Every soul shall taste death. We test you all with evil and good by way of trial. To Us you all must return. (35)

Reckoning Drawing Close

The *sūrah* is distinguished by a very powerful opening that shakes the careless who are preoccupied with the petty concerns of this world while the reckoning draws ever closer to them. Signs and indicators are given to them while they continue to turn their backs on divine guidance. The situation is grave, yet they remain totally unaware of its seriousness. Whenever they receive a new Qur'ānic warning, they respond with ridicule, persisting in their playful negligence. Their hearts can only attend to their own pleasure. It should be pointed out here that in Qur'ānic usage, the term, 'heart', is synonymous with mind as it refers to the faculty of contemplation, reflection and thought. "*Closer to people draws their reckoning, yet they continue to blithely turn away. Whenever there comes to them any new reminder from their Lord, they listen to it but take it in jest; their hearts set on pleasure. Yet, concealing their inner thoughts, the wrongdoers say to one another: 'Is this man anything but a human being like yourselves? Will you, then, follow his sorcery with your eyes open?'*" (Verses 1–3)

This is a picture of hearts that know no seriousness, jesting when the situation is most serious, and trifling with what is sacred. The reminder given to them here originates with 'their Lord', yet they are playful as they listen to it, showing no respect whatsoever. A soul that knows no seriousness, respect or sacredness ends up in a condition of barren triviality which makes it unsuitable for the fulfilment of any task of merit. Its life seems devoid of respect, cheap. A spirit which cares little or nothing for what is held as sacred is sick. Carelessness is the opposite of endurance. The latter is a serious effort indicating strength, while the former indicates insensitivity.

Such people responded inappropriately to Qur'ānic revelations that are meant to be a constitution regulating human life, and form a code for human dealings. They are hence warned of the imminent reckoning, but still they remain oblivious to it. Such people can be seen at all times. Whenever a person's spirit is devoid of seriousness and respect, it ends up in such a sick state that it makes of life a matter of jest, lacking real purpose.

By contrast, the believers received this *sūrah* with a due seriousness that made them care little for this world. In his biographical notes on 'Āmir ibn Rabī'ah, al-Āmidī says that he once received a bedouin guest and was typically very hospitable to him. Some time later, the bedouin called on him after having acquired a plot of land. He said to him, 'The Prophet has given me a valley in a nearby place of the Arab land. I would like to give you a piece of it to be yours to bequeath to your heirs.' 'Āmir said: "I have no need for your gift, because today a sūrah has been revealed which leaves us oblivious to all concerns of this life. It is the sūrah that starts with, '*Closer to people draws their reckoning, yet they continue to blithely turn away.*'"

This is the marked difference between a living heart which interacts with what it receives and a dead one which covers its lifelessness in a shroud of jest and play. The latter type does not respond to reminders because it is devoid of the elements of life.

"*Yet, concealing their inner thoughts,*" they plot among themselves and encourage one another in adopting an attitude that denies God's message. In reference to God's Messenger (peace be upon him), "*the wrongdoers say to one another: 'Is this man anything but a human being like yourselves? Will you, then, follow his sorcery with your eyes open?'*" (Verse 3)

Dead as their hearts were, they could not but be shaken by the Qur'ān. Hence they try to resist its influence with false excuses. They whisper to one another that Muḥammad is a man, and wonder how they could believe a message preached by a human being like themselves. They allege that what he says is plain magic, and ask how they could surrender themselves to sorcery when they have eyes with which to look.

The Prophet is instructed to leave the whole matter between him and the unbelievers to God, making it clear that He knows what they secretly say among themselves. He also informs him of their scheming by which they tried to divert the effect of the Qur'ān on themselves and on other people.

"*He says: My Lord knows whatever is spoken in heaven and earth. He is the One who hears all and knows all.*" (Verse 4) Whatever people may say in private is known to God, because He knows everything that takes place in heaven and earth. When they conspire and scheme, He is fully aware of their scheming. Nothing escapes His knowledge. They were at a loss as to how they should describe the Qur'ān in order to neutralize its appeal. Hence they variously alleged that it was sorcery, a series of confused dreams related by Muḥammad, poetry, or mere fabrication. The Qur'ān reported their claims as they uttered them. They say: "*Nay, it is but a medley of dreams! – Nay, he has invented it himself! – Nay, he is only a poet!*" (Verse 5) They could not agree on any one view or description to explain the magnetism the Qur'ān had on people. None of their allegations or justifications had any value. Hence, they roamed from one claim to another, betraying their puzzlement. Feeling themselves at a terrible loss, they decided to get around the whole question by demanding a miracle similar to those given to some early prophets: "*Let him, then, bring us some sign, as the prophets of old were sent with.*" (Verse 5)

Miraculous signs and events were given in the past, but the communities to which they were shown did not believe as a result. Hence they were destroyed in accordance with God's law which seals the fate of any community which continues to reject the truth after having been given a miraculous sign of it. "*Not one of the communities whom We destroyed in bygone days would ever believe.*" (Verse 6) When stubborn rejection of the truth reaches a point that it continues even after a tangible, physical, miraculous sign is given, then all excuses are invalid. People who continue with such rejection seal their own fate and they are destroyed as a result.

Miracles were given in plenty, but people still rejected the truth, and they were destroyed, one community after another. Is it likely then that those Arabs, similar as they were to earlier communities, would submit to miraculous evidence and accept the truth? "*Will these, then, believe?*" (Verse 6)

The Messengers God Sends

"*Before your time, We never sent [as Our messengers] any but men whom We inspired. Hence, ask the followers of earlier revelations if you do not know this. Neither did We give them bodies that did not eat food, nor were they immortal."* (Verses 7–8) In His infinite wisdom, God chose His messengers from among human beings. They received His revelations and called on people to believe in Him on the basis of such revelations. Those noble messengers of God were men with human bodies. God did not make them of a special type, so as not to eat food. Food is a basic necessity for human survival, and God's messengers, who were human, were not immortal. Such is the law God has set, and if those Arabs were unaware of it, then they should ask the people who received earlier revelations, because they knew earlier prophets.

Moreover, God chose His messengers from among human beings because He wanted them to experience human life. Thus, their own practical lives would demonstrate the practicality of divine law, and their daily actions set the example of what they called for. When words are confirmed by practice, they are far more effective, because people see their effect as they are implemented. Had God's messengers been of a different species, needing no food to eat, no going about in the markets to obtain their needs, and no intimacy with women, and had they had no experience of human emotion, they would have had no empathy with other people, and no understanding of their feelings and motives. In which case, people would not find in them relevant examples to follow.

Any advocate of a cause who does not interact with the people he addresses, neither sharing their feelings, nor letting them share his, remains on the margin of their lives, experiencing no mutual sympathy with them. Regardless of what he says to them, he will not be able to motivate them because of their mutual isolation. Likewise, an advocate whose actions do not endorse his words will not be able to reach people's hearts, no matter how lucid and eloquent he may be. Indeed a simple word that is felt to be genuine and endorsed by action is the one that motivates people to act.

Those who in times past suggested that God's messenger should be an angel, like their successors who today suggest that such a messenger of God should be far above human earthly feelings, indulge in futile argument. Furthermore, they are all oblivious to the fundamental fact that angels do not, by their very nature, experience human life. They can experience neither the physical needs and interactions of the human body, nor human feelings, emotions or concerns. A messenger from God must know all such feelings and motives, experiencing them in his own daily life so that he is able to provide practical guidance to those who respond to his message.

Furthermore, were the messenger to be an angel, people would have no motivation to follow his example in their life's details. They would feel that he belonged to a different race with a totally different nature. They will remain unable to follow his suit in their daily life. Needless to say, God's messengers have always provided their peoples with a good example to follow.

Furthermore, such a suggestion betrays ignorance of the honour God has bestowed on mankind. For He chose His messengers from among them, providing them with contact with the Supreme Society of heaven as they received instructions and revelations from Him.

For all these reasons, God, in His infinite wisdom, selected His messengers from among human beings, subjecting them to all that a human being experiences from the moment of birth to the moment of death, including emotions, reactions, hopes, pains, eating food, marriage, etc. It is God's wisdom that determined that the final and most perfect messenger to deliver His last and everlasting message should be the one who provided the most perfect example of human life on earth; a life full of motivation, experience, action and emotion.

Such has been God's law in selecting His messengers, and His law in saving them with their followers when He destroyed the wrongdoers who rejected the truth embodied in their messages: "*In the end, We fulfilled Our promise to them, and We saved them and all whom We willed [to save], and We destroyed those who transgressed beyond bounds.*" (Verse 9)

This is, then, a law set in operation, like that of sending God's messengers. He promised to save them along with those who truly believed in them and gave credence to their faith by action. He fulfilled His promise to them and destroyed those who were oppressors, transgressing all the bounds He set.

The Book Giving Distinction to Arabs

God reminds the pagan Arabs who oppressed the Prophet Muḥammad (peace be upon him), denying his message and persecuting him and his followers, that they are subject to His law for their transgression. He also makes it clear to them that it is an aspect of the grace He bestows on them that He has not sent them any physical miracle, because that would have spelt their doom if they continued to reject the truth as older communities did. Instead, He sent them a book which imparts honour to them, since it is in their own language. This book sets their life on the right footing and makes of them a community entitled to lead mankind and be respected by them. Moreover, this book invites thinking people to reflect on it and elevate themselves by implementing it: "*We have now revealed for you a book bringing you respect. Will you not, then, use your reason?*" (Verse 10)

The miracle of the Qur'ān is open to all generations. Thus, it is unlike the physical miracles given at a particular time and place. For the Arabs, the Qur'ān brought respect, honour and glory as they delivered its message to all people. Prior to the Qur'ān, the Arabs barely received mention in humanity's records. They had nothing to give humanity so as to ensure they were remembered. But as long as they upheld their book, they were honoured by the rest of mankind. Indeed, they assumed the leadership of humanity over many centuries, bringing happiness to themselves and to the rest of mankind. Then when they abandoned it, humanity left them aside, and they lost their position of respect. They were then at the tail end of humanity, suffering aggression from different quarters, in stark contrast with their glorious past when they enjoyed security while others suffered fear and anxiety.

The Arabs have nothing of value and no sound idea to give to humanity other than this guidance and the ideas it contains. Therefore, when they present their book to the world, they are known by it and they are given the honour they deserve, because humanity knows that they have what is of benefit to it. But when they present themselves as mere Arabs, such questions as – who are Arabs? – are asked. And what is the value of their ancestry when they do not have their book? Mankind has never accorded the Arabs any position of respect except when they showed themselves to be advocates of a faith which they implemented and conducted their affairs by and according to its teachings. By contrast, their being merely Arabs had no value in human history and no entry in the records of civilization. They are known only by being the standard-bearers of Islamic values, ideals and civilization. In history, this certainly has great value.

It is to this fact that the Qur'ān refers when it says to the Arab idolaters who rejected every idea it put to them and denied its truth: "*We have now revealed for you a book bringing you respect. Will you not, then, use your reason?*" (Verse 10)

It was an act of divine grace that God revealed the Qur'ān to them, rather than giving them the miracle they demanded. Had such a miracle been sent to them and had they continued to deny the truth, a calamity like those that destroyed earlier unbelievers would have brought about their doom. At this point the *sūrah* portrays a scene of total destruction and annihilation:

> *How many a community that persisted in evil-doing have We dashed into fragments, and raised another people in their stead. And as soon as they began to feel Our might they took to their heels and fled. Do not run away. Return to all your comforts and to your dwellings, so that you might be called to account. They said: 'Woe betide us! We were indeed wrongdoers!' And that cry of theirs did not cease until We caused them to become like a field mown down, still and silent as ashes.* (Verses 11–15)

The Arabic term *qaṣamnā*, rendered here as 'dashed into fragments', carries strong connotations of a strike that splits something into pieces. Moreover, its sound adds further connotations of complete destruction. Those communities persisted in their evil and met a sudden fate that left no trace of them. "*And [We] raised another people in their stead.*" We note also that the Arabic text uses the word *qaryah* which means village or town with the verb denoting the breaking into fragments, but it uses *qawm,* or 'people', when it speaks of raising a new community, because it is such people who build a new civilization. In this way, the destruction is rendered more powerful, which is in line with the distinctive characteristics of the Qur'ānic style.

Still, Silent and Lifeless

Indeed, the words the Qur'ān uses here add, by their very sound, strong connotations of an overwhelming strike that leaves everything lifeless. We look and see how those communities ran around frantically as God's power struck their land. They appear like trapped mice jumping here and there before they fall motionless: "*As soon as they began to feel Our might they took to their heels and fled.*" (Verse 12) They run so that they might leave a town which they felt was doomed. They run as though their very running will save them from God's power. It is not that they imagine that they are faster than God's strike; it is a thoughtless movement, like that of trapped mice.

They are then sarcastically told: "*Do not run away. Return to all your comforts and to your dwellings, so that you might be called to account.*" (Verse 13) You do not need to run away from your homes. Go back to your luxuries and comforts. You may perchance be asked about all this luxury and how you have used it. But the time for questioning is already over, and the Qur'ān delivers this final cataclysm as bitter sarcasm.

This brings their situation clearly before their eyes, for there is no means of escape. They cannot run away from or flee God's punishment. Hence, they change tactic and admit their faults: "*They said: Woe betide us! We were indeed wrongdoers!*" (Verse 14) But the time for all this is over. They can say what they like, but it is all to no avail. They are left to their devices until they are lifeless: "*And that cry of theirs did not cease until We caused them to become like a field mown down, still and silent as ashes.*" (Verse 15) But it is a field of humans, all of whom are motionless, lifeless; yet only a minute earlier, it was bustling, vibrant, full of life.

At this point the *sūrah* establishes a link between the faith already mentioned, its essential laws under which unbelievers are punished and the fundamental truth and seriousness which form the pivot around which the whole universe turns. If the unbelievers receive every new Qur'ānic revelation with jest and play, oblivious to its seriousness and the truth it outlines, heedless of the fast approaching Day of Reckoning and what awaits them on that day, then they should know that God's laws never fail. "*We have not created the heavens and the earth and all that is between them in mere idle play. Had We willed to indulge in a pastime, We would indeed have found one near at hand; if ever We were to do so! Nay, but We hurl the truth against falsehood, and it crushes the latter, and behold, it withers away. But woe to you for all your false claims.*" (Verses 16–18)

God has created the universe for a definite purpose, not to indulge in a pastime or idle play. He conducts its affairs in His infinite wisdom, and does not leave it to run aimlessly. One aspect of the seriousness involved in the creation of heaven and earth is that He has sent messengers, revealed books, and outlined for mankind their duties and obligations. We see, then, how seriousness is inherent in the nature of this universe and its laws, and in the faith God wants people to embrace and implement, as well as in the way He holds people accountable after they die.

Had God wanted to indulge in a pastime, He would have chosen something for Himself alone; it would have nothing to do with His mortal creatures. But this is merely a theoretical assumption: "*Had We willed to indulge in a pastime, We would indeed have found one near at hand.*" (Verse 17) The mode of expression here indicates that both parts of the conditional are negated. God has not willed to indulge in a pastime, and none has taken place. Besides, it never will, because God has not willed it in the first place: "*If ever We were to do so!*" (Verse 17)

Vanquishing Falsehood

It is all a theoretical argument given here in order to establish the basic truth that whatever relates to God is, like Him, ever-present and eternal. Hence, if God wants to enjoy some pastime, such pastime would not relate to anything that is created such as the heavens, the earth or anything in between. All these are new, in the sense that they are created at a certain point in time. What relates to God remains with Him, eternally, so as to fit in with His Majesty.

But the law that operates for all time is that there is no such thing as a pastime in respect of God. There are only seriousness and truth.

Thus, intrinsic truth will triumph over incidental falsehood: "*Nay, but We hurl the truth against falsehood, and it crushes the latter, and behold, it withers away. But woe to you for all your false claims.*" (Verse 18)

The Arabic particle *bal*, rendered here as 'nay', signifies turning away from whatever is at hand. Here it indicates putting aside this point about having a pastime to turn to a more serious point about the real world and the laws operating in it which ensure that falsehood is vanquished and the truth triumphant. The Qur'ānic verse paints this in a vivid picture, showing the truth as a missile hurled by God at falsehood, breaking its head and so utterly destroying it.

Such is the normal state of affairs: the truth is fundamental to the nature of the universe, deeply permeating its structure. Falsehood, on the other hand, is alien to it, lacking roots and power. God brands it as false and hurls the truth at it. When anything receives such a strike by God, it is bound to wither away and disappear.

People may sometimes feel that practical life goes on in a different direction to that stated by God, who knows all. This is particularly so when falsehood appears to be strong and overpowering, while the truth appears of small stature, shrinking in a corner, defeated. But this lasts only for a time, which God may extend as He pleases to expose people to a trial. Ultimately the law God has set in operation, to allow the heavens and the earth to remain and His message to flourish, is bound to run its course.

Those who believe in God entertain no doubt that His promise will come true, or that the truth enjoys prime position in the structure of the universe and its system. They are also certain that victory will eventually belong to the truth. Hence, if God tests them by allowing falsehood a temporary triumph, they realize that this is merely a test God puts them through so as to eradicate their weakness or give them what they lack. He wants them to be fit to receive the victorious truth, and to make them the tool by which He accomplishes His purpose. Thus, He lets them go through the test, to equip them properly for their role. If they hasten to remedy their weakness and redress their drawbacks, God will shorten their period of test and accomplish through them whatever He wishes. The ultimate result is a foregone conclusion: "*We hurl the truth against falsehood, and it crushes the latter, and behold, it withers away.*" (Verse 18) God accomplishes what He wills.

Thus the Qur'ān puts this fundamental fact before the unbelievers who are quick to hurl their false accusations at the Qur'ān and the Prophet (peace be upon him). They describe the Qur'ān as sorcery, poetry or mere fabrication, when it is the truth that smashes their falsehood and causes it to wither away. This is followed by a warning against the eventual outcome of their accusations: "*But woe to you for all your false claims.*" (Verse 18)

The *sūrah* goes on to show them a model of obedience to God and worshipping Him, contrasted with their rejection and turning away. The model shows creatures that are closer to God than them, yet they continue to worship Him, obeying His every order without fail: "*To Him belong all those who are in the heavens and on earth. Those that are with Him are never too proud to worship Him and never grow weary of that. They extol His limitless glory by night and day, tirelessly.*" (Verses 19–20)

'Those who are in the heavens and on earth' are known only to God who knows everything about them. Human knowledge is certain only of human existence, while believers are certain also of the existence of the angels and the *jinn* because both are mentioned in the Qur'ān. But we know of them only what God, their Creator, has told us. There may be other intelligent creatures on other planets, with forms and natures that are suited to those planets. But the knowledge of all this rests only with God.

Therefore when we read in the Qur'ān, "*To Him belong all those who are in the heavens and on earth,*" we know only of these whom we know, and we acknowledge that the Creator of the heavens and earth knows everyone else.

The phrase, '*those that are with Him,*' appears initially to refer to the angels, but we do not wish to attach particular meaning to this phrase, which is very general in its import, referring to the angels and other creatures. The expression here appears to mean those who are closer to God. When it applies to God, the phrase, 'with Him', does not signify a place or a description. The *sūrah* makes it clear that "*those that are with Him are never too proud to worship Him*", whilst the unbelievers demonstrate their arrogance by refusing to do so. Nor do they 'grow weary of' offering worship to Him. Indeed their lives are a continuous act of worship, as they ceaselessly glorify God.

Human beings are able to make their whole lives a continuous act of worship, without having to dedicate every minute to worship rituals and the glorification of God's name, as the angels do. Islam considers every move and every breath an act of worship if it is dedicated for God's sake, even when it involves partaking of the pleasures of this world.

Proof Is Required

Thus, the *sūrah* paints a picture of creatures glorifying God and extolling His praises at all times. At the same time, the unbelievers' claims about their multiple deities are strongly criticized. The *sūrah* provides irrefutable evidence of God's oneness by virtue of what we see in the constant system that permeates the universe, testifying that it is all run by the will of God, the One who manages and conducts all affairs. It also provides evidence from earlier scriptures given to other communities.

> *Or have they taken for worship some earthly deities who can restore the dead to life? Had there been in heaven or on earth any deities other than God, both would surely have fallen into ruin! But limitless in His glory is God, Lord of the Throne, and exalted is He above all that they attribute to Him! He cannot be questioned about whatever He does, whereas they shall be questioned. Or have they taken for worship some deities besides Him? Say: 'Produce your convincing proof. This is the message of those who are with me and the message of those before me.' But nay, most of them do not know the truth, and so they stubbornly turn away. Before your time We never sent a messenger without having revealed to him that there is no deity other than Me. Therefore, you shall worship Me alone.* (Verses 21–25)

The question the *sūrah* poses about the unbelievers' worship of different deities is, in effect, a denunciation of what they do. Yet the description of such deities as ones restoring the dead to life contains a strong note of ridicule. Indeed, one of the first qualities of the true God is that He is able to restore the dead to life. Hence, it is pertinent to ask whether the deities they worship can also do this. The answer is too clear to need to be stated. Indeed, they themselves do not claim that their deities initiate or restore life. As such, they do not have the very first quality of the Divine Being.

This is an argument based on the facts as we see them in our world. But there is another argument based on universal facts: "*Had there been in heaven or on earth any deities other than God, both would surely have fallen into ruin!*" (Verse 22)

The universe and its whole existence are based on a single system that brings all its parts together and ensures harmony between all those components. This system is devised by the single will of the One God. Had there been other entities, they would have had multiple wills and, consequently, multiple systems and laws. It goes without saying that a will is a manifestation of the entity that exercizes it, and the system is a manifestation of the active will. Hence, had there been other deities, the unity which provides coherence in the whole machinery of the universe, consistency and direction in its system, would totally disappear. Chaos, corruption and ruin would ensue. There would be no way of maintaining the coherence and harmony acknowledged by even the most hardened of atheists.

As it receives a clear message of the system governing the whole universe, a straight, uncorrupted nature will instinctively testify to the unity of the system and the will that has initiated it. It will acknowledge the oneness of the Creator who conducts all affairs in this consistent and harmonious universe, which suffers from no inherent defect in formation or from any impediment to its progress. "*But limitless in His glory is God, Lord of the Throne, and exalted is He above all that they attribute to Him!*" (Verse 22)

They assign partners to Him when He is in control of all and in need of none. For, He is "*Lord of the Throne*". A throne is a symbol of kingdom, real authority and exaltation. What they claim is absolutely false, and the universe, its system and freedom from corruptive elements, testifies to this.

"*He cannot be questioned about whatever He does, whereas they shall be questioned.*" (Verse 23) Since when could the One who controls the whole universe be questioned, and who could question Him when He holds sway over all His servants? Indeed, His will is free, unlimited, beyond restraint, even by the system His will has chosen to govern the universe. Questioning and accountability are subject to certain established criteria and defined limits. It is the free will that defines such limits and establishes such criteria, but such free will cannot be subject to these limits and criteria, while creatures are subject to them. Hence, they will undoubtedly be held to account.

Sometimes arrogance takes its hold of people, so that they impudently ask why has God done all this? And, furthermore, what is the wisdom behind it? The way they put these questions suggests that they see no purpose or wisdom in all this. Thus they overstep the limits of proper behaviour towards God Almighty. They also overlook the limits of human understanding dictated by its position in the universe. Needless to say, man remains ignorant of the reasons, causes, effects and objectives that apply to the universe.

It is the One who knows, manages and controls all that operates His will, conducts all matters and controls all things. It is He who "*cannot be questioned about whatever He does, whereas they shall be questioned.*" (Verse 23)

Having provided this irrefutable evidence based on the nature of the universe, the *sūrah* asks them whether they can support their claims about multiple deities with any evidence derived from their scriptures: "*Or have they taken for worship some deities besides Him? Say: 'Produce your convincing proof. This is the message of those who are with me and the message of those before me.' But nay, most of them do not know the truth, and so they stubbornly turn away.*" (Verse 24)

Here is the Qur'ān which incorporates the message given to the Prophet's contemporaries, and there are the scriptures containing the messages delivered by earlier messengers. In none of these is there any mention of partners with God. All divine faiths are based on the true concept of God's oneness. Where, then, did those unbelievers get this false concept of multiple deities when it cannot be supported by logical or religious argument? "*But nay, most of them do not know the truth, and so they stubbornly turn away.*" (Verse 24)

Claiming a Son for God

The *sūrah* then states the nature of what was revealed to all messengers sent to different communities before the Prophet Muḥammad's time: "*Before your time We never sent a messenger without having revealed to him that there is no deity other than Me. Therefore, you shall worship Me alone.*" (Verse 25) God's oneness is indeed the basic essential element in divine faith, ever since God sent His first messenger to mankind. Nothing has changed in that. God, the Creator who must be worshipped is One, without partners. The truth of Godhead and Lordship over the universe is a single issue that cannot be separated. God has no partners, whether in the sphere of Godhead or in that of worship. This fact ranks alongside the basic essential laws of the universe and is classified with them. Like them, its truth is unassailable.

The *sūrah* then picks up the claims of the unbelievers alleging that God has a son. This is one of the absurdities of ignorance:

> *They say: 'The Most Merciful has taken to Himself a son!' Limitless is He in His glory! No; they are but His honoured servants. They do not speak until He has spoken, and they act at His behest. He knows all that lies before them and all behind them. They do not intercede for any but those whom He has already graced with His goodly acceptance, since they themselves stand in reverent awe of Him. If any of them were to say, 'I am a deity beside Him,' We shall requite him with hell. Thus do We reward the wrongdoers.* (Verses 26–29)

The claim that God – limitless is He in His glory – has a son took several forms in the different communities that deviated from the path of truth. The pagan Arabs alleged that the angels were God's daughters, while unbeliever groups among the Jews alleged that Ezra was God's son. Similarly, deviant Christians alleged that Jesus Christ was God's son. All these are ignorant claims that deviate from the clear truth.

The *sūrah* is here especially concerned with the Arabs' claim that the angels were God's daughters. This claim is rebuffed by clarifying the nature of angels. They are not God's female offspring, rather, they are only His servants whom He has honoured. The angels do not suggest anything to God, because they know their limits and abide by them. They do what God bids them, without argument. God's knowledge encompasses all their affairs. They do not try to intercede on behalf of anyone other than those to whom He has gracefully granted His acceptance. Only on behalf of these does He accept intercession. By nature, the angels are in awe of God, revering Him, even though they are pure, honoured and obedient to Him. Needless to say, none of them ever makes a claim to Godhead. Had any of them, for argument's sake, made such a claim, they would have suffered the same fate as anyone else who makes such a claim. That fate is hell where goes everyone guilty of the worst type of wrongdoing, which is to make such a claim which runs against all right and is unjust to all creation.

The same applies to the unbelievers' false claims. They are hollow, absurd and irrational. Should anyone make such a claim, the same terrible fate will befall him.

The *sūrah* contrasts its image of the angels in obedience and awe of God with that of the unbelievers who make such absurd and impudent claims.

Universal Evidence of God's Oneness

The *sūrah* has so far given us several types of evidence drawn from the universe, all testifying to God's oneness, and stated a number of arguments denying any possibility of there being more than one God. It has also provided evidence that addresses people's hearts directly. Now the *sūrah* takes the human heart by the hand to contemplate some of the great phenomena in the universe, as it is wisely managed by God. Yet the unbelievers remain heedless of the clear signs revealed all about them. For those who look however, the universe reveals aspects of itself that leave our minds in total amazement when we contemplate them with an open heart and alert senses.

> *Are the unbelievers unaware that the heaven and the earth were once one single entity, which We then parted asunder? We have made out of water every living thing. Will they not, then, believe?* (Verse 30)

The statement that the heavens and the earth were split apart after having been a single entity is worth careful consideration. The more advanced theories of astronomy seeking to explain universal phenomena always tend to support this truth stated in the Qur'ān over 1,400 years ago. The theory that wins most acceptance today is that which claims that star constellations, such as our solar system which includes the sun, its planets and moons including our planet earth and its moon, were originally nebula. The nebula was then rent asunder and its parts took their circular shapes. The earth was also a piece of the sun that separated from it and cooled down.

However, this is merely an astronomical theory which may be fashionable today, but could be proven false tomorrow, only to be replaced by yet another assumption to explain universal phenomena. It thus gives birth to a different theory.[1] We, as believers, do not try to interpret a Qur'ānic statement in terms of a theory which is far from certain. We take Qur'ānic statements as they are. Scientific theories are different from true scientific facts which can be tried and tested, such as the fact that metals stretch when heated, or that water evaporates or freezes in severely cold weather.

The Qur'ān is not a book of scientific theories. Its field is not applied science. It is a constitution that regulates man's whole life. Its method is to set the human mind on the right track, so that it can function and be free within the limits set for it. It also sets society on the right lines

---

1. Since the author wrote this new theories about the origins of the earth have been advanced, with one speaking about a Big Bang, and another about string and fusion. Any of these may eventually be proven correct or abandoned in favour of new theories. This confirms the wisdom of the author's approach. – Editor's note.

so that it allows the mind to work and be free, without labouring on purely scientific detail. This area is left for the human mind to work out after it has been set free.

The Qur'ān may refer to some universal facts, like the one stated here: "*The heaven and the earth were once one single entity, which We then parted asunder.*" (Verse 30) We accept this as an absolute certainty simply because it is stated in the Qur'ān. We certainly do not know how the heavens and the earth were parted, or ripped one from the other. We accept astronomical theories which are not in conflict with this general fact mentioned in the Qur'ān. What we will not do however is take up the Qur'ānic text and try to fit it to any astronomical theory. We do not seek an endorsement of the Qur'ān through human theories, because the Qur'ān states only what is certain. The most we can say is that the astronomical theory accepted today is not in conflict with the general import of this Qur'ānic statement revealed many generations prior to it.

The next sentence of the verse states: "*We have made out of water every living thing.*" (Verse 30) This short sentence states a great and crucial fact. Indeed, scientists shower praise on Darwin for having identified that water was the first environment where life began.

It is indeed a fact that should capture all our attentions. That it is mentioned in the Qur'ān neither fills us with wonder nor increases our belief in the truth of the Qur'ān. Our belief in the absolute truth of everything it states is based on our unshakeable belief that it is God's revelation, not on its being confirmed by scientific discoveries or theories. The most that can be said here is that on this particular point, Darwin's evolutionary theory is not in conflict with what the Qur'ān states.

For fourteen centuries, the Qur'ān has drawn the attention of unbelievers to the great marvels God has placed in the universe, wondering how they could deny what they see everywhere: "*Will they not, then, believe?*" (Verse 30) How could they persist in their disbelief when everything around them in this universe inevitably leads to faith in God, the Creator, the Wise who conducts all affairs?

The *sūrah* continues to point out awesome scenes of the universe: "*We have also set firm mountains on earth, lest it sway with them.*"

(Verse 31) The Qur'ān, then, states that the mountains, firm as they are, maintain the balance of the earth so that it does not sway or shake. This balance may be maintained in various forms, such as setting a balance between the external pressure on the face of the earth and the one inside it, i.e. internally. Or it may be that the height of a mountain in one place is counterbalanced by a deep valley in another. Whatever the case may be, this statement confirms that the mountains have a direct bearing on the balance and stability of the earth. It is the domain of scientific study to identify and prove how this stability and balance are achieved. But it is the Qur'ānic text that invites us to contemplate such facts.

Let us now follow the magnificent aspects of God's creation in the wide universe: "*We have cut out there broad paths, so that they might find their way.*" (Verse 31) The pathways made in the mountains in the shape of depressions between its high peaks assist the traveller in finding his way yet there is also another subtle implication here that refers to faith. It may be that travellers will find their way to accepting the faith just as they find their way through the mountains along such paths.

"*And We have set up the sky as a well-secured canopy.*" (Verse 32) In Arabic, the sky refers to everything that is above us. We see above us something like a ceiling. The Qur'ān states that the sky is a well-secured canopy. It is secure from any defect or contamination, since it symbolizes the height from which God's revelations are bestowed. But "*they stubbornly turn away from all its signs.*" (Verse 32)

Finally a reference is made to time and place phenomena that are very close to man and his life on earth: "*It is He who has created the night and the day and the sun and the moon: each moves swiftly in its own orbit.*" (Verse 33)

The night and day are two universal phenomena, while the sun and the moon are two great celestial bodies that are closely related to human life on earth. When we contemplate the succession of the day and night and the movement of the sun and the moon, we realize that they are so accurate as to admit no defect, and so consistent as to allow no failure. Such contemplation is sufficient to guide our hearts and minds to the fact that the system that applies to them is one, the will governing them is one and their great Maker is one.

The Inevitable End of All People

This first passage of the *sūrah* concludes with an outline that links the laws relevant to creation, formation and sustenance with those relevant to the nature and destiny of human life:

> *Never have We granted life everlasting to any man before you. Should you yourself die, do they, perchance, hope to live forever? Every soul shall taste death. We test you all with evil and good by way of trial. To Us you all must return.* (Verses 34–35)

No human being has ever been granted immortality. Every creature is bound to die, and whatever has a beginning will certainly have an end. So if God's Messenger [peace be upon him] is also destined to die, why do they think they would be granted life everlasting? Since they cannot hope to live for ever, why do they not behave like ones who will inevitably taste death? Why do they not reflect and contemplate?

"*Every soul shall taste death.*" (Verse 35) This is the law that governs life. It has no exceptions or exemptions. The living, then, must take this into account and prepare themselves for it. This short journey on earth is bound to come to an end, and its end is the death of every living thing. All shall return to God. But whatever happens to us during this trip through life, whether good or bad, is meant as a test: "*We test you all with evil and good by way of trial.*" (Verse 35)

When we speak of being tested by something evil or hard, we can all easily understand this notion. It is a test to show the endurance and patience of the one who is being tested. It is the means to determine how unshakeable his trust in God, his Lord, is, and how much trust he places in God's mercy. But a test with good things needs to be explained.

To be tested with good things is more difficult than hardship, even though it may appear easier. For the fact is that many people can endure being tested by evil, but few can endure a test with the good. When the test takes the form of sickness and weakness, many are able to endure and withstand the hardship, but when its form is that of good health, strength and ability, then few are those who pass through successfully.

People may be able to withstand poverty and deprivation, maintaining their dignity in such situations, but few are those who succeed in a test with comfort and affluence. For the latter tempts us to satisfy all our desires.

Equally there are many who cannot be deterred by torture or physical harm. They are not overawed by such threats and actualities. By contrast, however, only a few can resist the temptations posited by wealth, position, comfort and desire.

It is not difficult to tolerate the hardships of struggle and the injuries that one sustains in such a struggle. But it is extremely hard to experience comfort and a carefree life without becoming so keen to maintain it even at the expense of one's dignity. Indeed such an experience could easily lead to accepting humiliation in order not to lose it.

A test with hardship may arouse within us a keen sense of dignity, encouraging us to resist. Thus, all our powers and faculties are directed at the hardship and enable us to pass through successfully. Affluence, on the other hand, has a calming effect which reduces our awareness of the test. Hence, many fail it. This applies to all human beings, except those that God helps and protects. They are the ones described by the Prophet as ending up with what is good in all situations: "Amazing is a believer's situation, because it all ends up in what is good. This applies to no one other than a believer. If he experiences what is good and pleasing, he will express his gratitude to God and this is good for him. On the other hand, if he experiences hardship, he will patiently persevere and this is good for him." [Related by Muslim] Hence to keep on the alert when being tested by affluence and comfort is more important than doing so when we go through a test with hardship. Maintaining a sound relation with God is the best guarantee in all situations.

2

A Warning Not to be Ignored

When the unbelievers see you, they make you the target of their mockery, saying [to one another], 'Is this the one who speaks against your gods?' Yet they are the ones who, at the mention of the Most Merciful, are quick to deny Him. (36)

وَإِذَا رَءَاكَ ٱلَّذِينَ كَفَرُوٓاْ إِن
يَتَّخِذُونَكَ إِلَّا هُزُوًا أَهَٰذَا ٱلَّذِى
يَذۡكُرُ ءَالِهَتَكُمۡ وَهُم بِذِكۡرِ
ٱلرَّحۡمَٰنِ هُمۡ كَٰفِرُونَ ٣٦

Man is a creature of haste. I shall show you My signs: do not, then, ask Me to hurry them on. (37)

خُلِقَ ٱلۡإِنسَٰنُ مِنۡ عَجَلٖۚ سَأُوْرِيكُمۡ
ءَايَٰتِى فَلَا تَسۡتَعۡجِلُونِ ٣٧

They say: 'When is this promise to be fulfilled, if what you say be true?' (38)

وَيَقُولُونَ مَتَىٰ هَٰذَا ٱلۡوَعۡدُ إِن
كُنتُمۡ صَٰدِقِينَ ٣٨

If only the unbelievers knew [that there will come] a time when they will not be able to shield their faces and their backs from the fire; a time when they will find no support. (39)

لَوۡ يَعۡلَمُ ٱلَّذِينَ كَفَرُواْ حِينَ لَا يَكُفُّونَ
عَن وُجُوهِهِمُ ٱلنَّارَ وَلَا عَن ظُهُورِهِمۡ
وَلَا هُمۡ يُنصَرُونَ ٣٩

Indeed, it will come upon them of a sudden, and will stupefy them. They will be unable to avert it, nor will they be allowed any respite. (40)

بَلْ تَأْتِيهِم بَغْتَةً فَتَبْهَتُهُمْ
فَلَا يَسْتَطِيعُونَ رَدَّهَا وَلَا هُمْ
يُنظَرُونَ ﴿٤٠﴾

Other messengers were derided before your time; but those who scoffed at them were [in the end] overwhelmed by the very thing that they derided. (41)

وَلَقَدِ ٱسْتُهْزِئَ بِرُسُلٍ مِّن قَبْلِكَ
فَحَاقَ بِٱلَّذِينَ سَخِرُوا۟ مِنْهُم
مَّا كَانُوا۟ بِهِۦ يَسْتَهْزِءُونَ ﴿٤١﴾

Say: 'Who could protect you, by night or by day, from the Most Merciful?' Yet, from the remembrance of their Lord do they stubbornly turn away. (42)

قُلْ مَن يَكْلَؤُكُم بِٱلَّيْلِ وَٱلنَّهَارِ مِنَ
ٱلرَّحْمَٰنِ ۗ بَلْ هُمْ عَن ذِكْرِ رَبِّهِم
مُّعْرِضُونَ ﴿٤٢﴾

Do they have gods other than Us to protect them? Those [alleged deities] are not even able to succour themselves, nor can they be given company by Us. (43)

أَمْ لَهُمْ ءَالِهَةٌ تَمْنَعُهُم مِّن دُونِنَا ۚ
لَا يَسْتَطِيعُونَ نَصْرَ أَنفُسِهِمْ
وَلَا هُم مِّنَّا يُصْحَبُونَ ﴿٤٣﴾

We have allowed these, and their fathers, to enjoy the good things of life for a great length of time. Can they not see that We gradually reduce the land from its outlying borders? Is it they, then, who will triumph? (44)

بَلْ مَتَّعْنَا هَٰٓؤُلَآءِ وَءَابَآءَهُمْ حَتَّىٰ
طَالَ عَلَيْهِمُ ٱلْعُمُرُ ۗ أَفَلَا يَرَوْنَ
أَنَّا نَأْتِى ٱلْأَرْضَ نَنقُصُهَا مِنْ
أَطْرَافِهَآ ۚ أَفَهُمُ ٱلْغَٰلِبُونَ ﴿٤٤﴾

Say: 'I do but warn you on the strength of divine revelation!' But the deaf cannot hear this call, however often they are warned. (45)

قُلْ إِنَّمَآ أُنذِرُكُم بِٱلْوَحْيِ ۚ وَلَا يَسْمَعُ
ٱلصُّمُّ ٱلدُّعَآءَ إِذَا مَا يُنذَرُونَ ﴿٤٥﴾

Yet, if but a breath of your Lord's punishment touches them, they are sure to cry, 'Oh, woe betide us! We were wrongdoers indeed.' (46)

وَلَئِن مَّسَّتْهُمْ نَفْحَةٌ مِّنْ عَذَابِ رَبِّكَ
لَيَقُولُنَّ يَٰوَيْلَنَآ إِنَّا كُنَّا ظَٰلِمِينَ ﴿٤٦﴾

We shall set up just scales on the Day of Resurrection, so that no human being shall be wronged in the least. If there be but the weight of a mustard seed, We shall bring it [to account]. Sufficient are We for reckoning. (47)

وَنَضَعُ ٱلْمَوَٰزِينَ ٱلْقِسْطَ لِيَوْمِ ٱلْقِيَٰمَةِ
فَلَا تُظْلَمُ نَفْسٌ شَيْـًٔا ۖ وَإِن كَانَ
مِثْقَالَ حَبَّةٍ مِّنْ خَرْدَلٍ أَتَيْنَا بِهَا ۗ
وَكَفَىٰ بِنَا حَٰسِبِينَ ﴿٤٧﴾

Overview

So far the *sūrah* has taken us on a long journey, showing us some of the laws of nature that operate in the universe, the rules that govern groups advocating God's message, people's fate, and the destruction of past communities. Now it picks up the point mentioned at the beginning of the *sūrah* about the way the unbelievers received God's Messenger and the revelations he was given, the mockery they hurled at him and their persistent disbelief.

The *sūrah* follows this by pointing out that, by nature, man is hasty. One manifestation of this haste is the unbelievers' attempts to hasten God's punishment. Hence, it warns them against such haste and makes it clear to them that they must refrain from mocking the Prophet if they wish to avoid the consequences of such unwarranted behaviour. It paints for them a picture of how those who wield power in this life find their authority dwindling, and in another scene demonstrates some aspects of the suffering in the hereafter meted out to persistent unbelievers.

This new passage concludes by emphasizing the accuracy of the reckoning in the hereafter and the suitability of the reward given on the Day of Judgement. Thus, the reckoning and the reward are linked to the rules operating in the universe, human nature and human life.

Protection to be Sought

> *When the unbelievers see you, they make you the target of their mockery, saying [to one another], 'Is this the one who speaks against your gods?' Yet they are the ones who, at the mention of the Most Merciful, are quick to deny Him.* (Verse 36)

The unbelievers deny the very existence of God, the Most Merciful, who has created the universe and set the rules that operate in it and sustain its existence. They object to the fact that God's Messenger, Muḥammad (peace be upon him), speaks out against their deities, showing such inanimate idols to be useless. Yet they themselves rudely deny God, the Most Merciful. How singular!

They hurl abuse and mockery at God's Messenger, saying that it is unacceptable that he should criticize their idol worship. They say to one another: "*Is this the one who speaks against your gods?*" (Verse 36) Yet they, creatures of God as they are, find nothing wrong with the arrogance that leads them to deny God's existence and reject the Qur'ān He has revealed to them. The irony of their attitude exposes to the full the far-reaching corruption that affects their nature and impairs their judgement.

What is more, they try to hasten the punishment against which the Prophet warns them. For, by nature, man is hasty: "*Man is a creature of haste. I shall show you My signs: do not, then, ask Me to hurry them on. They say: 'When is this promise to be fulfilled, if what you say be true?'*" (Verses 37–38)

"*Man is a creature of haste.*" Haste is present in man's very nature and constitution. He always stretches his eyes to what lies ahead, beyond the present moment, aiming to grasp it with his own hand. He wants to achieve, the moment it flashes in his mind, all that seems desirable. He wants to see all that is promised to him, even though it may be to his detriment. Such is man's nature, unless he establishes a firm relationship with God which gives him strength and reassurance. He will then trust to God's wisdom, leaving His will to run its course without hastening events. For faith combines trust with patience and reassurance.

Those unbelievers hastened God's punishment, wondering when the promise of punishment in the hereafter, as well as in this life, would be fulfilled. The Qur'ān paints here for them a scene of the suffering in the hereafter, while also warning them against a similar punishment to that which befell earlier communities which rejected the faith: "*If only the unbelievers knew [that there will come] a time when they will not be able to shield their faces and their backs from the fire; a time when they will find no support. Indeed, it will come upon them of a sudden, and will stupefy them. They will be unable to avert it, nor will they be allowed any respite. Other messengers were derided before your time; but those who scoffed at them were [in the end] overwhelmed by the very thing that they derided.*" (Verses 39–41)

If the unbelievers only knew what will happen, they would change their attitude completely. They would stop their mockery and hastening of what is bound to come. Let them, then, see what is bound to come. There they are surrounded by the fire on all sides. We visualize their frantic movements, described implicitly in the verse, to protect their faces and their backs against the fire, but their attempt is futile. It is as if the fire engulfs them on all sides. They can neither keep it away from themselves, nor retreat to seek protection. Nor is even a short respite from it possible.

That the punishment comes suddenly is only the response for their hastening it. They used to say time after time: "*When is this promise to be fulfilled, if what you say be true?*" (Verse 38) The answer is that it comes suddenly, perplexing their minds and paralysing their will. Thus they are unable to think or act, let alone enjoy a period of grace to mend their ways.

This applies to the punishment in the hereafter. As for this world's punishment, it certainly befell communities before them which ridiculed God's messengers. Just like those communities were unable to ward off a punishment that wiped them out altogether, so these unbelievers are unable to avert their defeat and captivity. They are thus warned not to deride God's Messenger, so as to avoid the punishment that befalls those who ridicule prophets. Such fate and punishment is bound to come, because it is part of God's law which will inevitably take effect, just as the destruction of earlier communities, guilty of the same offence, proves.

Or is it that they have someone other than God who protects them by night and day, ensuring that they will suffer no punishment either in this life or in the life to come? "*Say: 'Who could protect you, by night or by day, from the Most Merciful?' Yet, from the remembrance of their Lord do they stubbornly turn away. Do they have gods other than Us to protect them? Those [alleged deities] are not even able to succour themselves, nor can they be given company by Us.*" (Verses 42–43)

It is God who watches over every soul by night and day. He is the Most Merciful. Indeed, infinite mercy is His great attribute. Other than Him there is no one to watch over or protect anyone. Do the unbelievers know anyone else who can protect them? It is a rhetorical question, one which rebukes them for their turning away from God when it is He who watches over them at all times: "*Yet, from the remembrance of their Lord do they stubbornly turn away.*" (Verse 42)

The same question is put to them again in a different form: "*Do they have gods other than Us to protect them?*" (Verse 43) Could these gods be the ones who watch over, and protect, them? This cannot be, because such alleged deities "*are not even able to succour themselves,*" let alone support and protect anyone else. "*Nor can they be given company by Us,*" to derive strength from being on God Almighty's side. This is the sort of strength Moses and Aaron derived when their Lord said to them: "*Have no fear. I shall be with you: I hear all and see all.*" (20: 46)

Such false deities do not have power of their own. They do not have access to God's power. As such, they are utterly helpless.

This sarcastic argument exposes the absurdity of the unbelievers' beliefs. Hence, the *sūrah* stops arguing with them, but adds a moving touch which they feel in their hearts. It directs them to reflect on God's might as He folds the earth underneath triumphant armies. Thus the earth shrinks so that they are confined to a limited space, after they have wielded much power and authority. "*We have allowed these, and their fathers, to enjoy the good things of life for a great length of time. Can they not see that We gradually reduce the land from its outlying borders? Is it they, then, who will triumph?"* (Verse 44)

What has corrupted their nature, then, is that long enjoyment of the good things of life. It is luxury which corrupts the heart and stifles the senses. It leads to a weakening in their awareness of God and an inability to contemplate the signs He has placed in the universe, pointing to Him. This is a different kind of test God sets for human beings, making affluence the very means of this test. If a person allows himself to drift away from God, and forgets that He is the source of all the blessings he enjoys, then he is bound to fail this test.

Thus, the *sūrah* works on their hearts as it shows them the imagery of what occurs every day somewhere on earth. States that have had power begin to lose their grip and weaken. Their land soon shrinks as they are split into small states where once they formed great empires. They were once strong and triumphant; now they are weak and defeated. They had great armies and vast resources; now their armies are weak and their resources meagre.

In its inimitable style, the Qur'ān shows God's hand as it folds up the once vast space, making borders cave in, and reducing huge distances, in a splendid scene that combines fine movement and awesome feelings. It then asks rhetorically: "*Is it they, then, who will triumph?"* (Verse 44) Is it that what happens to others does not then apply to them?

Unheeded Warnings

At the height of this awesome scene, which leaves hearts trembling, the Prophet is instructed to deliver the final warning: "*Say: 'I do but warn you on the strength of divine revelation!' But the deaf cannot hear this call, however often they are warned.*" (Verse 45) Let them, then, beware lest they should be the deaf who do not hear! It is the deaf who will suffer the fate of having the earth shrunk beneath them, and the hand of the Almighty smashing their power, doing away with them and their luxuries.

The *sūrah* continues its discourse making a profound effect on people's hearts. It describes those very unbelievers as they begin to suffer God's punishment: "*Yet, if but a breath of your Lord's punishment touches them, they are sure to cry, 'Oh, woe betide us! We were wrongdoers indeed.'*" (Verse 46) In Arabic, the word, *nafḥah,* used in this verse for 'breath' is normally associated with mercy and grace, but here it is used in the context of suffering so as to imply that even the slightest breath of God's punishment is sufficient to make them ready to confess. Alas, confession is of no use now. Earlier in the *sūrah* we were shown past communities smitten by God's might, crying out with the same appeals: "*They said: 'Woe betide us! We were indeed wrongdoers!' And that cry of theirs did not cease until We caused them to become like a field mown down, still and silent as ashes.*" (Verses 14–15)

It is, then, a confession that comes too late. It is far better that they listen to the warnings contained in God's revelations when they still have time to act, before they are touched by such suffering.

Accurate Scales Ensuring Absolute Justice

The present passage concludes with a final scene from the Day of Reckoning: "*We shall set up just scales on the Day of Resurrection, so that no soul shall be wronged in the least. If there be but the weight of a mustard seed, We shall bring it [to account]. Sufficient are We for reckoning.*" (Verse 47) The mustard seed here represents the smallest and lightest thing our eyes can see. Yet not even a mustard seed is overlooked or ignored. The scales that are used are so accurate that a single mustard seed makes a difference.

Let people, then, reflect on what they put forward for that day. Let hearts be attentive to the warnings, and let those who turn their backs or indulge in ridicule be warned. They may be able to evade punishment in this life, but on Judgement Day the reckoning takes every little thing into account. The scales then are so accurate that even a tiny seed can make all the difference.

Thus the accurate scales of the hereafter, the unfailing laws of the universe, the rules applicable to advocates of the faith and the laws of human nature converge in perfect harmony, operated by the hand of the Almighty. This testifies to the truth of God's oneness, the theme that pervades this whole *sūrah*.

3

One Community of Believers

Indeed We vouchsafed to Moses and Aaron the standard by which to distinguish right from wrong, a guiding light and a reminder for the God-conscious (48)

وَلَقَدْ آتَيْنَا مُوسَىٰ وَهَارُونَ الْفُرْقَانَ
وَضِيَاءً وَذِكْرًا لِلْمُتَّقِينَ ﴿٤٨﴾

who fear their Lord in their most secret thoughts, and are weary of the Last Hour. (49)

الَّذِينَ يَخْشَوْنَ رَبَّهُمْ بِالْغَيْبِ وَهُمْ
مِنَ السَّاعَةِ مُشْفِقُونَ ﴿٤٩﴾

And this one, too, is a blessed reminder which We have bestowed from on high: will you, then, reject it? (50)

وَهَٰذَا ذِكْرٌ مُبَارَكٌ أَنْزَلْنَاهُ ۚ أَفَأَنْتُمْ
لَهُ مُنْكِرُونَ ﴿٥٠﴾

We formerly bestowed on Abraham his consciousness of what is right, and We were aware of him (51)

وَلَقَدْ آتَيْنَا إِبْرَاهِيمَ رُشْدَهُ مِنْ قَبْلُ
وَكُنَّا بِهِ عَالِمِينَ ﴿٥١﴾

when he said to his father and his people, 'What are these images to which you are so devoted?' (52)

إِذْ قَالَ لِأَبِيهِ وَقَوْمِهِ مَا هَٰذِهِ التَّمَاثِيلُ
الَّتِي أَنْتُمْ لَهَا عَاكِفُونَ ﴿٥٢﴾

They answered: 'We found our forefathers worshipping them.' (53)

قَالُواْ وَجَدۡنَآ ءَابَآءَنَا لَهَا عَٰبِدِينَ ٥٣

Said he: 'Indeed, you and your forefathers have been in evident error.' (54)

قَالَ لَقَدۡ كُنتُمۡ أَنتُمۡ وَءَابَآؤُكُمۡ فِي
ضَلَٰلٖ مُّبِينٖ ٥٤

They asked: 'Is it the truth you are preaching to us? Or are you one who jests?' (55)

قَالُوٓاْ أَجِئۡتَنَا بِٱلۡحَقِّ أَمۡ أَنتَ مِنَ ٱللَّٰعِبِينَ ٥٥

He replied: 'Indeed, your Lord is the Lord of the heavens and the earth, He who has brought them into being. And I am a witness to this [truth]. (56)

قَالَ بَل رَّبُّكُمۡ رَبُّ ٱلسَّمَٰوَٰتِ وَٱلۡأَرۡضِ
ٱلَّذِي فَطَرَهُنَّ وَأَنَا۠ عَلَىٰ ذَٰلِكُم
مِّنَ ٱلشَّٰهِدِينَ ٥٦

'By God, I shall most certainly bring about the downfall of your idols when you have turned your backs and gone away!' (57)

وَتَٱللَّهِ لَأَكِيدَنَّ أَصۡنَٰمَكُم بَعۡدَ أَن
تُوَلُّواْ مُدۡبِرِينَ ٥٧

So he broke the idols to pieces, [all] except for the biggest of them, so that they might turn back to him. (58)

فَجَعَلَهُمۡ جُذَٰذًا إِلَّا كَبِيرٗا لَّهُمۡ
لَعَلَّهُمۡ إِلَيۡهِ يَرۡجِعُونَ ٥٨

They said: 'Who has done this to our gods? He is definitely one of the wrongdoers.' (59)

قَالُواْ مَن فَعَلَ هَٰذَا بِـَٔالِهَتِنَآ إِنَّهُۥ لَمِنَ
ٱلظَّٰلِمِينَ ٥٩

They said: 'We heard a youth speak of them; he is called Abraham.' (60)

قَالُواْ سَمِعۡنَا فَتٗى يَذۡكُرُهُمۡ يُقَالُ لَهُۥٓ
إِبۡرَٰهِيمُ ٦٠

They said: 'Then bring him here in sight of all people, so that they may bear witness.' (61)

قَالُوا۟ فَأۡتُوا۟ بِهِۦ عَلَىٰٓ أَعۡيُنِ ٱلنَّاسِ لَعَلَّهُمۡ
يَشۡهَدُونَ ٦١

They said: 'Abraham, was it you who did this to our gods?' (62)

قَالُوٓا۟ ءَأَنتَ فَعَلۡتَ هَٰذَا بِـَٔالِهَتِنَا
يَٰٓإِبۡرَٰهِيمُ ٦٢

He answered: 'Nay, it was this one, the biggest of them, who did it. But ask them, if they can speak!' (63)

قَالَ بَلۡ فَعَلَهُۥ كَبِيرُهُمۡ هَٰذَا
فَسۡـَٔلُوهُمۡ إِن كَانُوا۟ يَنطِقُونَ ٦٣

So they turned to themselves, saying, 'Surely, it is you who are doing wrong.' (64)

فَرَجَعُوٓا۟ إِلَىٰٓ أَنفُسِهِمۡ فَقَالُوٓا۟ إِنَّكُمۡ
أَنتُمُ ٱلظَّٰلِمُونَ ٦٤

But then they relapsed into their old position and said, 'You know very well that these [idols] cannot speak!' (65)

ثُمَّ نُكِسُوا۟ عَلَىٰ رُءُوسِهِمۡ لَقَدۡ عَلِمۡتَ
مَا هَٰٓؤُلَآءِ يَنطِقُونَ ٦٥

Said [Abraham]: 'Do you then worship, instead of God, something that cannot benefit or harm you in any way? (66)

قَالَ أَفَتَعۡبُدُونَ مِن دُونِ ٱللَّهِ
مَا لَا يَنفَعُكُمۡ شَيۡـٔٗا وَلَا يَضُرُّكُمۡ ٦٦

Fie upon you and upon all that you worship instead of God! Will you not, then, use your reason?' (67)

أُفّٖ لَّكُمۡ وَلِمَا تَعۡبُدُونَ مِن دُونِ
ٱللَّهِۚ أَفَلَا تَعۡقِلُونَ ٦٧

They cried: 'Burn him, and succour your gods, if you are going to do [anything at all]!' (68)

قَالُوا۟ حَرِّقُوهُ وَٱنصُرُوٓا۟ ءَالِهَتَكُمۡ إِن
كُنتُمۡ فَٰعِلِينَ ٦٨

But We said: 'Fire, be cool to Abraham, and a source of inner peace [for him].' (69)

قُلْنَا يَٰنَارُ كُونِي بَرْدًا وَسَلَٰمًا عَلَىٰٓ
إِبْرَٰهِيمَ ٦٩

They sought to lay a snare for him, but We caused them to be the absolute losers. (70)

وَأَرَادُوا۟ بِهِۦ كَيْدًا فَجَعَلْنَٰهُمُ
ٱلْأَخْسَرِينَ ٧٠

We delivered him and Lot, [bringing them] to the land which We have blessed for all mankind. (71)

وَنَجَّيْنَٰهُ وَلُوطًا إِلَى ٱلْأَرْضِ ٱلَّتِى
بَٰرَكْنَا فِيهَا لِلْعَٰلَمِينَ ٧١

And We gave him Isaac and, as an additional gift, Jacob, and caused all of them to be righteous men, (72)

وَوَهَبْنَا لَهُۥٓ إِسْحَٰقَ وَيَعْقُوبَ نَافِلَةً ۖ
وَكُلًّا جَعَلْنَا صَٰلِحِينَ ٧٢

and We made them leaders to give guidance at Our behest. We inspired them to do good works, and to be constant in prayer, and to give regular charity. It is Us alone that they worshipped. (73)

وَجَعَلْنَٰهُمْ أَئِمَّةً يَهْدُونَ بِأَمْرِنَا
وَأَوْحَيْنَآ إِلَيْهِمْ فِعْلَ ٱلْخَيْرَٰتِ
وَإِقَامَ ٱلصَّلَوٰةِ وَإِيتَآءَ ٱلزَّكَوٰةِ ۖ
وَكَانُوا۟ لَنَا عَٰبِدِينَ ٧٣

And to Lot, too, We gave sound judgement and knowledge. We saved him from that community which was given to deeds of abomination. They were people lost in evil, depraved. (74)

وَلُوطًا ءَاتَيْنَٰهُ حُكْمًا وَعِلْمًا
وَنَجَّيْنَٰهُ مِنَ ٱلْقَرْيَةِ ٱلَّتِى
كَانَت تَّعْمَلُ ٱلْخَبَٰٓئِثَ ۗ إِنَّهُمْ
كَانُوا۟ قَوْمَ سَوْءٍ فَٰسِقِينَ ٧٤

Him We admitted to Our grace; for he was righteous. (75)

وَأَدْخَلْنَٰهُ فِى رَحْمَتِنَآ ۖ إِنَّهُۥ مِنَ
ٱلصَّٰلِحِينَ ﴿٧٥﴾

And long before that, Noah called out [to Us], and We responded to him and saved him with his household from the great calamity, (76)

وَنُوحًا إِذْ نَادَىٰ مِن قَبْلُ فَٱسْتَجَبْنَا
لَهُۥ فَنَجَّيْنَٰهُ وَأَهْلَهُۥ مِنَ ٱلْكَرْبِ
ٱلْعَظِيمِ ﴿٧٦﴾

and helped him against the people who had denied Our revelations. Lost in evil were they, and so We caused them all to drown. (77)

وَنَصَرْنَٰهُ مِنَ ٱلْقَوْمِ ٱلَّذِينَ كَذَّبُوا۟ بِـَٔايَٰتِنَآ ۚ
إِنَّهُمْ كَانُوا۟ قَوْمَ سَوْءٍ فَأَغْرَقْنَٰهُمْ
أَجْمَعِينَ ﴿٧٧﴾

And remember David and Solomon, when both gave judgement concerning the field into which some people's sheep had strayed and grazed by night. We were witness to their judgement. (78)

وَدَاوُۥدَ وَسُلَيْمَٰنَ إِذْ يَحْكُمَانِ فِى ٱلْحَرْثِ
إِذْ نَفَشَتْ فِيهِ غَنَمُ ٱلْقَوْمِ وَكُنَّا
لِحُكْمِهِمْ شَٰهِدِينَ ﴿٧٨﴾

We gave Solomon insight into the case. Yet We gave sound judgement and knowledge to both of them. And We caused the mountains to join David in extolling Our limitless glory, and likewise the birds. We are indeed able to do [all things]. (79)

فَفَهَّمْنَٰهَا سُلَيْمَٰنَ ۚ وَكُلًّا ءَاتَيْنَا
حُكْمًا وَعِلْمًا ۚ وَسَخَّرْنَا مَعَ دَاوُۥدَ
ٱلْجِبَالَ يُسَبِّحْنَ وَٱلطَّيْرَ ۚ وَكُنَّا
فَٰعِلِينَ ﴿٧٩﴾

And We taught him how to make garments for you, so that they may fortify you against all that which may cause you fear. Will you, then, give thanks? (80)

وَعَلَّمۡنَٰهُ صَنۡعَةَ لَبُوسٖ لَّكُمۡ
لِتُحۡصِنَكُم مِّنۢ بَأۡسِكُمۡۖ فَهَلۡ
أَنتُمۡ شَٰكِرُونَ ٨٠

To Solomon We subjected the stormy wind, so that it sped at his behest towards the land which We had blessed. It is We who have knowledge of everything. (81)

وَلِسُلَيۡمَٰنَ ٱلرِّيحَ عَاصِفَةٗ تَجۡرِي بِأَمۡرِهِۦٓ
إِلَى ٱلۡأَرۡضِ ٱلَّتِي بَٰرَكۡنَا فِيهَاۚ وَكُنَّا
بِكُلِّ شَيۡءٍ عَٰلِمِينَ ٨١

And of the evil ones, [We assigned him] some that dived for him into the sea and performed other works besides; but it was We who kept a watch over them. (82)

وَمِنَ ٱلشَّيَٰطِينِ مَن يَغُوصُونَ لَهُۥ
وَيَعۡمَلُونَ عَمَلٗا دُونَ ذَٰلِكَۖ وَكُنَّا
لَهُمۡ حَٰفِظِينَ ٨٢

And remember Job, when he cried out to his Lord: 'Affliction has befallen me, but of all those who show mercy You are the Most Merciful.' (83)

وَأَيُّوبَ إِذۡ نَادَىٰ رَبَّهُۥٓ أَنِّي مَسَّنِيَ
ٱلضُّرُّ وَأَنتَ أَرۡحَمُ ٱلرَّٰحِمِينَ ٨٣

We responded to him and relieved all the affliction he suffered. We restored to him his family and as many more with them, as an act of grace from Ourself, and as a reminder to all who worship Us. (84)

فَٱسۡتَجَبۡنَا لَهُۥ فَكَشَفۡنَا مَا بِهِۦ مِن
ضُرّٖۖ وَءَاتَيۡنَٰهُ أَهۡلَهُۥ وَمِثۡلَهُم
مَّعَهُمۡ رَحۡمَةٗ مِّنۡ عِندِنَا وَذِكۡرَىٰ
لِلۡعَٰبِدِينَ ٨٤

And remember Ishmael, Idrīs and Dhu'l-Kifl: they all were men of constancy and patience. (85)

وَإِسۡمَٰعِيلَ وَإِدۡرِيسَ وَذَا ٱلۡكِفۡلِۖ
كُلّٞ مِّنَ ٱلصَّٰبِرِينَ ٨٥

We admitted them to Our grace, for they were among the righteous. (86)

وَأَدْخَلْنَٰهُمْ فِى رَحْمَتِنَآ ۖ إِنَّهُم
مِّنَ ٱلصَّٰلِحِينَ ﴿٨٦﴾

And remember Dhu'l-Nūn, when he went away in anger, thinking that We would not force him into a tight situation! But then he cried out in the deep darkness: 'There is no deity other than You! Limitless are You in Your glory! I have done wrong indeed!' (87)

وَذَا ٱلنُّونِ إِذ ذَّهَبَ مُغَٰضِبًا فَظَنَّ أَن
لَّن نَّقْدِرَ عَلَيْهِ فَنَادَىٰ فِى ٱلظُّلُمَٰتِ
أَن لَّآ إِلَٰهَ إِلَّآ أَنتَ سُبْحَٰنَكَ إِنِّى
كُنتُ مِنَ ٱلظَّٰلِمِينَ ﴿٨٧﴾

So We responded to him and delivered him from his distress. Thus do We deliver those who have faith. (88)

فَٱسْتَجَبْنَا لَهُۥ وَنَجَّيْنَٰهُ مِنَ ٱلْغَمِّ ۚ
وَكَذَٰلِكَ نُۨجِى ٱلْمُؤْمِنِينَ ﴿٨٨﴾

And remember Zachariah when he cried out to his Lord: 'My Lord! Do not leave me alone, although You are the best of inheritors.' (89)

وَزَكَرِيَّآ إِذْ نَادَىٰ رَبَّهُۥ رَبِّ لَا تَذَرْنِى
فَرْدًا وَأَنتَ خَيْرُ ٱلْوَٰرِثِينَ ﴿٨٩﴾

So We responded to him and gave him John, having cured his wife for him. These [three] would vie with one another in doing good works, and would call on Us in yearning and awe. They were always humble before Us. (90)

فَٱسْتَجَبْنَا لَهُۥ وَوَهَبْنَا لَهُۥ يَحْيَىٰ
وَأَصْلَحْنَا لَهُۥ زَوْجَهُۥٓ ۚ إِنَّهُمْ كَانُوا۟
يُسَٰرِعُونَ فِى ٱلْخَيْرَٰتِ وَيَدْعُونَنَا
رَغَبًا وَرَهَبًا ۖ وَكَانُوا۟ لَنَا خَٰشِعِينَ ﴿٩٠﴾

And remember her who guarded her chastity, whereupon We breathed into her of Our spirit and caused her, together with her son, to become a sign to all mankind. (91)

وَٱلَّتِىٓ أَحْصَنَتْ فَرْجَهَا فَنَفَخْنَا
فِيهَا مِن رُّوحِنَا وَجَعَلْنَٰهَا
وَٱبْنَهَآ ءَايَةً لِّلْعَٰلَمِينَ ﴿٩١﴾

Surely, your community is but one community, and I am your only Lord. So, worship Me alone. (92)

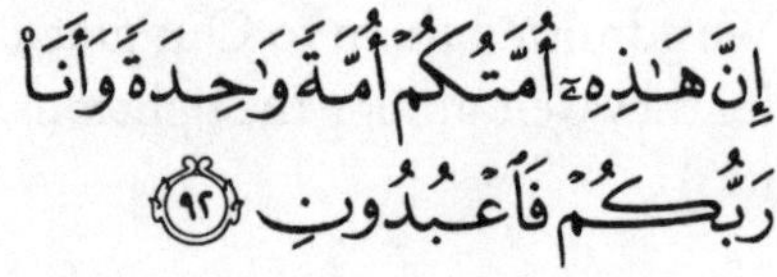

Overview

In this third passage the *sūrah* speaks about the communities that followed God's messengers, but it is not exhaustive in this respect. Some are not mentioned at all. Some are given only a brief mention, while others are referred to in some detail. We see in these references how God takes care of His messengers and bestows His grace on them. We also see the fate of those who continued to accuse their messengers of being liars, even though clear proof was given to them. We are further given an idea of how God tests His messengers, at times with delightful pleasures and at others with much affliction, and how they pass these tests.

The wisdom behind sending human messengers is also clear in this passage. The oneness of the faith and the way to be followed by all messengers, at all times, is also clearly apparent. We feel that they belong to a single community, despite the fact that they lived at different times and in different places. All this testifies to the oneness of the Maker, the will behind all events, and the consistency of the overall law that governs and unites the universe. It directs us all to one end: namely, to serve the One God worthy of worship: "*I am your only Lord. So, worship Me alone.*" (Verse 92)

Guidance and Light for Moses

Indeed We vouchsafed to Moses and Aaron the standard by which to distinguish right from wrong, a guiding light and a reminder for the God-conscious who fear their Lord in their most secret thoughts, and are weary of the Last Hour. And this one, too, is a blessed reminder which We have bestowed from on high: will you, then, reject it? (Verses 48–50)

We saw earlier in the *sūrah* how the Arab unbelievers used to ridicule God's Messenger (peace be upon him) on account of his being human. They also denied God's revelations, describing them as sorcery, poetry or mere fabrication. Now the *sūrah* shows that sending human messengers is a consistent norm, and it proceeds to give examples of such. Furthermore, the fact that God bestows books on His messengers is not a strange occurrence. For Moses and Aaron were also given a book by Him. Their book is here called '*al-Furqān*', which is the same description given to the Qur'ān. Thus, unity can be seen even in the names of these revealed books. All such books are revealed by God so as to serve as a standard distinguishing right from wrong, truth from falsehood, guidance from deviation. They also make clear the difference between ways of life. As such, each is a criterion for judgement. This is the quality which applies to both the Torah and the Qur'ān.

The Torah is also described as a '*guiding light*' which dispels all the darkness that may engulf the human mind, leading to errant beliefs. It also dispels the darkness that leads people astray and the darkness of falsehood. In such types of darkness both reason and conscience may find themselves at a loss. Indeed, the human heart remains in darkness until the light of faith is kindled within it. Faith thus sets it aglow, clearly setting its approach, guiding it to the path that should be followed, so that confusion does not arise from divergent values and concepts.

The Torah is further described as '*a reminder for the God-conscious*', reminding people of their true Lord, ensuring that they gain esteem and that they are always remembered by other people. In this respect, one only needs to ask what the status of the Children of Israel was before the revelation of the Torah! In essence they endured much humiliation under Pharaoh who slaughtered their male offspring, spared their women, and put them to hard labour and torture.

From among these God-conscious people, however, a certain group is singled out. These are the ones '*who fear their Lord in their most secret thoughts*'. (Verse 49) This is because those who fear God in their hearts when they have not seen Him, those who '*are weary of the Last Hour*', working hard to prepare themselves for its arrival, are indeed the ones who benefit by the light and follow its guidance. To them,

God's book provides an important reminder. Hence, they always remember God, and they are often favourably mentioned by other people.

This is as far as Moses and Aaron are deliberated upon here. A brief reference to the Qur'ān follows: "*And this one, too, is a blessed reminder which We have bestowed from on high.*" (Verse 50) It is not a new invention. It is nothing to wonder about since reminders were frequently revealed from on high. They are then asked rhetorically: "*Will you, then, reject it?*" (Verse 50) How could you, and on what basis, since earlier messages were vouchsafed to God's messengers in the past?

Having made this very brief reference to the two prophets, Moses and Aaron, as well as the book revealed to them, the *sūrah* now provides a detailed episode from the life of Abraham, the first grandfather of the Arabs. It was Abraham who built the Ka'bah in which the unbelievers now placed their idols and worshipped them. In fact he was the one who destroyed the idols worshipped by his own people. Hence, the *sūrah* portrays him standing up to idolatry and destroying its very symbols.

Questioning People's Beliefs

The episode narrated here is that of Abraham's message, given in a sequence of scenes that leave short gaps in between. It starts by mentioning that Abraham was initially given a sense of what is right, which here means God's oneness. In fact, it is the most important aspect of guidance which is clearly understood here as the referent of the phrase, '*what is right*': "*We formerly bestowed on Abraham his consciousness of what is right, and We were aware of him when he said to his father and his people, 'What are these images to which you are so devoted?'*" (Verses 51–52) This means that God gave Abraham his sense of what is right, knowing his aptitude to bear the trust given to His messengers.

"*He said to his father and his people, 'What are these images to which you are so devoted?'*" (Verse 52) The way he put this question is indicative of his sharp sense of what is right. He gave those stones and wooden shapes their true names, 'images'. He did not call them 'deities'. Indeed, he stated his disapproval of their worship of those images by using the word 'devoted', which indicates a permanent action. Needless to say, those people did not devote all their time to worshipping such idols, but they nonetheless attached great respect to them. This is, then, devotion in an abstract sense. The way Abraham put the question, describing them as permanent devotees to such idols, indicates that he considered their action absolutely absurd.

They defended their action by saying: "*We found our forefathers worshipping them.*" (Verse 53) Their answer indicates that they were in a stone-like inflexible state of mind that chained them to absurd traditions. They were far removed from freedom of thought, reflection and the proper evaluation of things and situations which belief in God generates as it breaks the chains of imaginary, baseless and traditional sanctities.

"*Said he: Indeed, you and your forefathers have been in evident error.*" (Verse 54) That such images were worshipped by their fathers could not impart to such objects any value which they did not have. Nor could it have given them any undeserved sanctity. Nor is real value derived from giving forefathers an elevated status and following in their footsteps. It is rather the result of proper, free and objective judgement.

When Abraham confronted them with such objectivity they asked: "*Is it the truth you are preaching to us? Or are you one who jests?*" (Verse 55) It is the kind of question asked only by someone who is unsure of his own beliefs, because he never questioned them to make sure they were right. Both his thinking and his soul are impaired by the myths and traditions he has thoughtlessly accepted. As such, he is uncertain about anything. Worship conversely must rely only on certainty, not on unsubstantiated myths. This is the state of loss that engulfs those who do not believe in a faith based on the clear truth of God's oneness that brings mind and conscience into perfect harmony.

Abraham, on the other hand, enjoys a state of complete certainty. He knows his Lord. His thoughts are full of the truth of His oneness. Hence, he says with absolute clarity: "*Indeed, your Lord is the Lord of the heavens and the earth, He who has brought them into being. And I am a witness to this [truth].*" (Verse 56) He is the Lord of man, the heavens and earth: a single Lord who is the Creator of all. Indeed, creation and Lordship are two qualities that go hand in hand. Such is the straight and clear faith. It is totally different from what unbelievers think when they claim that there are several deities, whilst at the same time conceding that none of them creates except God, the only Creator. Yet still they worship such deities knowing they are powerless to create.

Abraham reiterates his certainty like a witness testifying to a situation over which he has no doubt whatsoever: "*I am a witness to this truth.*" Abraham did not witness the creation of the heavens and the earth, nor did he witness his own creation, or that of his people. But the matter is so clear that true believers testify to it with absolute certainty. Everything in the universe confirms the oneness of the Creator who controls all. Moreover, every particle in man's constitution appeals to him to acknowledge this truth, as well as the unity of the law that governs the whole universe and conducts its affairs.

Abraham follows this with a declaration to his people that he is intent on doing something to their deities: "*By God, I shall most certainly bring about the downfall of your idols when you have turned your backs and gone away!*" (Verse 57) But he leaves his intent unclear. The *sūrah* does not mention the reply his people gave, because they relied on their feeling that a man like Abraham could not harm their deities. Hence, they left him and went away.

Abraham, however, went ahead with what he intended: "*So he broke the idols to pieces, [all] except for the biggest of them, so that they might turn back to him.*" (Verse 58) Thus, the idols which were the subject of worship were turned into small, broken pieces of stone and wood. But Abraham left the largest one untouched to see his people's reaction when they discovered what had happened. They might, for example, have wanted to ask the idol how all this happened and why it did not rise to their defence. They might even have reconsidered the whole issue and realized the absurdity of their beliefs and so begun to think properly.

A Debate to Open People's Eyes

Abraham's people returned to find the utter destruction of their idols except this largest one. But they did not question that idol or even ask themselves how their deities could suffer such a fate without defending themselves. Nor did they ask why the large idol did not take it upon itself to defend them all. They could not ask such questions, because the myths in which they believed rendered their minds useless, chaining their power of thought. Essentially, they could not consider the matter objectively, and were unable to ask the most logical question. They were only furious with the one who had brought all this upon their idols. "*They said: Who has done this to our gods? He is definitely one of the wrongdoers.*" (Verse 59) Then, those who had heard Abraham both object to his father's and peers' idol worship and threaten to destroy the same found their answer: "*They said: We heard a youth speak of them; he is called Abraham.*" (Verse 60)

It appears that Abraham (peace be upon him) was still a young man when God bestowed on him the gift of knowing what is right. Hence, he objected to the worship of idols and destroyed them when the chance presented itself. The question arises, however, as to whether he had already been given his message, or whether he acted on an inspiration that led him to the truth before he had received his message. In this latter case, his denunciation of idol worship and his call upon his father to follow his path were the result of that inspiration. This was most probably the case.

On the other hand, it is possible that Abraham's people's reference to him as 'a youth' was meant merely as a slight. This is supported by their words referring to him in the passive voice, '*he is called Abraham*'. They implied that he was unknown, and represented no threat. This is possible, but we think the first explanation to be more probable, viz. that he was only a young man at the time.

"*They said: Then bring him here in sight of all people, so that they may bear witness.*" (Verse 61) They wanted to denounce him in public so that people should know of his deeds and their consequences. And when he was brought before them, they said: "*Abraham, was it you who did this to our gods?*" (Verse 62) They continued to describe their idols as gods even when they had been smashed into pieces and formed little more than a heap of rubble. Abraham derided their thinking, and even though he faced them alone, mocked their stupidity. He was looking at the whole thing with an open mind and a clear heart. Hence, he gave them this mocking answer that fits their lowly level of thinking: "*He answered: Nay, it was this one, the biggest of them, who did it. But ask them, if they can speak!*" (Verse 63)

Derision is very clear in his answer. Hence there is no need to describe it as a lie and to try to find some justification for it, as commentators on the Qur'ān have done. The whole thing is much simpler than that. Abraham simply wanted to say to his people: these figures do not know who smashed them to pieces, nor whether it was me or this large idol which is as motionless as they were. All of them are inanimate and have no faculty of recognition. You are also deprived of your faculties, which accounts for your inability to distinguish between what is possible and what is impossible. You cannot even tell whether it was me who broke them or this big one. Hence, '*ask them, if they can speak!*'

It seems that his sarcasm shook them into some sort of reflection. "*So they turned to themselves, saying, 'Surely, it is you who are doing wrong.*'" (Verse 64) This was a good sign: not only were they aware of the absurdity of their stance but also how wrong it was to worship such statues. For once it seemed possible that they would open their eyes and see how untenable their position was.

Sadly, it was just a bright flash followed by utter darkness. Their minds seemed to see the light, but they soon sank back into lifelessness: "*But then they relapsed into their old position and said, 'You know very well that these [idols] cannot speak!*'" (Verse 65)

Their first reaction was one of returning to their senses, but their second was a relapse, a tumbling over their heads, as the Qur'ān describes. Initially, something had stirred them to reflect, but soon thereafter they had again lost their senses, lacking clear thought, and logical argument. Had there been any logic, their last statement gives Abraham a forceful argument against them. What more could he argue than the fact that those statues and deities were dumb, unable to speak? Hence, Abraham confronts them with impatience, which incidentally was very uncharacteristic of him. Basically, their absurdity was intolerable even for the most forbearing person: "*Said [Abraham]: Do you then worship, instead of God, something that cannot benefit or harm you in any way? Fie upon you and upon all that you worship instead of God! Will you not, then, use your reason?*" (Verses 66–67) Here we see Abraham's patience exhausted, as he expresses his amazement at their absurdity.

At this point, they resorted to tyranny which always prevails when tyrants are left speechless, unable to produce a coherent counter-argument. They resorted to brute force, rushing to inflict on him a painful suffering: "*They cried: Burn him, and succour your gods, if you are going to do [anything at all]!*" (Verse 68)

Yet what sort of deities are these which need the support of their servants, while they avail themselves of nothing? They are powerless, helpless.

When the Fire Was Made Cool

So, the unbelievers cried, '*burn him!*' A different word, however, was also said at this point to render everything they said meaningless, and to reduce their schemes to nothingness. This was the supreme word that can never be countered: "*But We said: Fire, be cool to Abraham, and a source of inner peace [for him].*" (Verse 69) And thus the fire was cool and a source of inner peace for Abraham to enjoy and relax in.

How is this possible? Yet why do we even ask about this when it is only the word, 'be', that needs to be said for worlds and universes to come into existence and for universal rules to be set in operation: "*When He wills a thing to be, He only says to it, 'Be' – and it is.*" (36: 82) We do not need to ask how the fire soothed rather than burnt Abraham when it is a well known phenomenon that fire burns all living tissues. For it was the One who said to the fire in the first place, 'burn' who also said to it in this instance, 'be cool and a source of inner peace'. It is the same word that initiates its object at the moment it is said, whatever that object may be, whether it is familiar to us or not.

Those who compare God's actions to those of human beings are the ones who ask how this could happen. On the other hand, those of us who understand that the two are widely different in both their nature and the means they employ neither ask such questions, nor do we try to find explanations, scientific or otherwise. The question is not one for analyses and explanations by human standards. Any method that tries to explain such miracles except by reference to God's absolute power suffers a basic defect. God's actions cannot be subjected to human standards or explained within the confines of man's limited knowledge.

All we need to do is to believe that this actually took place, because the One who did it is able to make it happen. What He did to the fire to make it cool so that it gave Abraham inner peace, and what He did to Abraham so that the fire did not burn him are points the Qur'ān does not explain because our limited minds fall short of understanding them. On the other hand, we have no source of evidence other than the Qur'ānic text.

Transforming the fire so as to give Abraham coolness and inner peace is only one example of God's infinite ability, even though they may not be totally contrary to what we are familiar with, as this one. There are countless other difficulties and circumstances that beset individuals and communities which, if allowed to run their course, would cause their total ruin. But then God administers just a small touch to bring about life instead of death, happiness instead of misery, and endless goodness instead of unmitigated evil. Thus we see how the command that made the fire cool, bringing peace to Abraham is frequently repeated in the life of individuals, groups and communities, as well as in the life of ideas and beliefs. This command is only a manifestation of the word which renders any scheme, effort or design futile, because it is the final say by the highest power.

"*They sought to lay a snare for him, but We caused them to be the absolute losers.*" (Verse 70) It is reported that the king who was Abraham's contemporary was the Nimrod, the Aramaic king of Iraq. He and his supporters were destroyed by some punishment inflicted by God. The reports we have differ as to the details of this punishment. We have no way of verifying them. However, all that we need to know is that God saved Abraham from the torture prepared for him while his opponents who schemed against him were the ones to suffer utter loss. They are described in the Qur'ān as the '*absolute losers*'.

"*We delivered him and Lot, [bringing them] to the land which We have blessed for all mankind.*" (Verse 71) It was to the land of Palestine that he and his nephew, Lot, emmigrated. This was the land to receive revelations from on high for a very long time and the area where prophets and messengers of Abraham's descent were raised. This area incorporates the holy land where the second house of worship was built. It is a fertile land with rich tillage. All these blessings were added to that of the generations of prophets living there.

> *And We gave him Isaac and, as an additional gift, Jacob, and caused all of them to be righteous men, and We made them leaders to give guidance at Our behest. We inspired them to do good works, and to be constant in prayer, and to give regular charity. It is Us alone that they worshipped.* (Verses 72–73)

Abraham left his home country where his family and community lived. So God compensated him with this blessed land as a better country to live in. He also gave him his son Isaac and grandson Jacob to be a better family than the one he had earlier. He also gave him a better community than his old one and raised from his offspring leaders to give mankind guidance. He inspired them to do all sorts of good works, to attend to their prayers and to give regular charity, or *zakāt*. They were obedient worshippers of God. All this was Abraham's blessed compensation given by God for his perseverance when he was tested. It was a goodly compensation to fit his endurance in adversity.

Endowed with Knowledge and Wisdom

> *And to Lot, too, We gave sound judgement and knowledge. We saved him from that community which was given to deeds of abomination. They were people lost in evil, depraved. Him We admitted to Our grace; for he was righteous.* (Verses 74–75)

The story of Lot is related in full detail elsewhere in the Qur'ān. Here we have only a brief reference to it, as he emmigrated from Iraq with his uncle, Abraham. Lot stayed in the township of Sodom, where the people resorted to repugnant practices. They were guilty of abominable, perverted sexual indecency, men with men, openly, without any sense of shame or guilt. Hence, God poured His punishment on the township and its people, as "*they were people lost in evil*". (Verse 74) God saved Lot and his household with the exception of his wife. "*Him We admitted to Our grace; for he was righteous.*" (Verse 75) The way this verse is phrased suggests that God's grace is a place of refuge into which God admits whomever He wills so that they find peace, comfort and blessings.

This is followed by a similarly short reference to Noah and his saviour: "*And long before that, Noah called out [to Us], and We responded to him and saved him with his household from the great calamity, and helped him against the people who had denied Our revelations. Lost in evil were they, and so We caused them all to drown.*" (Verses 76–77)

Again the reference here does not provide details. It is simply to confirm God's response to Noah when he appealed to Him. Noah lived at an earlier time than Lot, hence the reference, '*long before that*'. In Noah's case as well, he and his household were saved with the exception of his wife. As for his people, they were destroyed by the flood, which is described here as '*the great calamity*'. It is described in detail in *Sūrah* 11, *Hūd*.

Then follows a fairly detailed account of an episode in the story of David and Solomon:

> *And remember David and Solomon, when both gave judgement concerning the field into which some people's sheep had strayed and grazed by night. We were witness to their judgement. We gave Solomon insight into the case. Yet We gave sound judgement and knowledge to both of them. And We caused the mountains to join David in extolling Our limitless glory, and likewise the birds. We are indeed able to do [all things]. And We taught him how to make garments for you, so that they may fortify you against all that which may cause you fear. Will you, then, give thanks? To Solomon We subjected the stormy wind, so that it sped at his behest towards the land which We had blessed. It is We who have knowledge of everything. And of the evil ones, [We assigned him] some that dived*

for him into the sea and performed other works besides; but it was We who kept a watch over them. (Verses 78–82)

The story of the field over which David and Solomon gave judgement is detailed in some reports as stating that two men came to David. One of them had a field, or a vineyard according to some reports, while the other had a flock of sheep. The field's owner said: 'This man's sheep traversed my field at night, leaving it devastated.' David ruled that the owner of the field should take the sheep in compensation for his wasted crops. The sheep's owner then passed by Solomon and told him of David's judgement. Solomon went to his father and said: "Prophet of God, you should have judged differently." David asked: "How should I judge?" Solomon replied: "Give the sheep to the field's owner to benefit by them and give the field to the sheep's owner to tend until it is returned to its original state. Then each man returns to the other his property. Thus, the field's owner will get his field and the sheep's owner his sheep." David confirmed that that was the right judgement, and he ordered it to be carried out.

Both David and Solomon judged according to their own discretion, but God was observing their judgement. He inspired Solomon to give the verdict that was fairer. David's judgement aimed to compensate the field's owner for the damage done to him, which establishes justice. But Solomon's judgement added to justice a constructive dimension. Thus, justice became a motive to initiate constructive effort. This is a higher level of justice, one which was given by God's inspiration.

Both David and Solomon were given wisdom and knowledge: "*Yet We gave sound judgement and knowledge to both of them.*" (Verse 79) There was nothing wrong with David's judgement, but that of Solomon's went a step further because it was inspired.

The *sūrah* moves on to show what was given specifically to each of these prophets, starting with the father: "*And We caused the mountains to join David in extolling Our limitless glory, and likewise the birds. We are indeed able to do [all things]. And We taught him how to make garments for you, so that they may fortify you against all that which may cause you fear. Will you, then, give thanks?*" (Verses 79–80)

A Special Gift to a Special Man

David was famous for his Psalms, which were hymns that he chanted in his melodious voice. They were echoed by his surroundings, including the mountains and birds. When a human being feels his bond with God alive in his heart, he feels that the entire universe responds to him. All impediments and barriers separating different kinds of creatures are thus removed, so that they join together in one great, universal entity. In such moments of clarity, man's soul is united with all about it. It is no longer distinct from its surroundings. Indeed it is one with all that is around it.

As we read these verses we can imagine David chanting his Psalms, oblivious to his own separate entity, letting his soul move freely in the universe, looking at God's animate and inanimate creation. He feels that they echo his chanting and in this way respond to him. The entire universe thus becomes an orchestra singing a marvellous tune of God's praise and glorification. "*The seven heavens extol His limitless glory, as does the earth, and all who dwell in them. Indeed every single thing extols His glory and praise, but you cannot understand their praises.*" (17: 44) The one who understands such praises is a person who sheds all barriers and separations. He is one who turns to God.

"*We caused the mountains to join David in extolling Our limitless glory, and likewise the birds. We are indeed able to do [all things].*" (Verse 79) There is nothing difficult for God when He wills to have it done or put in place, regardless of whether it is familiar or not to mankind.

"*And We taught him how to make garments for you, so that they may fortify you against all that which may cause you fear. Will you, then, give thanks?*" (Verse 80) That was how God taught him to make shields using interconnected rings. Shields were previously made of long plates. Small, interconnected rings can make a shield that is easier to use and more flexible. It seems that it was David who invented this, as God instructed him to do. God reminds people of His favour in teaching David this art so as to protect them in wartime: "*So that they may fortify you against all that which may cause you fear.*" The verse ends with a question that encourages them to do the right thing: "*Will you, then, give thanks?*"

Human civilization has moved step by step in its discoveries, because the task that man was given to build life on earth allowed him to move one step at a time, to reorganize his life after each advance. Reorganizing life according to a new system is not easy for the human soul, because it shakes its foundations and alters its habits. A period of readjustment is thus needed until man settles into his new system. God in His wisdom has willed to allow a period of resettlement, long or short as it may be, after each leap forward.

In our own times, however, an important cause of anxiety that is characteristic is the rapidity of scientific and social changes which do not allow humanity a period of resettlement. Man is not given the chance to adapt to new conditions or recognize their merits.

The case of Solomon was even greater: "*To Solomon We subjected the stormy wind, so that it sped at his behest towards the land which We had blessed. It is We who have knowledge of everything. And of the evil ones, [We assigned him] some that dived for him into the sea and performed other works besides; but it was We who kept a watch over them.*" (Verses 81–82) Reports of all types are given about Solomon, most derived from Israelite sources and interwoven with unfounded myth. We will not go into this maze, but will rather confine our discussion to what is stated in the Qur'ān. Nothing else about Solomon is certain.

The Qur'ānic text here states that winds, in their stormy conditions, were made subservient to Solomon, moving at his bidding to the blessed land, which was most probably Palestine, given it was earlier described as such in Abraham's story. The question asked here though is how all this was done.

There is the story of the magic carpet which is said to have carried Solomon and his courtiers to Palestine and back in a very short period, while camel caravans took a month to cover the same distance. This report relies on what is mentioned in another *sūrah*: "*To Solomon [We made subservient] the wind: its morning course [covered the distance of] a month's journey, and its evening course, a month's journey.*" (34: 12) The Qur'ān though does not mention anything about a magic carpet, nor do we find it in any authentic report. Thus we cannot say anything further about it.

It is safer to explain this statement about the wind by saying that it was directed, by God's will, to the blessed land in a cycle lasting one month each way. How? As we have said, we cannot ask such a question about the operation of God's will, which is free and unrestrained. It is God's will that creates the laws of nature and sets them in operation. What we know of the laws operating in the universe is very little. There is nothing to preclude that other laws, about which we know nothing, are in operation, but their effects may surface only when God wills: "*It is We who have knowledge of everything.*" (Verse 81) Unlike human knowledge, God's knowledge is complete and perfect.

The same applies to making the *jinn* subservient to Solomon such that they dive into the depths of the sea, or deep into the earth, to bring him some of its hidden riches or to perform other works. The word *jinn* includes in its meaning everything that is concealed, hidden or unknown. Qur'ānic texts mention a type of creature unknown to us, called the Jinn. It was from among these that God assigned some to Solomon to dive in the sea and do his bidding. Furthermore, God kept watch over them so that they did not escape or rebel. It is He who holds sway over all His creatures, putting them to whatever purpose He chooses in any way He likes.

God tested David and Solomon with what pleases people. David was tested in connection with the administration of justice, while Solomon's test involved nobly bred, swift-footed steeds, as is detailed in *Sūrah* 38. So we will leave that for now. Both David and Solomon persevered, sought God's forgiveness and passed their tests. They remained grateful to God for His favours.

A Test of Hardship for a Prophet

The *sūrah* also provides us with the example of Job, the Prophet, (peace be upon him), being tested with hardship:

> *And remember Job, when he cried out to his Lord: 'Affliction has befallen me, but of all those who show mercy You are the most merciful.' We responded to him and removed all the affliction he suffered. We restored to him his family and as many more with*

them, as an act of grace from Ourself, and as a reminder to all who worship Us. (Verses 83–84)

Job's story is one of the finest that centres on a test. Qur'ānic texts mentioning Job only speak in general terms, giving few details. In this particular instance, the *sūrah* mentions Job's supplication and God's response, because the overall atmosphere of the *sūrah* is one of grace bestowed from on high on His prophets and the care He takes of them when He tests them. This applies in all test situations, including rejection by their peoples, as with Abraham, Lot and Noah; power and wealth as with David and Solomon; or hardship with Job.

Job's prayer, as mentioned here, does not go beyond describing his condition and emphasizing God's attributes: "*And remember Job, when he cried out to his Lord: 'Affliction has befallen me, but of all those who show mercy You are the most merciful.'*" (Verse 83) He does not appeal for his condition to be changed, because he wants to remain patient in adversity. Nor does he suggest anything to his Lord. His is an attitude of perfect humility before Him. Thus, he is God's model servant: neither panicking in a situation of adversity nor expressing frustration at the hardship he endures. Indeed, his is considered a test of the highest severity.[2] He is reluctant even to pray to God to lift his hardship. Therefore, he leaves the matter entirely to God, knowing that He knows his situation and does not need his prayer.

At the moment Job addressed his Lord with such confidence and humility, his prayer was answered and God's grace was bestowed on him in abundance. His test was over: "*We responded to him and relieved all the affliction he suffered. We restored to him his family and as many more with them.*" (Verse 84) His personal affliction was removed, and his health was restored. This indicates complete recovery, leaving no

2. There are numerous reports about what happened to Job, some of which are clearly exaggerated. Some suggest that he suffered an illness that made people turn away from him, unable to look at him. Thus was he left outside the city. We have no reliable evidence to support this. It is indeed contrary to what a messenger of God is like. What Qur'ānic texts suggest however is that he suffered hardship within himself and within his family. That is more than enough as a test for anyone. – Author's note.

trace of illness. The affliction which concerned his family was also lifted. God compensated him for the one he had lost by giving him twice as many. It is said that he had lost his children, and God gave him twice their number, or He might have given him new children and grandchildren.

All this was as "*an act of grace from Ourself*," because every blessing is an act of God's grace. It was also "*a reminder to all who worship Us.*" It reminds them of God and the tests He may put us through, and of His grace that will not fail to follow the hardship. The test to which Job was put provides an example for all mankind, and his patient endurance sets a model for all to follow.

The reference to those "*who worship Us*" within the context of hard tests is especially significant. Such worshippers may be subjected to tests and hardship. To endure with patience is a requirement of faith and worship. The whole matter is very serious. Faith is a trust which is given only to those who are able to shoulder its responsibility and endure its hardship. It is not mere words, carelessly uttered by anyone.

The *sūrah* then refers very briefly to three other prophets: "*And remember Ishmael, Idrīs and Dhu'l-Kifl: they all were men of constancy and patience. We admitted them to Our grace, for they were among the righteous.*" (Verses 85–86) Again with all three the quality of patience in adversity is highlighted. Ishmael showed his patience when he was required to submit himself for sacrifice, and he duly did so, saying to his father, Abraham: "*Father, do as you are bidden. You will find me, if God so wills, among those who are patient in adversity.*" (37: 102)

As for Idrīs, as we noted earlier, we know nothing about his time or where he lived. Some people suggest that he was Osiris, whom the Egyptians worshipped after his death and invented some legends concerning him. He is said to have been the first teacher of mankind, from whom farming and industry were learned. But we have no evidence to support this. We need only know that he was patient in some good way that merits a record in God's book.

Dhu'l-Kifl is also unknown: we cannot determine when or where he lived. Perhaps he was one of the Israelite prophets, or among their most pious and God-fearing people. It is also said that before one of their prophets died, he guaranteed that he would take care of the Children of Israel, giving a warrant that he would spend the night in worship, fast during the day and not allow anger to take hold of him when he ruled in a dispute. He honoured all his commitments. It is said that he was called Dhu'l-Kifl because of this, since his name refers to such practices.[3] But none of these details is supported by evidence. The Qur'ānic text here is sufficient to credit him with being patient in adversity, a highly rewarding quality.

"*We admitted them to Our grace, for they were among the righteous.*" (Verse 86) This is why they are mentioned in this *sūrah.*

Swallowed by the Whale

We then have a brief outline of Jonah's story to fit with the approach followed in this *sūrah*. It is however given in more detail in *Sūrah* 37, *al-Ṣāffāt*:

> *And remember Dhu'l-Nūn, when he went away in anger, thinking that We would not force him into a tight situation! But then he cried out in the deep darkness: 'There is no deity other than You! Limitless are You in Your glory! I have done wrong indeed!' So We responded to him and delivered him from his distress. Thus do We deliver those who have faith.* (Verses 87–88)

Jonah is here called Dhu'l-Nūn, which means 'man of the whale' because he was swallowed by the whale and then thrown out. He was sent to a particular city, and he called on its people to believe in God, but they rejected both him and his message. By way of response to their stubbornness, he left in anger. He showed little inclination to persevere with them on account of their rejection. He thought that God would not restrict him to a particular place, given there were many cities and communities, and that he would thus be directed to

3. The name Dhu'l-Kifl means 'the one giving a guarantee'. – Editor's note.

go somewhere else. This is what is meant by the expression rendered here as "*thinking that We would not force him into a tight situation!*"

Angry and frustrated, he walked away, and found himself sometime later by the sea, where he saw a laden boat. He boarded it. When the boat was in the middle of the sea, it was apparent that its load was too heavy. The shipmaster said that one passenger must be thrown overboard in order to give the rest a chance to survive. They all drew lots and the draw fell to Jonah. The other passengers threw him into the sea, or he might have jumped overboard. It was then that the whale swallowed him and he found himself in a most tight situation. He felt shrouded by several layers of darkness: the darkness of the whale's belly, the darkness of the deep blue sea and the darkness of the night. At this moment, he cried out: "*There is no deity other than You! Limitless are You in Your glory! I have done wrong indeed!*" (Verse 87) God answered his prayer and saved him from the distress he was suffering. The whale thus threw him out near the shore. The remainder of his story is taken up in *Sūrah* 37, *al-Ṣāffāt*.

There are in Jonah's story some significant points we need to reflect upon. First, Jonah did not initially show enough patience and willingness to endure the difficulties of delivering God's message. He quickly became fed up, abandoned his people and moved on, angry and frustrated. He felt his situation to be very tight. But God exposed him to a much tighter and harder distress as compared with the opposition of unbelievers. Had Jonah not turned to his Lord in repentance and admitted that he had wronged himself by leaving his position of duty, he would not have been relieved of his distress. It was God's care that saved him.

The advocates of a message must be ready to bear the burden involved in such advocacy, remain patient in the face of rejection and vicious opposition. When a person is certain of the truth of the message he advocates, he finds the opposition of people who accuse him of false inventions and deliberate lying difficult to handle. Yet to remain patient in the face of such adversity is only part of the duties of such advocacy. Those who are entrusted with delivering a message and advocate the truth must remain patient, face the difficulties and persevere with their advocacy. They must continue to present their message to people and call on them to believe in it, time after time.

Such advocates cannot give in to despair. They cannot give up on people, believing that they will never respond to the truth, no matter how much opposition they face, and how often they are rejected and accused of falsehood. If their hundred attempts to touch people's hearts meet with failure, their next attempt may have a positive result. Indeed, such a result may come only after one thousand and one attempts. Hence, if they have already tried a thousand times and failed, they should try once more in the hope that, with God's grace, their next attempt will be more successful.

The way a message must follow in order to touch people's hearts is neither easy nor comfortable. Positive responses may not be forthcoming. A great heap of false beliefs, erring practices, customs, traditions and situations weigh heavily on people's hearts and minds. This heap must be removed, and hearts must be revived in every possible way. A touch on every sensitive receptor must be made to try to find the effective nerve. With determination and diligence the right touch will inevitably be made, and a complete transformation of the addressee is achieved. We are often surprised that a thousand attempts may be made with one particular person, but without success. Then a casual gesture, coming at the right time, touches the right cord, and the person concerned goes through a complete transformation without any difficulty.

A comparison may be made with trying to find a particular radio station. We turn the tuning key to and fro, but we miss it despite taking full care to find it. Then suddenly a casual touch may hit upon it and we enjoy a good reception. The human heart is akin to a radio receiver. Advocates of the divine message must try hard to find the right spot that enables every heart to receive that message. When one thousand attempts have failed, the next one may succeed.

It is easy for an advocate of the divine message to be angry when people turn away from him. To give up and quit is always easy. It may enable us to cool down. But of what service is that to the message itself? It is the message that is most important, not its advocate. If we are angry, we should remain patient. It is infinitely better for us not to lose heart and not to give up.

An advocate is merely a tool in God's hand, and God preserves His message better than us. We must discharge our duty however hard the opposition we may face. We then leave the matter to God, and He gives guidance to whomever He pleases. In the story of Jonah we thus have a good example to reflect upon. His return to his Lord and acknowledgement of his error provide a good lesson. Furthermore, in the grace God showed him, answering the prayer he addressed through the compounded darkness, gives us great hope: "*Thus do We deliver those who have faith.*" (Verse 88)

One Community Throughout History

Along the same lines of its brief accounts of different prophets, the *sūrah* gives a quick reference to Zachariah and his son John, highlighting how God responded to Zachariah and answered his prayers:

> *And remember Zachariah when he cried out to his Lord: 'My Lord! Do not leave me alone, although You are the best of inheritors.' So We responded to him and gave him John, having cured his wife for him. They all would vie with one another in doing good works, and would call on Us in yearning and awe. They were always humble before Us.* (Verses 89–90)

The story of John's birth is given in detail in *Sūrahs* 19 and 3, *Maryam* and the *House of 'Imrān*. Here it is given very briefly to fit with the rest of the *sūrah*. It begins with Zachariah's prayer, '*My Lord, do not leave me alone,*' without a successor to take care of the temple. Zachariah was in charge of the temple where the Israelites offered their worship, before the birth of Jesus. However, Zachariah does not forget that the ultimate custodian of faith and property is God Himself: "*You are the best of inheritors.*" He only needs a successor who will attend well to the faith and to his family. People are the medium to fulfil God's will on earth.

The answer to this prayer was swift and direct at the same time. "*So We responded to him and gave him John, having cured his wife for him.*" (Verse 90) She was barren, unable to bear children. The *sūrah* overlooks all details to give us the ultimate result of God's response to Zachariah's prayer. "*They all would vie with one another in doing good works.*" Hence, God gave an immediate response to that prayer. They "*would call on Us in yearning and awe.*" They yearned to earn God's pleasure and were in awe of incurring His displeasure. Their hearts were alive, always hopeful. "*They were always humble before Us,*" showing no arrogance.

It was Zachariah's and his wife's good characteristics that deserved that God should bless them with a goodly son, John. Thus, the whole family was blessed, fully deserving of God's grace.

Finally, Mary is mentioned along with her son: "*And remember her who guarded her chastity, whereupon We breathed into her of Our spirit and caused her, together with her son, to become a sign to all mankind.*" (Verse 91)

We note that Mary is not mentioned here by name, because the main reference in the chain of prophets is to her son, while she is second to him in this account. Reference is made to her main quality that is related to her son.[4] Thus she is the one "*who guarded her chastity,*" keeping herself pure of all sexual contact. Normally, this expression of guarding one's chastity is used to refer to marriage, because it protects against sin. Here it refers to its primary meaning, which is purity of all contact, whether legitimate or not. Thus, Mary is held innocent of all accusations levelled by the Jews against her and against Joseph the carpenter, who was with her in the service of the temple. The Gospels now in circulation claim that he married her but did not consummate the marriage and she remained a virgin.

So, Mary guarded her chastity, and God breathed into her of His spirit. The breathing is left general here, unlike *Sūrah* 66, The

4. A number of eminent scholars, notably Ibn Ḥazm, rank Mary among prophets, citing in evidence her mention in this *sūrah*, as well as her listing in *Sūrah* 19, *Maryam*, with a number of prophets and then referring to them all in Verse 58 as prophets. – Editor's note.

Prohibition, where its location is mentioned. We discussed this in our commentary on *Sūrah* 19, *Maryam*. In order to stick to the general atmosphere generated by the text of this *sūrah*, we prefer not to add any details here, confining ourselves only to what is directly mentioned.

We "*caused her, together with her son, to become a sign to all mankind.*" (Verse 91) Indeed she was a unique sign, without similar example, whether in the past or in the future, a single such case in the history of mankind. Such a special case is worthy of our contemplation, for by doing so we recognize God's power, unrestricted as it is by anything whatsoever. It is the power that designs natural laws and sets them in operation, but which is not subservient to them. It remains free of all restrictions.

At the end of this fast moving round, referring to different messengers, types of tests, and forms of God's grace and mercy, the *sūrah* gives a final comment: "*Surely, your community is but one community, and I am your only Lord. So, worship Me alone.*" (Verse 92)

This is the community of prophets: a single community, sharing the same faith, following the same course, and turning to God alone. Thus we have a single community on earth, and a single Lord in heaven. He has no partners. No one can be worshipped but Him. This whole community follows the same line, acknowledging a single will in heaven and on earth. Thus, this whole round dovetails with the central theme of the *sūrah*, emphasizing the right faith based on the concept of God's oneness, which is confirmed by all universal laws.

4

A Mercy for Mankind

But people have divided themselves into factions. Yet to Us shall they all return. (93)

وَتَقَطَّعُوٓا۟ أَمْرَهُم بَيْنَهُمْ ۖ كُلٌّ
إِلَيْنَا رَٰجِعُونَ ﴿٩٣﴾

Whoever does righteous deeds and is a believer withal, his endeavour shall not be lost: We shall record it in his favour. (94)

فَمَن يَعْمَلْ مِنَ ٱلصَّٰلِحَٰتِ وَهُوَ
مُؤْمِنٌ فَلَا كُفْرَانَ لِسَعْيِهِۦ وَإِنَّا
لَهُۥ كَٰتِبُونَ ﴿٩٤﴾

It is forbidden that any community We have ever destroyed should not return [to Us]. (95)

وَحَرَٰمٌ عَلَىٰ قَرْيَةٍ أَهْلَكْنَٰهَآ
أَنَّهُمْ لَا يَرْجِعُونَ ﴿٩٥﴾

When Gog and Magog are let loose and swarm down from every corner, (96)

حَتَّىٰٓ إِذَا فُتِحَتْ يَأْجُوجُ وَمَأْجُوجُ
وَهُم مِّن كُلِّ حَدَبٍ يَنسِلُونَ ﴿٩٦﴾

when the true promise draws close [to its fulfilment], staring in horror shall be the eyes of the unbelievers, [and they will exclaim:] 'Oh, woe to us! Of this we were indeed heedless. We have assuredly done wrong.' (97)

وَٱقْتَرَبَ ٱلْوَعْدُ ٱلْحَقُّ فَإِذَا هِىَ
شَٰخِصَةٌ أَبْصَٰرُ ٱلَّذِينَ كَفَرُوا۟
يَٰوَيْلَنَا قَدْ كُنَّا فِى غَفْلَةٍ مِّنْ
هَٰذَا بَلْ كُنَّا ظَٰلِمِينَ ﴿٩٧﴾

You and all that you were wont to worship instead of God are but the fuel of hell: that is what you are destined for. (98)

إِنَّكُمْ وَمَا تَعْبُدُونَ مِن دُونِ
ٱللَّهِ حَصَبُ جَهَنَّمَ أَنتُمْ لَهَا
وَٰرِدُونَ ﴿٩٨﴾

If those [objects of your worship] had truly been divine, they would not have been destined for it. But there all shall abide. (99)

لَوْ كَانَ هَٰٓؤُلَآءِ ءَالِهَةً مَّا وَرَدُوهَا
وَكُلٌّ فِيهَا خَٰلِدُونَ ﴿٩٩﴾

There they will be groaning with anguish, and bereft of hearing. (100)

لَهُمْ فِيهَا زَفِيرٌ وَهُمْ فِيهَا
لَا يَسْمَعُونَ ﴿١٠٠﴾

But those for whom [the decree of] ultimate good has already gone forth from Us will be kept far away from that hell, (101)

إِنَّ ٱلَّذِينَ سَبَقَتْ لَهُم مِّنَّا ٱلْحُسْنَىٰٓ
أُو۟لَٰٓئِكَ عَنْهَا مُبْعَدُونَ ﴿١٠١﴾

hearing none of its hissing sound. They will abide in all that their souls have ever desired. (102)

لَا يَسْمَعُونَ حَسِيسَهَا ۖ وَهُمْ فِى
مَا ٱشْتَهَتْ أَنفُسُهُمْ خَٰلِدُونَ ﴿١٠٢﴾

The Supreme Terror will cause them no grief, since the angels will receive them with the greeting, 'This is your day which you were promised.' (103)

لَا يَحْزُنُهُمُ ٱلْفَزَعُ ٱلْأَكْبَرُ وَتَتَلَقَّىٰهُمُ
ٱلْمَلَٰٓئِكَةُ هَٰذَا يَوْمُكُمُ ٱلَّذِى
كُنتُمْ تُوعَدُونَ ﴿١٠٣﴾

On that day We shall roll up the heavens like a scroll of parchment. As We brought into being the first creation, so We shall bring it forth anew. That is a promise We willed upon Ourselves. We are indeed able to do all things. (104)

يَوْمَ نَطْوِى ٱلسَّمَآءَ كَطَىِّ ٱلسِّجِلِّ
لِلْكُتُبِ ۚ كَمَا بَدَأْنَآ أَوَّلَ
خَلْقٍ نُّعِيدُهُۥ ۚ وَعْدًا عَلَيْنَآ ۚ إِنَّا كُنَّا
فَٰعِلِينَ ﴿١٠٤﴾

We wrote in the Psalms, after the Reminder [given to Moses] that 'the righteous among My servants shall inherit the earth.' (105)

وَلَقَدْ كَتَبْنَا فِى ٱلزَّبُورِ مِنۢ بَعْدِ
ٱلذِّكْرِ أَنَّ ٱلْأَرْضَ يَرِثُهَا عِبَادِىَ
ٱلصَّٰلِحُونَ ﴿١٠٥﴾

In this, there is a message for people who worship God. (106)

إِنَّ فِى هَٰذَا لَبَلَٰغًا لِّقَوْمٍ
عَٰبِدِينَ ﴿١٠٦﴾

We have sent you as a [manifestation of Our] grace towards all the worlds. (107)

وَمَآ أَرْسَلْنَٰكَ إِلَّا رَحْمَةً لِّلْعَٰلَمِينَ ﴿١٠٧﴾

Say: 'It has been revealed to me that your God is the One and only God: will you, then, surrender yourselves to Him?' (108)

قُلْ إِنَّمَا يُوحَىٰٓ إِلَىَّ أَنَّمَآ إِلَٰهُكُمْ
إِلَٰهٌ وَٰحِدٌ فَهَلْ أَنتُم مُّسْلِمُونَ ﴿١٠٨﴾

If they turn away, say: 'I have proclaimed this in equity to all of you alike; but I do not know whether that which you are promised is imminent or far off. (109)

فَإِن تَوَلَّوْا۟ فَقُلْ ءَاذَنتُكُمْ عَلَىٰ
سَوَآءٍ وَإِنْ أَدْرِىٓ أَقَرِيبٌ أَم بَعِيدٌ
مَّا تُوعَدُونَ ﴿١٠٩﴾

He certainly knows all that is said openly, just as He knows all that you would conceal. (110)

إِنَّهُۥ يَعْلَمُ ٱلْجَهْرَ مِنَ ٱلْقَوْلِ
وَيَعْلَمُ مَا تَكْتُمُونَ ﴿١١٠﴾

For all I know, this may be but a trial for you, and a short reprieve.' (111)

وَإِنْ أَدْرِى لَعَلَّهُۥ فِتْنَةٌ لَّكُمْ
وَمَتَٰعٌ إِلَىٰ حِينٍ ﴿١١١﴾

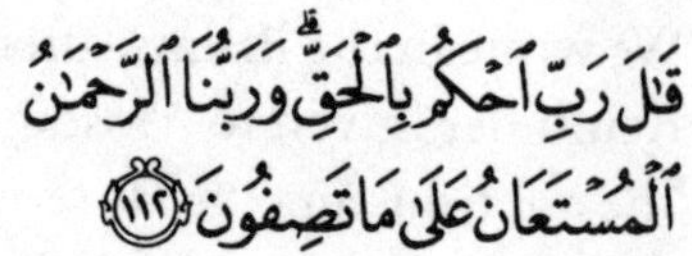

Say: 'My Lord, judge You in truth!' and [say]: 'Our Lord is the Most Merciful whose help is ever to be sought against all [the blasphemies] you utter.' (112)

Overview

This is the last passage of this *sūrah* which showed us first a number of God's universal laws that testify to the oneness of the Creator. It then showed us God's law in sending messengers to advocate a message testifying to the unity of the community of believers and their single faith. Now the *sūrah* gives us a scene of the Last Hour and its signs. We see here the destiny of those who associate partners with God as well as the destiny of those alleged partners. God is seen as the Lord of all who conducts the affairs of the entire universe. Following this, we have two statements: the first establishes the rule that governs who inherits the earth, while the second shows God's grace bestowed on all worlds in the form of sending His final Messenger, Muḥammad (peace be upon him).

At this point, the Prophet is ordered to leave the unbelievers alone to face their destiny which will be determined by God. The Prophet seeks God's help to face their opposition and ridicule, as well as their indulgence in idle pleasures when the Day of Reckoning is so near.

Rules That Never Fail

The followers of all God's messengers belong to one community, sharing the same faith and the same beliefs. The basis on which this community is built is the belief in God's oneness, which is testified to by universal laws. It is the central, unchanged belief advocated by all messengers, right from the very beginning to the last and final message. As new messages were given, certain details were added to the code of living that should be established on the basis of this central belief. These additions suited the abilities and development of each community and each new generation. They responded to the increased richness of human experience which makes new generations able to fulfil new types of legislation, meeting their increased needs and responding to their social and material advancement.

Despite the fact that the followers of all messengers constitute a single community, and despite the fact that all divine messages share the same basis, those followers divided themselves into factions. Each group took a portion and went away, allowing controversy to stir between them, and thus leading to division and hostility. Indeed this happened among the followers of a single messenger, with some eager to kill others in the name of the faith, which they all shared.

They have divided themselves into factions in this life, but they will all return to God in the life to come: "*Yet to Us shall they all return.*" (Verse 93) The end is with Him, when they will face the reckoning and He requites them for what they do in this present life.

"*Whoever does righteous deeds and is a believer withal, his endeavour shall not be lost: We shall record it in his favour.*" (Verse 94) This is the law of action and reward. No one shall suffer any loss of any good deed based on faith. All such deeds are recorded with God who never loses sight of anything.

It is essential that good action should be based on true faith in order to have its true value and to flourish. Moreover, good action is necessary so that faith can yield its fruits and prove its existence.

Faith is the central basis of life, because it provides true and real contact between man and the universe. Indeed faith is the bond that ties the universe and all living creatures to their only Creator. It outlines the single law that operates in the universe by God's will. No structure can be raised without a basis or a foundation. When we say that good action is the edifice, it has to stand upon a firm foundation, which is faith. Otherwise, it collapses.

Good action is the fruit of faith which proves its active presence in man's conscience. Islam in particular is an active faith: once it establishes its roots in man's conscience, it manifests itself in good action. It is like a ripe fruit pointing to the roots stretching below the surface.

Hence, the Qur'ān always associates faith with good deeds, whenever it mentions deeds and their reward. There is no reward for a belief that remains idle, motivating no good action. Nor is there any reward for action that is cut off from its roots of faith. A good action that is not based on faith is a mere coincidence, because it is not related to a well defined system or a consistent law. It is merely a whim that does not stem from the right motivation. The right motivation is faith in God who is pleased with good action, because it provides the means to build a sound structure in this universe and the means to achieve the excellence that God wants for this present life. Thus, good action is seen to be a movement towards an objective that is linked to the ultimate goal of life. It is never a fleeting whim or an aimless coincidence.

Reward for good action is given in the life to come, even though parts of it may be advanced in this present life. Those cities which suffered total destruction will inevitably return to receive their ultimate requital. It is not possible that they will not be returned: "*It is forbidden that any community We have ever destroyed should not return [to Us].*" (Verse 95)

The *sūrah* mentions these cities in particular, after the statement, "*Yet to Us shall they all return,*" because it may occur to us that their destruction in this life was their final reckoning and punishment. Hence the *sūrah* emphatically asserts that they will return. The assertion is given in a prohibited form whereby non-return is impossible. It is for sure a rather peculiar mode of expression. Therefore, some commentators and translators have interpreted it as a negation of a return of those communities to this present life after they were destroyed, or a negation of their turning back from their erring ways. Neither interpretation is necessary. It is better to take the text as it is, because its meaning is quite clear.

One Destiny for Idol and Worshipper

We are then presented with a scene of the Day of Resurrection, starting with a sign that signals its approach. This sign is the opening of the gates for Gog and Magog:

> *When Gog and Magog are let loose and swarm down from every corner, when the true promise draws close [to its fulfilment], staring in horror shall be the eyes of the unbelievers, [and they will exclaim:]*

'Oh, woe to us! Of this we were indeed heedless. We have assuredly done wrong.' (Verses 96–97)

When we discussed the account given in *Sūrah* 18, The Cave, of Dhu'l-Qarnayn and its reference to Gog and Magog, we said that the true promise of the hereafter may have already drawn close to its fulfilment when the Tartars swarmed eastwards to destroy states and empires. Indeed at the time of the Prophet himself, the Qur'ān states clearly: "*The Last Hour has drawn close.*" (54: 1) Nevertheless, its drawing close does not specify a particular time when it will actually take place. To God, time is totally different from our own calculation of days, months and years.

What is intended here is to describe what happens on that day when it actually arrives, and to introduce it with a miniature scene of what is familiar to human beings. This is the scene of Gog and Magog being let loose, and their swarming down from every corner in a fast moving image. The Qur'ān often uses notions that are familiar to man and elevates these to draw scenes of the hereafter.

The scene portrayed here stresses the element of surprise that takes the onlookers: Thus, "*staring in horror shall be the eyes of the unbelievers.*" (Verse 97) They shall not wink because of the great horror that has taken them by surprise. The text uses inversion here to bring forward the actual stirring in order to provide added emphasis.

The *sūrah* does not go on to describe their condition further. Instead, it shows them speaking to give more life to the scene: "*Oh, woe to us! Of this we were indeed heedless. We have assuredly done wrong.*" (Verse 97) This is the cry of one in utter distress. He is at a total loss, his eyes are stirring and he invokes a curse upon himself, acknowledging his past errors, and repents when repentance is no longer of any use.

When this confession is made in such shock, the final verdict is announced. It cannot be changed: "*You and all that you were wont to worship instead of God are but the fuel of hell: that is what you are destined for.*" (Verse 98)

The style employed here shows them as if they are now facing the ultimate reckoning, being taken to hell together with their worshipped idols. They are practically thrown in it mercilessly, as though they are small pebbles and hell is being stoned with them. At this moment, they are shown the falsity of their claims that these were deities. The proof is seen in that very scene: "*If those [objects of your worship] had truly been divine, they would not have been destined for it.*" (Verse 99) This is logical proof taken from a scene showing them, while they are still in this life, something that takes place in the hereafter. The *sūrah* then goes on to show them actually in hell, describing their abode and conditions in it. They are in a state that deprives them of their receptive faculties: "*But there all shall abide. There they will be groaning with anguish, and bereft of hearing.*" (Verses 99–100)

Believers, on the other hand, are spared all this hardship, because they have been promised a goodly life in the hereafter: "*But those for whom [the decree of] ultimate good has already gone forth from Us will be kept far away from that hell, hearing none of its hissing sound. They will abide in all that their souls have ever desired.*" (Verses 101–102)

The phrase, 'its hissing sound', or its one word equivalent in Arabic used here, *ḥasīsahā,* belongs to a number of Qur'ānic terms with sounds that impart meaning. It describes the sound of the fire as it rages and burns. It is an extremely frightening sound. Hence, those given the promise of a good destiny are spared that sound, let alone suffering it. They are saved from the terror that leaves the unbelievers in a state of utter loss. Instead they enjoy whatever they desire, in complete security and bliss. They are warmly received by the angels, who give them comforting company, when the general atmosphere is one of horror: "*The Supreme Terror will cause them no grief, since the angels will receive them with the greeting, 'This is your day which you were promised.'*" (Verse 103)

The scene is now drawn to its close, showing the ultimate state of the universe, which contributes to the great terror that overwhelms all on that day: "*On that day We shall roll up the heavens like a scroll of parchment.*" (Verse 104) Thus, the heavens are folded up since all matters have been settled, the reckoning is over, and the universe known to man has no further function to perform. A new world is born in a new universe: "*As We brought into being the first creation, so We shall bring it forth anew. That is a promise We willed upon Ourselves. We are indeed able to do all things.*" (Verse 104)

Who Inherits the World

Having drawn a strong image showing the end of the universe and all living creatures, the *sūrah* now makes clear the divine law that determines who inherits the earth. In the end it is God's righteous servants who will be the masters of the earth. The two scenes are interlinked: "*We wrote in the Psalms, after the Reminder [given to Moses] that 'the righteous among My servants shall inherit the earth.'*" (Verse 105)

As it is given in Arabic, this verse may be read in two ways. The first considers the Psalms as certain scriptures given in particular to the Prophet David (peace be upon him). In this case, the 'reminder' is a reference to the Torah which was revealed earlier than the Psalms. The other reading makes of the term *zabūr* a description of every revealed book, which is a portion of the original book recorded in the guarded Tablet, which in this case would be what the word 'reminder' refers to. This Tablet, thus, represents the complete version and the final authority to which all divine laws refer.

Be that as it may, the statement, '*We wrote in the Psalms, after the Reminder*,' is made here to explain the established rule God has put into operation concerning the succession to the earth. This means that '*the righteous among My servants shall inherit the earth.*' But what does this inheritance entail, and who are the righteous among God's servants?

God gave the earth to Adam so that he could fulfil his charge of building the earth, setting it on its right course so it could develop. This included utilization of its resources and treasures, and the exploitation of its apparent and concealed potentials so as to attain the highest possible standard that could be reached.

God set out a complete code or way of life for mankind to implement in their life on earth. This is based on faith and good action. God's final message includes a detailed account of this way of life, together with laws that ensure its freedom from distortion and which provide balance and harmony in its every step.

This code does not make the development of the earth and the use of its resources and utilization of potentials an aim in itself. It should rather be coupled with taking good care of man's conscience, so that man attains the highest standard he is capable of achieving. It protects man from sinking to the level of animals in the midst of a blooming material civilization. There must be no drop in the human side of man's life while great strides are made in the exploitation of apparent and latent resources.

On the way to achieving such balance and harmony the scales may tilt one way at one time and the other on a different occasion. It may happen that tyranny prevails, or that power may be concentrated in the hands of some unbelievers who are able to materially exploit the resources and wealth of the earth. All these will remain experiences that mankind has to go through at one stage or another, but the ultimate inheritance will fall to God's righteous servants who combine faith with good action. These two elements go hand in hand in their lives.

Whenever faith in the heart combines with the will to work in any community, it inherits the land. But when these two elements separate, then the scales tilt the other way, and tyranny or exploitation ensue. Power may fall to those who are keen to utilize all material resources, if those who claim to be believers neglect their utilization. This happens when believers are devoid of the true and genuine type of faith that provides the motivation to do good and build a proper human life on earth. It should be remembered that it is through such good work that man discharges the task assigned to him by God.

All the believers need do is bring into practice the full meaning of their belief, which is good action and the fulfilment of their duty, in order that God's promise of inheriting the earth is fulfilled. It is active and conscientious workers among believers that are described as God's righteous servants.

As the *sūrah* draws to its close, its rhythm takes on a similar note to that of its opening: "*In this, there is a message for people who worship God. We have sent you as a [manifestation of Our] grace towards all the worlds.*" (Verses 106–107) This Qur'ān, and the laws it reveals of nature, the universe, human destiny both in this present life and in the life to come, and the rules that govern action and reward, provide a clear message. This message is appreciated by those who are ready to receive God's guidance. These are the ones who are described here as '*people who worship God.*' For, a true worshipper is the one who has a soft heart, ready to receive a message, ponder over it and make use of it in his life.

A Manifestation of Grace

God has sent His last Messenger as a manifestation of His grace to all mankind. He takes them by the hand to show them divine guidance. It is only those who are ready to receive such guidance that benefit by it, but God's grace is bestowed on believers and unbelievers alike.

The code of living given to us through the Prophet Muḥammad (peace be upon him) is one that ensures the happiness of all mankind, and which will lead to the highest level of perfection humanity can attain. Muḥammad's message was given to mankind at a time when it attained its full mental maturity. Hence, it is a book open to all minds across all generations. It includes the unchangeable fundamentals of human life, and it is ready to meet changing needs that are known only to the One who created man, and who knows His creation well. He is most kind and aware of all things.

This book sets out the principles and the framework of a permanent code for an ever-renewing human life, leaving to human beings the task of deducing detailed rules necessary for organizing their relations as life progresses. It is also up to human beings to determine the methods and the means of implementation, according to their different situations and circumstances, without conflict with the principles of the permanent code.

Having guaranteed the right to freedom of thought and established the society that allows the human mind to think, this book also allows the human mind the freedom to determine what actions need to be taken. Thus, under Islam and within its fundamental principles, man is free to develop and progress towards the highest attainable standard of human life.

All human experience, up to the present moment, confirms that the Islamic system, in general, remains ahead of man's progress, able to provide the environment that ensures steady human progress in all directions. It will always be ahead of human life, providing the lead, and never restraining its march. In meeting human desire for development and progress, Islam never suppresses any human potential whether of individuals or the community. Nor does it deprive them of their ability to enjoy the fruits of their efforts or the pleasures of life.

The most important aspect of this code of living is that it is both balanced and coherent. It neither advocates physical torment in order to elevate man's spirit, nor does it neglect the spiritual dimension in order to indulge in physical pleasures. It neither imposes restrictions on the individual and his healthy, natural desires in order to serve the interests of the community or the state, nor does it give rein to the individual's deviant desires at the expense of the safety of the community.

It is clear that all the tasks the Islamic code of living assigns to man are within his ability and serve his interests. Moreover, he has been given the means and faculties that help him fulfil these tasks, looking at them as desirable, even though he may at times have to contend with difficulties and hardships in order to achieve them.

The message of Muḥammad (peace be upon him) was a manifestation of grace to his own people and to humanity at large. The principles he laid down sounded strange at first because humanity was then far removed from a truly sound practical and spiritual life. After the revelation of the message of Islam, humanity drew gradually closer to these principles, which then started to sound familiar, acceptable and easy to implement.

Islam calls for a humanity in which there is no room for ethnic or geographical distinction, united by its single faith and social system. To the human mind and in the prevailing conditions at the time, this sounded very strange. Noble classes then were accustomed to thinking of themselves as having a different make up to that of ordinary human beings. Yet humanity has been trying for nearly fourteen centuries to follow the lead of Islam, but it stumbles along the way because it does not benefit by the full light of Islam. It achieves only limited standards of the Islamic code, at least in what it professes to advocate. Still we find European and American countries holding on to disgraceful racial values which Islam removed at its very outset.

Islam advocated full equality between all people under the law. It did this at a time when all humanity used to divide people into classes with a different law for each class. In fact a master's will was the law in the age of slavery and feudalism. At that time it was very strange for humanity to hear a voice advocating the principle of full and universal equality under the law. Yet gradually humanity continues to try to achieve, at least theoretically, a measure of what Islam put in practice nearly 1,400 years ago.

Numerous other aspects confirm that Muḥammad's message was a manifestation of divine grace for all humanity, and that Muḥammad (peace be upon him) was certainly sent to bring mercy and grace to mankind, including those who did not believe in him. All humanity has been influenced, willingly or unwillingly, knowingly or unknowingly, by the code of living he outlined. This grace continues to be available in plenty for anyone who wishes to benefit by it. Its implementation enables humanity to enjoy the lovely breeze of heaven to dispel the burning heat of the earth, especially these days.

Today, humanity most urgently needs a fresh taste of this grace. Yet it persists in confusion as it gropes along in the maze of materialism, in the endless wars, and in the spiritual void in which it finds itself.

An Appeal for Judgement

Having highlighted this aspect of grace, the *sūrah* states an order given by God to His Messenger. He is to confront those who deny the truth and ridicule his efforts. He is to identify the essence of his message as one which brings grace and mercy to all mankind: "*Say: It has been revealed to me that your God is the One and only God: will you, then, surrender yourselves to Him?*" (Verse 108)

This is the most essential element of grace in the message of Islam. It is the belief in God's absolute oneness that saves humanity from the burdens of ignorant myth, senseless idolatry and from the pressures of superstition. It establishes life on a firm basis, bonding it with universal existence, according to clear and consistent laws, leaving no room for whim or fleeting desire. It ensures that every human being is able to stand up with heads held high. Heads bow only to God, the One who holds absolute sway over all that exists.

This is the path of grace: "*will you, then, surrender yourselves to Him?*" This is the only question God's Messenger is directed to ask those who deny his message and indulge in ridicule.

"*If they turn away, say: 'I have proclaimed this in equity to all of you alike.*" (Verse 109) I have given you all that I have, and now both you and I have the same knowledge. A proclamation of the sort this verse hints at is one that takes place at a time of war so as to indicate the end of peace. This *sūrah*, however, was revealed in Makkah, before war was made permissible in Islam. This means that the Prophet is commanded to declare to the unbelievers that he has given up on them, leaving them aware of their destiny, and of which he has warned them. Thus, they have no excuse. They will have to taste the bitter fruits of their actions, knowing full well what awaits them.

"*But I do not know whether that which you are promised is imminent or far off.*" (Verse 109) I have made my declaration to you in all equity, and I have no idea when what you are warned will befall you. It is part of what belongs to what God has kept to Himself. He alone knows its timing, and knows when He will inflict His punishment, whether in this life or in the life to come. He further knows what people say in private as well as what they say in public. Nothing is kept outside God's knowledge: "*He certainly knows all that is said openly, just as He knows all that you would conceal.*" (Verse 110)

Your situation is completely open. If He inflicts punishment on you, He does so on the basis of His perfect knowledge of all your affairs, public and private, overt or covert. On the other hand, when He delays punishment, He does so for a definite purpose. "*For all I know, this may be but a trial for you, and a short reprieve.*" (Verse 111) I have no knowledge of what God's intention is behind this delay. He may wish to put you to a certain trial, allowing you some reprieve until a certain date He might have determined. When that time comes, He may inflict on you very severe punishment.

With the issue left shrouded in mystery, the *sūrah* jolts their hearts, and leaves them with the realization that all possibilities remain open. They thus remain apprehensive of the great surprise they may be in for. Their minds are alert, realizing that the pleasures that they have been allowed to indulge in may be a prelude to a trial that brings trouble and hardship. When people expect that punishment may be inflicted at any time, they remain edgy, looking for reassurance while anticipating that the curtains may rise at any time to reveal what has thus far been kept hidden from them.

It is only human to overlook what may come at any time. Comforts and pleasures can be very deceptive, allowing people to forget that their knowledge is limited and that they do not know what God's will may bring about at any time. Hence, this warning is meant to encourage people to keep their hearts and minds alert. They have thus been warned, and they have no excuse if they fail to heed the warning.

Having discharged his trust, delivered his message, made his declaration in all fairness and warned people against forthcoming trials, the Prophet makes an appeal to his Lord. He requests God, the Most Merciful, to judge in fairness and in truth between him and those who ridicule his message. He seeks His help against their scheming, accusations and rejection, for help may be sought only from God: "*Say: 'My Lord, judge You in truth!' and [say]: 'Our Lord is the Most Merciful whose help is ever to be sought against all that you claim.'*" (112)

The emphasis placed here on God's abundant grace is significant. It is God, the Most Gracious and Merciful, who sent His Messenger and made this an act of His mercy. But he was met with rejection and ridicule by hardened unbelievers. It is He who can bestow His grace on His Messenger and give him support against their blasphemies.

Thus the *sūrah* ends on a powerful note, just as it opened with a powerful statement. The beginning and ending thus provide a profound and effective address.

SŪRAH 22

Al-Ḥajj

(The Pilgrimage)

Prologue

Parts of this *sūrah* were revealed in Makkah and other parts in Madīnah, as is evident from the topics addressed. We note in particular that verses 38–41, which give the Muslim community permission to fight, and verse 60, which speaks about meting out the same punishment that is inflicted on Muslims by others, were revealed in Madīnah. Muslims were only allowed to fight or to exact similar punishment after the Prophet's migration to Madīnah and the establishment of the Muslim state there. Prior to that, the Prophet stated that he had not received any directives allowing such action. He was replying to an offer made by the people of Madīnah who pledged their support to him. They stated that they were ready to kill all the unbelievers in Minā. In response, he said: "I have not been told to do such a thing." But when Madīnah became the land of the Muslim state, God permitted fighting to repel the unbelievers' aggression and to defend the freedom of belief and worship.

In its subject matter and its general ambiance, the *sūrah* appears closer to the Qur'ānic *sūrahs* revealed in Makkah. Issues like God's oneness, the warning to be watchful for the Last Hour, evidence for the inevitable resurrection of all mankind, the fallacy of pagan beliefs based on associating partners with God, the scenes of the Day of

Judgement, and drawing attention to universal signs pointing to God's existence and power, are all very prominent in the *sūrah*. Yet equally prominent are the many issues normally addressed in *sūrahs* revealed in Madīnah. Apart from giving permission to the Muslim community to fight for God's cause, the *sūrah* addresses freedom of worship, the promises of God's support to those who fight to repel aggression, and the order to fight for God's cause.

A Starting Jolt

The impressions the *sūrah* generates in its various scenes and cited examples are those of power, strength, toughness and awe. It delivers clear warnings and alerts our sense of God consciousness, of fearing Him and submitting to His will.

The scene of resurrection at the outset is one of power, striking fear in people's hearts: "*Mankind! Have fear of your Lord. The violent convulsion at the Last Hour will be awesome indeed. On the day when it comes, every suckling mother will utterly forget her nursling, and every woman heavy with child will cast her burden; and it will seem to you that all mankind are drunk, although they are not drunk. But severe indeed will be God's punishment.*" (Verses 1–2)

The same may be said of the scene describing punishment in the hereafter: "*For the unbelievers garments of fire shall be cut out; and scalding water will be poured over their heads, melting all that is in their bellies and their skin. In addition, there will be grips of iron for them. Whenever, in their anguish, they try to get out, they are returned there, and will be told: 'Taste the torment of fire.'*" (Verses 19–22)

A very vivid image is drawn showing the status of one who associates partners with God: "*He who associates partners with God is like one who is hurling down from the skies; whereupon he is snatched by the birds, or blown away by the wind to a far-off place.*" (Verse 31) Equally vivid is the description of the one who has lost hope of ever being granted God's support: "*If anyone thinks that God will not succour him in this world and in the life to come, let him stretch out a rope to the sky and then cut himself off; and then let him see whether his scheme will remove that which has enraged him.*" (Verse 15)

The scene depicting the townships destroyed on account of their wrongdoing also emits power: "*How many a township have We destroyed because it had been immersed in evildoing. Now they lie in desolate ruin. How many a well lies abandoned, and how many a proud palace lies empty.*" (Verse 45)

Such images of power and awe are coupled with serious orders and assigned tasks in addition to the justification given for the use of power to repel aggression and the firm promise to grant victory and power. This is re-emphasized in reference to God's might and the weakness of His alleged partners. Belonging to the first group is the following example: "*Permission to fight is given to those against whom war is waged, because they have been wronged. Most certainly, God has the power to grant them victory. These are the ones who have been driven from their homelands against all right for no other reason than their saying, 'Our Lord is God!' Were it not that God repels some people by means of others, monasteries, churches, synagogues and mosques – in all of which God's name is abundantly extolled – would surely have been destroyed. God will most certainly succour him who succours God's cause. God is certainly Most Powerful, Almighty. They are those who, if We firmly establish them on earth, attend regularly to their prayers, give in charity, enjoin the doing of what is right and forbid the doing of what is wrong. With God rests the final outcome of all events.*" (Verses 39–41)

An example of the second type is: "*Mankind! An aphorism is set forth; hearken, then, to it. Those beings whom you invoke instead of God cannot create a fly, even though they were to join all their forces to that end. If a fly robs them of anything, they cannot rescue it from him! Weak indeed is the seeker, and weak the sought! No true understanding of God have they. God is certainly Most Powerful, Almighty.*" (Verses 73–74)

Beyond all this we discern the repeated call to remain God-fearing and to stand in awe of God. The *sūrah* starts with this call in its first verse, and repeats it time and again: "*Mankind! Have fear of your Lord. The violent convulsion at the Last Hour will be awesome indeed.*" (Verse 1) "*Anyone who honours the symbols set up by God [shows evidence of] God-consciousness in people's hearts.*" (Verse 32) "*Your God is the One and Only God. Hence, surrender yourselves to Him. Give good news to those who are humble, whose hearts tremble with awe whenever God is mentioned.*" (Verses 34–35) "*Never does their meat or their blood reach God; it is your piety that reaches Him.*" (Verse 37)

The *sūrah* is also replete with scenes of the universe, the Day of Judgement, the fate of earlier communities, cited cases, images, reflections and lessons drawn. All aim to alert our feelings of faith, piety, and surrender to God. This is what characterizes the entire *sūrah* and gives it its distinctive mark.

When we read the *sūrah* in full, we find that it consists of four main parts. It begins with a general address to all mankind, calling on them to be God-fearing. They are warned against the violent convulsion which announces the arrival of the Day of Judgement. We also have a description of the horrific scenes accompanying it and a denunciation of disputing without knowledge about God and following every devil who inevitably leads his followers astray. It then highlights indications of the resurrection based on the stages of life a human embryo goes through, and the development of plant life, making a clear link between all types of life. These stages which follow well established and never failing laws God has set in operation are shown to be closely linked to a number of truisms: namely, that God is the truth; that He brings the dead to life; that He has power over all things; that the Last Hour will inevitably come, and that God will resurrect all those buried in their graves. All these are natural laws and facts closely related to the law that governs the life of the universe.

A second denunciation of ignorant disputes about God follows, since such disputes are devoid of guidance and follow no enlightening book or revelation. As this is made clear, a negative example is given showing the repugnant attitude of those who look at faith from a profit and loss point of view. When misfortune befalls such people, they are quick to seek help from sources other than God, in effect despairing of His help. This part of the *sūrah* concludes with a definitive statement that guidance and error are achieved by God's will. He will certainly judge, on the Day of Reckoning, between the followers of different faiths. It finally paints a horrific scene of the punishment suffered by unbelievers, contrasted with the perfect bliss enjoyed by believers.

The second part is clearly related to the first as it opens with a comment on the unbelievers who turn people away from God's path and from the Sacred Mosque in Makkah. Their action is strongly denounced since God has made the Sacred Mosque a place for all mankind, where those who live close by it and those who come from remote parts have the same rights and position. It then relates part of the history of building the Ka'bah, often referred to in the Qur'ān as the House, and the task assigned by God to Abraham to build it on the basis of His oneness, purifying it of all traces of idolatry. It goes on to mention some of the rituals of pilgrimage and how they strengthen people's piety, which is the aim of this great act of worship. This part of the *sūrah* concludes with giving permission to believers to fight in order to protect places and rites of worship against any aggression that seeks to turn them away from their belief in God alone.

The third part provides examples of past communities' denials of faith, the destruction of hardened unbelievers, and images of cities destroyed over the heads of wrongdoers. The purpose here is to explain God's law with regard to the messages He sends to mankind, to comfort the Prophet who was facing a determined campaign of rejection and opposition, and to reassure the believers as to their inevitable destiny. This part also includes certain aspects of Satan's scheming against prophets and messengers, and how God reasserts His message, setting His revelations on a solid basis. Thus, believers are reassured and unbelievers, whether weaklings or the arrogant and powerful, turn away, having been misled by Satan.

The final part of the *sūrah* states God's promise of support to anyone who is oppressed as he tries to repel such aggression. This promise is followed by highlighting some aspects of God's infinite power. Next to it we have a miserable image of the helplessness of the deities worshipped by those who associate partners with God. The *sūrah* concludes with an address to the believers to worship their Lord and strive for His cause, and to hold fast to His rope as they fulfil the duties required by their faith which goes back to the time of Abraham (peace be upon him).

I

The Pilgrimage

Al-Ḥajj (The Pilgrimage)

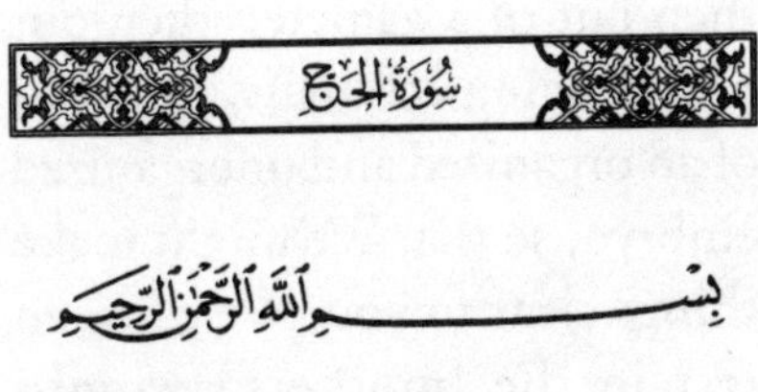

In the Name of God, the Merciful, the Beneficent

Mankind! Have fear of your Lord. The violent convulsion at the Last Hour will be awesome indeed. (1)

يَـٰٓأَيُّهَا ٱلنَّاسُ ٱتَّقُواْ رَبَّكُمْۚ إِنَّ
زَلْزَلَةَ ٱلسَّاعَةِ شَيْءٌ عَظِيمٞ ﴿١﴾

On the day when it comes, every suckling mother will utterly forget her nursling, and every woman heavy with child will cast her burden; and it will seem to you that all mankind are drunk, although they are not drunk. But severe indeed will be God's punishment. (2)

يَوْمَ تَرَوْنَهَا تَذْهَلُ كُلُّ مُرْضِعَةٍ
عَمَّآ أَرْضَعَتْ وَتَضَعُ كُلُّ ذَاتِ
حَمْلٍ حَمْلَهَا وَتَرَى ٱلنَّاسَ سُكَـٰرَىٰ
وَمَا هُم بِسُكَـٰرَىٰ وَلَـٰكِنَّ عَذَابَ
ٱللَّهِ شَدِيدٞ ﴿٢﴾

Yet some people argue about God without having any knowledge, and follow every rebellious devil. (3)

وَمِنَ ٱلنَّاسِ مَن يُجَـٰدِلُ فِي ٱللَّهِ بِغَيْرِ
عِلْمٖ وَيَتَّبِعُ كُلَّ شَيْطَـٰنٖ مَّرِيدٖ ﴿٣﴾

It is decreed for whoever entrusts himself to any [such devil] that he will lead him astray and guide him towards the suffering of the blazing flame. (4)

كُتِبَ عَلَيْهِ أَنَّهُ مَن تَوَلَّاهُ فَأَنَّهُ يُضِلُّهُ وَيَهْدِيهِ إِلَىٰ عَذَابِ السَّعِيرِ ﴿٤﴾

Mankind! If you are in doubt as to the resurrection, remember that We have created you out of dust, then out of a gamete,[1] then out of a clinging cell mass, then out of an organized and unorganized embryo, so that We might make things clear to you. We cause to rest in the [mothers'] wombs whatever We please for an appointed term, and then We bring you forth as infants, that you may grow up and attain your prime. Some of you die young, and some live on to abject old age when all that they once knew they know no more. You can see the earth dry and barren; and [suddenly,] when We send down water upon it, it stirs and swells and puts forth every kind of radiant bloom. (5)

يَا أَيُّهَا النَّاسُ إِن كُنتُمْ فِي رَيْبٍ مِّنَ الْبَعْثِ فَإِنَّا خَلَقْنَاكُم مِّن تُرَابٍ ثُمَّ مِن نُّطْفَةٍ ثُمَّ مِنْ عَلَقَةٍ ثُمَّ مِن مُّضْغَةٍ مُّخَلَّقَةٍ وَغَيْرِ مُخَلَّقَةٍ لِّنُبَيِّنَ لَكُمْ ۚ وَنُقِرُّ فِي الْأَرْحَامِ مَا نَشَاءُ إِلَىٰ أَجَلٍ مُّسَمًّى ثُمَّ نُخْرِجُكُمْ طِفْلًا ثُمَّ لِتَبْلُغُوا أَشُدَّكُمْ ۖ وَمِنكُم مَّن يُتَوَفَّىٰ وَمِنكُم مَّن يُرَدُّ إِلَىٰ أَرْذَلِ الْعُمُرِ لِكَيْلَا يَعْلَمَ مِن بَعْدِ عِلْمٍ شَيْئًا ۚ وَتَرَى الْأَرْضَ هَامِدَةً فَإِذَا أَنزَلْنَا عَلَيْهَا الْمَاءَ اهْتَزَّتْ وَرَبَتْ وَأَنبَتَتْ مِن كُلِّ زَوْجٍ بَهِيجٍ ﴿٥﴾

That is because God alone is the Ultimate Truth; and He alone brings the dead to life; and He has the power to will anything. (6)

ذَٰلِكَ بِأَنَّ اللَّهَ هُوَ الْحَقُّ وَأَنَّهُ يُحْيِي الْمَوْتَىٰ وَأَنَّهُ عَلَىٰ كُلِّ شَيْءٍ قَدِيرٌ ﴿٦﴾

---

1. For an explanation of the translation of this verse, please see the footnote on its commentary, p. 102.

And that the Last Hour is certain to come, beyond any doubt; and that God will certainly resurrect all who are in their graves. (7)

وَأَنَّ ٱلسَّاعَةَ ءَاتِيَةٌ لَّا رَيْبَ فِيهَا وَأَنَّ
ٱللَّهَ يَبْعَثُ مَن فِى ٱلْقُبُورِ ٧

Yet some people argue about God without having any knowledge, without guidance, and without any light-giving revelations. (8)

وَمِنَ ٱلنَّاسِ مَن يُجَـٰدِلُ فِى ٱللَّهِ بِغَيْرِ عِلْمٍ
وَلَا هُدًى وَلَا كِتَـٰبٍ مُّنِيرٍ ٨

They turn away in scorn so as to lead others astray from the path of God. Disgrace is in store for them in this world, and on the Day of Resurrection We shall make them taste suffering through fire. (9)

ثَانِىَ عِطْفِهِۦ لِيُضِلَّ عَن سَبِيلِ ٱللَّهِ ۖ لَهُۥ
فِى ٱلدُّنْيَا خِزْىٌ ۖ وَنُذِيقُهُۥ يَوْمَ ٱلْقِيَـٰمَةِ
عَذَابَ ٱلْحَرِيقِ ٩

[They shall be told:] 'This is the outcome of what your own hands have wrought. Never does God do the least wrong to His creatures.' (10)

ذَٰلِكَ بِمَا قَدَّمَتْ يَدَاكَ وَأَنَّ ٱللَّهَ
لَيْسَ بِظَلَّـٰمٍ لِّلْعَبِيدِ ١٠

Some people worship God on the border-line [of faith]. If good befalls such a person, he is content; but if a trial assails him, he turns away utterly; thus losing this world and the life to come. This is, indeed, a loss beyond compare. (11)

وَمِنَ ٱلنَّاسِ مَن يَعْبُدُ ٱللَّهَ عَلَىٰ حَرْفٍ ۖ
فَإِنْ أَصَابَهُۥ خَيْرٌ ٱطْمَأَنَّ بِهِۦ ۖ وَإِنْ
أَصَابَتْهُ فِتْنَةٌ ٱنقَلَبَ عَلَىٰ وَجْهِهِۦ
خَسِرَ ٱلدُّنْيَا وَٱلْءَاخِرَةَ ۚ ذَٰلِكَ هُوَ
ٱلْخُسْرَانُ ٱلْمُبِينُ ١١

He invokes, instead of God, something that can neither harm nor benefit him. This is the utmost that one can go astray. (12)

يَدْعُوا مِن دُونِ اللَّهِ مَا لَا يَضُرُّهُ
وَمَا لَا يَنفَعُهُ ذَٰلِكَ هُوَ الضَّلَٰلُ
الْبَعِيدُ ﴿١٢﴾

Indeed he invokes one that is far more likely to cause harm than benefit. Vile indeed is such a patron, and vile the friend. (13)

يَدْعُوا لَمَن ضَرُّهُ أَقْرَبُ مِن نَّفْعِهِ
لَبِئْسَ الْمَوْلَىٰ وَلَبِئْسَ الْعَشِيرُ ﴿١٣﴾

God will certainly admit those who believe and do righteous deeds into gardens through which running waters flow. God certainly does whatever He wills. (14)

إِنَّ اللَّهَ يُدْخِلُ الَّذِينَ ءَامَنُوا وَعَمِلُوا
الصَّٰلِحَٰتِ جَنَّٰتٍ تَجْرِي مِن
تَحْتِهَا الْأَنْهَٰرُ إِنَّ اللَّهَ يَفْعَلُ مَا يُرِيدُ ﴿١٤﴾

If anyone thinks that God will not succour him in this world and in the life to come, let him stretch out a rope to the sky and then cut himself off; and then let him see whether his scheme will remove that which has enraged him. (15)

مَن كَانَ يَظُنُّ أَن لَّن يَنصُرَهُ اللَّهُ فِي
الدُّنْيَا وَالْءَاخِرَةِ فَلْيَمْدُدْ بِسَبَبٍ إِلَى
السَّمَآءِ ثُمَّ لْيَقْطَعْ فَلْيَنظُرْ هَلْ يُذْهِبَنَّ
كَيْدُهُ مَا يَغِيظُ ﴿١٥﴾

Thus have We bestowed from on high this [Qur'ān] in clear verses. God guides him who wills [to be guided]. (16)

وَكَذَٰلِكَ أَنزَلْنَٰهُ ءَايَٰتٍ بَيِّنَٰتٍ
وَأَنَّ اللَّهَ يَهْدِي مَن يُرِيدُ ﴿١٦﴾

As for the believers, the Jews, the Sabians, the Christians, the Magians, and those who associate partners with God, God will decide between them on the Day of Judgement. God is witness to everything. (17)

إِنَّ ٱلَّذِينَ ءَامَنُواْ وَٱلَّذِينَ هَادُواْ
وَٱلصَّٰبِـِٔينَ وَٱلنَّصَٰرَىٰ وَٱلْمَجُوسَ
وَٱلَّذِينَ أَشْرَكُوٓاْ إِنَّ ٱللَّهَ
يَفْصِلُ بَيْنَهُمْ يَوْمَ ٱلْقِيَٰمَةِ إِنَّ
ٱللَّهَ عَلَىٰ كُلِّ شَىْءٍ شَهِيدٌ ١٧

Are you not aware that to God bow down in worship all those who are in the heavens and on earth, the sun, the moon, the stars, the mountains, the trees and the beasts, and a great number of human beings? But a great number also will inevitably have to suffer punishment. He whom God shall disgrace will have none who could bestow honour on him. God certainly does what He wills. (18)

أَلَمْ تَرَ أَنَّ ٱللَّهَ يَسْجُدُ لَهُۥ مَن فِى ٱلسَّمَٰوَٰتِ
وَمَن فِى ٱلْأَرْضِ وَٱلشَّمْسُ وَٱلْقَمَرُ
وَٱلنُّجُومُ وَٱلْجِبَالُ وَٱلشَّجَرُ وَٱلدَّوَآبُّ
وَكَثِيرٌ مِّنَ ٱلنَّاسِ ۖ وَكَثِيرٌ حَقَّ عَلَيْهِ
ٱلْعَذَابُ ۗ وَمَن يُهِنِ ٱللَّهُ فَمَا لَهُۥ مِن
مُّكْرِمٍ ۚ إِنَّ ٱللَّهَ يَفْعَلُ مَا يَشَآءُ ۩ ١٨

These two adversaries have become engrossed in contention about their Lord. For the unbelievers garments of fire shall be cut out; and scalding water will be poured over their heads, (19)

هَٰذَانِ خَصْمَانِ ٱخْتَصَمُواْ فِى رَبِّهِمْ ۖ
فَٱلَّذِينَ كَفَرُواْ قُطِّعَتْ لَهُمْ ثِيَابٌ مِّن نَّارٍ
يُصَبُّ مِن فَوْقِ رُءُوسِهِمُ ٱلْحَمِيمُ ١٩

melting all that is in their bellies and their skin. (20)

يُصْهَرُ بِهِۦ مَا فِى بُطُونِهِمْ وَٱلْجُلُودُ ٢٠

In addition, there will be grips of iron for them. (21)

وَلَهُم مَّقَٰمِعُ مِنْ حَدِيدٍ ٢١

Whenever, in their anguish, they try to get out, they are returned there, and will be told: 'Taste the torment of fire.' (22)

كُلَّمَآ أَرَادُوٓا۟ أَن يَخْرُجُوا۟ مِنْهَا مِنْ
غَمٍّ أُعِيدُوا۟ فِيهَا وَذُوقُوا۟ عَذَابَ
ٱلْحَرِيقِ ﴿٢٢﴾

God will certainly admit those who believe and do righteous deeds into gardens through which running waters flow, wherein they will be adorned with bracelets of gold and pearls, and where silk will be their raiment. (23)

إِنَّ ٱللَّهَ يُدْخِلُ ٱلَّذِينَ ءَامَنُوا۟ وَعَمِلُوا۟
ٱلصَّٰلِحَٰتِ جَنَّٰتٍ تَجْرِى مِن تَحْتِهَا
ٱلْأَنْهَٰرُ يُحَلَّوْنَ فِيهَا مِنْ أَسَاوِرَ
مِن ذَهَبٍ وَلُؤْلُؤًا وَلِبَاسُهُمْ فِيهَا
حَرِيرٌ ﴿٢٣﴾

For they were guided to the best of words; and so they were guided to the way that leads to the One to whom all praise is due. (24)

وَهُدُوٓا۟ إِلَى ٱلطَّيِّبِ مِنَ ٱلْقَوْلِ
وَهُدُوٓا۟ إِلَىٰ صِرَٰطِ ٱلْحَمِيدِ ﴿٢٤﴾

A Fear-Striking Opening

> *Mankind! Have fear of your Lord. The violent convulsion at the Last Hour will be awesome indeed. On the day when it comes, every suckling mother will utterly forget her nursling, and every woman heavy with child will cast her burden; and it will seem to you that all mankind are drunk, although they are not drunk. But severe indeed will be God's punishment.* (Verses 1–2)

This is how the *sūrah* begins: an awesome opening that makes hearts tremble. It addresses all mankind, calling on them to fear their Lord and warning them against what may happen on the eventful and terrible Day of Judgement. There is a clear element of mystery about it, one that is frightening and cannot be expressed in words. Thus we are told of a 'violent convulsion' which is then described as 'awesome indeed', but we have no clear indication as to its nature or substance.

When the details are given, we find them even more frightening. We have a picture of every suckling mother completely unaware of the child she is nursing: she looks but does not see, moves but only aimlessly. Every pregnant female miscarries because of the great shock that engulfs her. All people look drunk, but they are not. They only seem to be as they look into a void and walk unsteadily in all directions. It is a very busy scene, with a huge moving crowd. We almost see it with our eyes as the verses are recited, and we paint it in our imagination. Yet we hardly get the full view, because of the horror it describes. It is a horror that cannot be measured by volume or extent, but rather by its effect on human beings. Its measure is the suckling mother oblivious of the child on her breast. No mother can be so oblivious unless the horror she is encountering commands all her senses and faculties. It is also measured by the miscarrying pregnant women, and by the people behaving as if they are drunk yet who have not had a drink. All this is because God's punishment is severe indeed.

The Way Leading to Error

Despite this horror, we are told that some people dispute about God, having no fear of Him: "*Yet some people argue about God without having any knowledge, and follow every rebellious devil. It is decreed for whoever entrusts himself to any [such devil] that he will lead him astray and guide him towards the suffering of the blazing flame.*" (Verses 3–4)

Whether the dispute is about God's existence, oneness, power, knowledge or any of His attributes, it sounds extremely singular. How can anyone realize the extent of the horror that awaits us all, and from which the only escape is through piety and earning God's pleasure, yet continue to dispute about God? How can anyone with a mind to think and a heart to feel indulge in anything other than trying to avoid this violent convulsion whose horror threatens us all?

Had it been a dispute based on true knowledge, something might be said for it, but it is a dispute without knowledge. It is immersed in arrogance that seeks no firm evidence, and error that is the result of following Satan's bidding. Such people dispute about God "*and follow every rebellious devil,*" who boasts about turning away from the truth. Hence, "*it is decreed for whoever entrusts himself to any [such devil] that he will lead him astray and guide him towards the suffering of the blazing flame.*" (Verse 4) It is inevitable that such devils will lead their followers away from the truth in order to land them in hell. The *sūrah* sarcastically calls this 'guidance', which can only be the guidance of one who leads to destruction and doom.

Or is it that people are in doubt about the resurrection, or about the violent convulsion that signals the arrival of the Day of Judgement? If they are doubtful about returning to life, then they should reflect on how life is initiated. They should look at themselves, and at the earth around them. There are numerous indications that tell them that the whole thing is very close to them, but they pay little heed to the significance of the indicators within themselves and on earth, let alone appreciate them.

The Stages of Man's Creation

> *Mankind! If you are in doubt as to the resurrection, remember that We have created you out of dust, then out of a gamete, then out of a clinging cell mass, then out of an organized and unorganized embryo, so that We might make things clear to you. We cause to rest in the [mothers'] wombs whatever We please for an appointed term, and then We bring you forth as infants, that you may grow up and attain your prime. Some of you die young, and some live on to abject old age when all that they once knew they know no more. You can see the earth dry and barren; and [suddenly,] when We send down water upon it, it stirs and swells and puts forth every kind of radiant bloom.* (Verse 5)

Resurrection is a return to a life that has been in existence. Thus, by human standards, it is easier than the origination of life in the first place, although, by God's standards, the notion of easier or more difficult does not arise. To Him, initiating something out of nothing and restoring a life that had ended are the same. Both are the result of His will: "*When He wills a thing to be, He only says to it, 'Be' – and it is.*" (36: 82) But the Qur'ān addresses people according to their own standards, rational thinking and understanding. It directs their hearts to reflect on what they see happening at every moment in their lives. If only they would reflect on it carefully, they would realize that it is miraculous. But to appreciate it as such, they need to look at it with an open heart and a reflective mind. Alas! They rarely ever do so.

Let them ask themselves: what are these people all around them? What are they made of? Where have they come from? What were they before they took this shape and form? And what stages have they gone through?

"*We have created you out of dust.*" Man is a son of the earth. He originated, took form and lived out of its dust. Not a single element does man have in his constitution but has its parallel in the elements present in mother earth. The only exception is that gentle secret God placed in him when He breathed of His soul into man, thus bringing about the great difference between man and those elements constituting dust. The fact remains, however, that man is closely related to dust both in his constitution and his food. All tangible elements in man are from the dust of the earth.

Nevertheless, the gap is great between dust and man. The basic atoms that are present in dust are far removed from this highly complex creation that acts on his own behest and responds to others. The human creature is influenced by different factors in his surroundings and similarly influences others. His feet are placed on earth, but his soul and heart can fly to heaven. His mind floats to realms beyond that of the physical world that includes the dust from which he was first created.

It is a great divide separating the first status and the last. It points to the power that can bring about the resurrection, having brought about the initial creation.

Then out of a gamete, then out of a clinging cell mass, then out of an organized and unorganized embryo, so that We might make things clear to you. We cause to rest in the [mothers'] wombs whatever We please for an appointed term, and then We bring you forth as infants...[2] (Verse 5)

Again the gulf between the primitive, idle elements found in dust and the gamete, a single living cell, is great indeed. It enfolds the great secret of life about which human beings know only a very little, despite the passage of millions of years in which countless numbers of idle elements have been transformed into living cells in a continuous process that never stops. It is a secret that we can only observe and record, without ever being able to initiate, no matter how ambitious we may be. And then there are other secrets, like that of the transformation of

---

2. In rendering the terms used in the Qur'ān to denote the different stages that follow the fertilization of the female egg up to the birth of a child, translators of the Qur'ān have used different terms, as they thought to fit the Arabic ones most appropriately. In most cases, *nutfah* is rendered as 'sperm, drop of sperm, living germ, a drop of seed, etc.' while *'alaqah* is rendered as 'a clot of blood, a leech-like clot, a germ-cell, etc.' On the other hand, *muḍghah* is given as 'a morsel or lump of flesh, embryonic lump, etc.' All these were the outcome of commendable endeavours to match the original usage. However, nowadays when it is possible to monitor the development of a human embryo from the moment of conception, we need to give the Qur'ānic terms more accurate renderings that match the stages to which reference is made.

Thus 'gamete' is preferred as an equivalent of *nutfah* because this Arabic term does not refer only to the male sperm. The Prophet uses it in clear reference to a 'man's *nutfah* and a woman's *nutfah*', and the union of both. A *ḥadīth* related by Imām Aḥmad mentions that "a Jew came to the Prophet and said: 'Muḥammad! From what is man created?' The Prophet said to him: 'Jewish man! From both he is created: from the man's *nutfah* and the woman's *nutfah*.' The Jew said: 'Thus said the one's [i.e. prophets] before you.'" The Oxford Dictionary defines gamete as "A mature haploid germ cell (male or female) which unites with another of the opposite sex in sexual reproduction to form a zygote." As the fertilized egg gets implanted in the wall of the uterus, it clings to it. This is the reason for the use of the term *'alaqah* to denote the next stage. Hence, my rendering of the Arabic word as 'clinging cell mass'. Translators who use terms like 'clot' used a totally different sense of the Arabic word which also means 'leech', but it is clear now that there is no relation between this sense and the context in which the Qur'ānic term occurs. *Muḍghah* is the next stage, which is indeed the embryo.

The Qur'ānic verse, however, speaks here of the embryo as having two distinct parts: one having the beginning of different organs while the other has nothing of the sort, *mukhallaqah wa ghayr mukhallaqah*. Again these two parts are rendered by Qur'ānic translators in a variety of ways. My consultation with specialized doctors who are also conversant with the Qur'ānic terms reached the conclusion that the closest rendering is the one used above, 'organized and non-organized embryo', stressing that the reference here is to the organs that start to take shape at this stage, with the 'organized' part referring to the embryo itself and the 'non-organized' one referring to the placenta. – Editor's note.

the gamete into a clinging cell mass, and the transformation of this cell mass into an embryo which is then transformed into a human being.

What is this gamete, then? It begins with man's semen, a single drop of which contains many thousands of sperms. Yet only one of these countless sperms, or gametes, is needed to fertilize the woman's egg, which is then implanted in the uterus. In this little fertilized egg, implanted in the uterus, are stored, by God's will and power, all the unique characteristics of the human being yet to be born: his physical appearance including his height, stature, beauty, strength and health status as well as his mental and psychological characteristics, including his tendencies, natural likes and dislikes, abilities and talents.

Who can imagine that all this is stored in this little speck clinging to the uterus which, in time, becomes such a complex being? Yet every individual in this race is extremely different from all other individuals, to the extent that no two individuals are ever identical over any period of time.

Then this clinging cell mass is transformed into an embryo which at first is without shape or distinction. Subsequently a transformation overtakes it to give it a form that begins with a skeleton that is later fleshed up. Alternatively, the uterus may reject it if God wills not to let it complete its cycle.[3]

"*So that We might make things clear to you.*" (Verse 5) This clause indicates that there is a pause between the embryonic stage and the child. This clause refers to the numerous signs of God's limitless power, and the reference coincides with the appearance of organs in the embryo.

The verse moves on to refer to the next stage in the development of the foetus: "*We cause to rest in the [mothers'] wombs whatever We please for an appointed term.*" (Verse 5) Whatever God wills to complete its

3. The author follows earlier commentators in explaining the two descriptions of the embryo, saying that it either takes shape and form or does not do so. In this latter case, it aborts. Our advanced knowledge of the development of the foetus suggests that the verse has a different meaning, referring to the two parts of the embryo: the one which develops the organs and becomes a human being, and the one without organs, which is the placenta. – Editor's note.

cycle will rest in its mother's womb until its time of birth. "*Then We bring you forth as infants.*" (Verse 5) Again we say, what a wide gulf separating the first stage and this final one!

In terms of time, it is normally nine months, but in terms of the difference between the nature of the gamete and the nature of the child, it is far greater than that. The gamete cannot be seen by the naked eye, while the child is a highly complex and sophisticated creation, with numerous organs and systems, features, qualities, talents, tendencies and desires. An intelligent mind can only appreciate this great divide after it has humbly reflected, time and again, on the great power behind creation.

The *sūrah* continues with a new cycle that starts with the newborn child, after it has left its hiding place where it went through a series of great miracles, away from all beholders. Then it is time for a new phase, so that "*you may grow up and attain your prime.*" (Verse 5) You will attain your full growth: physically, mentally and psychologically. The gulf between a newborn child and an adult, in their respective characteristics, is much wider than the time separating one from the other. This gulf, however, is bridged by God's will who has given the little infant all the characteristics of a mature adult. What is more is that He has given this child a great variety of talents and potentialities that may rise to the surface at their appropriate times. It is the same divine will that gives the zygote, as it is implanted in the uterus, all the qualities of a human child. Yet that fertilized egg is the product of worthless fluid.

"*Some of you die young, and some live on to abject old age when all that they once knew they know no more.*" (Verse 5) The one who dies young meets at an early stage the end of every living thing. As for the ones who live to old age, they provide an important case for reflection. Although each one was a person of knowledge, maturity and wisdom, now they are again children in their feelings, reactions, awareness, knowledge, dealings and management. Like a child, one little thing may give them great pleasure, and another may cause them to cry. Their memory retains very little and retrieves very little. And like a child, they take events individually, unable to relate them to one another or to look ahead to the conclusion to which they lead. They simply forget the beginning before they reach the end. It is like God says: "*When all that they once knew they know no more.*" They lose the knowledge that once was a source of pride to them, leading them even to argue about God, His existence and His attributes. Now all such knowledge disappears from their minds and consciousness.

The verse then moves on to portray other scenes of creation and living creatures on earth and in the world of plants. "*You can see the earth dry and barren; and [suddenly,] when We send down water upon it, it stirs and swells and puts forth every kind of radiant bloom.*" (Verse 5) The state of being 'dry and barren', which is expressed in the Arabic text with one word, *hāmidah*, is a state in between life and death. This is how the earth is when it is starved of water, the basic ingredient for life and the living. Thus, when rain water is poured over it, '*it stirs and swells.*' This is a remarkable movement which the Qur'ān recorded many centuries before human science. When soil is very dry and then rain falls over it, it makes a movement like shaking or stirring. It absorbs the water and swells. It is then full of life, bringing forth blooming vegetation that radiates pleasure. Is there anything more pleasing to the eye than seeing life bloom in an area that has long remained barren?

Here we see how the Qur'ān speaks of a bond between all living creatures, citing them all as one of God's numerous signs. This is a remarkable reference to the fact that the essence of life is one in all the living, and to the unity of the will that brings life into being on earth, as in plants, animals and man.

The Ultimate Truth

> *That is because God alone is the Ultimate Truth; and He alone brings the dead to life; and He has the power to will anything. And that the Last Hour is certain to come, beyond any doubt; and that God will certainly resurrect all who are in their graves.* (Verses 6–7)

All that has been said about the origins of man and his creation out of dust, the various stages an embryo goes through, and the next cycle of a child and his life, and also about life blooming out of a dry and barren earth are closely related to the fact that God is the Ultimate

Truth. All these aspects are constant laws initiated and operated by God, the Truth, whose laws will never fail. The progress of life in such a fashion, moving from one stage to another, is indicative of the great will that determines its moves and stages. The link is clear between the fact that God is the Ultimate Truth and this consistency of an unfailing cycle of life.

"*He alone brings the dead to life.*" (Verse 6) Bringing the dead to life is to re-initiate life in what has been dead. The One who originated life in the first instance is the One who brings it back in the final stage. "*God will certainly resurrect all who are in their graves.*" (Verse 7) They will then be given their reward for whatever they did in this first life. Such resurrection is dictated by the purpose of creation.

The cycles both embryo and child go through indicate that the wise will which has set them in motion will inevitably allow man to attain his ultimate perfection in a world of perfection. In this life on earth, perfection is unattainable because man's advancement stops at a certain point before he retreats so far as to reach a stage when '*all that he once knew, he knows no more.*' It is, then, absolutely necessary that a second life should take place to allow man to attain perfection.

Thus, these cycles, with all their stages, give a dual indication of the resurrection. They establish first that the Creator who initiates life is able to bring the dead back to life. They also show that the wise will that has set all this in operation will undoubtedly complete man's perfection in the life to come. Thus, the laws of creation and return, life and resurrection, as well as reckoning and reward, all unite to testify to the power of God, the Creator, who conducts and controls the entire universe. His existence and power admit no doubt whatsoever.

But despite all this evidence some people continue to dispute God's existence: "*Yet some people argue about God without having any knowledge, without guidance, and without any light-giving revelations. They turn away in scorn so as to lead others astray from the path of God. Disgrace is in store for them in this world, and on the Day of Resurrection We shall make them taste suffering through fire. [They shall be told]: This is the outcome of what your own hands have wrought. Never does God do the least wrong to His creatures.*" (Verses 8–10)

Argument about God in the face of all this evidence is singularly stupid. How much more ridiculous is it then when such argument has no basis in knowledge, evidence, fact, or revelation to enlighten the heart and mind and give a clear account of the truth?

The *sūrah* paints a picture of this type of conceited person who '*turns away in scorn*'. Such a person realizes that his attitude lacks sound knowledge and tries to compensate for it by becoming arrogant. His aim is '*to lead others astray from the path of God.*' He is not satisfied to be astray himself. He wants others to follow his suit.

Such deviant arrogance which leads people astray must be stopped and dealt with severely. Hence, '*disgrace is in store for them in this world.*' Such disgrace befalls them in contrast with their arrogance. God does not ignore such arrogant people who lead others astray but instead He smashes their arrogance and brings them low, even if this is not immediate. God may give them respite for a while so that their disgrace becomes that much more effective and their punishment in the hereafter that much more severe: "*On the Day of Resurrection We shall make them taste suffering through fire.*" (Verse 9)

And in a brief moment, the threatened punishment becomes a reality we see with our own eyes. This is achieved by the change of style from a statement to an address: "*This is the outcome of what your own hands have wrought. Never does God do the least wrong to His creatures.*" (Verse 10) We almost see them being severely rebuked as well as the punishment of fire that they must endure.

A Conditional Approach to Faith

The *sūrah* then paints a picture of another type of person. Although this type was definitely present in the early days of the Islamic message, it is also present in every generation. It is the type that weighs up faith against what profit or loss he is likely to achieve as a result. Thus, his approach to faith is the same as any business transaction he conducts.

> *Some people worship God on the border-line [of faith]. If good befalls such a person, he is content; but if a trial assails him, he turns away*

utterly; thus losing this world and the life to come. This is, indeed, a loss beyond compare. He invokes, instead of God, something that can neither harm nor benefit him. This is the utmost that one can go astray. Indeed he invokes one that is far more likely to cause harm than benefit. Vile indeed is such a patron, and vile the friend. (Verses 11–13)

Faith is the mainstay of a believer's life. The world may be swayed and shaken here or there, but the believer stays his ground supported by this mainstay. Events may pull him in this or that direction, but he remains firm in his resolve. Support may crumble all around him, but he is certain that faith gives him the kind of support that never fails. Such is the value of faith in the life of a believer. Hence, he or she must ensure that they have the right faith, trust to its unfailing support, entertain no hesitation and wait for no immediate reward. Indeed, faith itself is a reward for believers, because it gives them all the support they need. It is indeed a reward for a heart that opens up to the light of faith and seeks guidance. Because of this, God grants them faith to provide them with all the reassurance they need. A believer realizes that faith is a reward and appreciates its value when he sees people all around him moving aimlessly, pulled here and there, worried, thrown off-course, while he himself is certain of his footsteps, calm, reassured by his strong bond with God.

Contrasted with this is the person who looks at faith as a commercial endeavour: "*If good befalls such a person, he is content.*" He would say that faith is beneficial, bringing in material gains, allowing plants to grow, efforts to be fruitful, goods to sell well and transactions to be profitable. But if it turns out otherwise, then he takes a totally different stance: "*If a trial assails him, he turns away utterly; thus losing this world and the life to come.*" (Verse 11) His loss in this life is reflected in the misfortune he cannot tolerate, and the calamity that did not bring him back to complete reliance on God. Hence he also loses the hereafter by turning away from faith, rejecting the guidance that was made available to him.

This is a very vivid picture. For such a person's worship of God is shown to be on the edge, or on the border line. Faith has not penetrated him; his worship is suspect. Hence, he moves unsteadily, liable to fall at the slightest push. Hence, when misfortune does befall him, it causes him to turn away completely. In fact, lack of surety shows him to be all too ready for such a roundabout turn.

A computation of profit and loss may be suitable for commercial dealings, but it is utterly unsuited to faith, because faith represents the truth and it is embraced for nothing other than its truth. It addresses the heart which receives light and guidance and inevitably reacts to them. Moreover, faith brings its own rewards in the form of satisfaction, pleasure and reassurance. It does not seek any reward other than itself.

A good believer worships God in gratitude to Him for having guided him, and for the reassurance he feels in being close to God. Should there be any further reward, it comes by the grace of God, and it is given for one's acceptance of the faith or for one's worship. Moreover, a believer does not put God to the test. On the contrary, he accepts everything that God determines for him, contented with whatever comes his way, be it pleasant or otherwise. There is no question of a market deal here between a buyer and a seller. All that takes place is submission to the Creator who initially gives people existence and who ultimately determines fates.

Undoubtedly, the person who turns away from faith once hardship befalls him exposes himself to utter loss: "*This is, indeed, a loss beyond compare.*" (Verse 11) He is deprived of trust, reassurance and contentedness, in addition to his loss of wealth, children, health or other losses with which God puts His servants to the test. For God requires His servants to demonstrate their trust in Him, to patiently persevere in the face of adversity, as well as to dedicate their lives to His cause and to His will. Moreover, he loses the life to come and all that it promises of bliss, happiness and being close to God. This is indeed a great loss.

So where does the person who worships God on the border line go when he strays from God? In simple terms, "*he invokes, instead of God, something that can neither harm nor benefit him.*" (Verse 12) He may invoke an idol or a statue in old fashioned ignorance, or *jāhiliyyah*, or he may invoke a person, or some authority, or interest, like the different forms of *jāhiliyyah* that exist at any time or place, whenever human beings abandon belief in God's oneness and turn their backs on His guidance. But what does all this represent? It is all going astray from the only method in which invocation is of use: "*This is the utmost that one can go astray.*" (Verse 12) Indeed when anyone resorts to invoking such beings instead of God, he takes himself very far away from the truth and the right way leading to it.

"*Indeed he invokes one that is far more likely to cause harm than benefit,*" be that an idol, Satan, or a human being providing support or protection. None of these can cause the invoker either harm or benefit; indeed, they are more likely to bring him harm than benefit. This harm results, in the spiritual world, from overburdening one's heart with myth and humiliation. As for the material world, its harm is self-evident. And above all, it brings about utter loss in the life to come. Hence, the *sūrah* states: "*Vile indeed is such a patron,*" which is powerless, able to cause neither harm nor benefit. "*And vile the friend,*" who brings on such utter loss. All this applies equally to whether the patron and the friend are idols and statues, or human beings raised to the status of deities or semi-deities.

Judgement Between All Creeds

As for those who truly believe in God's oneness, God prepares for them what is much better than all the material comforts and benefits this life may provide: "*God will certainly admit those who believe and do righteous deeds into gardens through which running waters flow. God certainly does whatever He wills.*" (Verse 14) Therefore, anyone who endures adversity or a test should remain steadfast and persevere. He must also continue to place his trust in God and His mercy and support, believing that only He can relieve his adversity and reward him for his perseverance.

A person who loses his trust in God's help, both in this life and in the life to come, and despairs of God's grace when he finds himself under severe pressure or adversity, may do with himself whatever he is able to do. But nothing he does will ever change his lot or relieve him of his problems: "*If anyone thinks that God will not succour him in this world and in the life to come, let him stretch out a rope to the sky and then cut himself off; and then let him see whether his scheme will remove that which has enraged him.*" (Verse 15)

This verse paints a moving scene of the rage such a person feels and the action that results from such rage. It magnifies this state when one is at breaking point. Needless to say, a person in adversity who despairs of God's grace loses every source of light and every comforting thought or hope. His worry increases manifold and his stress weighs heavily on his heart. Thus, his adversity is multiplied. Therefore, the verse tells anyone who thinks that God will not grant him His help, either in this world or in the life to come, to stretch a rope to the sky and to climb up holding to it, or to tie the rope round his neck and then cut the rope so that he falls, or cut his own breath so as to choke. Let him then look to see whether this removes his hardship or not.

The fact remains that the only way to endure hardship is to trust in God's help and hope for His grace. There is simply no way to rise above one's trials except by hard work, seeking God's support. No desperate measure can bring anything other than an increase in stress and adversity. Feelings of pressure and hardship may multiply leading to utter desperation. Therefore, anyone who is enduring such adversity should keep the window of hope and trust in God's help open, as only it brings comfort and mercy.

With such a clear exposition of examples of people who benefit by, and follow, divine guidance as well as those who go astray, God has sent this Qur'ān from on high. Thus, people who open their hearts to it will benefit by it and receive God's guidance: "*Thus have We bestowed from on high this [Qur'ān] in clear verses. God guides him who wills [to be guided].*" (Verse 16)

God has willed that guidance and error are to be granted. Therefore, whoever seeks guidance will have it in fulfilment of God's will and according to His law. The same applies to one who wishes to follow error and to stray from the truth. The *sūrah* here only mentions guidance because this is what fits with the context.

As for the different sects and their divergent beliefs, it is God who judges them all on the Day of Judgement. He is perfectly aware of whatever each of them incorporates of the truth and what falsehood they contain: "*As for the believers, the Jews, the Sabians, the Christians, the Magians, and those who associate partners with God, God will decide between them on the Day of Judgement. God is witness to everything.*" (Verse 17)

Human beings determine the way they follow according to their ideas, tendencies and desires. By nature, the rest of the universe submits to its Creator, prostrating itself before Him:

> *Are you not aware that to God bow down in worship all those who are in the heavens and on earth, the sun, the moon, the stars, the mountains, the trees and the beasts, and a great number of human beings? But a great number also will inevitably have to suffer punishment. He whom God shall disgrace will have none who could bestow honour on him. God certainly does what He wills.* (Verse 18)

When we reflect on this verse we find countless creatures, some of which we know and some we do not; and we glance at an infinite number of worlds, many of which we do not begin to know; as also an endless variety of mountains, trees and beasts that live on earth, man's abode. All these, without exception, join a single procession that prostrates itself in humble submission to God, addressing its worship, in perfect harmony, to Him alone. And out of all these creatures, man alone has a special case, as people diverge: "*a great number of human beings [bow down in worship], but a great number also will inevitably have to suffer punishment,*" because of their rejection of the truth. Thus, man stands out on his own, unique in that great, harmonious procession.

The verse concludes with a statement making clear that whoever deserves punishment will inevitably be humbled and disgraced: "*He whom God shall disgrace will have none who could bestow honour on him.*" (Verse 18) How could such a person be honoured when all honour and respect are granted by God. In other words, anyone who submits to any being other than God Almighty, to whom the entire universe willingly submits, will be disgraced.

Widely Divergent Ends

The next passage draws a scene of the Day of Judgement when the honour bestowed by God on His faithful servants and the humiliation suffered by the others are shown as though they are happening here and now.

> *These two adversaries have become engrossed in contention about their Lord. For the unbelievers garments of fire shall be cut out; and scalding water will be poured over their heads, melting all that is in their bellies and their skin. In addition, there will be grips of iron for them. Whenever, in their anguish, they try to get out, they are returned there, and will be told: 'Taste the torment of fire.' God will certainly admit those who believe and do righteous deeds into gardens through which running waters flow, wherein they will be adorned with bracelets of gold and pearls, and where silk will be their raiment.* (Verses 19–23)

It is a violent scene with loud noises and bustling movements. The descriptive style imparts a sense of long duration, with ever renewing action raised before our imagination. We see garments being cut out and tailored, and fiercely boiling water being poured over people's heads. Its temperature is so high that the moment it touches the heads of those at the receiving end, whatever is in their bellies is melted, as does their skin. We also see whips made of red-hot iron to flog those condemned to such punishment. The suffering is intensified and becomes unbearable. The unbelievers make a sudden move to try to escape this torment, but they are fiercely returned into it. They are strongly rebuked and told: '*Taste the torment of fire.*'

Our imagination continues to repeat this scene from its first movement right up to the point where the unbelievers are repelled when they try to escape. It then starts all over again. The only way to turn away from this self-repeating scene is to look at the other destiny portrayed in the *sūrah*. The starting point is that there are two adversaries contending about their Lord. We have just seen the sad end of those who refuse to believe in Him. The believers, on the other hand, are in gardens through which running waters flow. Their clothes are unlike those of the first group: they are made of silk. On top of these they have adornments and jewellery made of gold and pearls. God also guides them to the best of words and to the way leading to the One worthy of all praise. Thus, they encounter no difficulty either in word or in direction. Such guidance is a great blessing, because it gives them a sense of ease, comfort and reassurance.

Such is the end of contention about God: people are ranked into two groups with two greatly different ends. Anyone who continues to argue about God, without knowledge, guidance or a light-giving divine book, unsatisfied with the clear evidence of the truth God has given us, should reflect before he faces this inevitable end.

2

The Ka'bah and Pilgrimage

The unbelievers who debar others from the path of God and the Sacred Mosque which We have set up for all people alike, both those who dwell there and those who come from abroad... Anyone who seeks to profane it by evildoing We shall cause to taste grievous suffering. (25)

إِنَّ ٱلَّذِينَ كَفَرُواْ وَيَصُدُّونَ عَن سَبِيلِ
ٱللَّهِ وَٱلۡمَسۡجِدِ ٱلۡحَرَامِ ٱلَّذِى جَعَلۡنَٰهُ
لِلنَّاسِ سَوَآءً ٱلۡعَٰكِفُ فِيهِ وَٱلۡبَادِۚ
وَمَن يُرِدۡ فِيهِ بِإِلۡحَادِۭ بِظُلۡمٖ نُّذِقۡهُ
مِنۡ عَذَابٍ أَلِيمٖ ٢٥

When We assigned to Abraham the site of the [Sacred] House, [We said]: 'Do not associate anything as partner with Me. Purify My House for those who will walk around it, and those who will stand before it, and those who will bow down and prostrate themselves in prayer. (26)

وَإِذۡ بَوَّأۡنَا لِإِبۡرَٰهِيمَ مَكَانَ ٱلۡبَيۡتِ
أَن لَّا تُشۡرِكۡ بِى شَيۡـٔٗا وَطَهِّرۡ بَيۡتِىَ
لِلطَّآئِفِينَ وَٱلۡقَآئِمِينَ وَٱلرُّكَّعِ
ٱلسُّجُودِ ٢٦

Proclaim to all people the duty of pilgrimage. They will come to you on foot and on every kind of fast mount. They will come from every far-away quarter, (27)

وَأَذِّن فِى ٱلنَّاسِ بِٱلۡحَجِّ يَأۡتُوكَ
رِجَالٗا وَعَلَىٰ كُلِّ ضَامِرٖ
يَأۡتِينَ مِن كُلِّ فَجٍّ عَمِيقٖ ٢٧

لِيَشْهَدُوا مَنَافِعَ لَهُمْ وَيَذْكُرُوا
اسْمَ اللَّهِ فِي أَيَّامٍ مَعْلُومَاتٍ عَلَىٰ
مَا رَزَقَهُمْ مِنْ بَهِيمَةِ الْأَنْعَامِ فَكُلُوا
مِنْهَا وَأَطْعِمُوا الْبَائِسَ الْفَقِيرَ ﴿٢٨﴾

so that they might experience much that shall be of benefit to them, and that they might extol the name of God on the days appointed [for sacrifice], over whatever heads of cattle He may have provided for them. Eat, then, of such [sacrificed cattle] and feed the unfortunate poor. (28)

ثُمَّ لْيَقْضُوا تَفَثَهُمْ وَلْيُوفُوا
نُذُورَهُمْ وَلْيَطَّوَّفُوا بِالْبَيْتِ
الْعَتِيقِ ﴿٢٩﴾

Thereafter let them complete the rites prescribed for them, fulfil their vows, and again walk around the Ancient House.' (29)

ذَٰلِكَ وَمَنْ يُعَظِّمْ حُرُمَاتِ اللَّهِ فَهُوَ
خَيْرٌ لَهُ عِنْدَ رَبِّهِ وَأُحِلَّتْ لَكُمُ
الْأَنْعَامُ إِلَّا مَا يُتْلَىٰ عَلَيْكُمْ
فَاجْتَنِبُوا الرِّجْسَ مِنَ الْأَوْثَانِ
وَاجْتَنِبُوا قَوْلَ الزُّورِ ﴿٣٠﴾

All this [is ordained by God]. Whoever honours God's sanctities, it will be better for him with his Lord. All kinds of cattle have been made lawful to you, except for what is specified to you [as forbidden]. Shun, then, the loathsome evil of idolatrous beliefs and practices; and shun every word that is untrue. (30)

حُنَفَاءَ لِلَّهِ غَيْرَ مُشْرِكِينَ بِهِ وَمَنْ يُشْرِكْ
بِاللَّهِ فَكَأَنَّمَا خَرَّ مِنَ السَّمَاءِ فَتَخْطَفُهُ
الطَّيْرُ أَوْ تَهْوِي بِهِ الرِّيحُ فِي مَكَانٍ
سَحِيقٍ ﴿٣١﴾

Be true to God, turning away from all that is false, associating no partners with Him. For he who associates partners with God is like one who is hurling down from the skies; whereupon he is snatched by the birds, or blown away by the wind to a far-off place. (31)

This is [to be borne in mind]. Anyone who honours the symbols set up by God [shows evidence of] God-consciousness in people's hearts. (32)

ذَٰلِكَ وَمَن يُعَظِّمْ شَعَـٰٓئِرَ ٱللَّهِ فَإِنَّهَا مِن
تَقْوَى ٱلْقُلُوبِ ﴿٣٢﴾

You have benefit in them for a term appointed; and in the end their place of sacrifice is near the Ancient House. (33)

لَكُمْ فِيهَا مَنَـٰفِعُ إِلَىٰٓ أَجَلٍ مُّسَمًّى ثُمَّ
مَحِلُّهَآ إِلَى ٱلْبَيْتِ ٱلْعَتِيقِ ﴿٣٣﴾

For every community We have appointed [sacrifice as] an act of worship, so that they might extol the name of God over whatever heads of cattle He may have provided for them. Your God is the One and Only God. Hence, surrender yourselves to Him. Give good news to those who are humble, (34)

وَلِكُلِّ أُمَّةٍ جَعَلْنَا مَنسَكًا لِّيَذْكُرُوا۟
ٱسْمَ ٱللَّهِ عَلَىٰ مَا رَزَقَهُم مِّنۢ بَهِيمَةِ
ٱلْأَنْعَـٰمِ ۗ فَإِلَـٰهُكُمْ إِلَـٰهٌ وَٰحِدٌ فَلَهُۥٓ
أَسْلِمُوا۟ ۗ وَبَشِّرِ ٱلْمُخْبِتِينَ ﴿٣٤﴾

whose hearts tremble with awe whenever God is mentioned, and who patiently bear whatever befalls them, attend regularly to their prayer and spend in charity out of what We provide for them. (35)

ٱلَّذِينَ إِذَا ذُكِرَ ٱللَّهُ وَجِلَتْ قُلُوبُهُمْ
وَٱلصَّـٰبِرِينَ عَلَىٰ مَآ أَصَابَهُمْ وَٱلْمُقِيمِى
ٱلصَّلَوٰةِ وَمِمَّا رَزَقْنَـٰهُمْ يُنفِقُونَ ﴿٣٥﴾

The sacrifice of camels We have ordained for you as one of the symbols set up by God, in which there is much good for you. Hence, extol the name of God over them when they are lined up

وَٱلْبُدْنَ جَعَلْنَـٰهَا لَكُم مِّن شَعَـٰٓئِرِ
ٱللَّهِ لَكُمْ فِيهَا خَيْرٌ ۖ فَٱذْكُرُوا۟ ٱسْمَ ٱللَّهِ عَلَيْهَا

[for sacrifice]; and after they have fallen lifeless to the ground, eat of their meat, and feed the poor who is contented with his lot, as well as the one who is forced to beg. It is to this end that We have made them subservient to your needs, so that you might have cause to be grateful. (36)

صَوَآفَّ فَإِذَا وَجَبَتْ جُنُوبُهَا فَكُلُوا۟
مِنْهَا وَأَطْعِمُوا۟ ٱلْقَانِعَ وَٱلْمُعْتَرَّ كَذَٰلِكَ
سَخَّرْنَٰهَا لَكُمْ لَعَلَّكُمْ تَشْكُرُونَ ﴿٣٦﴾

Never does their meat or their blood reach God; it is your piety that reaches Him. It is to this end that He has made them subservient to your needs, so that you might glorify God for all the guidance with which He has graced you. Give good news to those who do good. (37)

لَن يَنَالَ ٱللَّهَ لُحُومُهَا وَلَا دِمَآؤُهَا وَلَٰكِن
يَنَالُهُ ٱلتَّقْوَىٰ مِنكُمْ كَذَٰلِكَ سَخَّرَهَا
لَكُمْ لِتُكَبِّرُوا۟ ٱللَّهَ عَلَىٰ مَا هَدَىٰكُمْ
وَبَشِّرِ ٱلْمُحْسِنِينَ ﴿٣٧﴾

God will certainly defend those who believe. For certain, God does not love anyone who betrays his trust and is bereft of gratitude. (38)

إِنَّ ٱللَّهَ يُدَٰفِعُ عَنِ ٱلَّذِينَ ءَامَنُوٓا۟ إِنَّ
ٱللَّهَ لَا يُحِبُّ كُلَّ خَوَّانٍ كَفُورٍ ﴿٣٨﴾

Permission to fight is given to those against whom war is waged, because they have been wronged. Most certainly, God has the power to grant them victory. (39)

أُذِنَ لِلَّذِينَ يُقَٰتَلُونَ بِأَنَّهُمْ ظُلِمُوا۟
وَإِنَّ ٱللَّهَ عَلَىٰ نَصْرِهِمْ لَقَدِيرٌ ﴿٣٩﴾

These are the ones who have been driven from their homelands against all right for no other reason than their saying, 'Our Lord is God!' Were it not that God repels some people by means of others, monasteries, churches, synagogues and mosques – in all of which God's name is abundantly extolled – would surely have been destroyed. God will most certainly succour him who succours God's cause. God is certainly Most Powerful, Almighty. (40)

ٱلَّذِينَ أُخۡرِجُواْ مِن دِيَٰرِهِم بِغَيۡرِ حَقٍّ
إِلَّآ أَن يَقُولُواْ رَبُّنَا ٱللَّهُۗ وَلَوۡلَا دَفۡعُ
ٱللَّهِ ٱلنَّاسَ بَعۡضَهُم بِبَعۡضٖ لَّهُدِّمَتۡ
صَوَٰمِعُ وَبِيَعٞ وَصَلَوَٰتٞ وَمَسَٰجِدُ
يُذۡكَرُ فِيهَا ٱسۡمُ ٱللَّهِ كَثِيرٗاۗ
وَلَيَنصُرَنَّ ٱللَّهُ مَن يَنصُرُهُۥٓۚ إِنَّ
ٱللَّهَ لَقَوِيٌّ عَزِيزٌ ٤٠

They are those who, if We firmly establish them on earth, attend regularly to their prayers, give in charity, enjoin the doing of what is right and forbid the doing of what is wrong. With God rests the final outcome of all events. (41)

ٱلَّذِينَ إِن مَّكَّنَّٰهُمۡ فِي ٱلۡأَرۡضِ أَقَامُواْ
ٱلصَّلَوٰةَ وَءَاتَوُاْ ٱلزَّكَوٰةَ وَأَمَرُواْ
بِٱلۡمَعۡرُوفِ وَنَهَوۡاْ عَنِ ٱلۡمُنكَرِۗ وَلِلَّهِ
عَٰقِبَةُ ٱلۡأُمُورِ ٤١

Overview

The first passage ended with a description of the inevitable destiny of those who engage in futile dispute about God, making it clear that such people will have no escape from the burning of hell. By contrast, the *sūrah* also describes the bliss to be enjoyed by the believers. This new passage is closely linked to the end of the first, as it speaks about the unbelievers who turn people away from God's path and from the Sacred Mosque in Makkah. The reference here is to those who opposed the message of Islam when it started in Makkah, and who sought to turn people away from it. They also confronted the Prophet and his

Muslim Companions seeking to debar their entry into the Sacred Mosque at the Ka'bah. It then speaks about the basis on which this mosque was founded when God assigned its building to Abraham (peace be upon him) and ordered him to call on all people to visit it for pilgrimage. Abraham's instructions were very clear: that this mosque must be established on the clear basis of God's oneness, so as to prevent any form of associating partners with God from being practised in or near it. It must be kept open to all people, whether they reside nearby or come from afar. None is to be denied entry, and none is to claim its ownership. The *sūrah* then outlines some of the rituals of pilgrimage and how they enhance people's consciousness and constant remembrance of God. It also stresses the need to protect the Sacred Mosque against any aggression by those who try to turn people away from it or change the basis on which it is founded. Those who fulfil their duties of protecting the purity of the faith are promised victory.

The First Sanctuary

> *The unbelievers who debar others from the path of God and the Sacred Mosque which We have set up for all people alike, both those who dwell there and those who come from abroad... Anyone who seeks to profane it by evildoing We shall cause to taste grievous suffering.* (Verse 25)

Such was the Quraysh's practice: they turned people away from the faith that God had established for mankind, providing a direct way to Him. They fought hard to prevent people from following the code He had chosen for human life. They also stopped Muslims from offering the pilgrimage and *'umrah,* as was the case in the sixth year of the Islamic calendar when the events that started with such prevention led to the signing of a peace agreement at al-Ḥudaybiyah. God made this mosque an area of peace and safety for all people, where they have no fear of anyone. This applied to everyone living in Makkah, and to all those who travelled from distant areas to visit the mosque. Thus, the Ka'bah and the mosque around it form a House of God where all people are equal. None can claim any right of ownership or any distinction whatsoever: "*The Sacred Mosque which We have set up for all people alike, both those who dwell there and those who come from abroad.*" (Verse 25)

This law God established for His Sacred House preceded all attempts by human beings to establish a sanctuary where no arms are allowed, opponents are safe, bloodshed is ended and everyone enjoys peace and security. No one can claim any favour for observing these rules. They are a privilege equally extended to all people at all times.

Scholars have different views on the permissibility of ownership of houses in Makkah which are not used for personal living. Scholars who accept such ownership also differ on whether such houses may be let. Al-Shāfi'ī believes that such houses may be owned, inherited and let out. The basis of his view is the authentic report that 'Umar ibn al-Khaṭṭāb bought from Ṣafwān ibn Umayyah a house for 4,000 dirhams to make it a prison. Isḥāq ibn Rāhawayh, on the other hand, says that such homes may neither be inherited nor let. He argues: "At the times when God's Messenger, Abū Bakr and 'Umar died, dwellings in Makkah were known only as *sawā'ib* [which means 'left vacant']: whoever needed a place could live in any of them, and whoever had what was surplus to his own needs gave it to others." 'Abdullāh ibn 'Umar is quoted as saying: "It is not permissible to sell or let houses in Makkah." Ibn Jurayj mentions that 'Aṭā', an early scholar, "used to warn against letting homes in the Ḥaram area. He further told me that 'Umar ibn al-Khaṭṭāb used to order the people of Makkah not to have front doors for their homes, so that pilgrims might feel free to stop anywhere. The first person to put up a door to his home was Suhayl ibn 'Amr. 'Umar sent to him for an explanation and he replied, saying: 'Let me explain: I am engaged in trade and I only wanted to have two doors so that my camels would stay within them.' 'Umar accepted his explanation and allowed him these doors."

'Umar is further quoted as addressing the people of Makkah, saying: "Do not put up front doors to your homes. Let the travelling pilgrims stop wherever they wish." Imām Aḥmad ibn Ḥanbal takes a middle line that satisfies all reported statements. Thus, he says that homes in Makkah may be owned and inherited, but may not be let.

We see how Islam was far ahead of the rest of humanity, establishing an area of peace and security for all, as well as a home open to every human being. Indeed, the Qur'ān threatens with painful suffering anyone who tries to cause any deviation from this well-defined system: "*Anyone who seeks to profane it by evildoing We shall cause to taste grievous suffering.*" (Verse 25) What is, then, the punishment meted out to a person who does not stop at seeking to profane the Sacred Mosque, but goes on to actually do it? The Qur'ānic verse threatens with grievous suffering anyone who either seeks this, or has the intention of doing so. This makes the warning much more powerful and far-reaching.

Another aspect of the fine style of the Qur'ān is the omission of the predicate in the first sentence of the verse. Thus, the sentence states: "*The unbelievers who debar others from the path of God and the Sacred Mosque...*" (Verse 25) It does not say what happens to them, or what punishment they will receive. Thus, the verse suggests that their mere mention and description is more than enough to determine their fate.

Establishing the Sanctuary

The *sūrah* now refers to the establishment of this Sacred Mosque which the idolaters had usurped. They worshipped idols there and prevented believers in God's oneness, who had purged themselves from idolatry, from entering it. Yet it was built by Abraham (peace be upon him) on God's own instructions. The *sūrah* also mentions the fundamental basis of God's oneness which served as the basis of the foundation of the Sacred Mosque. It also adds the purpose of its building as a place to worship God alone, a place where the dedicated could walk around it, and stand before it in submission to God:

> *When We assigned to Abraham the site of the [Sacred] House, [We said]: 'Do not associate anything as partner with Me. Purify My House for those who will walk around it, and those who will stand before it, and those who will bow down and prostrate themselves in prayer. Proclaim to all people the duty of pilgrimage. They will come to you on foot and on every kind of fast mount. They will come from every far-away quarter, so that they might experience much*

that shall be of benefit to them, and that they might extol the name of God on the days appointed [for sacrifice], over whatever heads of cattle He may have provided for them. Eat, then, of such [sacrificed cattle] and feed the unfortunate poor. Thereafter let them complete the rites prescribed for them, fulfil their vows, and again walk around the Ancient House.' (Verses 26–29)

It was for celebrating the glory of God alone that this House was built. God showed its place to Abraham, and gave him clear instructions so that he raised it on proper foundations: "*Do not associate anything as partner with Me.*" It belongs to God alone, without partners of any sort. Abraham was also required to purify the House for those who come to it to perform the pilgrimage and for those who stand up in prayer there. "*Purify My House for those who will walk around it, and those who will stand before it, and those who will bow down and prostrate themselves in prayer.*" (Verse 26) It is for those who worship God alone that this House was built. It has nothing to do with others who associate partners with Him or address their worship to anyone other than Him.

Announcing the Pilgrimage

When Abraham completed building the Ka'bah as instructed, he was ordered to declare the duty of pilgrimage as binding on all people, and to call on them to fulfil this duty. God also promised him that people would respond to his call, and that they would come from all corners of the globe, either on foot, or using every kind of fast mount that becomes thin as a result of a long journey: "*Proclaim to all people the duty of pilgrimage. They will come to you on foot and on every kind of fast mount. They will come from every far-away quarter.*" (Verse 27)

God's promise to Abraham continues to be fulfilled, even today, and it is certain to continue well into the future. People's hearts aspire to visiting the Ka'bah, passionately longing to see and walk around it. A person of good means will use some form of transport, while a poor person will still come, even though he may have to cover a long distance on foot. Tens of thousands flock to it from far away corners of the earth, every year, in response to Abraham's proclamation of this duty made thousands of years ago.

The *sūrah* then mentions some aspects and objectives of the pilgrimage: "*so that they might experience much that shall be of benefit to them, and that they might extol the name of God on the days appointed [for sacrifice], over whatever heads of cattle He may have provided for them. Eat, then, of such [sacrificed cattle] and feed the unfortunate poor. Thereafter let them complete the rites prescribed for them, fulfil their vows, and again walk around the Ancient House.*" (Verses 28–29)

The benefits that pilgrims receive are manifold. The pilgrimage is a season of trade and worship, and a conference where people get to know each other and establish close cooperation. It is a religious duty in which objectives pertaining to this life converge with those that pertain to the life to come. Near and distant memories of true faith are also grouped together. Business people find pilgrimage to be a high season for their merchandise. Fruits of every type are brought to the sanctified city of Makkah from all corners. Pilgrims come from every country and area of the world bringing with them their best goods that have different seasons. Thus, in Makkah all these are found in the same season, making of the pilgrimage an all-embracing exhibition and an annual international market place.

It is at the same time a season of worship, when souls feel their purity as they sense that they are close to God in His Sacred House. People's spirits roam around the House, recalling memories that are associated with it, and see near and distant images. The memory of Abraham as he abandons his small child, Ishmael, born to him in old age, yet whom he left alone with his mother. As he turned away to leave, he addressed a prayer to God, one which clearly reflected an issuing from an apprehensive heart: "*Our Lord, I have settled some of my offspring in a valley without cultivation, by Your Sacred House, so that they may establish regular prayers. So, cause You people's hearts to incline towards them, and provide them with fruits, so that they may give thanks.*" (14: 37)

We remember Hagar as she tries to find water for herself and her young child in that exceedingly hot place where the Sacred House was yet to be built. We see her dashing to and fro between the two hills of al-Ṣafā and al-Marwah, feel her exceeding thirst, and watch her fear for her child as she's weighed down with the strenuous effort involved. She returns after covering the distance seven times, feeling something approaching despair, only to find water springing up between the blessed child's hands. That water was the Well of Zamzam, a spring of mercy in the middle of a barren desert

We recall the memory of Abraham and his vision: how he had no hesitation in offering his first son as a sacrifice. He carries a believer's submission to its highest standard: "*He said: Dear son! I have seen in a dream that I should sacrifice you. Consider, then, what would be your view.*" (37: 102) And he is answered with equal obedience that demonstrates self-surrender to God in its clearest sense: "*He answered: Father! Do as you are bidden. You will find me, if God so wills, one who is patient in adversity.*" (37: 102) But then God's grace is bestowed upon them and the son is released with a sacrifice sent by God: "*We called out to him: Abraham, you have already fulfilled that dream-vision! Thus indeed do We reward those who do good. All this was indeed a trial, clear in itself. And We ransomed him with a tremendous sacrifice.*" (37: 104–107)

We also see the image of Abraham and Ishmael, many years later, as they raise the foundations of the House, praying to God with submission and humility: "*Our Lord, accept this from us; You are the One that hears all and knows all. Our Lord, make us surrender ourselves to You, and make out of our offspring a community that will surrender itself to You. Show us our ways of worship and accept our repentance; You are the One who accepts repentance, the Merciful.*" (2: 127–128)

Such memories follow one upon the other until we see ʿAbd al-Muṭṭalib, the Prophet's grandfather, pledging that, if God would give him ten sons, he would sacrifice one of them. As lots are drawn, the choice falls on ʿAbdullāh, his youngest son. We see ʿAbd al-Muṭṭalib keen to fulfil his pledge, and we see his people objecting, then suggesting a ransom sacrifice. He draws the lots again and again, increasing the ransom every time, but the draw continues to be against ʿAbdullāh, until the ransom reaches 100 camels, although only 10 were normally required. At this point, his offering is accepted and 100 camels are sacrificed to save ʿAbdullāh. But his salvation is short-lived. He lives only long enough to give his wife, Āminah, whom he has just wed, the pregnancy that leads to the birth of the most noble person in human history, the one loved most by God. ʿAbdullāh dies soon afterwards. It is as if God had saved him from being sacrificed only to accomplish the honourable task of being the father of Muḥammad (peace be upon him).

Further images and memories come thick and fast. We see Muḥammad, God's Messenger, in his childhood running near this House, and we see him a man close to maturity, lifting the black stone with his blessed hands to place it in its position, to prevent discord among the various tribes and clans. We see him praying at the Sacred Mosque, performing the *ṭawāf*, i.e., walking around the Kaʿbah, delivering a speech or absorbed in his devotion. The steps he takes there are vividly painted before our eyes. Deep in their thoughts, pilgrims almost see these steps as though they were being taken by him now. We also see his Companions as they walk around the House, the Kaʿbah, and we almost hear them as they talk.

The Pilgrimage Conference

But the pilgrimage is also a conference at which all Muslims gather. In it they find the beginning of their community, going back ages in time to none other than their first father, Abraham (peace be upon him): "*It is He who has chosen you, and has laid no hardship on you in [anything that pertains to] religion; the creed of your forefather Abraham. It is He who has named you Muslims, in bygone times and in this [book].*" (Verse 78) There at the pilgrimage, they find the force that brings them all together, their *qiblah* to which they all turn as they stand up in prayer. They also find the banner under which they unite, namely, the banner of faith under which all distinctions of race, colour or nationality are non-existent. They sense their power, of which they may often be oblivious; that is the power of their unity which is capable of sweeping everything before it, when they are united by faith alone.

The pilgrimage is a conference where Muslims have the opportunity to get to know one another, discuss their affairs, coordinate their plans, group their forces, exchange commodities, information, experiences and other benefits. They organize their single well-integrated Muslim world once every year, under God's banner, close to His House, in the light of devotion to Him alone and the memories outlined, in the best place, time and atmosphere.

It is to this blessing that the verse refers: "*so that they might experience much that shall be of benefit to them.*" (Verse 28) This applies to every generation according to its prevailing circumstances, needs, experience, and requirements. This is part of what God wants the pilgrimage to be, ever since He made it a duty incumbent upon all Muslims, and ordered Abraham to proclaim this duty to mankind.

The *sūrah* refers to some of the rituals of the pilgrimage and their purpose: "*They might extol the name of God on the days appointed [for sacrifice], over whatever heads of cattle He may have provided for them.*" (Verse 28) This is a reference to the animal sacrifice that pilgrims offer on the four days of *'Īd*. The Qur'ānic verse refers first to the practice of extolling God's name at the time of the slaughter, highlighting the fact that the whole atmosphere is one of worship, and the purpose of the sacrifice is to get closer to God. Hence, the *sūrah* stresses the mentioning of God's name at the point of sacrifice, as though such mention is the aim of the whole sacrificial ritual.

The sacrifice itself commemorates the sacrifice that was given as a ransom for Ishmael. Thus, it commemorates a sign given by God, and the act of obedience by His two noble servants, Abraham and Ishmael, in addition to the element of charity involved as most of its meat is given to the poor. The 'heads of cattle' mentioned in the Qur'ānic verse refer to camels, cows, sheep and goats that are normally sacrificed. "*Eat, then, of such [sacrificed cattle] and feed the unfortunate poor.*" (Verse 28) The order to eat of one's sacrifice is one of permissibility and recommendation, while the order to feed the poor is one of duty and obligation. Perhaps the order that one should eat of one's own sacrifice is meant to show the poor that it is wholesome and of a quality that the person offering it does not disdain to eat from.

The sacrifice signals the end of the state of consecration, or *iḥrām*, which means that the pilgrim may now shave his head, or cut his hair. Other *iḥrām* restrictions, such as prohibiting the plucking of armpit hair and nail cutting, are also relaxed. All this is referred to in this

Qur'ānic verse: "*Thereafter let them complete the rites prescribed for them, fulfil their vows...*" (Verse 29) These vows are concerned with whatever people might have pledged to God, other than the sacrifice that is part of the pilgrimage rituals. "*And again walk around the Ancient House.*" (Verse 29) This is a reference to the *ṭawāf* of *ifāḍah*, which falls due after attendance at 'Arafāt. This *ṭawāf* is also different from the *ṭawāf* of farewell which is offered shortly before departing from Makkah.

The Ancient House refers to the Sacred Mosque which God made immune from the power of all tyrants, and against collapse through the passage of time. It continues to be visited, ever since the time of Abraham, and will continue to be so for as long as God wills.

Fall, Snatch and the Deep End

This is the story of how the Sacred House in Makkah was built and the basis on which it was founded. It was God who ordered His friend, Abraham (peace be upon him), to raise this House making belief in God's oneness its solid foundation. He further ordered Abraham to purify it of all idolatry, and to proclaim to mankind the duty of offering the pilgrimage to the House, where they mention God's name, not the names of false deities, over what they sacrifice of cattle He provides for them. They are to eat of it and to feed the needy and the poor in praise of God's name, not the name of anyone or anything else. This means that it is a sacred House where God's sanctities are respected. Paramount among these are the belief in God's oneness, the opening of the House to worshippers who walk around it, stand before it in prayer, and bow and prostrate themselves to God, in addition to the prevention of bloodshed, the honouring of covenants and treaties, and the maintenance of peace.

> *All this [is ordained by God]. Whoever honours God's sanctities, it will be better for him with his Lord. All kinds of cattle have been made lawful to you, except for what is specified to you [as forbidden]. Shun, then, the loathsome evil of idolatrous beliefs and practices; and shun every word that is untrue. Be true to God, turning away*

from all that is false, associating no partners with Him. For he who associates partners with God is like one who is hurling down from the skies; whereupon he is snatched by the birds, or blown away by the wind to a far-off place. (Verses 30–31)

Honouring God's sanctities instils a keen, watchful sense lest one should violate them. In God's measure, this is better for us. It is better in the realm of conscience and feeling, and better in this life generally. A watchful conscience is one which wants to remain pure, untainted. A community where God's sanctities are inviolable ensures a life of peace where people are secure, fearing no aggression or persecution, reassured of their comfort and safety.

The idolaters in Makkah used to consider as sacred certain animals, such as a slit-ear she-camel, a she-camel let loose for pasture, idol sacrifices for animal twin-births, and stallion-camel freed from work. They falsely attributed sanctity for such animals, while they violated God's clear sanctities. Therefore, the *sūrah* makes clear at this juncture that all cattle are lawful to eat, except for those specified as forbidden, such as carrion, blood, the flesh of swine and any animal at the slaughter of which any name other than God's is invoked: "*All kinds of cattle have been made lawful to you, except for what is specified to you [as forbidden].*" (Verse 30) This has been made clear so that none other than God's sanctities are acknowledged, none enacts any legislation except God, and no one exercises judgement according to any law other than that of God.

While all cattle are made lawful, the *sūrah* gives an order to steer away from the abomination of venerating idols. The idolaters used to slaughter their animals before idols that personified evil. Associating partners with God is also an evil that contaminates people's hearts and consciences in the same way as an impurity contaminates a garment or a place. Since the association of partners with God is an act of fabricating falsehood against Him, the *sūrah* warns against saying anything untrue: "*Shun, then, the loathsome evil of idolatrous beliefs and practices; and shun every word that is untrue.*" (Verse 30)

The Qur'ānic statement magnifies the offence of fabricating falsehood, putting it on a par with associating partners with God. A *ḥadīth* related by Imām Aḥmad states: "One day, the Prophet offered dawn prayers. When he stood up to leave, he said: 'Perjury is equal to associating partners with God.' He then recited this verse."

What God wants of all people is that they should steer away from all types of associating partners with Him, as also steer away from saying anything untrue. They must maintain in absolute purity their belief in God's oneness: "*Be true to God, turning away from all that is false, associating no partners with Him.*" (Verse 31) The *sūrah* then paints a violent scene of a person who slips away from this pure concept of God's oneness, and who falls into the depths of associating partners with Him. He is totally lost, as though he has never come to life. "*For he who associates partners with God is like one who is hurling down from the skies; whereupon he is snatched by the birds, or blown away by the wind to a far-off place.*" (Verse 31)

In this scene we see a person falling from a great height, so as to be '*hurling down from the skies.*' In no time, he breaks into pieces, and is '*snatched by the birds.*' Alternatively, he may be blown away by the wind or thrown into a bottomless depth. We note here the rapid and violent movement, with scenes shown in quick succession and then disappearing completely.

It is a very true picture and an apt description of one who associates partners with God. He falls from the sublime height of faith to land where he is totally lost, as he deprives himself of the firm basis of belief in God's oneness. He is also deprived of the haven to which he could have returned safely. Hence, he is snatched away by his desires, like one who is snatched by birds of prey. False beliefs and myths throw him off course, just like storms might do. How could he avoid such a fate when he has abandoned the most firm bond and the solid foundation that provides him with a firm link with the world around him?

A Sacrifice of Distinction

Having mentioned those who honour God's sanctities and the need to preserve and protect such sanctities, the *sūrah* now speaks of honouring the symbols set up by God, which, in this instance, refers to the animals sacrificed as part of the pilgrimage rituals. This honour is manifested by choosing the best and most valuable animals for sacrifice:

> *This is [to be borne in mind]. Anyone who honours the symbols set up by God [shows evidence of] God-consciousness in people's hearts. You have benefit in them for a term appointed; and in the end their place of sacrifice is near the Ancient House.* (Verses 32–33)

A link is established here between the sacrifice offered by pilgrims and the way hearts are made conscious of God. The whole purpose of all pilgrimage rituals is to enhance believers' God-fearing sense. All these rituals are symbols confirming submission to God, the Lord of the Ka'bah, the Sacred House, as also obeying Him in all situations. They may also involve reminders of old events, from the time of Abraham and later generations, but these are reminders of complete submission to God, obeying His rules and looking up to Him for guidance. Such is the mark of the Muslim community ever since its earliest days. Hence, these symbols are to be treated on an equal footing with prayer.

Animals marked for sacrifice on the day when pilgrims are due to release themselves from consecration may be used by their owners. The owner may ride such animals, if they are suitable for such purpose, or he may use their milk, until they reach the place of sacrifice, which is in the vicinity of the Ancient House. They are then sacrificed there, when the owners may partake of their meat, but they must give much of it to the poor.

At the Prophet's time, Muslims used to choose the best animals for sacrifice, paying the best prices for them, as a gesture of honouring the symbols set up by God. Their only motive was their God-fearing sense. 'Abdullāh ibn 'Umar reports that his father received a superb she-camel as a gift. He was offered 300 dinars for it, (which was a very high price). He reported this to the Prophet and asked whether he should sell it to buy instead several camels for sacrifice. The Prophet said: "No. Make this one your sacrifice."

We note here that 'Umar did not wish to sell the camel in order to save part of its price. He simply wanted to buy instead several camels or cows and sacrifice them all, although he was aware that one camel or cow was sufficient to fulfil the sacrificial duty of seven pilgrims. The Prophet, however, advised him to sacrifice the precious animal itself, for the very reason that it was so precious. While the alternative suggested by 'Umar could have provided much more meat to go round, the moral aspect was intended here, because it is a demonstration of honouring the symbols set up by God. This is what the Prophet wished to highlight as he ordered 'Umar to sacrifice that particular she-camel.

The Qur'ān mentions that such a sacrifice ritual was known in many communities. It was left to Islam, however, to put it on its right course, offered for God alone:

> *For every community We have appointed [sacrifice as] an act of worship, so that they might extol the name of God over whatever heads of cattle He may have provided for them. Your God is the One and Only God. Hence, surrender yourselves to Him. Give good news to those who are humble, whose hearts tremble with awe whenever God is mentioned, and who patiently bear whatever befalls them, attend regularly to their prayer and spend in charity out of what We provide for them.* (Verses 34–35)

Islam purifies feelings and intentions, setting them all for one goal. Thus, intentions, actions, worship and customs all serve a common purpose, setting life on the sound basis of pure faith.

This is the underlying reason for prohibiting eating any meat at the slaughter of which any name other than God's is invoked. Indeed it is essential to invoke God's name at the sacrifice, giving prominence to such invocation, as if the sacrifice is done merely to invoke His name: "*For every community We have appointed [sacrifice as] an act of worship, so that they might extol the name of God over whatever heads of cattle He may have provided for them.*" (Verse 34) This is followed by a clear statement of God's oneness: "*Your God is the One and Only God.*" (Verse 34) An order of submission to Him is the logical conclusion: "*Hence, surrender yourselves to Him.*" (Verse 34) Such surrender should be an act of choice, done with complete reassurance and without any compulsion: "*Give good news to those who are humble, whose hearts tremble with awe whenever God is mentioned.*" (Verses 34–35) The mere mention of God's name stirs in them a feeling of awe that manifests itself in their actions. "*Who patiently bear whatever befalls them.*" (Verse 35) They do not object to whatever happens to them by God's will. They also "*attend regularly to their prayer,*" showing thus that they worship God as He wishes to be worshipped. Moreover, they do not grudgingly hold on to what they have. Rather, they "*spend in charity out of what We provide for them.*" (Verse 35)

Thus a close link is established between faith and worship rituals. The latter derive from faith and are manifestations of it. Hence, they are described as symbols set up by God. What is important in all this is that life itself derives its colour from faith, ensuring unity between beliefs and actions.

The *sūrah* continues to emphasize the link between faith and worship rituals as it outlines some pilgrimage duties, speaking here of the sacrifice of cows and camels: "*The sacrifice of camels We have ordained for you as one of the symbols set up by God, in which there is much good for you.*" (Verse 36)

Camels are mentioned here in particular because they are the largest and most valuable of sacrificial animals. The *sūrah* states that there is much good for mankind in camels: they serve as good mounts and provide plenty of milk. When they are sacrificed, they provide much meat to eat and give for charity. In return for all these benefits, people should invoke God's name, making their purpose clear and their sacrifice purely for God's sake. This should be clear in their minds as they bring the camels forward for sacrifice: "*Hence, extol the name of God over them when they are lined up.*" (Verse 36) Camels are slaughtered standing on three legs, while the fourth is tied. "*After they have fallen lifeless to the ground, eat of their meat, and feed the poor who is contented with his lot, as well as the one who is forced to beg.*" (Verse 36) The owners of the slaughtered sacrifice are recommended to partake of its meat, but they are required to give gifts to the poor who are contented and do not ask for charity, as well as those whose poverty makes them beg. It is because all these benefits are provided that people should give thanks to God: "*It is to this end that We have made them subservient to your needs, so that you might have cause to be grateful.*" (Verse 36)

As people are commanded to slaughter their sacrifice invoking God's name, it is made clear to them that "*never does their meat or their blood reach God.*" (Verse 37) He has no need of them. What reaches Him, however, is people's piety and consciousness of Him. It is the intention behind any action that gives it its worth. Compare this with the practice of the Quraysh idolaters who used to splatter the blood of their sacrifices over their idols. How crude and ugly!

> *It is to this end that He has made them subservient to your needs, so that you might glorify God for all the guidance with which He has graced you.* (Verse 37)

It is He who has guided you to the proper and true faith of submission to Him alone. Thus, you have become aware of the proper relation between man and God and the true meaning of action undertaken purely for God's sake. "*Give good news to those who do good,*" putting their beliefs, worship and life activities on a proper footing.

Thus Muslims turn to God with every move they make, at any time of the day or night, conscious of His majesty, seeking His pleasure. With this attitude, life becomes a series of acts of worship, fulfilling God's purpose of creation. Life on earth is set on its proper basis, with a solid link between this world and the next.

Permission to Fight

It is imperative that such worship rituals be conducted safely away from those who turn people from God's path. No aggression against the freedom of belief and worship or the sanctity of mosques and places of worship can be tolerated. Believers should have the freedom to implement the divine code of living, based on faith, and aiming to achieve every benefit for man. Therefore, when the early Muslims settled in Madīnah after enduring persecution in Makkah for years, God permitted them to fight the idolaters so as to repel any aggression against themselves and their faith.

Given at a time when such aggression had reached its peak, the permission to fight also aimed to ensure freedom of belief and worship for themselves and for all other people. God promised the believers that they would achieve victory and establish their authority, provided that they fulfilled their duties, required by their faith, as detailed in the following verses:

> *God will certainly defend those who believe. For certain, God does not love anyone who betrays his trust and is bereft of gratitude. Permission to fight is given to those against whom war is waged, because they have been wronged. Most certainly, God has the power to grant them victory. These are the ones who have been driven from their homelands against all right for no other reason than their saying, 'Our Lord is God!' Were it not that God repels some people by means of others, monasteries, churches, synagogues and mosques – in all of which God's name is abundantly extolled – would surely have been destroyed. God will most certainly succour him who succours God's cause. God is certainly Most Powerful, Almighty. They are those who, if We firmly establish them on earth, attend regularly to their prayers, give in charity, enjoin the doing of what is right and forbid the doing of what is wrong. With God rests the final outcome of all events.* (Verses 38–41)

Forces of evil are active in this world. The fight between goodness, divine guidance and forces of faith on the one hand and evil, falsehood and tyrannical forces on the other has raged since man's creation. What is more is that evil and falsehood command great firepower. They have no hesitation in using their arsenal and weaponry to achieve their aims. With such power and false temptation, they strive hard to turn people away from the true faith. Hence, it is imperative that faith, goodness and truth should have enough power to repel aggression and to make all wicked schemes futile.

It has not been God's will to leave unarmed the advocates of faith, truth and goodness so that they face the forces of evil and falsehood relying only on the power of their faith, or on the depth of goodness in their hearts. The material power of evil can be very strong, able to shake people and blind their eyes. Besides, people can only endure hardships and trials up to a certain point. God knows all this and the limits of people's ability. Hence, He wanted the believers to endure the hardship only for a short period during which they would acquire the means to resist and to defend themselves. When they achieved this, they were given permission to fight aggression.

Before stating this permission for self defence, God also tells them that it is He who will defend them: "*God will certainly defend those who believe.*" (Verse 38) He also tells them that He dislikes their enemies because of their treachery and ingratitude. "*For certain, God does not love anyone who betrays his trust and is bereft of gratitude.*" (Verse 38) He has judged their position to be fully justified, because they are the ones who have endured injustice and persecution. They do not resort to aggression against others: "*Permission to fight is given to those against whom war is waged, because they have been wronged.*" (Verse 39) Because they are the ones at the receiving end of wrongful aggression, they are reassured that God will grant them His support and protection: "*Most certainly, God has the power to grant them victory.*" (Verse 39)

Furthermore, they have all the justification for going to war. They have been chosen to undertake a great humanitarian task, the benefits of which will not be theirs alone. Indeed these benefits will accrue to all believers. Their fight will ensure that people shall enjoy the freedom of belief and worship. Besides, they are the ones who have been wronged, the ones driven out of their homes without valid justification: "*These are the ones who have been driven from their homelands against all right for no other reason than their saying, 'Our Lord is God!'*" (Verse 40)

It is the most truthful word any person can say, and the word everyone should say. Yet, it is because of their saying this that they have been driven out of their homes. Hence why such injustice does not carry any semblance of right action. The Qur'ānic statement makes it clear that these victims of aggression have no personal objective to fight for; instead, they fight only for their faith. They seek no worldly gain. Personal and national interests that give rise to conflicts, alliances and wars are of no appeal to them.

Beyond that, we have the general rule that makes it clear that faith needs to be defended: "*Were it not that God repels some people by means of others, monasteries, churches, synagogues and mosques – in all of which*

God's name is abundantly extolled – would surely have been destroyed." (Verse 40)

We note here that the verse mentions monasteries where priests devote all their time to worship, as well as places of public worship for Christians, Jews and Muslims. They are all vulnerable and can be destroyed, despite their sanctity and dedication for worship. Evil will not respect the fact that these places are made for extolling God's name. They are protected only through people's efforts, with the advocates of faith standing up to repel falsehood's aggression. Indeed, falsehood and evil will not stop their aggression unless they realize that the truth has enough power to counter their own. Truth may be valued by people, but such value is not enough to provide it with protection against aggression in man's world. It requires the appropriate means of self defence.

In Defence of the Believers

We need to reflect a little on these short statements that provide profound insight into human nature. The first thing to note is that the permission to fight back is granted by God to those against whom the idolaters had waged a wrongful aggression. This permission starts with a statement that God defends the believers and dislikes aggressors: "*God will certainly defend those who believe. For certain, God does not love anyone who betrays his trust and is bereft of gratitude.*" (Verse 38)

This is a guarantee given by God to the believers that He is the one to defend them, and whoever is defended by God will certainly come to no harm at the hands of his enemies. He will certainly be victorious. Why do they, then, need permission to fight? Why are they required to go to war, suffer casualties, endure hardship and make sacrifices of themselves, when the result is a forgone conclusion and God is able to ensure it without any effort on their part?

The answer is that God's wisdom is absolutely perfect. We as human beings may discern certain aspects of it. Thus, on the basis of our experience and perception we may say that part of God's wisdom may be that He does not want the advocates of His cause to be a group of idle and lazy people who sit relaxing, waiting for victory to be granted them without effort. They do not deserve victory merely because they attend to their prayers, recite the Qur'ān and appeal to God for help and support whenever they suffer hardship or aggression.

It is true that believers should always attend to their prayers, read the Qur'ān and turn to God for help in situations of ease and hardship alike. However, such worship, on its own, does not qualify them as advocates and defenders of God's cause. This worship is merely part of the equipment they need in their fight against the forces of evil. It is their unfailing ammunition in their hard battle. They must face evil with weapons like the ones it uses against them, but they need to add the most effective weaponry of faith, a God-fearing sense, and a solid bond with God.

God has willed that His defence of the believers be through them, so that as they go through battle, they achieve maturity. Nothing brings about latent human resources better than danger. It is only when people realize that they are being attacked that they muster all their resources. Thus, every cell comes forward to play its role, joining ranks with all other cells, each doing its utmost to attain the highest level it can achieve in this life. A community entrusted with God's cause needs to have all its cells ready, its resources brought to the fore, and all its forces mobilized so that it attains its full maturity and is able to discharge its great trust.

A speedy victory gratuitously given to people who make little effort will not tap such latent resources and abilities. There is simply no incentive for them to bring such resources into play. Furthermore, victory achieved easily is lost easily. To start with, it comes cheap, requiring no real sacrifice. Moreover, those who achieve it do not have the necessary training to maintain it. Since they did not have to mobilize their resources to win it, they are not mobilized to defend it.

Moreover, when the Muslim community has to go to war and utilize its resources in attack and defence, feeling its weakness at times and strength at others, retreating one day and moving forward the next, it gains valuable experience. It will experience contrasting feelings such as hope and pain, joy and sorrow, anxiety and reassurance, weakness and strength. It will also experience unity in faith, a readiness to sacrifice all, as well as the bringing together of all elements before, during and after the battle. It will learn what points of strength it has so as to enhance them, and what areas of weakness it has and how to redress them. All these are needed for a community entrusted with the divine faith and its advocacy.

For all this and other reasons known to God, He does not make of victory a free gift granted to believers in a package that falls to them from the sky. Indeed, God accomplishes His defence of the believers through their own efforts.[4]

Assured Victory

Yet victory may be slow in coming to those who are driven out of their homes against all right and for no reason other than their declaration of their belief in God as the only Lord in the universe. If it is slow in coming, then there must be a reason for this.

Victory may be slow in coming because the Muslim community has not as yet attained full maturity. It may not have mobilized all its resources or tapped its potentials. Should victory be given to it then, it would not be able to protect it for long, and so would soon lose it. Victory may also be delayed until the community of believers has given its all, sacrificing every cherished thing, demonstrating that it holds nothing too dear.

It may happen that victory is not granted until the community of believers has tried all its efforts and realized that such efforts, on their own, cannot guarantee victory unless they are supported by God.

---

4. We need to add here that Islam does not consider fighting an end or an objective in itself. It permits fighting for a goal that is greater than achieving a state of *modus vivendi.* As stated in many other Qur'ānic verses, peace is the goal Islam wants to achieve. But peace must be free of aggression, injustice and oppression. When oppression or injustice is perpetrated against any aspect of human dignity, such as the freedom of belief and worship, justice, fair distribution of benefits, responsibilities, rights and duties, and conscientious observance of divine rules by individuals and the community alike, then Islam adopts a different attitude. Whether such aggression and injustice are perpetrated by an individual, a group or a state, and the victim of such aggression is similarly an individual, a group or a state, Islam will not countenance any peace that sanctions such aggression. Peace, according to Islam, does not mean the absence of war; it means complete justice, according to the code God has chosen for human life.

Victory is granted by God only when believers have done their best, placing all their trust in Him alone. Likewise, victory may be delayed so that the community of believers strengthens its bonds with God. It will suffer and render sacrifices, realizing that it cannot turn for support to anyone other than God. It is such a bond with God that guarantees that it will continue to follow the right path after victory. This is a crucial objective. The Muslim community must never swerve from the path of truth and justice through which its victory is achieved.

Victory may also be slow in coming if the community of believers does not dedicate all its struggle and sacrifices to God alone. It may be fighting for something it wants to gain, or for national interests, or to demonstrate its bravery. But God wants its struggle to be purely for Him, untinged by any other feeling or objective. The Prophet was once asked about a person fighting to support his community, one fighting out of bravery, and one fighting to be seen in battle: "Which of them is for God's sake?" He replied: "Only he who fights so that God's word becomes supreme fights for God's cause." [Related by al-Bukhārī and Muslim]

Victory may be delayed because the evil the believers are fighting may still be mingled with a residue of goodness. God may determine that such a residue should be finally separated so that the evil becomes pure, without any trace of goodness, when it is finally defeated.

Furthermore, victory may be delayed because the falsehood that the believers fight is not seen in its true reality by all people. If it is defeated at such a juncture, it could still find support by those who continue to be deceived by it, unconvinced that it is absolutely false. In this situation, God may determine that falsehood remains until its reality is seen by all, so that no one feels sorry for it when it ultimately collapses.

Victory may also be slow in coming because the general environment is not yet ready to receive the truth and justice that the community of believers represents. If the believers are granted victory in such circumstances, they will have to face resistance by the environment they work in. Therefore, the struggle continues until such time as the whole area is ready to receive the truth triumphant.

For all these reasons, and others known to God alone, victory may be slow in coming. This means in effect more sacrifices and more suffering by the believers. Nevertheless, God will continue to defend them and grant them victory in the end.

When Victory is Granted

When granted by God, victory brings about new duties and responsibilities:

> *God will most certainly succour him who succours God's cause. God is certainly Most Powerful, Almighty. They are those who, if We firmly establish them on earth, attend regularly to their prayers, give in charity, enjoin the doing of what is right and forbid the doing of what is wrong. With God rests the final outcome of all events.* (Verses 40–41)

God's true promise which will never fail is that He supports those who support Him. The question that arises here is who are these people that support God and thus deserve His support which means certain victory? Their qualities are outlined in this verse. They are those who, when given victory by God and are established in a position of authority, "*attend regularly to their prayers.*" They worship God alone, submitting themselves to Him willingly and strengthening their bonds with Him. They "*give in charity*", thus they meet the liability imposed on their property. By so doing, they demonstrate their ability to overcome greed and self interest, and they help their community to provide help to the poor and needy. They thus demonstrate a practical example of the Prophet's description of the Muslim community: "In their mutual love, sympathy and compassion, the believers are like one body: when any organ is in complaint, the rest of the body shares its complaint with symptoms of sleeplessness and fever." The third quality is that they "*enjoin the doing of what is right.*" They advocate every good thing and encourage people to practise it. By contrast, they also "*forbid the doing of what is wrong.*" They resist evil and corruption. In this way, they demonstrate a very important characteristic of the Muslim community which does not tolerate any wrong if it can change it, and does not hesitate to do any right thing if it is within its ability.

These are the people who give succour to God, as they implement the way of life He has chosen for mankind. They rely on God alone, to the exclusion of any other power. It is such people that God promises victory, and His promise is most assured. It will never fail.

Here we see again that the victory granted to the Muslim community relies on the fulfilment of its conditions and the discharge of certain responsibilities. All matters rest with God who determines what course events should take. He may change a defeat into victory or a victory into defeat when the foundation is not solid or responsibilities are ignored: "*With God rests the final outcome of all events.*" (Verse 41)

The victory granted by God is one that leads to the establishment of His code in human life. It is a code that ensures that truth, justice and freedom are fulfilled so that they can bring goodness into human life. No individual self-aggrandizement is allowed; no personal greed or desire tolerated. Such a victory has well-defined conditions, duties and a price. It is not granted as a personal favour to anyone. Nor does it continue when its objectives and duties are not fulfilled.

3

The Sights, Blind Hearts

If they accuse you of falsehood, before their time, the people of Noah, the 'Ād and Thamūd similarly accused [their prophets] of falsehood, (42)

وَإِن يُكَذِّبُوكَ فَقَدْ كَذَّبَتْ قَبْلَهُمْ
قَوْمُ نُوحٍ وَعَادٌ وَثَمُودُ ﴿٤٢﴾

as did the people of Abraham and the people of Lot, (43)

وَقَوْمُ إِبْرَٰهِيمَ وَقَوْمُ لُوطٍ ﴿٤٣﴾

and the dwellers of Madyan; and so too was Moses accused of falsehood. [In every case] I gave rein, for a while, to the unbelievers, but then I took them to task. How awesome was the way I rejected them. (44)

وَأَصْحَٰبُ مَدْيَنَ ۖ وَكُذِّبَ مُوسَىٰ
فَأَمْلَيْتُ لِلْكَٰفِرِينَ ثُمَّ أَخَذْتُهُمْ ۖ
فَكَيْفَ كَانَ نَكِيرِ ﴿٤٤﴾

How many a township have We destroyed because it had been immersed in evildoing. Now they lie in desolate ruin. How many a well lies abandoned, and how many a proud palace lies empty. (45)

فَكَأَيِّن مِّن قَرْيَةٍ أَهْلَكْنَٰهَا وَهِيَ
ظَالِمَةٌ فَهِيَ خَاوِيَةٌ عَلَىٰ عُرُوشِهَا
وَبِئْرٍ مُّعَطَّلَةٍ وَقَصْرٍ مَّشِيدٍ ﴿٤٥﴾

أَفَلَمْ يَسِيرُوا۟ فِى ٱلْأَرْضِ فَتَكُونَ لَهُمْ
قُلُوبٌ يَعْقِلُونَ بِهَآ أَوْ ءَاذَانٌ يَسْمَعُونَ
بِهَا ۖ فَإِنَّهَا لَا تَعْمَى ٱلْأَبْصَـٰرُ وَلَـٰكِن
تَعْمَى ٱلْقُلُوبُ ٱلَّتِى فِى ٱلصُّدُورِ ﴿٤٦﴾

Have they never journeyed through the lands, letting their hearts gain wisdom, and their ears hear? It is not eyes that go blind; but blind indeed become the hearts that are in people's breasts. (46)

وَيَسْتَعْجِلُونَكَ بِٱلْعَذَابِ وَلَن يُخْلِفَ
ٱللَّهُ وَعْدَهُۥ ۚ وَإِنَّ يَوْمًا عِندَ رَبِّكَ كَأَلْفِ
سَنَةٍ مِّمَّا تَعُدُّونَ ﴿٤٧﴾

They challenge you to hasten the coming upon them of God's punishment; but God never fails to fulfil His promise. Well, in your Lord's sight a day is like a thousand years of your reckoning. (47)

وَكَأَيِّن مِّن قَرْيَةٍ أَمْلَيْتُ لَهَا وَهِىَ
ظَالِمَةٌ ثُمَّ أَخَذْتُهَا وَإِلَىَّ ٱلْمَصِيرُ ﴿٤٨﴾

To how many a township that was immersed in evildoing have I given rein for a while! But then I took it to task. With Me is the end of all journeys. (48)

قُلْ يَـٰٓأَيُّهَا ٱلنَّاسُ إِنَّمَآ أَنَا۠ لَكُمْ
نَذِيرٌ مُّبِينٌ ﴿٤٩﴾

Say: 'Mankind, I am but a plain warner, sent to you!' (49)

فَٱلَّذِينَ ءَامَنُوا۟ وَعَمِلُوا۟ ٱلصَّـٰلِحَـٰتِ
لَهُم مَّغْفِرَةٌ وَرِزْقٌ كَرِيمٌ ﴿٥٠﴾

Those who believe and do righteous deeds shall be granted forgiveness of sins and a most excellent sustenance; (50)

وَٱلَّذِينَ سَعَوْا۟ فِىٓ ءَايَـٰتِنَا مُعَـٰجِزِينَ
أُو۟لَـٰٓئِكَ أَصْحَـٰبُ ٱلْجَحِيمِ ﴿٥١﴾

whereas those who strive against Our revelations, seeking to defeat their purpose, are destined for the blazing fire. (51)

Whenever We sent forth a messenger or a prophet before you, and he was hoping for something, Satan would throw some aspersion on his wishes. But God renders null and void whatever aspersion Satan may cast; and God makes His messages clear in and by themselves. God is All-Knowing, Wise. (52)

وَمَآ أَرۡسَلۡنَا مِن قَبۡلِكَ مِن رَّسُولٖ
وَلَا نَبِيٍّ إِلَّآ إِذَا تَمَنَّىٰٓ أَلۡقَى ٱلشَّيۡطَٰنُ
فِيٓ أُمۡنِيَّتِهِۦ فَيَنسَخُ ٱللَّهُ مَا يُلۡقِي
ٱلشَّيۡطَٰنُ ثُمَّ يُحۡكِمُ ٱللَّهُ ءَايَٰتِهِۦۗ
وَٱللَّهُ عَلِيمٌ حَكِيمٞ ٥٢

He may cause whatever aspersion Satan may cast to become a trial for all in whose hearts is disease and all whose hearts are hardened. Indeed, all who are thus sinning are most deeply in the wrong. (53)

لِّيَجۡعَلَ مَا يُلۡقِي ٱلشَّيۡطَٰنُ فِتۡنَةٗ لِّلَّذِينَ
فِي قُلُوبِهِم مَّرَضٞ وَٱلۡقَاسِيَةِ قُلُوبُهُمۡۗ
وَإِنَّ ٱلظَّٰلِمِينَ لَفِي شِقَاقِۭ بَعِيدٖ ٥٣

And those who are endowed with knowledge may realize that this [Qur'ān] is the truth from your Lord, and thus they may believe in it, and their hearts may humbly submit to Him. God will surely guide those who believe to a straight path. (54)

وَلِيَعۡلَمَ ٱلَّذِينَ أُوتُواْ ٱلۡعِلۡمَ أَنَّهُ ٱلۡحَقُّ
مِن رَّبِّكَ فَيُؤۡمِنُواْ بِهِۦ فَتُخۡبِتَ لَهُۥ
قُلُوبُهُمۡۗ وَإِنَّ ٱللَّهَ لَهَادِ ٱلَّذِينَ ءَامَنُوٓاْ
إِلَىٰ صِرَٰطٖ مُّسۡتَقِيمٖ ٥٤

Yet the unbelievers will not cease to be in doubt about Him until the Last Hour comes suddenly upon them, or suffering befalls them on a day with no more [days] to follow. (55)

وَلَا يَزَالُ ٱلَّذِينَ كَفَرُواْ فِي مِرۡيَةٖ مِّنۡهُ
حَتَّىٰ تَأۡتِيَهُمُ ٱلسَّاعَةُ بَغۡتَةً أَوۡ يَأۡتِيَهُمۡ
عَذَابُ يَوۡمٍ عَقِيمٍ ٥٥

On that day, all dominion shall belong to God. He shall judge between them. Thus, all who believe and do righteous deeds shall find themselves in gardens of bliss, (56)

ٱلْمُلْكُ يَوْمَئِذٍ لِّلَّهِ يَحْكُمُ بَيْنَهُمْ ۚ
فَٱلَّذِينَ ءَامَنُوا۟ وَعَمِلُوا۟ ٱلصَّٰلِحَٰتِ
فِى جَنَّٰتِ ٱلنَّعِيمِ ﴿٥٦﴾

whereas for the unbelievers who have denied Our revelations there shall be shameful suffering in store. (57)

وَٱلَّذِينَ كَفَرُوا۟ وَكَذَّبُوا۟ بِـَٔايَٰتِنَا
فَأُو۟لَٰٓئِكَ لَهُمْ عَذَابٌ مُّهِينٌ ﴿٥٧﴾

Overview

The previous passage finished with permission granted to fight unbelievers in order to protect and preserve faith and worship, coupled with God's promise to grant victory to those who fulfil their responsibilities towards faith and implement the divine law in life. Now that the task entrusted to the community of believers has been clearly spelt out, the *sūrah* reassures the Prophet that God's power will intervene to provide him with the help he needs ensuring the failure of his enemies. The same power intervened in the past to support earlier prophets and messengers, and to punish those who denied and opposed them. The unbelievers are directed to reflect on the doom suffered by earlier communities; even though such reflection benefits only hearts and minds that are open and receptive. It is not only eyes that can be blind, for real blindness is that of the heart.

The Prophet is also reassured on another count, namely that God protects His messengers from Satan's wicked scheming, just like He protects them from their opponents' plots. He renders all Satan's attempts futile, keeps His revelations pure and clear, so that people with sound mind reflect on them. Those that are sick at heart and those who deny the true faith will continue to be in doubt, and their doubts will lead them to the worst destiny anyone can ever have. Thus, this new passage is a study of how God's power plays a vital role in the fortunes of the advocates of His message.

Past Communities Punished

> *If they accuse you of falsehood, before their time, the people of Noah, the 'Ād and Thamūd similarly accused [their prophets] of falsehood, as did the people of Abraham and the people of Lot, and the dwellers of Madyan; and so too was Moses accused of falsehood. [In every case] I gave rein, for a while, to the unbelievers, but then I took them to task. How awesome was the way I rejected them.* (Verses 42–44)

It is the same pattern seen over and over again, in all past messages up to the final one. Messengers are given signs and revelations, and there will always be those who deny the truth. Thus, when the idolaters in Makkah denied the message of the Prophet Muḥammad, it was by no means a new trend nor did the Prophet experience an unknown pattern of hostility. However, the outcome is well known, and what happened with earlier communities is bound to happen again: "*The people of Noah, the 'Ād and Thamūd similarly accused [their prophets] of falsehood, as did the people of Abraham and the people of Lot, and the dwellers of Madyan.*" (Verses 42–44)

Moses, however, is mentioned on his own as though the reference to him constitutes a special paragraph: "*And so too was Moses accused of falsehood.*" (Verse 44) Unlike other messengers, Moses was not accused of falsehood by his own people. It was Pharaoh and his chiefs that opposed Moses, levelling all sorts of accusations on him. Moreover, Moses was given very clear and numerous signs. Nevertheless, in all these cases, God granted the unbelievers respite for a while, in the same way as He now gave the Quraysh, the Prophet's own people who fiercely opposed him, time to reflect. He then punished all those past communities very severely.

This is followed by a rhetorical question that stresses the frightening effect of God's punishment: "*How awesome was the way I rejected them?*" (Verse 44) The Arabic word, *nakīr*, used here for 'rejection', carries added connotations of violent change. The question needs no answer, as it is well known: it was a rejection demonstrated through great floods, destruction, earthquakes, fearful hurricanes, and the like.

Having made this very quick reference to the fate suffered by those communities, the *sūrah* adds a general reference to past communities which suffered because of their attitude to the divine message: "*How many a township have We destroyed because it had been immersed in evildoing. Now they lie in desolate ruin. How many a well lies abandoned, and how many a proud palace lies empty.*" (Verse 45) Numerous indeed were those towns and cities which suffered their inevitable doom as a result of their evildoing. Their fate is shown here most effectively: "*Now they lie in desolate ruin.*" Roofs are caved in as walls are made to collapse, leaving a depressing sight of total, lifeless ruin. The scene invites contemplation, because ruins have a very strong effect on people, causing them to reflect.

Next to these desolate remains of destroyed cities lie abandoned wells, reminding visitors of past days when people gathered around them for fresh water. And next to these are deserted palaces that once stood proudly in the past, but which now lie empty, evoking only images and memories of a glorious past.

As the *sūrah* portrays these scenes, it adds another rhetorical question about their effects on unbelievers:

> *Have they never journeyed through the lands, letting their hearts gain wisdom, and their ears hear? It is not eyes that go blind; but blind indeed become the hearts that are in people's breasts.* (Verse 46)

Emphasis is here placed on the location of hearts in people's bodies, which serves to amplify the blindness of those hearts in particular. Had those hearts been able to reflect on the scenes portrayed, they would have remembered and people's eyes would have been tearful. They would have moved towards faith, at least as a result of fearing an end like the ones that befell other communities.

But the Quraysh unbelievers did not wish to reflect on such scenes demonstrating God's punishment. Instead they tried to hasten their own punishment which God had delayed until a particular point in time known only to Him:

> *They challenge you to hasten the coming upon them of God's punishment; but God never fails to fulfil His promise. Well, in your Lord's sight a day is like a thousand years of your reckoning.* (Verse 47)

It is the same story with the unbelievers in all generations. They see with their eyes the ruins of cities destroyed for their wrongdoing, and they hear their histories, but they, nevertheless, follow in their footsteps overlooking their fate. If they are reminded of what happened to earlier communities, they nonetheless consider it unlikely that they will suffer the same fate. But if God grants them respite to test them further, they grow arrogant and heedless. They even ridicule anyone reminding them that they could suffer as people before them suffered. What is more they add to such ridicule a request for their punishment to be hastened. Here they are told that '*God never fails to fulfil His promise.*' Such a promise or warning will inevitably come to pass at the time God, in His infinite wisdom, determines. If people hasten its fulfilment, it will not be made to come before its appointed time, because its delay is for a purpose known to God, and that purpose will not fail so as to grant human beings their ignorant wishes. Moreover, time is calculated differently by God: "*In your Lord's sight a day is like a thousand years of your reckoning.*" (Verse 47)

He gave respite to many past communities, but such respite did not save them from punishment when they persisted in their wrongdoing. This is a rule which God has set in operation and it cannot fail: "*To how many a township that was immersed in evildoing have I given rein for a while! But then I took it to task. With Me is the end of all journeys.*" (Verse 48) Why would the Arab unbelievers, then, hasten their own punishment and deride God's warning when it is only a temporary respite that God grants such people?

A Parting of the Ways

At this point in the narrative describing the fate of past communities, and outlining the rule concerning those who persist in denying God's messages, the *sūrah* addresses the Prophet instructing him to warn people and explain the inevitable outcome:

> *Say: 'Mankind, I am but a plain warner, sent to you!' Those who believe and do righteous deeds shall be granted forgiveness of sins and a most excellent sustenance; whereas those who strive against Our revelations, seeking to defeat their purpose, are destined for the blazing fire.* (Verses 49–51)

We note that in this context, the Prophet's task is clearly stated as one of giving people a clear and plain warning, that leaves no room for ambiguity. This fits the immediate situation of stubborn rejection of God's message that makes people hasten their own doom.

The final destiny is clearly stated. Those who believe and put their faith into practice, so as to 'do righteous deeds' will have their reward which consists of forgiveness by their Lord of all sins that they may have committed or duties they may have omitted to do. Such forgiveness is coupled with '*a most excellent sustenance*' that they receive with dignity.

Those who endeavour to stop God's revelations from addressing people's hearts, and God's laws from being implemented in their life, will be the ones to suffer in the blazing fire. The expression the *sūrah* uses makes them the owners of this fire, which is in stark contrast with the excellent sustenance the believers receive.

God always protects His message from the wicked designs of unbelievers who try to prevent its implementation. Similarly, He protects it from Satan's scheming and his attempts to manoeuvre his way into the hopes entertained by God's messengers who are, after all, human. Although God's messengers are given immunity from Satan, their human nature makes them hope that their efforts in advocating divine faith will be enough to remove all impediments and ensure a speedy victory. Satan tries to exploit these hopes in order to force the message out of its fundamental principles and proper methods. But God renders all Satan's schemes futile, preserves His message, making its principles and values clear, perfects His revelations and removes all doubt that may surround its values and method of action.

Whenever We sent forth a messenger or a prophet before you, and he was hoping for something, Satan would throw some aspersion on his wishes. But God renders null and void whatever aspersion Satan may cast; and God makes His messages clear in and by themselves. God is All-Knowing, Wise. He may cause whatever aspersion Satan may cast to become a trial for all in whose hearts is disease and all whose hearts are hardened. Indeed, all who are thus sinning are most deeply in the wrong. And those who are endowed with knowledge may realize that this [Qur'ān] is the truth from your Lord, and thus they may believe in it, and their hearts may humbly submit to Him. God will surely guide those who believe to a straight path. (Verses 52–54)

There are many reports about the events leading to the revelation of these verses, but Ibn Kathīr describes all these reports as lacking in authenticity. The most detailed of these reports is attributed to al-Zuhrī, a leading *Ḥadīth* scholar of the generation that followed the Prophet's Companions. It mentions that *Sūrah* 53, The Star, was revealed at a time when some idolaters said to one another that they would leave Muḥammad and his Companions alone if only he would say a good word about the idols they worshipped. The report goes as follows:

They felt that the Prophet did not criticize the Jews and Christians who opposed him in the same way as he denounced the practices of the idolaters. The Prophet was very grieved by their continued denial of his message and the persecution they inflicted on his Companions. He still hoped that they would be able to recognize divine guidance. God then revealed the *sūrah,* The Star, including the following verses: '*Have you ever considered al-Lāt and al-'Uzzā, as well as Manāt, the third and last [of this triad]? Why [would you choose] for yourselves only male offspring, whereas to Him [you assign] females?*' (53: 19–21) At this mention of the Quraysh's worshipped idols, Satan added the words, 'these are the sublime birds, whose intercession is to be hoped for.' These were nothing but the rhyming words of Satan's invention, but they touched the hearts of all idolaters in Makkah who kept repeating them and expressing their delight to one another, claiming that Muḥammad had returned to his old religion, practised by his people.

When the Prophet completed the recitation of the *sūrah*, he prostrated himself, and all those present, Muslims and idolaters alike, also prostrated themselves. The only exception was al-Walīd ibn al-Mughīrah, an old man, who took a handful of dust and placed his forehead over it. Both parties were amazed at this common prostration when the Prophet prostrated himself. Muslims were amazed that the idolaters should prostrate themselves when they did not believe in God, particularly because they were unaware of what Satan made the idolaters hear. The idolaters, on the other hand, were reassured by what Satan had introduced through the Prophet's hopes and implied to them that the Prophet read those words as he recited the *sūrah*. Hence, they prostrated themselves because their idols were praised.

All this was soon widely known, and Satan helped to circulate it. Before long, the news travelled to Abyssinia, where some Muslims had sought refuge, including 'Uthman ibn Maẓ'ūn. They were told that the people of Makkah had embraced Islam and prayed with the Prophet. They also came to know of al-Walīd ibn al-Mughīrah's gesture of prostration on a handful of dust he raised to his forehead. They felt that Muslims were now safe in Makkah, which prompted some of them to speedily return. But then God nullified Satan's aspersion and made His revelation clear and perfect, preserving it from Satanic fabrication. It was as God said: '*Whenever We sent forth a messenger or a prophet before you, and he was hoping for something, Satan would throw some aspersion on his wishes. But God renders null and void whatever aspersion Satan may cast; and God makes His messages clear in and by themselves. God is All-Knowing, Wise. He may cause whatever aspersion Satan may cast to become a trial for all in whose hearts is disease and all whose hearts are hardened. Indeed, all who are thus sinning are most deeply in the wrong.*" (Verses 52–53) When God made His judgement clear and purged from it the Satanic rhyme, the idolaters of the Quraysh increased their persecution of the Muslims.

Foiling Satan's Efforts

In his commentary on the Qur'ān, Ibn Kathīr says that al-Baghawī includes several versions consolidated from reports by Ibn 'Abbās, Muḥammad ibn Ka'b and others, giving similar accounts. He then asks: "How could this take place, given that God guaranteed the Prophet's infallibility in conveying His message?" He then quotes answers to this question by different people. One of the most interesting is that Satan could only delude the idolaters into thinking that they heard these words from the Prophet when it was not so in reality. It was all Satan's work, not the words of God's Messenger.

Al-Bukhārī reports Ibn 'Abbās's explanation, making the Arabic word, *umniyyatih*, rendered in translation as 'on his wishes', as meaning 'his discourse'. Thus the verse means that when the Prophet spoke, Satan added something into his speech, but God causes Satan's efforts to be futile and makes His own message clear. Mujāhid, on the other hand, explains the reference to any of God's messengers 'hoping for something' as meaning his speech, or his recitation. Al-Baghawī says that most commentators say that it means his reading of God's revelations. It is in his recitation that Satan may add something. Ibn Jarīr describes this explanation as an exercise in giving special meaning to words.

This is a summary of this story which is known as 'The story of the birds, or *gharānīq*.' From the point of view of its transmission, the story is very flimsy. *Ḥadīth* scholars maintain that it was not reported by anyone who may be graded as an accurate reporter; nor was it ever related with an uninterrupted chain of reliable transmitters. Al-Bazzār says: "We do not know that this ḥadīth was ever reported with a chain of transmitters worth mentioning, and leading to the Prophet. From the viewpoint of its subject matter, it is in conflict with a fundamental principle of faith, which is the infallibility of the Prophet (peace be upon him) and the impossibility of Satan being able to introduce anything into the delivery of his message."

Orientalists and opponents of Islam[5] have taken up this report, circulated it and decorated it with much importance. The fact is that it

5. The most recent opponent of Islam to make a fuss of this absurd story was Salman Rushdie in his infamous work *Satanic Verses*. – Editor's note.

is a false report that cannot hold its own in discussion. Indeed, it is unworthy of even being a subject of debate.

The Qur'ānic text itself contains what refutes the claim, namely that such a single event was the reason for the revelation of these verses, which clarify a rule applicable to all divine messages and all God's messengers: "*Whenever We sent forth a messenger or a prophet before you, and he was hoping for something, Satan would throw some aspersion on his wishes. But God renders null and void whatever aspersion Satan may cast; and God makes His messages clear in and by themselves.*" (Verse 52) This statement refers to a general rule indicating a characteristic common to all messengers who are, after all, human beings. This rule is not, for certain, contrary to the principle of the messengers' infallibility.

When God's messengers are entrusted with delivering His message to mankind, they love nothing better than to see people flock to them and realize that all the goodness they advocate comes from God, so that they accept it. But there are numerous impediments that stand in their way. God's messengers are human beings, with a limited lifespan. They know this fact well. Hence, they hope to persuade people to accept their message without delay. They may wish to give people a period of grace in respect of habits and traditions that are close to their hearts. They may think that if they can attract people to accept divine guidance while giving them this period of grace, they will then be able to wean them off such useless rituals, habits and traditions. They may also wish to compromise with them over a small portion of their desires so as to attract them to the faith, and hope to subsequently eliminate such lingering desires through education.

They may entertain other wishes concerning the spread of their message and its gaining supremacy. But God wants His message to follow its own principles and to be guided by its own values. People can choose to believe or not. According to divine standards, which are not subject to human weaknesses and mistakes, the divine message makes its true gains by following its own principles and values, even though it may lose individuals at the start. Strict adherence to principles and values inevitably wins over those people, or others better than them. What is more is that the message remains pure, intact and faultless.

Satan may find in such hopes and wishes, as well as their expressions, a chance to plot against the message and force it out of its tried and tested method. He endeavours to raise doubts in people's minds about its integrity. But God makes all Satan's endeavours come to nothing. He spells out the final ruling on people's words and actions, instructing His messengers to make His verdict clear to people, including what the messengers themselves might have done by mistake. This was the case with regard to some actions of the Prophet Muḥammad (peace be upon him), which were subject to clear verdicts in the Qur'ān.

Thus does God foil Satan's scheming and make His revelations clear so that the right course to be followed is clearly mapped. "*God is All-Knowing, Wise.*" Those with sickness and disbelief in their hearts and minds find in such situations fertile ground for controversy: "*All who are thus sinning are most deeply in the wrong.*" (Verse 53) At the opposite end, people endowed with true knowledge and wisdom are reassured by God's clear verdict: "*And those who are endowed with knowledge may realize that this [Qur'ān] is the truth from your Lord, and thus they may believe in it, and their hearts may humbly submit to Him. God will surely guide those who believe to a straight path.*" (Verse 54)

Messengers' Great Hopes

We find some examples during the Prophet's life and in Islamic history to confirm this. Thus there is no need for the sort of unsupported interpretation reported by some scholars.

One such example is that of the incident involving Ibn Umm Maktūm, a poor and blind Companion of the Prophet. He once went to the Prophet and asked him repeatedly to teach him something of what he had been taught by God. The Prophet was very busy speaking to al-Walīd ibn al-Mughīrah and a number of Quraysh notables, entertaining hopes that they might accept Islam. Ibn Umm Maktūm did not know that the Prophet was busy, but the Prophet was unhappy about his repeated request, and this was clear on his face. This was the subject of a strong reproach of the Prophet by God: "*He frowned and turned away when the blind man came to him. How could you tell? He might have sought to purify himself. He might have been reminded and the reminder might have profited him. But to the one who considered himself self-sufficient you were all attention. Yet the fault would not be yours if he remained uncleansed. As to him who comes to you with zeal, and with a feeling of fear in his heart, him you ignore. No indeed! This is an admonition. Let him who will, bear it in mind.*" (80: 1–12)

Thus, God set the message back on its right course, holding on to its proper standard and appropriate values. The Prophet's behaviour in this incident was also corrected. His motive was his desire to see those Quraysh notables become Muslims, because that would have ensured that large numbers of their followers would do likewise. But God explained to the Prophet that maintaining the proper Islamic values in addressing the message to people is far more important than gaining a few notables to the cause. Satan's attempts to divert the advocacy of the message through the Prophet's hopes was thus rendered futile. God made His message clear, and the believers were reassured.

Subsequently, the Prophet treated Ibn Umm Maktūm very kindly, welcomed him whenever he saw him, saying: "Welcome to the man on whose account God reproached me." The Prophet would ask him if he could help him in any way. Furthermore, the Prophet chose Ibn Umm Maktūm to deputize for him in Madīnah more than once when he was away on a journey or expedition.[6]

Another incident is related by Muslim in his collection of authentic *aḥādīth*. "Sa'd ibn Abī Waqqāṣ reports: Six of us were with the Prophet when some unbelievers asked him to turn us away so that they could have his full attention. With me was 'Abdullāh ibn Mas'ūd, a man from the Hudhayl tribe, Bilāl and two other men whose names I have forgotten. The Prophet felt whatever he might have felt, and thoughts occurred to him. But God revealed to him the verse that says: "*Do not drive away those who call on their Lord morning and evening, seeking only to win His pleasure.*" (6: 52)

Again in this incident, God sets the message back on its proper course, rendering futile Satan's attempts to divert it by agreeing to the wishes

6. This story is explained in detail in the commentary on *Sūrah* 80, with comments on its practical effects on Muslim society: Vol. XVIII, pp. 50–65. – Editor's note.

of the Quraysh elders. They wanted to retain their position of distinction and not mix with the poor and weak. To maintain proper Islamic values is far more important than those notables, even though they might have accepted Islam, together with thousands others of their followers. God knows best the source of strength for His message. Such strength is derived from maintaining proper values that brook no compromise based on personal preference or social tradition.

A third example may be seen in the case of Zaynab bint Jaḥsh, the Prophet's cousin whom he married to Zayd ibn Ḥārithah. Prior to Islam, Zayd was the Prophet's adopted son. But God wanted to stop adoption altogether, giving Qur'ānic orders that forbade calling someone the son or daughter of anyone other than their own parents: "*He never made your adopted sons truly your sons … Call them by their real fathers' names: this is more equitable in God's sight.*" (33: 4–5) Zayd was very dear to the Prophet. This is why he chose his own cousin to be Zayd's wife, but their life together was not smooth.

Prior to Islam, the Arabs did not approve of a man marrying the divorcee of his adopted son. But God wanted to put an end to this, as He stopped calling a son or daughter after anyone other than their real fathers. He told His Messenger to marry Zaynab after Zayd had divorced her, so that his marriage might be the practical action that put an end to the effects of adoption. But the Prophet concealed this when Zayd complained to him that his life with Zaynab could not go on. He told him to hold on to his wife, thinking of what people would say when he married her after Zayd had divorced her. He continued to keep this whole thing to himself, until Zayd actually divorced his wife. God then revealed in the Qur'ān what thoughts were in the Prophet's mind, making clear the rules He wished to put in place on this whole issue: "*You said to the one to whom God had shown favour and to whom you had shown favour, 'Hold on to your wife, and remain God-fearing!' Thus would you hide within yourself something that God was about to bring to light – for you feared [what] people [might think], whereas it was God alone of whom you should stand in awe! Then, when Zayd had come to the end of his union with her, We gave her to you in marriage, so that no blame should attach to the believers for [marrying] the spouses of their adopted children when the latter have come to the end of their union with them. Thus, God's will was done.*"[7] (33: 37)

'Ā'ishah was right when she said: "Had Muḥammad concealed anything God revealed to him in His book, he would have suppressed the statement: "*Thus would you hide within yourself something that God was about to bring to light – for you feared [what] people [might think], whereas it was God alone of whom you should stand in awe!*" (33: 37)

Thus God made His law very clear, exposing the thoughts entertained by His own Messenger, concerning people's dislike of his marriage to the divorcee of his former adopted son. But Satan's attempts to achieve gain in this way were brought to nothing. Yet those with sick or hardened hearts will continue to exploit this event in their attempts to show Islam in a bad light.

Such is the meaning we feel these verses convey. It is God who gives guidance and shows the right way.

Hasty Hopes

Enthusiasm may also be an important factor with advocates of the divine message, in all generations. Their long cherished desire to see the message spread and triumph may encourage them to try to win over certain individuals or influential people, even if this requires them to initially overlook some requirements that they may think to be of no great importance. They may even try to accommodate some of these practices so that people do not adopt a hostile attitude to the divine message.

In their keenness to achieve success for their cause, they may go even further and adopt means and methods that are inconsistent with the strict standards of Islam or with its line of action. They link their haste with what they consider to be the interests of Islam. But these are truly served only by strict adherence to the approach and method of

7. These verses and the events to which they refer will be discussed more fully in the commentary on *Sūrah* 33, in Vol. XIV. – Editor's note.

action adopted by Islam. Future results are known only to God. Hence, the advocates of Islam must not concern themselves with such results, as they are not accountable for them. Their duty is to follow the proper Islamic approach and clear line of action. They must leave the results to be determined by God, knowing that they can only be good and serve the interests of His cause.

These Qur'ānic verses provide a warning for the advocates of Islam, making it clear that Satan will try to exploit their hasty hopes to undermine their very cause. God has protected His messengers and prophets, bringing to nothing all Satan's schemes to exploit their natural human keenness. Others, however, who are not similarly infallible, must take extra care so that they leave no room for Satan to exploit their sincere desires to ensure success for God's message, or what they may term 'the interests of the cause'. This phrase must be removed from their lexicon, because it is a trap which Satan sets for them when he is unable to deceive them through their personal interests. Indeed, in some situations, 'the interests of the cause' may become an idol worshipped by its advocates who tend then to forget the proper Islamic method of operation. The advocates of Islam must always follow its own method, regardless of what such adherence brings about of results that may seem to involve risks for them and what they advocate. The only danger they must try hard to avoid is that of deviation from the Islamic method of action, even a minor one, for whatever reason. God knows best what serves the interests of His cause. They are not required to look after such interests. What they are required to ensure is that they do not deviate from the method and line of action shown to them by God's Messenger.

The *sūrah* adds a comment on the fact that God protects His message against Satan's scheming, emphasizing that those who reject it will be vanquished, and that humiliating torture awaits them.

> *Yet the unbelievers will not cease to be in doubt about Him until the Last Hour comes suddenly upon them, or suffering befalls them on a day with no more [days] to follow. On that day, all dominion shall belong to God. He shall judge between them. Thus, all who*

believe and do righteous deeds shall find themselves in gardens of bliss, whereas for the unbelievers who have denied Our revelations there shall be shameful suffering in store. (Verses 55–57)

Such is the unbelievers' attitude to the Qur'ān in general. It is mentioned here as it closely relates to their attitude to whatever aspersion Satan may try to cast in the hopes of God's prophets and messengers, i.e., the two situations are inter-linked. They continue to have doubts about the Qur'ān because their hearts have not felt the sort of pleasure and happiness it imparts so that they appreciate the truth it advocates. They continue to be in such state of doubt "*until the Last Hour comes suddenly upon them, or suffering befalls them on a day with no more [days] to follow.*" (Verse 55) Such suffering befalls them on the Day of Judgement, which is described in the Qur'ānic text as *'aqīm,* or sterile, in the sense that it is not followed by any other day.

On that day, no one other than God will have any dominion, not even the superficial type that people in this world tend to cherish. Judgement on that day is also exercised by God alone, who gives every party its just deserts: "*Thus, all who believe and do righteous deeds shall find themselves in gardens of bliss, whereas for the unbelievers who have denied Our revelations there shall be shameful suffering in store.*" (Verses 56–57) Such suffering is the right recompense for their scheming against the divine faith, denying God's clear revelations, and for their wilful refusal to obey Him.

4

Abraham's Choice of Name

As for those who leave their homes to serve God's cause, and are then slain or die, God will most certainly grant them a goodly provision. God is indeed the most munificent provider. (58)

وَٱلَّذِينَ هَاجَرُواْ فِي سَبِيلِ ٱللَّهِ
ثُمَّ قُتِلُوٓاْ أَوۡ مَاتُواْ لَيَرۡزُقَنَّهُمُ
ٱللَّهُ رِزۡقًا حَسَنٗاۚ وَإِنَّ ٱللَّهَ لَهُوَ
خَيۡرُ ٱلرَّٰزِقِينَ ٥٨

He will most certainly admit them to a place with which they shall be well pleased. God is surely All-Knowing, Most Forbearing. (59)

لَيُدۡخِلَنَّهُم مُّدۡخَلٗا يَرۡضَوۡنَهُۥۗ
وَإِنَّ ٱللَّهَ لَعَلِيمٌ حَلِيمٞ ٥٩

Thus shall it be. If one retaliates only to the extent of the injury he has received, and then is wronged again, God will certainly succour him. God is certainly the One who absolves sin, who is Much-Forgiving. (60)

ذَٰلِكَۖ وَمَنۡ عَاقَبَ بِمِثۡلِ مَا عُوقِبَ
بِهِۦ ثُمَّ بُغِيَ عَلَيۡهِ لَيَنصُرَنَّهُ ٱللَّهُۚ
إِنَّ ٱللَّهَ لَعَفُوٌّ غَفُورٞ ٦٠

Thus it is, because God causes the night to pass into the day, and the day to pass into the night; and because God hears all and sees all. (61)

ذَٰلِكَ بِأَنَّ ٱللَّهَ يُولِجُ ٱلَّيۡلَ فِي
ٱلنَّهَارِ وَيُولِجُ ٱلنَّهَارَ فِي ٱلَّيۡلِ
وَأَنَّ ٱللَّهَ سَمِيعُۢ بَصِيرٞ ٦١

Thus it is, because God alone is the Ultimate Truth, and all that people invoke beside Him is sheer falsehood, and because God alone is Most High, Great. (62)

ذَٰلِكَ بِأَنَّ ٱللَّهَ هُوَ ٱلْحَقُّ وَأَنَّ
مَا يَدْعُونَ مِن دُونِهِۦ هُوَ ٱلْبَٰطِلُ
وَأَنَّ ٱللَّهَ هُوَ ٱلْعَلِيُّ ٱلْكَبِيرُ ٦٢

Are you not aware that God sends down water from the skies, whereupon the earth becomes green. God is unfathomable in His wisdom, All Aware. (63)

أَلَمْ تَرَ أَنَّ ٱللَّهَ أَنزَلَ مِنَ ٱلسَّمَآءِ
مَآءً فَتُصْبِحُ ٱلْأَرْضُ مُخْضَرَّةً ۗ إِنَّ
ٱللَّهَ لَطِيفٌ خَبِيرٌ ٦٣

To Him belongs all that is in the heavens and on earth. God alone is indeed free of all want, worthy of all praise. (64)

لَّهُۥ مَا فِى ٱلسَّمَٰوَٰتِ وَمَا فِى ٱلْأَرْضِ ۗ
وَإِنَّ ٱللَّهَ لَهُوَ ٱلْغَنِىُّ ٱلْحَمِيدُ ٦٤

Do you not see that God has made subservient to you all that is on earth, and the ships that sail the sea at His bidding? He it is who holds the celestial bodies, so that they may not fall upon the earth except by His leave. Most compassionate is God, and merciful to mankind. (65)

أَلَمْ تَرَ أَنَّ ٱللَّهَ سَخَّرَ لَكُم مَّا فِى ٱلْأَرْضِ
وَٱلْفُلْكَ تَجْرِى فِى ٱلْبَحْرِ بِأَمْرِهِۦ
وَيُمْسِكُ ٱلسَّمَآءَ أَن تَقَعَ عَلَى
ٱلْأَرْضِ إِلَّا بِإِذْنِهِۦٓ ۗ إِنَّ ٱللَّهَ بِٱلنَّاسِ
لَرَءُوفٌ رَّحِيمٌ ٦٥

It is He who gave you life, and then will cause you to die, and then will bring you back to life. Bereft of all gratitude is man. (66)

وَهُوَ ٱلَّذِىٓ أَحْيَاكُمْ ثُمَّ يُمِيتُكُمْ
ثُمَّ يُحْيِيكُمْ ۗ إِنَّ ٱلْإِنسَٰنَ لَكَفُورٌ ٦٦

To every community We have appointed ways of worship, which they should observe. Let them not draw you into disputes on this score, but call [them all] to your Lord. You are indeed on the right way. (67)

لِّكُلِّ أُمَّةٍ جَعَلْنَا مَنسَكًا هُمْ
نَاسِكُوهُ فَلَا يُنَٰزِعُنَّكَ فِى
ٱلْأَمْرِ وَٱدْعُ إِلَىٰ رَبِّكَ إِنَّكَ لَعَلَىٰ
هُدًى مُّسْتَقِيمٍ ٦٧

Should they argue with you, say: 'God knows best what you are doing.' (68)

وَإِن جَٰدَلُوكَ فَقُلِ ٱللَّهُ أَعْلَمُ
بِمَا تَعْمَلُونَ ٦٨

God will judge between you on the Day of Resurrection with regard to all on which you dispute. (69)

ٱللَّهُ يَحْكُمُ بَيْنَكُمْ يَوْمَ ٱلْقِيَٰمَةِ
فِيمَا كُنتُمْ فِيهِ تَخْتَلِفُونَ ٦٩

Do you not know that God knows all that occurs in heaven as well as on earth? Indeed it is all in a record. All this is easy for God. (70)

أَلَمْ تَعْلَمْ أَنَّ ٱللَّهَ يَعْلَمُ مَا فِى ٱلسَّمَآءِ
وَٱلْأَرْضِ إِنَّ ذَٰلِكَ فِى كِتَٰبٍ إِنَّ
ذَٰلِكَ عَلَى ٱللَّهِ يَسِيرٌ ٧٠

And yet they worship beside God something for which He has never bestowed any warrant from on high, and of which they cannot have any knowledge. The wrongdoers shall have none to help them. (71)

وَيَعْبُدُونَ مِن دُونِ ٱللَّهِ مَا لَمْ يُنَزِّلْ
بِهِۦ سُلْطَٰنًا وَمَا لَيْسَ لَهُم بِهِۦ عِلْمٌ
وَمَا لِلظَّٰلِمِينَ مِن نَّصِيرٍ ٧١

As it is, whenever Our revelations are recited to them in all their clarity, you can perceive utter repugnance in the faces of unbelievers. They would almost assault those who recite Our revelations to them. Say: 'Shall I tell you of something worse than that? It is the fire which God has promised to those who deny Him. How vile an end!' (72)

وَإِذَا تُتْلَىٰ عَلَيْهِمْ ءَايَٰتُنَا بَيِّنَٰتٍ تَعْرِفُ
فِى وُجُوهِ ٱلَّذِينَ كَفَرُوا۟ ٱلْمُنكَرَ ۖ
يَكَادُونَ يَسْطُونَ بِٱلَّذِينَ يَتْلُونَ
عَلَيْهِمْ ءَايَٰتِنَا ۗ قُلْ أَفَأُنَبِّئُكُم بِشَرٍّ
مِّن ذَٰلِكُمُ ۗ ٱلنَّارُ وَعَدَهَا ٱللَّهُ ٱلَّذِينَ
كَفَرُوا۟ ۖ وَبِئْسَ ٱلْمَصِيرُ ﴿٧٢﴾

Mankind! An aphorism is set forth; hearken, then, to it. Those beings whom you invoke instead of God cannot create a fly, even though they were to join all their forces to that end. If a fly robs them of anything, they cannot rescue it from him! Weak indeed is the seeker, and weak the sought! (73)

يَٰٓأَيُّهَا ٱلنَّاسُ ضُرِبَ مَثَلٌ فَٱسْتَمِعُوا۟
لَهُۥٓ ۚ إِنَّ ٱلَّذِينَ تَدْعُونَ مِن دُونِ
ٱللَّهِ لَن يَخْلُقُوا۟ ذُبَابًا وَلَوِ ٱجْتَمَعُوا۟
لَهُۥ ۖ وَإِن يَسْلُبْهُمُ ٱلذُّبَابُ شَيْـًٔا
لَّا يَسْتَنقِذُوهُ مِنْهُ ۚ ضَعُفَ ٱلطَّالِبُ
وَٱلْمَطْلُوبُ ﴿٧٣﴾

No true understanding of God have they. God is certainly Most Powerful, Almighty. (74)

مَا قَدَرُوا۟ ٱللَّهَ حَقَّ قَدْرِهِۦٓ ۗ إِنَّ ٱللَّهَ
لَقَوِىٌّ عَزِيزٌ ﴿٧٤﴾

God chooses message bearers from among the angels and from among men. God hears all and sees all. (75)

ٱللَّهُ يَصْطَفِى مِنَ ٱلْمَلَٰٓئِكَةِ رُسُلًا
وَمِنَ ٱلنَّاسِ ۚ إِنَّ ٱللَّهَ سَمِيعٌۢ بَصِيرٌ ﴿٧٥﴾

He knows all that lies open before them and all that is hidden from them. To God all things shall return. (76)

يَعْلَمُ مَا بَيْنَ أَيْدِيهِمْ وَمَا خَلْفَهُمْ ۗ
وَإِلَى ٱللَّهِ تُرْجَعُ ٱلْأُمُورُ ﴿٧٦﴾

يَٰٓأَيُّهَا ٱلَّذِينَ ءَامَنُوا۟ ٱرْكَعُوا۟
وَٱسْجُدُوا۟ وَٱعْبُدُوا۟ رَبَّكُمْ وَٱفْعَلُوا۟
ٱلْخَيْرَ لَعَلَّكُمْ تُفْلِحُونَ ۩ ﴿٧٧﴾

Believers! Bow down and prostrate yourselves, and worship your Lord alone, and do good, so that you might be successful. (77)

وَجَٰهِدُوا۟ فِى ٱللَّهِ حَقَّ جِهَادِهِۦ ۚ هُوَ
ٱجْتَبَىٰكُمْ وَمَا جَعَلَ عَلَيْكُمْ فِى ٱلدِّينِ
مِنْ حَرَجٍ ۚ مِّلَّةَ أَبِيكُمْ إِبْرَٰهِيمَ ۚ هُوَ
سَمَّىٰكُمُ ٱلْمُسْلِمِينَ مِن قَبْلُ وَفِى
هَٰذَا لِيَكُونَ ٱلرَّسُولُ شَهِيدًا عَلَيْكُمْ
وَتَكُونُوا۟ شُهَدَآءَ عَلَى ٱلنَّاسِ ۚ فَأَقِيمُوا۟
ٱلصَّلَوٰةَ وَءَاتُوا۟ ٱلزَّكَوٰةَ وَٱعْتَصِمُوا۟
بِٱللَّهِ هُوَ مَوْلَىٰكُمْ ۖ فَنِعْمَ ٱلْمَوْلَىٰ وَنِعْمَ
ٱلنَّصِيرُ ﴿٧٨﴾

And strive hard in God's cause as you ought to strive. It is He who has chosen you, and has laid no hardship on you in [anything that pertains to] religion; the creed of your forefather Abraham. It is He who has named you Muslims, in bygone times and in this [book], so that the Messenger might bear witness for you, and that you might bear witness for all mankind. Thus, attend regularly to your prayer, and pay out your *zakāt*, and hold fast to God. He is your Guardian: the best of guardians and the best to give support. (78)

Overview

The previous passage ended with an outline of the opposite destinies of the believers and those who deny God's message. On the day when all dominion belongs to God alone, they end up in contrasting positions. All this is given within the context of God's support of His messengers, protection of His message and the reward He has in store for those who believe and those who refuse to believe.

This passage begins with a reference to those who migrate for God's cause. They have already been permitted to fight in defence of their faith and to defend themselves against injustice. They have been driven out of their homes against all right, for no reason other than their declaration that they believed in God alone. The passage also clarifies that God will compensate them for the property they left behind when they migrated.

A general verdict follows which applies to those who find themselves unjustly attacked and who try to repel aggression, but are then subjected to further tyranny and hostility. They are given a clear and assured promise of support. This firm promise is followed by listing some indicators of God's power which ensures that His promises will always come true. These indicators are seen in the universe around us. It thus suggests that God's help to those who suffer injustice, despite their attempts to repel aggression, is a certainty in the same vein as other universal laws.

At this point in the passage, the Prophet receives a direct address that each community is shown a course of action, suitable for its own circumstances. Therefore, he should not be preoccupied with arguments with unbelievers. He must not allow them a chance to dispute his method. Should they seek to argue with him, he should leave them to God who judges between them on the Day of Judgement over everything which they differed. He is the One who knows the truth of what they follow, as He knows everything in the heavens and on earth.

The *sūrah* also refers to their worship of deities that have no sanction from God, as well as their worship of beings they do not know. They are criticized for being hard hearted and for their dislike of hearing the truth. In fact they would not shrink from attacking those who recite God's revelations to them. They are threatened with the fire which will be their ultimate abode. This is a promise that will never fail.

This is followed by an announcement to all mankind, making it clear that those whom they worship instead of God are devoid of power. Their weakness is shown in a humble image that carries no exaggeration, but the way it is presented brings their shameful weakness into sharp relief. They are shown as incapable of contending with flies, or of retrieving what a fly takes from them. Yet, unbelievers claim that such beings are deities.

The passage and the *sūrah* end with an address to the community of believers requiring them to fulfil their duties as leaders of humanity. They should prepare themselves for their task with prayer, worship and good action, seeking God's help and protection.

A Fitting Reward

> *As for those who leave their homes to serve God's cause, and are then slain or die, God will most certainly grant them a goodly provision. God is indeed the most munificent provider. He will most certainly admit them to a place with which they shall be well pleased. God is surely All-Knowing, Most Forbearing.* (Verses 58–59)

Migration, or leaving one's home, to serve God's cause represents a desertion of every comfort whether it be family, community and childhood memories, or property and material comforts. When one puts one's faith ahead of all this for no other reason than to earn God's pleasure, one demonstrates that such a prize is more valuable than all material goods. Migration was possible before Makkah fell to Islam and the Islamic state was established. After that, migration was invalid. The requirement now is to strive in serving God's cause. Whoever strives thus for God's cause and dedicates himself to its service receives a similar reward to that of migration.

"*As for those who leave their homes to serve God's cause, and are then slain or die, God will most certainly grant them a goodly provision.*" (Verse 58) This applies whether they die in battle, earning martyrdom, or die normally in their homes. They left their homes and property ready to face any eventuality only to serve Him. They sought martyrdom in any way it might come, sacrificing every worldly comfort. Therefore, God compensates them richly for what they abandoned on His account: "*God will most certainly grant them a goodly provision. God is indeed the most munificent provider.*" (Verse 58) Such provisions are better than everything they leave behind.

"*He will most certainly admit them to a place with which they shall be well pleased.*" (Verse 59) They departed in a way that pleased God, and in return He promises that they will be well pleased with the position into which He will admit them. It is indeed a clear aspect of the honour God grants them when He makes sure of answering their wishes and ensuring that they are pleased with what they receive from Him. "*God is surely All-Knowing, Most Forbearing.*" (Verse 59) He is well aware of what they have suffered of injustice and what makes them feel well compensated. He is also forbearing, giving the unbelievers respite in order that they realize that they are in the wrong. He eventually gives fitting reward to those who suffer injustice and fitting punishment to those who inflict injustice.

Those who are targets of human aggression may not be able to tolerate such treatment or bear it with patience. They would rather respond in kind, measure for measure. If aggressors persist, and continue with their oppression, God is certain to support the oppressed and help them against those who are unjust: "*Thus shall it be. If one retaliates only to the extent of the injury he has received, and then is wronged again, God will certainly succour him. God is certainly the One who absolves sin, who is Much-Forgiving.*" (Verse 60) The condition that must be fulfilled for God's help to be forthcoming is that the action must be one of retaliation, seeking to repel aggression. Such help is not forthcoming for aggression of any sort. Moreover, retaliation must not be excessive; rather it must be limited in scale, replying, measure for measure, to the original aggression.

The comment made in the verse on the nature of this retaliation is that "*God is certainly the One who absolves sin, who is Much-Forgiving.*" It is He who forgives and absolves. Human beings have no say in this. Indeed they may prefer to retaliate and to repel aggression. Given their nature, they are allowed to pursue such retaliatory action. God will help them to achieve victory.

God's promise of help to victims of aggression is linked to universal laws that testify to His power. These laws operate most accurately, without fail, which, in turn, suggests that God's help to those at the receiving end of aggression is one of the unfailing universal laws He has set in operation. "*Thus it is, because God causes the night to pass into the day, and the day to pass into the night; and because God hears all and sees all.*" (Verse 61)

This refers to a natural phenomenon which people observe morning and evening, day and night, winter and summer. The night passes into the day at sunset, and the day passes into the night at sunrise. And the night takes more of the day as we go into the winter, while the day takes up more of the night as summer approaches. People see both phenomena of the two parts of the daily cycle passing into each other, but long familiarity makes them oblivious to their accuracy and unfailing regularity. Nevertheless, these phenomena are witnesses to God's power which controls the universe and all its events.

The *sūrah* wants people to open their eyes and hearts to these often overlooked phenomena that are indicative of God's superior power that controls the movement and length of both day and night, with absolute accuracy. The same may be said about God's help to those who suffer aggression and try to repel it. It is as accurate and regular as the passing of the day into the night and the passing of the night into the day. God always smites the power of tyrant oppressors and allows justice to triumph. Again, people tend to be oblivious of this phenomenon, just as they overlook signs and pointers indicating God's power and control of the universe.

Absolute Truth

All this relates to the essential fact that God is the ultimate and absolute truth. His is the truth that controls the universe and operates its systems. Everything else is false, irregular, and cannot be maintained: "*Thus it is, because God alone is the Ultimate Truth, and all that people invoke beside Him is sheer falsehood, and because God alone is Most High, Great.*" (Verse 62)

This is an adequate explanation and a guarantee that truth and justice will inevitably triumph, while falsehood and aggression are certain to be defeated. It is the same guarantee that the laws of the universe will operate without fail. One of these laws and phenomena is that the truth will be victorious and falsehood will suffer a humiliating defeat. God is certainly far superior to any absolute ruler who seeks to demonstrate his power over the weak. The verse concludes with this comment: "*God alone is Most High, Great.*" Hence, He will not allow aggression to swell, or injustice to be everlasting.

Further natural phenomena are shown as permanent indicators of God's power: "*Are you not aware that God sends down water from the skies, whereupon the earth becomes green. God is unfathomable in His wisdom, All Aware.*" (Verse 63) We see this happening all the time: rain pours down from the skies and the earth becomes green within a very short period, but again long familiarity makes us oblivious to this. However, to people with open minds the scene arouses a host of feelings. At times, you look at a green shoot poking out through the black earth and you feel its freshness. It reminds you of young children smiling happily to the world around them, and who almost fly with delight when they see the spreading light.

If we have such feelings, we can properly understand the comment at the end of the verse: "*God is unfathomable in His wisdom, All Aware.*" It is as profound a comment as our feelings when we look at this delightful scene and contemplate its nature. It is part of God's unfathomable wisdom to initiate such subtle movements within the depths of the earth, bringing forth a green shoot, fresh but weak and slim. With God's power, it stretches out into the air, moving against the law of gravity. It is God's knowledge that determines the amount of rain that falls from the sky and its timing, so that water mixes with the earth and allows vegetation to grow.

Water falls from God's sky to His earth to initiate life and provide nutrition and wealth. But then God owns both the heavens and earth and all that they contain, yet He needs nothing of them. He gives provisions to all living things, through water and plants. But He is free of all need. "*To Him belongs all that is in the heavens and on earth. God alone is indeed free of all want, worthy of all praise.*" (Verse 64) He is in need of nothing of what lives in the heavens and earth. Indeed all praise is due to Him for the favours He bestows on all His creatures.

Mercy Without Limit

Once more the *sūrah* points out some of the aspects of God's power as seen in nature: "*Do you not see that God has made subservient to you all that is on earth, and the ships that sail the sea at His bidding? He it is who holds the celestial bodies, so that they may not fall upon the earth except by His leave. Most compassionate is God, and merciful to mankind."* (Verse 65) This draws people's attention to the earth they live on, which contains a wide variety of powers and wealth which God has made subservient to man. Yet man remains oblivious of God's favours which he enjoys night and day.

God has placed everything on earth at man's disposal, by making the laws of nature affecting the earth compatible with man's nature and abilities. Had these been at variance with the natural laws of the earth, human life would not have been possible on this planet, and man would not have been able to utilize its resources to his benefit. Had he been physically different from the condition which allows him to tolerate the earth's atmosphere, breathe its air, eat its food and drink its water, man could not have survived on earth for even a very brief time. Had the density of the earth or the human constitution been different, man would not have been able to walk or stand upright on earth; he would either fly in the air or sink into the earth. Had the earth been without an atmosphere, or had the air been heavier or lighter than its present condition, man would have suffocated or been unable to breathe. Thus, it is the compatibility of all these natural elements with human nature that makes man able to live on earth and benefit by its resources. This is only feasible through God's will.

Moreover, God made the earth subservient to man through the powers and abilities He gave man. Without these man would not have been able to tap the resources of the earth to his benefit. As it is, man discovers these resources one by one. Whenever he needs something new for his life, he uncovers new treasures; and whenever he feels that the earth's reserves of an essential material are running short, he finds new ones or alternative materials. Today, although there remain plenty of oil supplies and other minerals, yet the vast potential of nuclear energy has become available.[8] But man is still like a child who plays

8. Nuclear energy is cited in this case as an example of alternatives to coal and oil. The important point is that God has placed in man's world different means and resources to support life, growth and development. – Editor's note.

with fire, and can easily burn himself and those around him. Hence, he needs to abide by the code of living God has laid down so that he can make full use of the earth's resources to build a better human life and fulfil his mission.

"*Do you not see that God has made subservient to you all that is on earth, and the ships that sail the sea at His bidding?*" (Verse 65) It is God who created the laws that allow ships to sail through the sea, and who gave man the necessary means to discover these laws and utilize them to his benefit. Had the nature of the sea, or the ships, or man's powers of understanding and learning been different, none of this could have happened.

"*He it is who holds the celestial bodies, so that they may not fall upon the earth except by His leave. Most compassionate is God, and merciful to mankind.*" (Verse 65) It is He who created the universe and chose its appropriate system. It is He who has made its laws which ensure that celestial bodies remain far apart from each other.

Every theory explaining this universal system is no more than an attempt to understand the laws that ensure the maintenance of the balance that God has placed in the universe. Yet some people overlook this essential fact. They think that if they learn how the universe works, then they are negating God's role and His power which operates it. This is a particularly singular way of thinking. To explain how a certain law of nature works does not negate that it has been devised by the One who set it in operation in the first place, or that He continues to ensure that such a law remains in operation. Besides, all that man has come up with is a host of theories that attempt to explain natural phenomena. They may be right, and may equally be wrong.

God Almighty '*holds the celestial bodies so that they may not fall upon the earth*' through the system He has devised for the universe. He keeps them from falling '*except by His leave.*' This is a reference to a time when He may decide to stop this system for a purpose He, in His infinite wisdom, wishes to happen.

The *sūrah* completes its reference to aspects of God's power and the perfection of natural laws by speaking of the human soul. It talks of human existence, life and death: "*It is He who gave you life, and then will cause you to die, and then will bring you back to life. Bereft of all gratitude is man.*" (Verse 66) The first life is a miracle renewed with every child born at every moment of the night and day. Its secret continues to fill man's mind with wonder and to leave a vast area for us to contemplate. Death is also a secret that man cannot fathom. It occurs within a brief moment, yet the gulf between the nature of life and that of death is vast indeed, leaving a similarly vast area for contemplation. Life after death is something that lies beyond our faculties of perception, but our present life provides ample evidence for it. This is a further area for contemplation.

Yet man seldom reflects or contemplates, because man is '*bereft of all gratitude.*' The *sūrah* shows all these aspects and draws our attention to them within the context of assuring victims of oppression that they will have God's support as they try to repel such hostility. Such is the Qur'ānic method in using universal scenes to arouse human feelings, and in linking the laws of justice to the laws governing universal existence.

No Room for Argument

At this point the *sūrah* addresses the Prophet (peace be upon him) instructing him to follow his own way, paying no attention to the unbelievers and their futile arguments. He must not allow them to divert him from the method God chose for him, as He assigned him the task of delivering His message to mankind.

> *To every community We have appointed ways of worship, which they should observe. Let them not draw you into disputes on this score, but call [them all] to your Lord. You are indeed on the right way. Should they argue with you, say: 'God knows best what you are doing.' God will judge between you on the Day of Resurrection with regard to all on which you dispute. Do you not know that God knows all that occurs in heaven as well as on earth? Indeed it is all in a record. All this is easy for God.* (Verses 67–70)

Every community has its own way of life, thought, behaviour and beliefs, and these are subject to the consistent and accurate laws God has set to regulate people's nature, thinking, feelings and reactions to outside influences. A community that opens its hearts to the pointers to divine guidance and responds to relevant pointers in the universe and within the human soul finds its way to God. In this, it will benefit by the numerous signs pointing to His oneness and encouraging compliance with His orders. By contrast, a community that shuts its mind to all this is in the wrong, sinking deeper into error.

Since God has appointed a certain way for each community, then the Prophet need not trouble himself with arguments he may put to the unbelievers when they turn away from the path of divine guidance and persist in following error. God instructs him not to allow the unbelievers any chance to dispute with him over his mission, or the way of life he advocates. He must continue to implement it, paying no heed to anyone who wants to engage in argument and dispute. His is a straightforward way, as God Himself testifies: "*You are indeed on the right way.*" (Verse 67) This gives him all the reassurance he needs to follow divine guidance.

If unbelievers try to dispute with him, he should cut short such arguments. It is no use wasting time and effort: "*Should they argue with you, say: 'God knows best what you are doing.'*" (Verse 68) Argument can be useful with people whose hearts and minds are open to receive guidance, seeking knowledge and seriously searching for the right evidence. But argument is futile with those who persist in their erring ways, turning a blind eye to all the indicators and pointers they see in the universe and within themselves. The Prophet is told to leave these people to God who will judge between all creeds and ways of life and their followers: "*God will judge between you on the Day of Resurrection with regard to all on which you dispute.*" (Verse 69) He is the judge to whom no one can object, because on that day all argument is abandoned. Nor can there be any argument about the final judgement.

God makes His judgement on the basis of His perfect knowledge. He does not lose sight of any circumstances, and no motive or feeling is withheld from Him. He knows everything in the heavens and the earth, including people's intentions, motives, actions and reactions: "*Do you not know that God knows all that occurs in heaven as well as on earth? Indeed it is all in a record. All this is easy for God.*" (Verse 70)

God's knowledge is not subject to any of the influences that erase things from memory or cause forgetfulness. His record is complete and perfect.

The human mind becomes overwhelmed when it merely contemplates some of what we see in the heavens and the earth, and tries to imagine how God knows all these perfectly, down to the most minute details of people, their thoughts, intentions and actions. But all this is very little compared to God's full knowledge and power. Hence the verse concludes with the statement: "*All this is easy for God.*" (Verse 70) Having made it clear to the Prophet that he must not allow the unbelievers a chance to dispute with him over his right way, the *sūrah* shows how flawed and flimsy the way followed by the unbelievers is. It betrays total ignorance of the truth. They are deprived of God's help, and as such they have none to help them:

> *And yet they worship beside God something for which He has never bestowed any warrant from on high, and of which they cannot have any knowledge. The wrongdoers shall have none to help them.* (Verse 71)

No situation or system can have any real power except for what is granted by God. What lacks the source of power given by God remains weak and unsupportable. Such unbelievers worship different deities, some of which are idols and statues, and some are human; or they may even worship Satan. All these are devoid of God's power; hence they are weak. Besides, they do not worship these deities on the basis of any solid and convincing evidence. Their basis is myth and superstition. Having been denied God's help, they will not receive any from any other source.

The most singular thing is that while they worship false deities of which they have no knowledge, they refuse to listen to the voice of truth. They are hardened in their attitude, threatening to strike at those who recite God's revelations to them:

> *As it is, whenever Our revelations are recited to them in all their clarity, you can perceive utter repugnance in the faces of unbelievers. They would almost assault those who recite Our revelations to them.* (Verse 72)

They cannot answer an argument with an equally valid counter argument, or reply to evidence with anything that is similarly powerful. Instead, they resort to heavy-handed tactics, violence and oppression, realizing that they have no leg to stand on. This is always the case with tyrants who think only of suppressing the truth, knowing that they have no other way to answer it.

Hence, the Qur'ān delivers a clear warning, pointing to the inevitable outcome: "*Say: Shall I tell you of something worse than that?*" (Verse 72) What is worse than the evil they harbour within themselves, and the oppression they embark upon? "*It is the fire which God has promised to those who deny Him.*" (Verse 72) This is the right reply for the oppression they engage in. And the final comment is: "*How vile an end!*" (Verse 72)

Powerless Man

The *sūrah* now makes a powerful, universal declaration that all deities people associate with God, including the ones to which the wrongdoers appeal for help, are weak and powerless. Their weakness is shown in a bustling and captivating scene:

> *Mankind! An aphorism is set forth; hearken, then, to it. Those beings whom you invoke instead of God cannot create a fly, even though they were to join all their forces to that end. If a fly robs them of anything, they cannot rescue it from him! Weak indeed is the seeker, and weak the sought!* (Verse 73)

The address is universal, it includes everyone anywhere in the world, and the declaration is loud and clear: "Mankind!" When people have been gathered to listen, they are told that they are about to be given a statement of a general principle, not a particular case applicable on a certain occasion. "*An aphorism is set forth; hearken, then, to it.*" It is a statement of fact that applies in all situations: "*Those beings whom you invoke instead of God cannot create a fly, even though they were to join all their forces to that end.*" All false deities, whether they be idols and statues, human beings, traditions and values, to whom you appeal for support and with whom you seek to achieve victory and high esteem, are incapable of creating a fly, even if they muster all their forces, utilize all their knowledge and channel all their resources into one supreme effort. Indeed, the creation of a mere fly, that small and abject creature, defies all the harnessed powers of such false gods.

Creating a fly is just as impossible, for anyone or thing other than God, as creating a camel or an elephant, because the fly also demonstrates the great secret of life. Hence, it is placed on the same level as camels and elephants, with regard to its miraculous creation. The Qur'ānic aphorism, however, cites the case of a little, insignificant fly in order to generate a more profound feeling of powerlessness, without compromising the underlying principle.

The *sūrah* adds another dimension in describing their powerlessness: "*If a fly robs them of anything, they cannot rescue it from him!*" (Verse 73) False deities, be they idols or humans, cannot retrieve anything from a fly when it robs them of it. Flies can rob people of that which is precious indeed. At the same time, a fly carries agents of some very serious diseases, such as tuberculosis, typhoid, dysentery and conjunctivitis. It can deprive a person of his eyes or other organs, or indeed deprive him of his life. A weak and contemptible fly can rob a human being of what he can never retrieve.

Here again we note how the Qur'ānic style uses facts in the most effective way. Had the text referred to lions and similar wild animals adding that men cannot rescue anything such animals rob them of, it would have generated an air of strength and force, rather than weakness. Besides, the most powerful animals cannot rob man of anything greater than what a fly can rob him of.

This powerful image stating a clear aphorism concludes with a simple comment: "*Weak indeed is the seeker, and weak the sought!*" (Verse 73) This comment further emphasizes the effects generated by the verse as a whole.

At this moment when we realize how weak and contemptible these false deities are, the *sūrah* denounces the unbelievers for their faulty concept of God, clearly stating God's power: "*No true understanding of God have they. God is certainly Most Powerful, Almighty.*" (Verse 74) How could they understand Him as He really is when they associate with Him such powerless deities that cannot even create a fly? What understanding of God have they, when they see His highly sophisticated creation and yet they consider as equal to Him beings that cannot create even a little fly? They even invoke such powerless creatures which cannot retrieve anything flies take away from them, instead of invoking God. So, how can it be claimed that they have a proper concept of God? This is a damning comment at a point which should arouse feelings of submission to God alone.

The *sūrah* then mentions that God Almighty chooses His angel messengers to deliver His revelations to prophets, and chooses His human messengers to address mankind. All this is done on the basis of immaculate knowledge and total ability:

> *God chooses message bearers from among the angels and from among men. God hears all and sees all. He knows all that lies open before them and all that is hidden from them. To God all things shall return.* (Verses 75–76)

The choice of both angel and human messenger is made by the Almighty, and it was from the Almighty that Muḥammad received the message of Islam. It was God who chose Muḥammad to be His Messenger to mankind. How could he be compared to those who rely on deities that are both weak and contemptible?

"*God hears all and sees all,*" and as such "*He knows all that lies open before them and all that is hidden from them.*" His knowledge is perfect, immaculate, complete. Nothing present or absent, near or distant escapes God's knowledge.

"*To God all things shall return.*" (Verse 76) He is the ultimate arbiter, who has power over all things.

Striving for the Right Cause

Having exposed the absurdity of the idolaters' beliefs and the ignorance their worship rituals reflect, the *sūrah* makes a final address to the Muslim community, urging it to be true to its beliefs and to stick to the right way of life.

Believers! Bow down and prostrate yourselves, and worship your Lord alone, and do good, so that you might be successful. And strive hard in God's cause as you ought to strive. It is He who has chosen you, and has laid no hardship on you in [anything that pertains to] religion; the creed of your forefather Abraham. It is He who has named you Muslims, in bygone times and in this [book], so that the Messenger might bear witness for you, and that you might bear witness for all mankind. Thus, attend regularly to your prayer, and pay out your zakāt, *and hold fast to God. He is your Guardian: the best of guardians and the best to give support.* (Verses 77–78)

Indeed these two verses sum up the code of living God has laid down for the Muslim community and the duties He has assigned to it. They define its role and mark out its course of action, past, present and future, provided that it follows His guidance.

The first instruction given here requires the believers to pray, highlighting two distinctive actions of Islamic prayer, namely bowing down and prostrating before God. Thus, prayer is given a real image and a noteworthy movement so that we see it clearly before our eyes. In this way, the mode of expression is that much more effective.

Next we have a general instruction to worship God. This is far more comprehensive than prayer, because worship includes all duties and adds every action, thought or feeling that is addressed to God alone. Indeed every human activity becomes part of worship when it is intended for God's sake. This even includes pleasure and personal enjoyment which become part of worship earning reward from God. All it needs is that we should remember God who has granted us these pleasures and who intends them as means to strengthen our resolve to follow the way He has chosen for us. Nothing of the nature of such pleasures and enjoyments changes, but their purpose is changed, and thus they become part of worship.

The last instruction in the first of these two verses is that believers must do every good thing, particularly in their dealings with fellow human beings, just as they do good in their relations with God, offering prayer and worship. All these instructions are given to the Muslim community so that it can be successful, because these are the means to success. Worship maintains its relation with God so that life is established on the right footing, and follows the way leading to the ultimate goal. Doing good means that the life of the community is firmly established on the basis of right belief.

When the Muslim community has such a proper relation with God and an appropriate lifestyle, it can discharge its awesome responsibility: "*And strive hard in God's cause as you ought to strive.*" This is a veracious and comprehensive description, indicating a massive responsibility that requires adequate preparation and the mustering of equipment and resources.

"*And strive hard in God's cause as you ought to strive.*" (Verse 78) This includes striving against one's enemies, laziness, evil and corruption. All these must be equally resisted. It is God who has assigned to you this massive responsibility and chosen you to fulfil it: "*It is He who has chosen you.*" This choice adds to the seriousness of the responsibility, which means that it cannot be shrugged off or abandoned. Indeed it is an honour God has bestowed on the Muslim community for which it should be infinitely grateful.

Moreover, the assigned task is entwined with God's grace: He "*has laid no hardship on you in [anything that pertains to] religion.*" Indeed, the religion of Islam, with all its duties, worship and laws always observes man's nature and abilities. It aims to satisfy human nature and release man's abilities so that they are used constructively. Human nature must neither be suppressed nor left without control.

Moreover, the Islamic way of life has a long history in human life, linking the past with the present. It is "*the creed of your forefather Abraham.*" It is the system that has continued on earth since the time of Abraham, without any long gap that allows the divine faith to be totally distorted, as happened in some periods prior to Abraham's time.

God has given the name 'Muslim' to the community that believes in His oneness, and this name remained the same whether in olden days or in the Qur'ān: "*It is He who has named you Muslims, in bygone times and in this [book].*"

Islam means surrendering oneself totally to God, attributing no share of Godhead to anyone else. Thus, the Muslim community has enjoyed the same system across successive generations, and with successive messages and messengers, up to the time of the Prophet Muḥammad (peace be upon him). It was then that the divine message was entrusted to the Muslim community. Thus, the past, present and future are interlinked as God wants. Thus, "*the Messenger might bear witness for you, and that you might bear witness for all mankind.*" The Prophet is, thus, a witness defining the way the Muslim community should follow, pointing out right and wrong, and the Muslim community fulfils the same task with regard to humanity at large. It occupies the position of trustee by virtue of the standards established by its laws, education and concepts relating to life and to the universe. Needless to say, the Muslim community cannot fulfil this role unless it implements God's message fully in life. When the Muslim community abandoned this role and deviated from the divine code of living, God removed it from this leadership, leaving it trailing well behind. It will continue to be in this humiliating position until it resumes its role chosen for it by God.

To ensure such a return, it must be fully prepared for it. Hence the order: "*Attend regularly to your prayer, and pay out your* zakāt, *and hold fast to God. He is your Guardian: the best of guardians and the best to give support.*" (Verse 78) Prayer provides a link between the weak and mortal individual and the source of power, while *zakāt* provides a strong link between members of the community, ensuring security for all. Holding fast to God is the strong tie that is never severed.

With such resources, the Muslim community can resume the role of human leadership for which God has chosen it. It will also be able to utilize the material resources people consider to be sources of strength. The Qur'ān does not overlook these; on the contrary, it wants the Muslim community to be equipped with them, alongside the resources that are available only to believers who strive to enrich life with all that is good and right.

The great advantage of the divine way of life is that it takes humanity by the hand along the way that raises it to the highest position of perfection achievable in this life. It is far removed from systems that care only for worldly pleasures and the satisfaction of carnal desires.

Sublime human values aim to satisfy the needs of material life, but do not stop there. This is what Islam wants for humanity, under the wise trusteeship of the community that implements the divine message.

SŪRAH 23

Al-Mu'minūn

(The Believers)

Prologue

This *sūrah*, The Believers, or *al-Mu'minūn*, is defined by its name which makes its subject matter very clear. It begins with an outline of the believers' qualities, and presents an exposition on the indicators of faith in both the human soul and the universe at large. It then moves on to present the essence of faith as expostulated by God's messengers since the time of Noah up to Muḥammad, the last of all prophets and messengers, (peace be upon them all). It also discusses the fallacies of those who deny faith, their objections and determined opposition that compel God's messengers to appeal to Him for help. At this point, God punishes the rejecters and saves the believers. The *sūrah* then refers to the fact that, after God's messengers have passed away, people fall into contention about this truth that admits no variation. This provides an opportunity to discuss and denounce the unjustified attitude the Arab idolaters took to God's last messenger, Muḥammad (peace be upon him). The *sūrah* closes with a scene of the Day of Judgement in which we see the fate suffered by those who reject the truth of faith. They are strongly reproached for their attitude. This scene concludes with a statement re-emphasizing the truth of God's absolute oneness and a prayer for His mercy and forgiveness.

As such, the *sūrah* is what its titles say, The Believers, or the *sūrah* of faith with all its issues, aspects and nature. Faith then provides its central theme.

The *sūrah* may be divided into four parts. The first begins with a statement that success is assured for the believers: "*Truly, successful shall be the believers.*" (Verse 1) It provides a detailed account of the qualities of those believers who are certain to be successful. Referring to signs that encourage and endorse faith, which are found both in human beings and in the universe at large, this part mentions the different stages of human life from its early beginnings to its final end. It elaborates much when it mentions the different stages an embryo goes through while providing only a brief outline of other stages. It then follows human life up to the Day of Resurrection before moving on to signs of faith in the wide universe, referring to the creation of the heavens, rain falling from the sky, bringing forth vegetation, plants and fruits. It also mentions animals that are placed at the disposal of human beings, ships traversing the seas and man's ability to use such ships and animals for transport.

The second part takes us from the indicators pointing out the reality of faith to a discussion of the truth of faith as advocated by all God's messengers, without exception: "*My people, worship God alone: for you have no deity other than Him.*" (Verse 23) This is a statement made by Noah, and by every messenger that followed him, up to Muḥammad, God's final Messenger. The unbelievers always made the same objections: "*This man is but a mortal like yourselves,*" and "*had God willed, He would have surely sent down angels.*" (Verse 24) Another objection refers to the promise made by God's messengers: "*Does he promise you that, after you have died and become dust and bones, you shall be brought forth to life?*" (Verse 35) The result was always that messengers appealed to God for support. He answered their appeals and destroyed the unbelievers. This part concludes with an address to all messengers: "*Eat of that which is wholesome, and do good deeds: I certainly have full knowledge of all that you do. This community of yours is one single community, and I am your only Lord. Therefore, fear Me alone.*" (Verses 51–52)

The third part speaks about the fact that after God's messengers had gone, people were divided and fell into contention over this essential truth: "*People have divided themselves into factions, each delighting in what they have.*" (Verse 53) It further speaks about people being oblivious of the fact that God tests them with the blessings He bestows on them. They are deluded by the riches they enjoy. The believers, on the other hand, remain God-fearing, worship Him alone and associate no partners with Him. At the same time they remain fully alert, with awe in their hearts: "*Their hearts [are] filled with awe, knowing that to their Lord they shall certainly return.*" (Verse 60) At this point, an image is portrayed showing those who were oblivious of the truth of faith being overwhelmed by God's punishment. They cry out for help, but they are strongly reproached: "*Time and again were My revelations recited to you, but every time you would turn about on your heels, revelling in your arrogance, and talking senselessly far into the night.*" (Verses 66–67) The *sūrah* denounces their attitude towards God's Messenger whom they knew well to be honest and truthful. Now that he has come to them with the message of the truth, asking for no wages, how can they reject him and the truth he advocates? Although they acknowledge that to God belongs all that is in the heavens and the earth, which are all under His control as He is their only Lord, they reject the very concept of resurrection. They go further in their falsehood, claiming that God has a son and associating partners with Him. "*Sublimely exalted is He above anything they associate as partner with Him.*" (Verse 92)

The final part turns away from them and their claims in order to address the Prophet, telling him to repel evil with what is better, and to seek refuge with God from the evil of satans. He must not be angered or grieved by what they say. In addition, we have here a scene of the Day of Judgement describing the punishment, suffering and humiliation that await them there. The *sūrah* concludes by stating that God always remains exalted above all that they say about Him: "*Sublimely exalted is God, the Ultimate Sovereign, the Ultimate Truth. There is no deity other than Him, the Lord of the Glorious Throne.*" (Verse 116) It also asserts that the unbelievers will never be successful, whereas the believers' success is confirmed at the beginning of the *sūrah*:

"*He that invokes besides God any other deity – a deity for whose existence he has no evidence – shall be brought to account before his Lord. Most certainly, the unbelievers shall never be successful.*" (Verse 117) Again, an instruction is given to seek God's mercy and forgiveness: "*Say: My Lord! Forgive and have mercy. You are the best of those who show mercy.*" (Verse 118)

The *sūrah* spreads an air of explanation and factual statement, mixed with calm argument, pure logic and inspiration. Its subject matter is faith, and faith gives it its special ambience. At the beginning we see the believers "*who humble themselves in their prayer,*" and in the middle they are described in the following terms: "*They give away whatever they have to give with their hearts filled with awe, knowing that to their Lord they shall certainly return.*" (Verse 60) For an example of the inspiration of the *sūrah* we may take: "*It is He who has endowed you with hearing, and sight, and minds: how seldom are you grateful.*" (Verse 78). Indeed the entire *sūrah* reflects a gentle air of faith.

I

Man, Faith and the Universe

Al-Mu'minūn (The Believers)

In the Name of God, the Merciful, the Beneficent

Truly, successful shall be the believers, (1)

who humble themselves in their prayer, (2)

who turn away from all that is frivolous, (3)

who are active in deeds of charity, (4)

who refrain from sex (5)

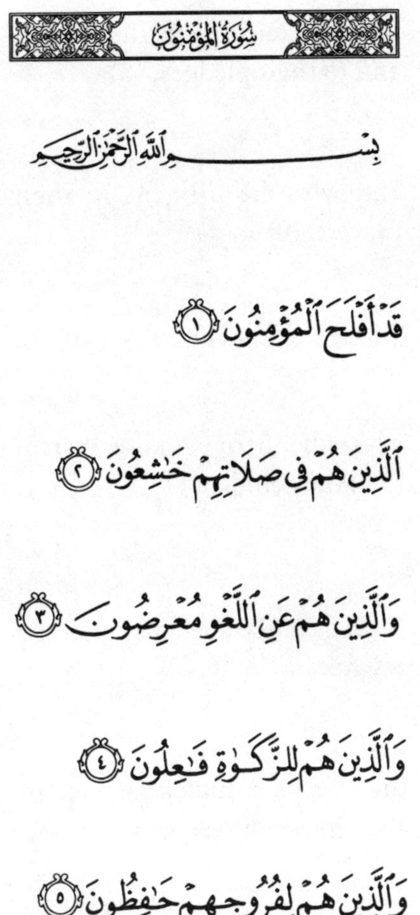

سورة المؤمنون

بسم الله الرحمن الرحيم

قد أفلح المؤمنون ١

الذين هم في صلاتهم خاشعون ٢

والذين هم عن اللغو معرضون ٣

والذين هم للزكوة فاعلون ٤

والذين هم لفروجهم حافظون ٥

إِلَّا عَلَىٰٓ أَزْوَٰجِهِمْ أَوْ مَا مَلَكَتْ
أَيْمَٰنُهُمْ فَإِنَّهُمْ غَيْرُ مَلُومِينَ ﴿٦﴾

except with those joined to them in marriage, or those whom they rightfully possess – for then, they are free of all blame, (6)

فَمَنِ ٱبْتَغَىٰ وَرَآءَ ذَٰلِكَ فَأُو۟لَٰٓئِكَ هُمُ
ٱلْعَادُونَ ﴿٧﴾

whereas those who seek to go beyond that [limit] are indeed transgressors, (7)

وَٱلَّذِينَ هُمْ لِأَمَٰنَٰتِهِمْ وَعَهْدِهِمْ
رَٰعُونَ ﴿٨﴾

who are faithful to their trusts and to their pledges, (8)

وَٱلَّذِينَ هُمْ عَلَىٰ صَلَوَٰتِهِمْ يُحَافِظُونَ ﴿٩﴾

and who are diligent in their prayers. (9)

أُو۟لَٰٓئِكَ هُمُ ٱلْوَٰرِثُونَ ﴿١٠﴾

These shall be the heirs, (10)

ٱلَّذِينَ يَرِثُونَ ٱلْفِرْدَوْسَ هُمْ
فِيهَا خَٰلِدُونَ ﴿١١﴾

who will inherit paradise; therein shall they abide. (11)

وَلَقَدْ خَلَقْنَا ٱلْإِنسَٰنَ مِن سُلَٰلَةٍ
مِّن طِينٍ ﴿١٢﴾

Indeed, We create man out of the essence of clay, (12)

ثُمَّ جَعَلْنَٰهُ نُطْفَةً فِى قَرَارٍ مَّكِينٍ ﴿١٣﴾

then We place him, a gamete,[1] in a safe place of rest. (13)

1. For an explanation of the translation of the Qur'ānic terms denoting the stages of human development during pregnancy, please refer to the footnote on verse 5 of *Sūrah* 22, in this volume, p. 102. – Editor's note.

Then We create out of the gamete a clinging cell mass, and out of the clinging cell mass We create an embryo. Then We create within the embryo bones, then We clothe the bones with flesh. We then bring this into being as another creation. Exalted be God, the best of creators. (14)

ثُمَّ خَلَقْنَا ٱلنُّطْفَةَ عَلَقَةً فَخَلَقْنَا ٱلْعَلَقَةَ
مُضْغَةً فَخَلَقْنَا ٱلْمُضْغَةَ عِظَـٰمًا
فَكَسَوْنَا ٱلْعِظَـٰمَ لَحْمًا ثُمَّ أَنشَأْنَـٰهُ خَلْقًا
ءَاخَرَ ۚ فَتَبَارَكَ ٱللَّهُ أَحْسَنُ ٱلْخَـٰلِقِينَ ﴿١٤﴾

And then, after all this, you are destined to die; (15)

ثُمَّ إِنَّكُم بَعْدَ ذَٰلِكَ لَمَيِّتُونَ ﴿١٥﴾

and then, you shall be restored to life on the Day of Resurrection. (16)

ثُمَّ إِنَّكُمْ يَوْمَ ٱلْقِيَـٰمَةِ تُبْعَثُونَ ﴿١٦﴾

We have created above you seven [celestial] orbits; and never are We unmindful of [Our] creation. (17)

وَلَقَدْ خَلَقْنَا فَوْقَكُمْ سَبْعَ طَرَآئِقَ
وَمَا كُنَّا عَنِ ٱلْخَلْقِ غَـٰفِلِينَ ﴿١٧﴾

We send down water from the skies in accordance with a set measure, and We cause it to lodge in the earth; and We are most certainly able to take it all away. (18)

وَأَنزَلْنَا مِنَ ٱلسَّمَآءِ مَآءًۢ بِقَدَرٍ فَأَسْكَنَّـٰهُ فِى
ٱلْأَرْضِ ۖ وَإِنَّا عَلَىٰ ذَهَابٍۭ بِهِۦ لَقَـٰدِرُونَ ﴿١٨﴾

And by means of this water We bring forth for you gardens of date-palms and vines, yielding abundant fruit, and from which you eat, (19)

فَأَنشَأْنَا لَكُم بِهِۦ جَنَّـٰتٍ مِّن نَّخِيلٍ
وَأَعْنَـٰبٍ لَّكُمْ فِيهَا فَوَٰكِهُ كَثِيرَةٌ
وَمِنْهَا تَأْكُلُونَ ﴿١٩﴾

as well as a tree that grows on Mount Sinai yielding oil and relish for all to eat. (20)	وَشَجَرَةً تَخْرُجُ مِن طُورِ سَيْنَاءَ تَنۢبُتُ بِٱلدُّهْنِ وَصِبْغٍ لِّلْآكِلِينَ ﴿٢٠﴾
In the cattle too there is a lesson for you: We give you to drink of that which is in their bellies, and you gain many other benefits from them, and you eat of their flesh. (21)	وَإِنَّ لَكُمْ فِي ٱلْأَنْعَٰمِ لَعِبْرَةً نُّسْقِيكُم مِّمَّا فِي بُطُونِهَا وَلَكُمْ فِيهَا مَنَٰفِعُ كَثِيرَةٌ وَمِنْهَا تَأْكُلُونَ ﴿٢١﴾
By them, as by the ships you are carried. (22)	وَعَلَيْهَا وَعَلَى ٱلْفُلْكِ تُحْمَلُونَ ﴿٢٢﴾

Success Guaranteed by Faith

"*Truly, successful shall be the believers.*" (Verse 1) It is a true promise; nay, it is a firm decision ensuring success for the believers. If we take it as a promise, we know God never fails to honour His promises; and if we say that it is His decision, then no one can ever foil a decision by God. What is promised is success in the life of this world and in the life to come; success for the individual believer and for the community of believers. A believer will feel this success in his heart and will see it coming true in his day to day life. The success God promises includes all that human beings associate with success and what God keeps in store for His faithful servants.

So, who are those faithful servants, the believers who receive this document written by God, containing this promise and a clear declaration of success? Who are the believers promised all goodness, victory, happiness, success and goodly provisions in this life on earth; and further promised to be successful in the hereafter, when they receive God's reward and enjoy His pleasure? They will also have much more that is known only to God, and this will be given in their two lives. Who are these believers who will inherit paradise where they will abide?

Verses 2–9 give us a detailed list of their characteristics. They are the ones "*who humble themselves in their prayer, who turn away from all that is frivolous, who are active in deeds of charity, who refrain from sex except with those joined to them in marriage, or those whom they rightfully possess – for then, they are free of all blame, whereas those who seek to go beyond that [limit] are indeed transgressors, who are faithful to their trusts and to their pledges, and who are diligent in their prayers.*" (Verses 2–9) So, what do we make of these characteristics?

Together they draw for us the character of a Muslim at its highest level. That is the level of Muḥammad (peace be upon him), God's Messenger and the most perfect human being ever to walk on the face of the earth. He was educated and given a refined character by God, and God certified to his noble character and way of life: "*Truly, yours is a sublime nature.*" (68: 4) 'Ā'ishah, the Prophet's wife, was asked about his character. Her answer was: "His character was the Qur'ān in practice." She then recited verses 1–9 of the present *sūrah*, and commented, "Such was God's Messenger." [Related by al-Nasā'ī]

But we ask again: what value do these characteristics give to the life of the individual, the community and to human life in general?

"*Who humble themselves in their prayer.*" (Verse 2) They feel the reverence associated with prayer, as they stand up to address God, and their hearts are thus filled with awe, which is, in turn, reflected in their features and movements. Their spirits feel God's majesty as they realize that they stand in His presence. Thus, all their preoccupations and distractions disappear. Their thoughts and feelings are all concentrated on their discourse with Him. In His sublime presence, they are heedless of all their surroundings. They see and feel nothing but His majesty. Their minds and hearts are purged of even the slightest alien thought or feeling. In such a situation, a stray atom is reunited with its source, a wandering spirit finds its way, and a heart that has been long in isolation finds its company. Thus, all values, concerns and considerations diminish, except for the ones that are related to God in some way.

"*Who turn away from all that is frivolous.*" (Verse 3) This includes all frivolity, in words, actions, or concerns. A believer's heart has its own preoccupations which steer it away from frivolity. It is full with the remembrance of God and with reflection on His majesty and His signs that we see everywhere in the universe and within ourselves. Indeed, every scene in the universe fills our minds with wonder and gives a clear message to our hearts. Moreover, the duties required by faith keep a believer preoccupied with maintaining the purity of his or her heart, soul and conscience. Believers' duties include those of behaviour which aim at maintaining the very high standards required by faith. Moreover, the task of enjoining what is right and forbidding what is wrong aims at preventing any deviation in the life of the Muslim community. *Jihād* is also a duty that aims to repel aggression, protect the Muslim community and maintain its position and sovereignty. These duties are always there, and believers do not shirk their responsibilities. These are either individual or collective duties, sufficient to preoccupy people throughout their lives. Man's energy is limited, and it may either be spent in what serves and improves human life, or in frivolity and idle pursuit. By his faith, a believer is required to spend all his energy in what promotes life and sets it on the course of success and prosperity.

This does not preclude relaxation and seeking comfort when it is needed. But this is totally different from indulging in frivolous and idle pursuits.

Social and Moral Qualities

"*Who are active in deeds of charity.*" (Verse 4) Having come forward to declare their submission to God and demonstrate this in their prayer, and having turned away from all that is frivolous, true believers complement this by being active in charity. The term used in Arabic for charity is *zakāt*, but this word is often used in a wider sense that goes far beyond the obligatory financial worship with which it is normally associated. Such charity purifies man's heart and money. It purges hearts of selfishness and greed, and overcomes Satan's whispers of discouragement as he raises before us the spectre of poverty, and demonstrates our trust in God. It also makes our money, or what is left of it, pure and good, free of all obligations and doubts concerning its being lawful. Furthermore, charity protects the Muslim community against the imbalance that results from the extremes of poverty on the one side and affluence on the other. It provides social security for all individuals in the Muslim community, particularly the weaker elements, and it protects the community against disintegration.

"*Who refrain from sex...*" (Verse 5) This is a pointer to the purity of the human soul, the home and the community, and to the way of protecting oneself, family and society. It is all the result of refraining from indulgence in sin and turning people's hearts only to what is permissible. Thus, the Muslim community is protected from the unrestrained promiscuity that undermines the family and allows dubious parenthood to increase and become acceptable.

A community with no restraint on desire is wont to find its very social fabric corrupted, because it deprives itself of the sanctity for the family. The family home is the basic unit in the structure of the community. It is the cradle where children grow up. To serve as a healthy cradle, it needs purity and security, both of which give reassurance to the husband and wife so that each has full trust in the other. Thus, they cooperate to safeguard their home and ensure the healthy upbringing of their young ones.

A community where unrestrained desire becomes commonplace is a filthy community that occupies a very lowly position in humanity's esteem. Self control, willpower and the appropriate regulation of natural instincts to ensure their healthy and productive fulfilment are the best way to gauge human advancement. Thus, children feel no shame about the way they start their existence in this world, for they know who their fathers are. This is far removed from what animals are like.

The Qur'ān defines here the clean and healthy way which allows a man to place the seeds of life in the right place: "*Who refrain from sex except with those joined to them in marriage, or those whom they rightfully possess – for then, they are free of all blame.*" (Verses 5–6) As for married couples, no argument is raised here, because marriage is respected in all human communities. The other form, referring to 'rightfully possessed' women, needs some explanation.

We have spoken about the question of slavery and the Islamic approach to it elsewhere in this book.[2] As we have stated, when Islam was revealed, slavery was a universal system. Captives of war were made slaves, and this was an international institution. It was not possible for Islam at the time, when it was engaged in military battles against its enemies who were trying hard to stop its spread with military force, to abolish slavery unilaterally. This would have meant that Muslim captives would remain enslaved by the enemies of Islam, while Islam would set enemy captives free. Hence, while putting an end to all other sources of slavery, Islam made a provisional exception in the case of captives of war. Abolition of this remaining source was delayed until a new international system to regulate the question of war captives could be put in place.

With this source of slavery remaining, captive women continued to come into Islamic society. To give them equal treatment, on the basis of the system then operating throughout the world, meant that they should be slaves. Their enslavement did not allow them to become wives through normal marriage. Hence, Islam allowed intercourse with them by their masters only, unless they were freed through the many ways Islam provided for the same.

We see also in this permission a way to satisfy the natural needs of the women slaves themselves, so that they did not resort to immorality. We see this happening today, despite the international treaties prohibiting slavery, when women are taken captive in war. Islam, however, does not condone such promiscuity. But Islam did open up several ways for women slaves to gain their freedom: one of which automatically came into operation when the slave woman gave birth to her master's child. In this case, she became free on her master's death. Alternatively, her master may give her her freedom, either voluntarily or in atonement for some offence he might have committed. Or, she may choose to buy her own freedom. A different situation applied if her master hit her across the face. He was, then, required to free her by way of compensation. There were further ways to freedom as well.

---

2. Reference to slavery is made in Vol. I, pp. 333–5, Vol. III, pp. 38–9, and further details will be discussed in this volume, pp. 339–40.

Anyway, allowing slavery through war was a temporary necessity in order to maintain equal treatment in a world where all war captives became slaves. It was, however, not a part of the Islamic social system *per se*.

"*Whereas those who seek to go beyond that [limit] are indeed transgressors.*" (Verse 7) The limit is that of wives and women rightly possessed. There can be no other legitimate way. Whoever tries to go beyond this limit actually breaks the boundaries of permissibility and falls in sin. He becomes an assailant of human honour. There can be no lawful relationship except through marriage or the results of war undertaken for the sake of Islam. When transgression beyond these well defined limits takes place, the individual concerned becomes corrupt, like a sheep grazing out of bounds, and the family is undermined because of the lack of security felt by its members. Indeed the whole community feels endangered because its wolves have been set loose. Islam is keen to avoid all that.

Qualities Guaranteeing Admission to Heaven

"*Who are faithful to their trusts and to their pledges.*" (Verse 8) They, individuals and community alike, honour their pledges and discharge their trust. Both the individual and the community have many types of trust to maintain, the first of which is the trust encapsulated in their own nature, i.e. they are created by God in an upright fashion so as to be in harmony with the rest of the universe to which they belong. This testifies to God's oneness by the natural feeling of unity that governs the universe. Believers are faithful to this great trust, and they protect their nature from deviation so that it continues to testify to God's oneness. Other trusts are derived from this basic element.

The first pledge is that God has taken from, and made ingrained in human nature, committing it to believe in His existence and His oneness. All other pledges, covenants and treaties derive from this first one. When a believer commits himself to something, he makes God his witness. Honouring his commitments is, to a believer, part of being God-fearing, of *taqwā*.

The Muslim community is also responsible for honouring its public trust, and for the fulfilment of its pledges to God and the duties that result from these pledges. The *sūrah* gives its statement in very general terms so as to include every type of trust and pledge. Believers are faithful to all these, at all times. Being faithful is part of their character. No community can hope to have a straightforward life unless pledges and trusts are fulfilled, so that every individual and group are certain of this basic rule of community life. It is the rule that gives everyone a sense of trust and security.

"*And who are diligent in their prayers.*" (Verse 9) They do not neglect their prayers or miss them through laziness. Nor do they fail to attend to them as prayer should be attended to. They offer them on time, attending to obligatory and recommended parts, making them complete, omitting nothing essential. Their prayer is alive, filling their hearts and interacting with their consciences. Prayer maintains a bond between God and human hearts. Therefore, a person who does not attend regularly to his prayer is unlikely to attend diligently and conscientiously to his bonds with other people. The qualities of believers outlined in this *sūrah* start with prayer and finish with prayer, so as to stress its unrivalled importance in the structure of faith. After all, prayer is the most perfect form of worship addressed to God.

These characteristics delineate the character of believers who are certain to be successful. While they are characteristics of individuals, they are decisive in giving the Muslim community its collective character and shaping the type of life it lives. It is an honourable life that befits man, the creature God has honoured and allowed to move up on the way to perfection. It is clear that God does not want man to live like animals, merely eating and indulging in pleasure.

Since life on earth does not achieve the perfection God wants for mankind, He has willed that believers who follow His way should attain their goal in paradise, where they live forever, in complete security, and where they have no fear: "*These shall be the heirs who will inherit paradise; therein shall they abide.*" (Verses 10–11) This is the ultimate success God has determined for believers. There is no goal beyond this.

The Origins of Man

Having given a detailed account of the qualities and characteristics of believers, the *sūrah* moves on to point out the indications available within man himself that lead to faith. It speaks of the various stages of development of a human being, starting with the very beginning of human origin, and ending with resurrection on the Day of Judgement, to establish a firm link between this life and the life to come:

> *Indeed, We create man out of the essence of clay, then We place him, a gamete, in a safe place of rest. Then We create out of the gamete a clinging cell mass, and out of the clinging cell mass We create an embryo. Then We create within the embryo bones, then We clothe the bones with flesh. We then bring this into being as another creation. Exalted be God, the best of creators. And then, after all this, you are destined to die; and then, you shall be restored to life on the Day of Resurrection.* (Verses 12–16)

The gradual formation of man, following the same sequence, confirms first the truth of the Originator, and also the deliberate planning in the course such formation follows. This cannot be the result of blind coincidence. Nor can it be a random beginning leading to a consistent line that never fails or deviates. The truth is that human beings come into existence in the way they do, rather than any other possible way, because our Creator wants it this way, and He does things according to His own plan and design.

Moreover, by giving this full picture with the different stages shown to follow each other without fail also indicates that belief in the Creator who plans everything and following the course of action believers follow, as indicated in the first eleven verses of the *sūrah*, is the only way to achieve the perfect standard human beings can achieve both in this life and in the hereafter. Thus, the two opening passages of the *sūrah* are interlinked.

"*Indeed, We create man out of the essence of clay.*" (Verse 12) This statement implies that there are stages in the creation of human beings, without specifying them. The implication is much clearer in the Arabic original where the term *sulālah*, given in English as 'essence', also connotes a chain of development. Hence, it means that man goes through different stages, one leading to the other, from the very first beginning of clay to the eventual creation, man. This is a truth we get to know from the Qur'ān. We do not need any confirmation of it from scientific theories concerned with the origins of man or other living things.

The Qur'ān establishes this truth of God's work and design. Thus, we can contemplate the great divide between the clay and man who came from that clay through a succession of stages. The details of this succession are not mentioned because it is unimportant to the wider aims of the Qur'ān. Scientific theories try to find a definite ladder for our origins and evolution. In their attempts, these theories may come up with some true conclusions and they may make mistakes. We cannot, however, confuse the truth established in the Qur'ān, which mentions the succession of stages, with the attempts made by scientists to establish these different stages of succession. These attempts are always open to error, proving today what they may disprove tomorrow in the light of advanced techniques and technologies.

This truth is sometimes expressed very briefly in the Qur'ān, when it says that man's creation began with clay, giving no reference to the stages which the process of creation then went through. The ultimate reference then is the most detailed Qur'ānic text, which refers to a 'succession of stages'. We should remember that the Qur'ān uses a more general or shorter text, only because it is more suited to the context in which it occurs.

The Qur'ān does not explain how man evolved from the essence of clay, because such explanation is not part of its objectives. The stages of this succession may be exactly as scientific theories suggest, or they may be different. It may happen that man will be able to formulate an accurate idea of such succession. However, the parting point between the Qur'ānic view of man and the way scientific theories look at him is that the Qur'ān honours man, stating that a measure of God's spirit was breathed into him to make of him a man with the qualities and characteristics that distinguish man from animals. In this, the Islamic view is fundamentally different from that of all materialist theories. God certainly tells the truth.

Different Stages in the Creation of Man

This applies to the origin of the human race: it starts from an essence of clay. As for individual human beings, they go through well known stages: "*Then We place him, a gamete, in a safe place of rest.*" (Verse 13) The creation formula that brings about new individuals of the human race, and their method of reproduction, follows a line set by God. A drop of fluid is discharged from the man to settle in the woman's uterus. It is not the whole drop; rather, a single cell out of hundreds of thousands forming this drop. It settles in this safe enclosure in the uterus which is supported by the hip bones, protecting it from the shocks and knocks that occur to the body as one moves about.

The Qur'ānic text makes the gamete a stage in the succession of man's creation, coming immediately after man's existence. This is true, but it also deserves contemplation. A human being in his full stature, and with all his features, elements and characteristics, is enclosed within this gamete. It then develops into an embryo when it begins its new existence through a new series of stages.

The gamete stage leads to that of a cell mass after the male sperm fertilizes the female egg, and then the cell mass clings to the wall of the uterus. The cell mass grows and becomes an embryo. This little creation continues in this line that never changes or deviates from its course. It moves along its marked line, using its latent energy according to God's law which combines perfect design with elaborate planning.

The next stage is that of the emergence of bones: "*Then We create within the embryo bones,*" which is followed by another stage in which the bones are clothed with flesh. We are overwhelmed with amazement here at this fact in the development of the embryo which is stated in the Qur'ān long before it was confirmed by embryology. This is the fact that bones are made of cells that are totally different from those of flesh. It has been confirmed beyond any shadow of doubt that bones are formed first in the embryo. In fact, not a single cell of flesh could be seen before the whole skeleton of the embryo is finally in place. This is what the Qur'ān states: "*Then We create within the embryo bones, then We clothe the bones with flesh.*" (Verse 14) Limitless is God in His glory. He is indeed All-Knowing, All-Aware.

"*We then bring this into being as another creation.*" (Verse 14) This is now man with his distinctive features. It is true that the human embryo is similar to animal embryos, but only in its physical stages. For then the human embryo is given a different sort of creation to make up this distinguished creature that we know, with his potential to achieve excellence. The animal embryo, on the other hand, remains within the animal grade, possessing nothing of the distinctive features and qualities of man.

The human embryo is given special qualities that in time lead it along its human way. It is given 'another creation' as it completes its embryonic stages, while the animal embryo stops at that stage because it does not have the same qualities. Hence, no animal can go beyond its animal status, so as to automatically evolve into the same high status as man. The two are totally different, and the difference is caused by the breathing of divine spirit that brings the essence of clay into a human being, which is a different creation. This means that man and animals are similar in their biological make-up, but animals do not go beyond their status, while man is brought into being as a different creation, able to achieve a totally different level of perfection through the distinctive qualities God has willed to give him in order to complete His design of creation.[3]

"*Exalted be God, the best of creators.*" (Verse 14) God is certainly the only One who creates. The superlative form is not used here in a comparative sense; rather, it indicates perfection in God's creation.

"*Exalted be God, the best of creators.*" (Verse 14) It is He who has given human nature the ability to move from one stage to the next, in accordance with the law He has set, which will never change or be modified. It will not fail to continue until man achieves the degree of perfection assigned to him, on the basis of a perfect order.

---

3. The theory of evolution seeks to prove the opposite, making man another stage of animal evolution, and giving animals the capability to attain human status. The facts we see disprove the existence of any such relation between man and animal, showing that no animal has the necessary qualities to evolve into human status. It will always remain within animal boundaries. Its animal evolution may be proven according to Darwin's theory or in some other way, but mankind remains a higher type of creation distinguished by certain qualities that make man what he is, and this could never have come about as a result of mechanical development. It is a gift from a higher power.

People look with amazement at what they term as 'scientific miracles' when man invents a machine that works automatically, without human interference. But how does this compare with the development of an embryo in all its phases and stages, each of which is hugely different from the preceding one, ushering in total transformations. But people tend to overlook such miraculous events, closing their eyes and minds to them, because long familiarity tends to disguise their miraculous nature. The mere thought that man, very complex as he is, is summed up within a single cell that cannot be seen with the naked eye, yet carries all his qualities, distinctive features and special characteristics fills us with wonder. In fact, all these distinctive qualities, features and characteristics grow and take full shape during the different stages of the development of the embryo, and then appear in full when the embryo is brought back as a different and new creation. Then they are visibly seen in the child, or they make their presence in the newborn child felt. Indeed, every child carries its own genetic features in addition to general human features and qualities. Both types are latent in the original cell but emerge later. When we reflect on this fact, which occurs all the time, our hearts and minds are bound to acknowledge this remarkable design by our Creator.

Further Aspects of Creation

The *sūrah* continues to depict the different stages of life to complete the journey. Human life that began on earth does not however end there, because an element from outside the earth forms an essential part of it, influencing the path it travels. The breathing of God's spirit in it has given human life a goal different from that of the body, and a destination unlike that of the destination of flesh and blood. Hence it achieves its completeness somewhere other than this earth, in a totally different world: "*And then, after all this, you are destined to die; and then, you shall be restored to life on the Day of Resurrection.*" (Verses 15–16)

Thus, death is the end of human life on earth, forming a bridge between the life we know and the life to come. As such, it is a stage in human life, not its end.

Then comes resurrection which heralds the last stage, when the perfect life begins, free of all the failings of earthly life, physical needs, fear and worry, and leading to no other stage because it represents the level of perfection human beings can attain. This, however, applies only to those who follow the way leading to such perfection, outlined in the opening verses of this *sūrah*. It is the way followed by believers. By contrast, those who in this life sink to the level of animals go further down in the life to come so that they are right at the bottom. They are no longer human beings, because they become part of the fuel of hell, fed by stones and men.

The *sūrah* moves on to point out well known, yet often forgotten, aspects in the universe which should lead people to faith:

> *We have created above you seven [celestial] orbits; and never are We unmindful of [Our] creation. We send down water from the skies in accordance with a set measure, and We cause it to lodge in the earth; and We are most certainly able to take it all away. And by means of this water We bring forth for you gardens of date-palms and vines, yielding abundant fruit, and from which you eat, as well as a tree that grows on Mount Sinai yielding oil and relish for all to eat. In the cattle too there is a lesson for you: We give you to drink of that which is in their bellies, and you gain many other benefits from them, and you eat of their flesh. By them, as by the ships you are carried.* (Verses 17–22)

All these indicators are cited here as aspects of God's power and perfect planning. In their constitutions, functions and roles they move in perfect harmony and in the same direction. They are subject to the same law. They function in unison and serve man, the creature God has honoured. Therefore, these aspects of the universe are shown to be interlinked with the stages of human life as outlined in the *sūrah*.

"*We have created above you seven [celestial] orbits; and never are We unmindful of [Our] creation.*" (Verse 17) The Arabic word used here, *ṭarā'iq*, carries different meanings. It may mean seven layers, one above the other, or next to one another. It may also mean seven orbits, (as we chose in our translation), but it could also mean seven celestial systems like our solar system, or seven nebulae, or clusters of stars. Be that as it may, the term signifies seven celestial creatures above us, which means that they are higher than the level of the earth in the universe. God created them all according to His planning and to suit His purpose. He protects and preserves them according to a definite law He has set in operation: "*Never are We unmindful of Our creation.*"

Blessings All Around Us

"*We send down water from the skies in accordance with a set measure, and We cause it to lodge in the earth; and We are most certainly able to take it all away.*" (Verse 18) Here we have a direct link between those seven orbits or bodies and the earth. Water falls from the sky, and has a direct link with those bodies. In fact, it is the perfect order controlling the universe that allows water to so fall from the sky and settle into the earth.

It is only recently that geologists developed their theory that underground water comes from surface water and rain, which seeps through the earth. Before this theory was advanced, the general perception was that underground water was independent of surface water. Yet the Qur'ān stated this fact more than 1,400 years ago.

"*We send down water from the skies in accordance with a set measure.*" It is all according to an elaborate plan. It is neither too much so as to cause flooding and devastation, nor too little so as to cause drought and famine. Nor does it come at the wrong time when it would be of little use.

"*And We cause it to lodge in the earth.*" The picture here is akin to that of the fertilized egg that is implanted in the uterus, which is described in the Qur'ān as '*a safe place of rest.*' Both the egg and the water have their settled and safe places of settlement in order to give rise to life. Here we see yet another example of the Qur'ānic method of artistic arrangement of scenes and images.

"*We are most certainly able to take it all away.*" It can sink into the depths of the earth, through a schism in the rocky layer under it, or by some other means. The One who kept it stored in its place is also able to allow it to go beyond man's reach. Keeping it in its place is part of God's grace.

It is from water that life derives: "*And by means of this water We bring forth for you gardens of date palms and vines, yielding abundant fruit, and from which you eat.*" (Verse 19) Date trees and vines are only two types of plant life for the emergence of which water is essential. By the same token, the sperm, or fluid man discharges, is essential for the emergence of human life. Both examples are easily understood by those addressed by the Qur'ān. They also point to the numerous other examples that depend on water for life.

Of these other types the olive tree is chosen for particular mention: "*as well as a tree that grows on Mount Sinai yielding oil and relish for all to eat.*" (Verse 20) It is one of the most useful trees for man, with its oil, fruit and wood. The closest area to Arabia where it was planted was Mount Sinai, close to the blessed valley mentioned in the Qur'ān. Hence, this particular area is mentioned here. In that area, it is fed by groundwater.

Then the *sūrah* leaves aside all plants to refer to the animal kingdom:

> *In the cattle too there is a lesson for you: We give you to drink of that which is in their bellies, and you gain many other benefits from them, and you eat of their flesh. By them, as by the ships you are carried.* (Verses 21–22)

These creatures have been made subservient to man by God's power and design, as also by His distribution of qualities and functions in the entire universe. Anyone who looks at them with open eyes and mind will not fail to recognize the wisdom behind this planning. He will realize that we drink the milk that comes from their bellies, which means that it comes from what these cattle feed on and digest. Their special glands turn it into this tasty and highly beneficial fluid.

"*You gain many other benefits from them.*" These benefits are given first in this general statement, and then two are chosen for particular emphasis: "*You eat of their flesh. By them, as by the ships you are carried.*" Permission is given to man to eat of these animals, which include camels, oxen, sheep and goats, but man is forbidden to inflict pain on these animals or to torture them. Eating them provides real benefit, while torture and pain are only indicative of a sadistic nature. Causing pain and inflicting torture bring no benefit to man.

The *sūrah* compares man's riding of animals and his being carried on board boats and ships. Both are made possible through the system God has perfected for this universe which organizes the functions of all creatures and establishes coherence and coordination between them all. It is the way God has made water, ships and the atmosphere around them both that allows ships to float on water. If the composition of any of the three alters or changes, it would not be possible for ships to travel the seas. People realized this very early in human life, and they continue to benefit by it.

All these are signs that lead to faith when they are properly understood. They are relevant to both the preceding and the following parts of the *sūrah*, and fit with them in perfect harmony.

2

One Message for All Mankind

We sent forth Noah to his people, and he said: 'My people! Worship God alone, for you have no deity other than Him. Will you not be God-fearing?' (23)

وَلَقَدۡ أَرۡسَلۡنَا نُوحًا إِلَىٰ قَوۡمِهِۦ فَقَالَ
يَٰقَوۡمِ ٱعۡبُدُواْ ٱللَّهَ مَا لَكُم مِّنۡ إِلَٰهٍ
غَيۡرُهُۥٓۚ أَفَلَا تَتَّقُونَ ٢٣

The unbelieving elders of his people said: 'This man is but a mortal like yourselves who wants to make himself superior to you. Had God willed, He would surely have sent down angels. We have never heard anything like this ever happening to our forefathers. (24)

فَقَالَ ٱلۡمَلَؤُاْ ٱلَّذِينَ كَفَرُواْ مِن قَوۡمِهِۦ مَا هَٰذَآ
إِلَّا بَشَرٞ مِّثۡلُكُمۡ يُرِيدُ أَن يَتَفَضَّلَ عَلَيۡكُمۡ
وَلَوۡ شَآءَ ٱللَّهُ لَأَنزَلَ مَلَٰٓئِكَةٗ مَّا سَمِعۡنَا
بِهَٰذَا فِيٓ ءَابَآئِنَا ٱلۡأَوَّلِينَ ٢٤

He is but a madman; so bear with him for a while.' (25)

إِنۡ هُوَ إِلَّا رَجُلُۢ بِهِۦ جِنَّةٞ فَتَرَبَّصُواْ
بِهِۦ حَتَّىٰ حِينٖ ٢٥

He said: 'My Lord, help me against their accusation of lying.' (26)

قَالَ رَبِّ ٱنصُرۡنِي بِمَا كَذَّبُونِ ٢٦

We revealed to him to 'build the ark, under Our eyes, and according to Our inspiration. When Our judgement comes to pass, and water gushes forth over the face of the earth, place on board this ark one pair of every species, as well as your family, except those on whom sentence has already been passed. Do not plead with Me for the wrongdoers; for they shall be drowned. (27)

فَأَوْحَيْنَآ إِلَيْهِ أَنِ ٱصْنَعِ ٱلْفُلْكَ بِأَعْيُنِنَا
وَوَحْيِنَا فَإِذَا جَآءَ أَمْرُنَا وَفَارَ ٱلتَّنُّورُ
فَٱسْلُكْ فِيهَا مِن كُلٍّ زَوْجَيْنِ ٱثْنَيْنِ
وَأَهْلَكَ إِلَّا مَن سَبَقَ عَلَيْهِ ٱلْقَوْلُ
مِنْهُمْ وَلَا تُخَٰطِبْنِى فِى ٱلَّذِينَ ظَلَمُوٓا۟
إِنَّهُم مُّغْرَقُونَ ﴿٢٧﴾

When you and those who are with you are settled in the ark, say: 'All praise is due to God who has saved us from those wrongdoing folk.' (28)

فَإِذَا ٱسْتَوَيْتَ أَنتَ وَمَن مَّعَكَ عَلَى
ٱلْفُلْكِ فَقُلِ ٱلْحَمْدُ لِلَّهِ ٱلَّذِى نَجَّىٰنَا
مِنَ ٱلْقَوْمِ ٱلظَّٰلِمِينَ ﴿٢٨﴾

And also say: 'My Lord! Let my landing be blessed. You are the best to bring us to safe landing.' (29)

وَقُل رَّبِّ أَنزِلْنِى مُنزَلًا مُّبَارَكًا وَأَنتَ
خَيْرُ ٱلْمُنزِلِينَ ﴿٢٩﴾

Surely, in that there are signs. Indeed, We always put [people] to a test. (30)

إِنَّ فِى ذَٰلِكَ لَءَايَٰتٍ وَإِن كُنَّا لَمُبْتَلِينَ ﴿٣٠﴾

Then after these people We raised a new generation. (31)

ثُمَّ أَنشَأْنَا مِنۢ بَعْدِهِمْ قَرْنًا ءَاخَرِينَ ﴿٣١﴾

And We sent forth to them a messenger from among themselves, and he said: 'My people! Worship God alone, for you have no deity other than Him. Will you not be God-fearing?' (32)

فَأَرْسَلْنَا فِيهِمْ رَسُولًا مِّنْهُمْ أَنِ ٱعْبُدُوا۟ ٱللَّهَ
مَا لَكُم مِّنْ إِلَٰهٍ غَيْرُهُۥٓ ۖ أَفَلَا تَتَّقُونَ ﴿٣٢﴾

The unbelieving elders of his people, who denied the life to come and to whom We granted ease and plenty in this worldly life, said: 'This man is but a mortal like yourselves, eating of what you eat and drinking of what you drink. (33)

وَقَالَ ٱلْمَلَأُ مِن قَوْمِهِ ٱلَّذِينَ كَفَرُوا۟
وَكَذَّبُوا۟ بِلِقَآءِ ٱلْءَاخِرَةِ وَأَتْرَفْنَٰهُمْ
فِى ٱلْحَيَوٰةِ ٱلدُّنْيَا مَا هَٰذَآ إِلَّا بَشَرٌ
مِّثْلُكُمْ يَأْكُلُ مِمَّا تَأْكُلُونَ مِنْهُ
وَيَشْرَبُ مِمَّا تَشْرَبُونَ ﴿٣٣﴾

Indeed, if you pay heed to a mortal like yourselves, you will certainly be the losers. (34)

وَلَئِنْ أَطَعْتُم بَشَرًا مِّثْلَكُمْ إِنَّكُمْ
إِذًا لَّخَٰسِرُونَ ﴿٣٤﴾

Does he promise you that, after you have died and become dust and bones, you shall be brought forth to life? (35)

أَيَعِدُكُمْ أَنَّكُمْ إِذَا مِتُّمْ وَكُنتُمْ تُرَابًا
وَعِظَٰمًا أَنَّكُم مُّخْرَجُونَ ﴿٣٥﴾

Improbable, improbable indeed is what you are promised! (36)

هَيْهَاتَ هَيْهَاتَ لِمَا تُوعَدُونَ ﴿٣٦﴾

There is no life beyond this, our present life; we die and we live, and we shall never be restored to life. (37)

إِنْ هِىَ إِلَّا حَيَاتُنَا ٱلدُّنْيَا نَمُوتُ
وَنَحْيَا وَمَا نَحْنُ بِمَبْعُوثِينَ ﴿٣٧﴾

إِنْ هُوَ إِلَّا رَجُلٌ ٱفْتَرَىٰ عَلَى ٱللَّهِ كَذِبًا
وَمَا نَحْنُ لَهُۥ بِمُؤْمِنِينَ ﴿٣٨﴾

He is nothing but a man who attributes his lies to God. Never will we believe in him.' (38)

قَالَ رَبِّ ٱنصُرْنِى بِمَا كَذَّبُونِ ﴿٣٩﴾

He said: 'My Lord, help me against their accusation of lying.' (39)

قَالَ عَمَّا قَلِيلٍ لَّيُصْبِحُنَّ نَٰدِمِينَ ﴿٤٠﴾

Said [God]: 'Before long they shall certainly come to rue it.' (40)

فَأَخَذَتْهُمُ ٱلصَّيْحَةُ بِٱلْحَقِّ فَجَعَلْنَٰهُمْ
غُثَآءً ۚ فَبُعْدًا لِّلْقَوْمِ ٱلظَّٰلِمِينَ ﴿٤١﴾

Then the blast overtook them in all justice, and We caused them to be like dead leaves. And so – away with those wrongdoing folk! (41)

ثُمَّ أَنشَأْنَا مِنۢ بَعْدِهِمْ قُرُونًا ءَاخَرِينَ ﴿٤٢﴾

Then after them We raised new generations. (42)

مَا تَسْبِقُ مِنْ أُمَّةٍ أَجَلَهَا وَمَا يَسْتَـْٔخِرُونَ ﴿٤٣﴾

No community can forestall the end of its term nor delay it. (43)

ثُمَّ أَرْسَلْنَا رُسُلَنَا تَتْرَا ۖ كُلَّ مَا جَآءَ أُمَّةً رَّسُولُهَا
كَذَّبُوهُ ۚ فَأَتْبَعْنَا بَعْضَهُم بَعْضًا وَجَعَلْنَٰهُمْ
أَحَادِيثَ ۚ فَبُعْدًا لِّقَوْمٍ لَّا يُؤْمِنُونَ ﴿٤٤﴾

And We sent forth Our messengers, one after another. Every time their messenger came to a community, they accused him of lying. So, We caused them to follow one another, and let them become mere tales. And so – away with the folk who would not believe. (44)

ثُمَّ أَرْسَلْنَا مُوسَىٰ وَأَخَاهُ هَٰرُونَ
بِـَٔايَٰتِنَا وَسُلْطَٰنٍ مُّبِينٍ ﴿٤٥﴾

And then We sent forth Moses and his brother Aaron, with Our signs and with clear authority, (45) to Pharaoh and his nobles; but these behaved with arrogance, for they were haughty people. (46)

إِلَىٰ فِرْعَوْنَ وَمَلَإِيْهِۦ فَٱسْتَكْبَرُوا۟
وَكَانُوا۟ قَوْمًا عَالِينَ ﴿٤٦﴾

And so they said: 'Are we to believe two mortals like ourselves, even though their people are our slaves?' (47)

فَقَالُوٓا۟ أَنُؤْمِنُ لِبَشَرَيْنِ مِثْلِنَا وَقَوْمُهُمَا
لَنَا عَٰبِدُونَ ﴿٤٧﴾

Thus, they gave the lie to them, and earned their place among the doomed. (48)

فَكَذَّبُوهُمَا فَكَانُوا۟ مِنَ ٱلْمُهْلَكِينَ ﴿٤٨﴾

We had indeed given Moses the Book, so that they might be guided. (49)

وَلَقَدْ ءَاتَيْنَا مُوسَى ٱلْكِتَٰبَ لَعَلَّهُمْ
يَهْتَدُونَ ﴿٤٩﴾

And We made the son of Mary and his mother a symbol, and provided them with an abode in a lofty place of lasting restfulness and a fresh spring. (50)

وَجَعَلْنَا ٱبْنَ مَرْيَمَ وَأُمَّهُۥٓ ءَايَةً وَءَاوَيْنَٰهُمَآ
إِلَىٰ رَبْوَةٍ ذَاتِ قَرَارٍ وَمَعِينٍ ﴿٥٠﴾

Messengers! Eat of that which is wholesome, and do good deeds: I certainly have full knowledge of all that you do. (51)

يَٰٓأَيُّهَا ٱلرُّسُلُ كُلُوا۟ مِنَ ٱلطَّيِّبَٰتِ وَٱعْمَلُوا۟
صَٰلِحًا ۖ إِنِّى بِمَا تَعْمَلُونَ عَلِيمٌ ﴿٥١﴾

This community of yours is one single community, and I am your only Lord. Therefore, fear Me alone. (52)

وَإِنَّ هَٰذِهِۦٓ أُمَّتُكُمْ أُمَّةً وَٰحِدَةً وَأَنَا۠
رَبُّكُمْ فَٱتَّقُونِ ﴿٥٢﴾

Overview

Having highlighted some of the indicators of the truth of God's oneness that are widely available in the universe and within man himself, the *sūrah* now speaks about the truth of faith preached by all God's messengers. It shows how people received this same truth that admits no alteration or amendment at any time or with the successive messages given to God's messengers, starting with Noah (peace be upon him). We behold the procession of the community of messengers sent by God to deliver to mankind the same message expressed in one word, with a single import and a single direction. Although this message was given in the numerous languages God's messengers spoke to their communities, it is given in the same wording in Arabic. Thus, Noah's statement expressing this message is repeated in exactly the same wording by every messenger sent later, and mankind always give the same answer using the same words.

The First Messenger

> *We sent forth Noah to his people, and he said: 'My people! Worship God alone, for you have no deity other than Him. Will you not be God-fearing?' The unbelieving elders of his people said: 'This man is but a mortal like yourselves who wants to make himself superior to you. Had God willed, He would surely have sent down angels. We have never heard anything like this ever happening to our forefathers. He is but a madman; so bear with him for a while.'* (Verses 23–25)

"*My people! Worship God alone, for you have no deity other than Him.*" (Verse 23) This is the unchanging word of truth. The whole universe is based on this truth and everything in it testifies to it. "*Will you not be God-fearing?*" (Verse 23) Do you not fear the consequences of denying the most fundamental truth that gives rise to all other truths? Do you not appreciate that by denying it you are distorting the bright image of the truth, and this will inevitably cause you to incur God's severe punishment?

However, the noblemen in his community who deny what he advocates are not prepared to discuss his statement or consider the evidence supporting it. They are unable to shed their narrow vision that concentrates on their own status and that of the messenger who calls them to accept the truth. They are not prepared to elevate themselves to the broader level from where they can better appreciate this great truth on its own. They cannot isolate it from personalities. Hence, they disregard this most fundamental truth in the universe, speaking instead about Noah as an individual: "*This man is but a mortal like yourselves who wants to make himself superior to you.*" (Verse 24)

From this very narrow angle the people of Noah looked at the great truth advocated by him. Hence, they could not appreciate its nature or see its truth. Their limited concerns and narrow interests thus blinded them to its essence, preventing their minds and hearts from appreciating it. Thus, to them the whole question was one of a single man from among themselves, who had nothing to distinguish him from the rest of them, wanting to have superiority over them, giving himself status above their own.

In their haste to prevent Noah from attaining what they imagine he is after, they not only deny Noah's status, but also the status of mankind in general. They refuse to accept that God may honour this human race. They simply do not believe that God would send a human messenger, if He sends messengers at all. "*Had God willed, He would surely have sent down angels.*" (Verse 24)

This is because they do not find in their own souls the sublime quality that links mankind with the Supreme Society. It is the quality that enables those whom God selects to receive the grace embodied in His message and deliver it to their fellow human beings, guiding them to its noble source.

In their futile argument they refer to familiar precedents, rather than to wise logic: "*We have never heard anything like this ever happening to our forefathers.*" (Verse 24) This always happens when blind imitation suppresses free thinking. Thus people do not look at what they have and try to relate it to reality in order to arrive at the right conclusion to questions in hand. They rather look to history for precedents. If they fail to find such a precedent, they are prepared to reject the question in its entirety.

Devoid of thought and imagination, such communities of unbelievers accept that what happened in the past may happen again. By contrast, what did not happen in the past cannot come into existence. What a narrow vision of human life this is, freezing it at a particular point of their forefathers' lives.

They are incapable of understanding that they are imprisoned within their narrow walls, unable to break into the wide universe! They accuse those who advocate freedom of thought of being mad, calling on them to think and reflect. When they are reminded of the pointers to the truth all around them, their reply is full of arrogance, reiterating accusations: "*He is but a madman; so bear with him for a while.*" (Verse 25) Bear with him until he dies when we will be relieved of him, his message and his persistent advocacy of faith.

Drowned in a Great Flood

At this moment Noah could not find any way by which he could soften such stone-hearted people. He could only protect himself against their ridicule by putting his complaint to God and seeking His support: "*He said: My Lord, help me against their accusation of lying.*" (Verse 26)

When the living decide to freeze in this way, while life wants to move forward towards the high standards it can achieve, such people constitute a clear impediment. Hence, they are either broken or life moves on, leaving them where they are. The former is what happened to Noah's people, for God willed that they should be removed:

> *We revealed to him to build the ark, under Our eyes, and according to Our inspiration. When Our judgement comes to pass, and water gushes forth over the face of the earth, place on board this ark one pair of every species, as well as your family, except those on whom sentence has already been passed. Do not plead with Me for the wrongdoers; for they shall be drowned.* (Verse 27)

It was God's will that the road should be cleared of obstacles so that human life could continue its march along the road assigned to it.

Humanity had become prematurely old by Noah's time. It was like a young tree affected by a pest that stops it from growing. It soon dries up and dies whilst still young. At the time of Noah, humanity was in a similar position. Therefore, the remedy was the great flood that swept away everything, washing off the soil and leaving the land ready for a new crop with healthy seeds and a clean environment.

"*We revealed to him to build the ark, under Our eyes, and according to Our inspiration.*" (Verse 27) The ark was the means of safety at the time of the flood. It also served to preserve the seeds of life so that they could grow again. God had willed that Noah should make the ark with his own hands, because man must take responsible action and utilize all means, doing his utmost so that he deserves God's help. Divine help is not given to those who sit on their laurels waiting for something to happen. Since Noah was chosen by God to be the second father of humanity, God instructed him to take the necessary measures, helping him and teaching him how to build the ark so that His purpose was accomplished and His will was done.

God gave Noah a sign which would announce this total process of purification of the entire planet: "*When Our judgement comes to pass, and water gushes forth over the face of the earth...*" At this point Noah was to move quickly and place on board the ark the new seeds of life: "*Place on board this ark one pair of every species.*" These included all types of animal, bird and plant that were known to Noah at the time, and which man could easily handle. He was also to place on board his "*family, except those on whom sentence has already been passed.*" This is a reference to the unbelievers who denied the word of God and incurred His displeasure. They thus deserved to endure the working of God's law that engulfed with His punishment those who persistently denied His signs.

Noah was ordered not to argue about anyone or try to save anyone even though they may be very close to him: "*Do not plead with Me for the wrongdoers; for they shall be drowned.*" (Verse 27) God's law does not try to appease anyone. It does not change its course for the sake of any friend or relative.

The *sūrah* does not give any details here of what happened to Noah's people after that. The whole matter is settled with the statement: "*They shall be drowned.*" Noah, however is taught how to show his gratitude to God and praise Him, seeking His guidance:

> *When you and those who are with you are settled in the ark, say: 'All praise is due to God who has saved us from those wrongdoing folk.' And also say: 'My Lord! Let my landing be blessed. You are the best to bring us to safe landing.'* (Verses 28–29)

This is the right way to praise God and to turn to Him, giving Him His rightful attributes and acknowledging His signs. All people, including prophets who provide the lead for others to follow should show such humility before God.

The *sūrah* then comments on the whole story and the aspects of God's power and wisdom it demonstrates: "*Surely, in that there are signs. Indeed, We always put [people] to a test.*" (Verse 30) Tests come in different types. Some are designed to demonstrate perseverance, some to show gratitude, some to earn reward, others to give guidance, purge unsound elements, or to rectify people's direction, etc. In the story of Noah there are several tests for him, his people and his future offspring.

Along the Same Way to Ruin

The *sūrah* moves on to portray another scene of unbelievers denying the message that continues to be the same across all generations and communities.

> *Then after these people We raised a new generation. And We sent forth to them a messenger from among themselves, and he said: 'My people! Worship God alone, for you have no deity other than Him. Will you not be God-fearing?'* (Verses 31–32)

The stories of earlier prophets referred to in this *sūrah* are not meant to give a full account or to provide details. They are meant to emphasize the unity of the message given to all of them, and to make clear that they received the same response from all their different communities. Hence these accounts commence with Noah to indicate the starting point, and finish with Moses and Jesus to define the last point before the final message. No names are mentioned in between the start and the finish of this long chain. This serves to indicate the similarity of all intervening episodes. However, in every new case the essence of the message and the way it was received are clearly mentioned to serve the purpose of the *sūrah*.

"*Then after these people We raised a new generation.*" (Verse 31) The community in question is not specified, but it is most likely that the reference here is to the 'Ād, the Prophet Hūd's people.

> *And We sent forth to them a messenger from among themselves, and he said: My people! Worship God alone, for you have no deity other than Him. Will you not be God-fearing?* (Verse 32)

It is exactly the same message given by Noah to his people. It is expressed here in the very same words, although these communities spoke totally different languages. But what was the answer?

Their answer was almost identical to that given by Noah's people:

> *The unbelieving elders of his people, who denied the life to come and to whom We granted ease and plenty in this worldly life, said: 'This man is but a mortal like yourselves, eating of what you eat and drinking of what you drink. Indeed, if you pay heed to a mortal like yourselves, you will certainly be the losers.'* (Verses 33–34)

This oft repeated objection concentrates on the fact that the messenger sent to them is a human being. Those who raise it are people who enjoy power and wealth and whose hearts no longer feel the spiritual bond between man and his Creator. Affluence corrupts human nature, blunts sensitivities, closes receptive faculties and weakens the heart's ability to feel and respond. Hence Islam combats the accumulation of wealth and establishes a social system that does not allow the very rich to emerge in the Muslim community simply because to do so encourages corruption.

The corrupt rich add in this case a denial of resurrection. They wonder at this messenger who alerts them to such life after death, considering it very strange:

> *Does he promise you that, after you have died and become dust and bones, you shall be brought forth to life? Improbable, improbable indeed is what you are promised! There is no life beyond this, our present life; we die and we live, and we shall never be restored to life.* (Verses 35–37)

Such people cannot understand the ultimate purpose of life, the elaborate planning of its different stages until it reaches its eventual destination. This purpose will not be achieved in full in this present life on earth. Goodness is not fully rewarded in this life, nor does evil receive its just deserts. All rewards are given in the life to come. Good believers achieve the ultimate form of life that is free of fear, worry and hardship and continues as God wishes. On the other side, those who cling to evil in this life go to the lowest depths of life where their humanity comes to an end and they become as hard as stones.

Such people cannot understand such concepts. They fail to look at the early stages of life which were outlined at the beginning of the *sūrah* in order to realize the nature of its final stages. They cannot imagine that the Mighty Power that controlled those stages will not cause life to end at the point of death when the body decays. Hence they are full of amazement at the messenger who promises them that they will be resurrected. In their ignorance, they consider this far-fetched. They categorically state that there is only one life and one death. Generation succeeds generation, and those who have already died and are reduced to dust and bones cannot come back to life as the prophet promises them.

Yet unbelievers do not stop at this juncture betraying their own ignorance and their inability to reflect on the early stages of human life detailed at the opening of the *sūrah*. They go further than this and accuse God's messenger of lying and fabricating things that he attributes to God. They do not know God except in the context of making false accusations against His messenger: "*He is nothing but a man who attributes his lies to God. Never will we believe in him.*" (Verse 38)

Facing the Same Rejection

At this point, the messenger finds no alternative but to seek God's help like Noah did before him. He uses the same wording as Noah: "*He said: My Lord, help me against their accusation of lying.*" (Verse 39)

God responded to His messenger when the people refused to take the chance afforded to them. Nothing good could be expected from them after they had persisted in their denial of the truth. The messenger's appeal receives this answer: "*Said [God]: Before long they shall come to rue it.*" (Verse 40) But then no regret will be of any avail. There is no turning back: "*Then the blast overtook them in all justice, and We caused them to be like dead leaves.*" (Verse 41) The Arabic word, *ghuthā'*, describing their status contains even more connotations as it refers to what floods may carry of dead plants and other discarded, worthless items that serve no purpose. Having discarded the qualities with which God has honoured them, overlooked the purpose of their existence in this life and severed their relation with the Supreme Society, they no longer deserve honourable treatment. Hence, they are like the scum that the flood carries. No one pays any regard to it.

To this humiliation is added the fact that they are deprived of God's grace; thus no-one pays any attention to them: "*And so – away with those wrongdoing folk!*" (Verse 41) Far removed are they in real life and from people's memories and consciences.

The *sūrah* goes on to look at other generations and communities:

> *Then after them We raised new generations. No community can forestall the end of its term nor delay it. And We sent forth Our messengers, one after another. Every time their messenger came to a community, they accused him of lying. So, We caused them to follow one another, and let them become mere tales. And so – away with the folk who would not believe.* (Verses 42–44)

This gives us a very brief summary of the advocacy of the truth, and establishes the normal trend that God operates in human life, right from the time of Noah and Hūd at the beginning to Moses and Jesus at the end. Every generation gets its term and departs: "*No community can forestall the end of its term nor delay it.*" (Verse 43) Every community denies the truth given to them through God's messenger: "*Every time their messenger came to a community, they accused him of lying.*" (Verse 44) And each time they do this, they are punished according to God's law: "*So, We caused them to follow one another.*" (Verse 44) The lesson remains there for anyone who wishes to learn: "*We let them become mere tales,*" told by one generation to the next.

This brief summary concludes with an emphatic rejection of such communities. Thus, they are cast away: "*And so – away with the folk who would not believe.*" (Verse 44)

Moses' story and Pharaoh's denial of his message is then told in a very brief account that fits with the general style of the *sūrah* and purpose.

> *And then We sent forth Moses and his brother Aaron, with Our signs and with clear authority, to Pharaoh and his nobles; but these behaved with arrogance, for they were haughty people. And so they said: 'Are we to believe two mortals like ourselves, even though their people are our slaves?' Thus, they gave the lie to them, and earned their place among the doomed.* (Verses 45–48)

Again in this account we note that the same objection is given to the fact that the messenger was merely a human being: "*They said: Are we to believe two mortals like ourselves?"* (Verse 47) A specific consideration connected with the Israelites' situation in Egypt is also added: "*Even though their people are our slaves?"* (Verse 47) They are subservient to us and they do our bidding. In this situation, Moses and Aaron deserve, in Pharaoh's and his people's view, to be looked down upon. As for the revelations and the signs they have been given by God, and the clear authority granted to them, these count for nothing according to these people, focused as they are on earthly considerations and false values.

This is followed by a similarly brief reference to Jesus and his mother, highlighting the great miracle in his creation. Again, those who were bent on denying the truth of God and creation rejected this sign clearly pointing to God's power:

We had indeed given Moses the Book, so that they might be guided. And We made the son of Mary and his mother a symbol, and provided them with an abode in a lofty place of lasting restfulness and a fresh spring. (Verses 49–50)

There are a number of different reports about the hill described here as a 'lofty place' and its exact location. Was it in Egypt, Damascus or Jerusalem? These were the places where Mary went with her son during his childhood and youth, as mentioned in Christian Scriptures. But knowing the exact location is not of vital importance. It is more important to know that God gave them both a goodly abode where fine plants grew and clear water was plentiful. Thus, they felt that God took care of them both.

At this point in its quick references to earlier messengers the *sūrah* makes its address to the followers of all messengers, as though they were all gathered together. Thus, the separating gulfs of time and place are shown to be meaningless when compared to the true bond of faith that unites them all:

Messengers! Eat of that which is wholesome, and do good deeds: I certainly have full knowledge of all that you do. This community of yours is one single community, and I am your only Lord. Therefore, fear Me alone. (Verses 51–52)

This address to His messengers requires them to live as human beings, which is the very thing that those who opposed them questioned: "*Eat of that which is wholesome.*" Eating is a human need, but choosing only what is wholesome is the aspect that elevates human beings and makes them grow in purity. It enables them to establish a bond with the Supreme Society.

They are also required to "*do good deeds.*" While taking action is common to all human beings, insisting on doing good is the characteristic of goodly people, providing a measure of control and a clear goal for their deeds. Again such people look up to the Supreme Society when they embark on anything.

No messenger of God was ever required to abandon his humanity. Rather, what they were asked to do was to elevate this humanity to the highest standard God has made possible for human beings to achieve. Thus, the Prophets provided the role model and the ideal which other people should try to emulate. It is left to God to judge their actions according to His own fine measure: "*I certainly have full knowledge of all that you do*." (Verse 51)

Emphasis is placed on the fact that neither time nor place is of any significance when compared with the single truth that all messengers preached. They all shared a very distinctive nature, were given their messages by the One Creator of all, and worked towards the same goal: "*This community of yours is one single community, and I am your only Lord. Therefore, fear Me alone*." (Verse 52)

3

A Book Stating the Truth

But people have divided themselves into factions, each delighting in what they have. (53)

فَتَقَطَّعُوٓا۟ أَمْرَهُم بَيْنَهُمْ زُبُرًا ۖ كُلُّ حِزْبٍۭ
بِمَا لَدَيْهِمْ فَرِحُونَ ٥٣

So, leave them alone, lost in ignorance, till a time appointed. (54)

فَذَرْهُمْ فِى غَمْرَتِهِمْ حَتَّىٰ حِينٍ ٥٤

Do they think that by all the wealth and offspring We provide for them (55)

أَيَحْسَبُونَ أَنَّمَا نُمِدُّهُم بِهِۦ مِن مَّالٍ
وَبَنِينَ ٥٥

We hasten to them all that is good? By no means! But they are devoid of perception. (56)

نُسَارِعُ لَهُمْ فِى ٱلْخَيْرَٰتِ ۚ بَل لَّا يَشْعُرُونَ ٥٦

Truly, those who stand in reverent awe of their Lord, (57)

إِنَّ ٱلَّذِينَ هُم مِّنْ خَشْيَةِ رَبِّهِم
مُّشْفِقُونَ ٥٧

and who believe in their Lord's revelations, (58)

وَٱلَّذِينَ هُم بِـَٔايَٰتِ رَبِّهِمْ يُؤْمِنُونَ ٥٨

and who do not associate any partners with their Lord, (59)

وَٱلَّذِينَ هُم بِرَبِّهِمْ لَا يُشْرِكُونَ ٥٩

وَٱلَّذِينَ يُؤۡتُونَ مَآ ءَاتَواْ وَّقُلُوبُهُمۡ وَجِلَةٌ أَنَّهُمۡ
إِلَىٰ رَبِّهِمۡ رَٰجِعُونَ ٦٠

and who give away whatever they have to give with their hearts filled with awe, knowing that to their Lord they shall certainly return: (60)

أُوْلَـٰٓئِكَ يُسَٰرِعُونَ فِي ٱلۡخَيۡرَٰتِ وَهُمۡ
لَهَا سَٰبِقُونَ ٦١

these vie with one another in doing good works, and they are the ones who are foremost in them. (61)

وَلَا نُكَلِّفُ نَفۡسًا إِلَّا وُسۡعَهَاۖ وَلَدَيۡنَا كِتَٰبٌ
يَنطِقُ بِٱلۡحَقِّۚ وَهُمۡ لَا يُظۡلَمُونَ ٦٢

We do not charge a soul with more than it can bear. We have a record that speaks the truth. None shall be wronged. (62)

بَلۡ قُلُوبُهُمۡ فِي غَمۡرَةٍ مِّنۡ هَٰذَا وَلَهُمۡ أَعۡمَٰلٌ
مِّن دُونِ ذَٰلِكَ هُمۡ لَهَا عَٰمِلُونَ ٦٣

Nay, their hearts are blind to all this. But apart from all that, they have deeds which they will continue to commit. (63)

حَتَّىٰٓ إِذَآ أَخَذۡنَا مُتۡرَفِيهِم بِٱلۡعَذَابِ إِذَا
هُمۡ يَجۡـَٔرُونَ ٦٤

Then, when We shall have overwhelmed with suffering those of them that live in luxury, they cry out in belated supplication. (64)

لَا تَجۡـَٔرُواْ ٱلۡيَوۡمَۖ إِنَّكُم مِّنَّا لَا تُنصَرُونَ ٦٥

[But they will be told:] Do not cry out this day, for from Us you shall receive no help. (65)

قَدۡ كَانَتۡ ءَايَٰتِي تُتۡلَىٰ عَلَيۡكُمۡ فَكُنتُمۡ
عَلَىٰٓ أَعۡقَٰبِكُمۡ تَنكِصُونَ ٦٦

Time and again were My revelations recited to you, but every time you would turn about on your heels, (66) revelling in your arrogance, and talking senselessly far into the night. (67)

مُسْتَكْبِرِينَ بِهِۦ سَٰمِرًا تَهْجُرُونَ ٦٧

Have they, then, never tried to understand this word [of God]? Or has there come to them something that never came to their forefathers of old? (68)

أَفَلَمْ يَدَّبَّرُوا۟ ٱلْقَوْلَ أَمْ جَآءَهُم مَّا لَمْ يَأْتِ
ءَابَآءَهُمُ ٱلْأَوَّلِينَ ٦٨

Or do they not recognize their Messenger, and so they deny him? (69)

أَمْ لَمْ يَعْرِفُوا۟ رَسُولَهُمْ فَهُمْ لَهُۥ
مُنكِرُونَ ٦٩

Or do they say that there is in him a touch of madness? Nay, he has brought them the truth; and the truth do most of them detest. (70)

أَمْ يَقُولُونَ بِهِۦ جِنَّةٌۢ ۚ بَلْ جَآءَهُم بِٱلْحَقِّ
وَأَكْثَرُهُمْ لِلْحَقِّ كَٰرِهُونَ ٧٠

Had the truth been in accord with their desires, the heavens and the earth, together with all that lives in them, would surely have been in utter corruption. Nay, We have given them all that brings them glory. Yet from this their glory they turn away. (71)

وَلَوِ ٱتَّبَعَ ٱلْحَقُّ أَهْوَآءَهُمْ لَفَسَدَتِ
ٱلسَّمَٰوَٰتُ وَٱلْأَرْضُ وَمَن فِيهِنَّ ۚ
بَلْ أَتَيْنَٰهُم بِذِكْرِهِمْ فَهُمْ عَن
ذِكْرِهِم مُّعْرِضُونَ ٧١

Or do you ask of them any recompense? But the recompense given by your Lord is best, since He is the best of providers. (72)

أَمْ تَسْـَٔلُهُمْ خَرْجًا فَخَرَاجُ رَبِّكَ خَيْرٌ ۖ
وَهُوَ خَيْرُ ٱلرَّٰزِقِينَ ٧٢

Most certainly, you call them to a straight path. (73)

وَإِنَّكَ لَتَدْعُوهُمْ إِلَىٰ صِرَٰطٍ مُّسْتَقِيمٍ ٧٣

وَإِنَّ ٱلَّذِينَ لَا يُؤْمِنُونَ بِٱلْـَٔاخِرَةِ عَنِ
ٱلصِّرَٰطِ لَنَـٰكِبُونَ ٧٤

But those who will not believe in the life to come are bound to deviate from the right path. (74)

وَلَوْ رَحِمْنَـٰهُمْ وَكَشَفْنَا مَا بِهِم مِّن ضُرٍّ
لَّلَجُّوا۟ فِى طُغْيَـٰنِهِمْ يَعْمَهُونَ ٧٥

Even were We to show them mercy and remove whatever distress might afflict them, they would still persist in their overweening arrogance, blindly stumbling to and fro. (75)

وَلَقَدْ أَخَذْنَـٰهُم بِٱلْعَذَابِ فَمَا ٱسْتَكَانُوا۟
لِرَبِّهِمْ وَمَا يَتَضَرَّعُونَ ٧٦

Indeed, We took them to task, but they neither humbled themselves before their Lord, nor do they submissively entreat [Him]. (76)

حَتَّىٰٓ إِذَا فَتَحْنَا عَلَيْهِم بَابًا ذَا عَذَابٍ
شَدِيدٍ إِذَا هُمْ فِيهِ مُبْلِسُونَ ٧٧

Yet when We open before them a gate of truly severe suffering, they will plunge in despair. (77)

وَهُوَ ٱلَّذِىٓ أَنشَأَ لَكُمُ ٱلسَّمْعَ وَٱلْأَبْصَـٰرَ
وَٱلْأَفْـِٔدَةَ ۚ قَلِيلًا مَّا تَشْكُرُونَ ٧٨

It is He who has endowed you with hearing, and sight, and minds. How seldom are you grateful. (78)

وَهُوَ ٱلَّذِى ذَرَأَكُمْ فِى ٱلْأَرْضِ
وَإِلَيْهِ تُحْشَرُونَ ٧٩

And He it is who caused you to multiply on earth; and to Him you shall be gathered. (79)

وَهُوَ ٱلَّذِى يُحْىِۦ وَيُمِيتُ وَلَهُ ٱخْتِلَـٰفُ
ٱلَّيْلِ وَٱلنَّهَارِ ۚ أَفَلَا تَعْقِلُونَ ٨٠

And He it is who grants life and causes death; and to Him is due the alternation of night and day. Will you not, then, use your reason? (80)

But they say like the people of old times used to say. (81)

بَلْ قَالُوا۟ مِثْلَ مَا قَالَ ٱلْأَوَّلُونَ ﴿٨١﴾

They say: 'What! After we have died and become dust and bones, shall we be raised to life? (82)

قَالُوٓا۟ أَءِذَا مِتْنَا وَكُنَّا تُرَابًا
وَعِظَٰمًا أَءِنَّا لَمَبْعُوثُونَ ﴿٨٢﴾

This we have been promised before, we and our forefathers! This is nothing but fables of the ancients.' (83)

لَقَدْ وُعِدْنَا نَحْنُ وَءَابَآؤُنَا هَٰذَا مِن قَبْلُ
إِنْ هَٰذَآ إِلَّآ أَسَٰطِيرُ ٱلْأَوَّلِينَ ﴿٨٣﴾

Say: 'To whom belongs the earth and all that lives therein? [Tell me] if you know.' (84)

قُل لِّمَنِ ٱلْأَرْضُ وَمَن فِيهَآ إِن
كُنتُمْ تَعْلَمُونَ ﴿٨٤﴾

They will reply: 'To God.' Say: 'Will you not, then, reflect?' (85)

سَيَقُولُونَ لِلَّهِ ۚ قُلْ أَفَلَا تَذَكَّرُونَ ﴿٨٥﴾

Say: 'Who is the Lord of the seven heavens, and the Lord of the Supreme Throne?' (86)

قُلْ مَن رَّبُّ ٱلسَّمَٰوَٰتِ ٱلسَّبْعِ وَرَبُّ
ٱلْعَرْشِ ٱلْعَظِيمِ ﴿٨٦﴾

They will reply: '[They all belong] to God.' Say: 'Will you not, then, fear Him?' (87)

سَيَقُولُونَ لِلَّهِ ۚ قُلْ أَفَلَا تَتَّقُونَ ﴿٨٧﴾

Say: 'In whose hand rests the sovereignty of all things, protecting all, while against Him there is no protection? [Tell me] if you know.' (88)

قُلْ مَنۢ بِيَدِهِۦ مَلَكُوتُ كُلِّ شَىْءٍ
وَهُوَ يُجِيرُ وَلَا يُجَارُ عَلَيْهِ إِن
كُنتُمْ تَعْلَمُونَ ﴿٨٨﴾

سَيَقُولُونَ لِلَّهِ ۚ قُلْ فَأَنَّىٰ تُسْحَرُونَ ﴿٨٩﴾

They will reply: '[They all belong] to God.' Say: 'How, then, can you be so deluded?' (89)

بَلْ أَتَيْنَٰهُم بِٱلْحَقِّ وَإِنَّهُمْ لَكَٰذِبُونَ ﴿٩٠﴾

Nay, We have revealed to them the truth; and yet, they are certainly lying. (90)

مَا ٱتَّخَذَ ٱللَّهُ مِن وَلَدٍ وَمَا كَانَ مَعَهُۥ
مِنْ إِلَٰهٍ ۚ إِذًا لَّذَهَبَ كُلُّ إِلَٰهٍۭ بِمَا خَلَقَ
وَلَعَلَا بَعْضُهُمْ عَلَىٰ بَعْضٍ ۚ سُبْحَٰنَ ٱللَّهِ
عَمَّا يَصِفُونَ ﴿٩١﴾

Never did God take to Himself any offspring, nor has there ever been any deity alongside Him. [Had there been any] each deity would surely have taken away his own creation, and they would surely have tried to establish superiority over one another. Limitless in His glory is God, far above all that which they attribute to Him. (91)

عَٰلِمِ ٱلْغَيْبِ وَٱلشَّهَٰدَةِ فَتَعَٰلَىٰ
عَمَّا يُشْرِكُونَ ﴿٩٢﴾

He knows all that is beyond the reach of human perception, and all that can be witnessed. Sublimely exalted is He above anything they associate as a partner with Him. (92)

قُل رَّبِّ إِمَّا تُرِيَنِّى مَا يُوعَدُونَ ﴿٩٣﴾

Say: 'My Lord! If it be Your will to show me that which they are warned against, (93)

رَبِّ فَلَا تَجْعَلْنِى فِى ٱلْقَوْمِ
ٱلظَّٰلِمِينَ ﴿٩٤﴾

then, my Lord, do not let me be one of those wrongdoing folk.' (94)

We are most certainly able to show you that which We promise them. (95)	وَإِنَّا عَلَىٰٓ أَن نُّرِيَكَ مَا نَعِدُهُمْ لَقَٰدِرُونَ ﴿٩٥﴾
Repel evil with that which is best. We are fully aware of all that they say. (96)	ٱدْفَعْ بِٱلَّتِى هِىَ أَحْسَنُ ٱلسَّيِّئَةَ ۚ نَحْنُ أَعْلَمُ بِمَا يَصِفُونَ ﴿٩٦﴾
And say: 'My Lord! I seek refuge with You from the promptings of the evil ones; (97)	وَقُل رَّبِّ أَعُوذُ بِكَ مِنْ هَمَزَٰتِ ٱلشَّيَٰطِينِ ﴿٩٧﴾
and I seek refuge with You, my Lord, lest they come near me.' (98)	وَأَعُوذُ بِكَ رَبِّ أَن يَحْضُرُونِ ﴿٩٨﴾

Overview

This third passage begins by showing the state mankind reached after the generations which witnessed God's messengers. This is the state God's last Messenger found them in. They were in dispute over the single truth preached by all God's messengers.

The *sūrah* shows people oblivious of the truth the final Messenger put before their eyes. In their ignorance, they were totally unaware of the consequences they were bound to face. By contrast, believers worship God alone, do good deeds and remain apprehensive of what lies before them. They are in awe over the fact that they will inevitably be returned to God. The two situations are in perfect contrast: a believer is alert, cautious and heeding the warnings, while an unbeliever is deep in ignorance, unaware of what lies ahead.

The passage addresses them in different ways, at times denouncing their attitude, and at others discussing their doubts and providing clear answers to them. The passage also addresses their finer nature, pointing out what encourages people to believe, whether it be within themselves or in the universe at large. It also picks up some of what they take for granted, using these as argument against them.

As the passage concludes, it leaves them to their inevitable destiny. It tells the Prophet Muḥammad (peace be upon him) that he should continue his efforts, explaining his message. He should not be distressed at their obstinate rejection. He should repel their evil deeds with good ones, and seek refuge with God against Satan who tries hard to lead mankind along the path of error.

Competing in Good Works

> *But people have divided themselves into factions, each delighting in what they have. So, leave them alone, lost in ignorance, till a time appointed. Do they think that by all the wealth and offspring We provide for them We hasten to them all that is good? By no means! But they are devoid of perception.* (Verses 53–56)

All messengers (peace be upon them all) belonged to a single nation, preaching the same message, worship and pursuing the same direction. But when the messengers had gone, mankind splintered into different groups which could not agree on what line to follow.

The Qur'ān portrays such divergence as people in conflict, splitting into factions, quarrelling and pulling apart from each other. The picture drawn here is full of effort and movement. In the end each faction is left with only a portion of the whole, delighting at their ability to hold on to this. Hence, no faction thinks of anything other than what it supposedly possesses. Each goes its separate way, shutting up all inlets so that no ray of light or fresh breath of air comes through. All live in their isolated quarters, busy with what they have, ignorant of everything else.

Once this image has been drawn, the *sūrah* addresses God's Messenger: "*So, leave them alone, lost in their ignorance, till a time appointed.*" (Verse 54) Let them take their time, preoccupied with their own affairs, until their appointed time inevitably comes, spelling out their destiny.

The *sūrah* adds a derisive question that highlights their lack of awareness. They think that the time they have been given, and the wealth and offspring they are allowed to enjoy means that they are favoured with blessings. "*Do they think that by all the wealth and offspring We provide for them We hasten to them all that is good?*" (Verses 55–56) Little do they realize the truth that it is all but a test which they have to go through: "*By no means! But they are devoid of perception.*" (Verse 56) They simply do not perceive the destiny to which they are heading after having enjoyed what has been given in this life.

By contrast, the believers are always on the alert, taking necessary precautions:

> *Truly, those who stand in reverent awe of their Lord, and who believe in their Lord's revelations, and who do not associate any partners with their Lord, and who give away whatever they have to give with their hearts filled with awe, knowing that to their Lord they shall certainly return: these vie with one another in doing good works, and they are the ones who are foremost in them.* (Verses 57–61)

Here we see how faith affects hearts, imparting to them a special kind of refinement, sensitivity and aspiration to attain perfection. They are the ones who consider the consequences of their actions. They are always ready and willing to do their duties.

We see that believers are always in awe of their Lord, God-fearing, believing in His revelations and His signs, attributing no share of Godhead to anyone other than Him, fulfilling the duties He requires of them. Beyond all this, they '*give away whatever they have to give with their hearts filled with awe, knowing that to their Lord they shall certainly return.*' This is a manifestation of their feeling that they actually fall short of what they should do. It is true that they have done their utmost, but they consider it far from adequate.

'Ā'ishah reports that she asked the Prophet about this verse, saying: "Does the expression '*those who give away whatever they have to give with their hearts filled with awe...*' refer to people who may steal, commit adultery and drink intoxicants but fear God?" He said: "No. It refers to a person who offers prayers, fasts, gives away to charity and at the same time fears God." [Related by al-Tirmidhī]

A believer senses God's care and feels His favours with his every breath and heartbeat. Hence, he thinks that whatever he offers of worship and good action is too little by comparison. At the same time, every grain in a believer feels God's greatness and power. With all his faculties he perceives how God regulates everything around him. Hence, he stands in awe of Him. He dreads meeting God, for fear of having fallen short of fulfilling his duties towards Him, or not having given Him what is due to Him of worship and gratitude.

It is these people who vie with one another in doing what is good. They are the ones who hasten to do good deeds, and are in the lead among those who do good. Their watchful eyes, alert hearts and minds prompt them to do what is required of them. Theirs is a totally different situation from the others who are lost in ignorance, thinking that God's blessings are given to them because they are favoured. They are no better than game animals rushing towards bait. Such people are everywhere: they are overwhelmed with what they are given of life's comforts, distracted from their duties, full of their own importance. But then they only wake up to their fate when it is too late.

Will They Not Reflect?

Islam ensures that its followers' hearts are always alert. This is an alertness generated by faith right from the moment it settles in a person's heart. It neither defies human power, nor is too hard for man to sustain. It is a question of sensitivity enhanced by a believer's bond with God and his watchfulness in all situations, guarding against sin. It is perfectly within people's power when the light of faith shines in their hearts: "*We do not charge a soul with more than it can bear. We have a record that speaks the truth. None shall be wronged.*" (Verse 62)

God has established people's duties as He knows their inclinations and abilities. He will hold them to account on the basis of what they do within their ability. He neither charges them with what they cannot bear, nor dismisses any little thing they do. All their deeds are documented in a '*record that speaks the truth*,' highlighting it in its full value. Needless to say, God is precise in His reckoning.

People, however, tend to overlook the truth because their hearts are not touched by its invigorating light. Hence, they remain preoccupied with petty concerns, lost in a perpetual maze. They are only awakened when faced with inevitable doom, looking at the suffering that awaits them and enduring a humiliatingly and strong reproach:

> *Nay, their hearts are blind to all this. But apart from all that, they have deeds which they will continue to commit. Then, when We shall have overwhelmed with suffering those of them that live in luxury, they cry out in belated supplication. [But they will be told:] Do not cry out this day, for from Us you shall receive no help. Time and again were My revelations recited to you, but every time you would turn about on your heels, revelling in your arrogance, and talking senselessly far into the night.* (Verses 63–67)

Thus, the reason for their headlong pursuit of worldly affairs is nothing like being burdened with what they cannot bear. It is simply that their hearts are blinded, unable to see the truth as clearly stated in the Qur'ān. They are wont to follow a line different from the course charted by the Qur'ān: "*They have deeds which they will continue to commit.*" (Verse 63)

The *sūrah* then paints a picture of their being awakened by a sudden calamity: "*When We shall have overwhelmed with suffering those of them that live in luxury, they cry out in belated supplication.*" (Verse 64) People who live in luxury are indeed the ones who are most preoccupied with life's comforts, totally oblivious to what lies ahead. Now they find themselves suddenly overtaken by suffering, and they cry out for mercy, making a passionate appeal for it to be lifted. It is a picture that contrasts with the life of luxury and arrogance they lead in this world. Hence, they receive a strong reproach: "*Do not cry out this day, for from Us you shall receive no help.*" (Verse 65) The scene is described as though it is taking place now. They are strongly reproached, made certain of having no support, and reminded of what they used to do in life: "*Time and again were My revelations recited to you, but every time you would turn about on your heels, revelling in your arrogance, and talking senselessly far into the night.*" (Verses 66–67) It is as though what was being recited was a danger or a calamity you needed to avoid. You were too proud to submit to the truth. Indeed, you compounded your insolence, adding insult to injury, speaking ill of the Prophet and his message, but you, nevertheless, are willing to spend hours in idle chit-chat.

It was common practice for them to use obscene language when they gathered in circles around the Ka'bah, close to the idols they worshipped. Now the Qur'ān paints for them a scene of when they are called to account for their indulgence, showing them raising their voices with cries for help. It is at this point that they are reminded of what they do now in their circles, as though both take place at the same time. This is a familiar method of the Qur'ān, frequently depicting the Day of Judgement as though it were actually occurring at that precise moment.

In their hostility towards the Prophet and with their disparaging remarks about him and the Qur'ān in their gatherings, the unbelievers represent an ignorant arrogance that is blinded to the truth. With such blind ignorance, the truth becomes the subject of derision and ridicule. Such people are encountered no matter what the time or place. Yet the state of ignorance that prevailed in Arabia at the time when the Islamic message was revealed serves as an example of similar past and future situations where ignorance prevails.

The Line the Truth Follows

Having shown the unbelievers this scene of reproach in the hereafter, the *sūrah* takes them back to this world, questioning them about their attitude: what stops them from accepting what they are told by God's Messenger, whom they know to be a man of trust? What doubts do they have to prevent them from following divine guidance? Why do they turn away from it, ridiculing it when it represents the absolute truth?

> *Have they, then, never tried to understand this word [of God]? Or has there come to them something that never came to their forefathers of old? Or do they not recognize their Messenger, and so they deny*

him? Or do they say that there is in him a touch of madness? Nay, he has brought them the truth; and the truth do most of them detest. Had the truth been in accord with their desires, the heavens and the earth, together with all that lives in them, would surely have been in utter corruption. Nay, We have given them all that brings them glory. Yet from this their glory they turn away. Or do you ask of them any recompense? But the recompense given by your Lord is best, since He is the best of providers. Most certainly, you call them to a straight path. But those who will not believe in the life to come are bound to deviate from the right path. (Verses 68–74)

The message Muḥammad, God's Messenger, preached could not be rejected by anyone who looks at it carefully, using his reason. It is a model of beauty, perfection, consistency and attraction. It fits with human nature, addresses people's minds and hearts, outlines a course to elevate human life, and lays down a fine constitution to follow and a perfect code of justice. It also includes what answers the needs of human nature and what helps its development and advancement. "*Have they, then, never tried to understand this word [of God]?*" (Verse 68) This is, then, the secret behind their attitude.

"*Or has there come to them something that never came to their forefathers of old?*" (Verse 68) If so, it would have been strange for them and for their forefathers that a messenger came to call on them to believe in God's oneness. But the history of divine messages proves that messengers followed one another, and all of them preached the same message advocated by Muḥammad, God's last Messenger.

"*Or do they not recognize their Messenger, and so they deny him?*" (Verse 69) Could this have been the reason for their insolent rejection? Yet they knew their Messenger well. They knew his birth and ancestry. They also knew his character, honesty and integrity. Long before he received his message, they nicknamed him *al-amīn*, which means 'the trustworthy'.

"*Or do they say that there is in him a touch of madness?*" (Verse 70) Some of the lowest in their ranks used to say this about him, knowing full well that he was the wisest and most reasonable person among them. They never knew him slip once.

None of such possibilities had any foundation whatsoever. The fact is that most of them hated the truth because it deprived them of their false values and contradicted their desires and preferences: "*Nay, he has brought them the truth; and the truth do most of them detest.*" (Verse 70)

The truth cannot be subservient to personal desires and preferences. For it is on the basis of truth that the universe is sustained, life flourishes and the laws of nature function: "*Had the truth been in accord with their desires, the heavens and the earth, together with all that lives in them, would surely have been in utter corruption.*" (Verse 71)

The truth is unique and consistent, while desires are numerous and changing. It is on the basis of the unique truth that the whole universe moves along the course that ensures its existence. Thus, its laws are not made to deviate or change in order to accommodate fleeting desires. Had the universe been subject to such changing or sudden desires it would have become corrupted. Indeed, human life, values, standards and systems would also have become corrupted. They would have staggered to and fro, in response to anger, pleasure, hatred, caprice, fear, laziness, activity, reaction and influence. But the physical universe and its progress towards its goal requires consistency and reliability as well as the following of a clearly charted course that is subject to no modification or deviation.

Bearing this in mind, Islam considers legislation for human life to be part of the universal law, formulated by the same hand that conducts the affairs of the universe and establishes coherence between all its parts. Human beings are part of the universe and subject to its law. Hence, it is only fitting that the One who legislates for the entire universe should also legislate for human life. When this is done, human life is no longer subjected to personal desires and preferences. Thus, it is immune to corruption: "*Had the truth been in accord with their desires, the heavens and the earth, together with all that lives in them, would surely have been in utter corruption.*" (Verse 71)

The community addressed by Islam should be keen to follow its truth, not only because it is the truth, but also because it represents its glory. Without Islam, it would have had no place in history: "*Nay, We have given them all that brings them glory. Yet from this their glory they turn away.*" (Verse 71) The Arabs were ignored throughout history until they were given the message of Islam. Since then, this community continued to be glorious as long as it adhered to Islam. Its position on the world stage, however, gradually shrank when it abandoned Islam, until it reached its present low depth. It will not recover its glory until it reverts to its true, guiding light.

The *sūrah* resumes its questioning of their attitude and the doubts that may be the cause for their refusal to believe in the Messenger: "*Or do you ask of them any recompense?*" (Verse 72) Had you demanded any wages from them, such a request might be their cause for refusal. The fact is that you seek nothing from them, because "*the recompense given by your Lord is best, since He is the best of providers.*" (Verse 72) What could a prophet seek from human beings, poor and needy as they are, when he has access to God's inexhaustible favours? Indeed, what would a prophet's followers hope to gain of this world's comforts when they seek what may be provided by God who grants everything people have? The fact is that when a human heart is in touch with God, this whole universe, with all that it contains, dwindles into insignificance.

You only seek to guide them to the best method: "*Most certainly, you call them to a straight path*"; a path that brings them into line with the law that governs their nature. It bonds them with the rest of the universe, guiding them straight, without deviation, to God, the Creator of all.

Yet, like everyone else who does not believe in the life to come, these people deviate from the perfect way: "*But those who will not believe in the life to come are bound to deviate from the right path.*" (Verse 74) Had they been well guided, they would have reflected on the stages of their existence, because such reflection is bound to lead to belief in the hereafter, when perfection and absolute justice are attainable. The life to come is merely a stage in the line God has charted for all existence.

Inspiring Signs

These unbelievers are people who have lost their way and no longer benefit from the tests to which they are exposed, be they tests of plenty and affluence or those of hardship. Hence, when they are tested with favour "*they think that by all the wealth and offspring We provide for them We hasten to them all that is good?"* (Verses 55–56) Even if they are tested with difficulty and hardship, their hearts are not softened, nor are their consciences awakened. They do not turn back to God, appealing to Him to remove their hardship. They remain in such a condition until, on the Day of Judgement, they are visited with an even greater suffering. Then they will be truly desperate and bewildered.

> *Even were We to show them mercy and remove whatever distress might afflict them, they would still persist in their overweening arrogance, blindly stumbling to and fro. Indeed, We took them to task, but they neither humbled themselves before their Lord, nor do they submissively entreat [Him]. Yet when We open before them a gate of truly severe suffering, they will plunge in despair.* (Verses 75–77)

These are common features among such people. They are hard hearted, oblivious of their duties to God, and they deny the hereafter. The idolaters who opposed the Prophet when he delivered his message were of the same type.

Showing humility at a time of hardship, and turning to God, entreating Him and recognizing Him as the only refuge and resort are indicative of a change of heart and a returning to faith. A heart which establishes such links with God is bound to soften. Reflection and remembrance then provide protection against further slips and errors. Thus, hardship brings about real benefit. But the person who persists in arrogance is a lost case, without hope. He is left to his destiny when he will be overwhelmed with suffering in the life to come. He will then plunge into despair, finding neither refuge nor support.

The *sūrah* then takes the unbelievers on a further round of reflection, in the hope that their hearts will awaken when they see the pointers to faith within themselves and in the universe at large:

> *It is He who has endowed you with hearing, and sight, and minds. How seldom are you grateful. And He it is who caused you to multiply on earth; and to Him you shall be gathered. And He it is who grants life and causes death; and to Him is due the alternation of night and day. Will you not, then, use your reason?* (Verses 78–80)

Indeed if man would only reflect on his own form and constitution, the multi-faceted potential he has been given, and the faculties of perception with which he has been blessed, he would certainly acknowledge God. His guidance would be all these great faculties within him that testify to God's oneness. No one other than God Almighty could produce such a creation with all these miraculous aspects, large and small. For example, how does our sense of hearing function? How are sounds picked up and distinguished? How does our eyesight function, sorting out shapes and shades of light? And then, what about our mind and how it works? How does it recognize forms and things? How does it understand meanings, concepts, values, feelings and physical forms?

The mere understanding of the nature of these senses and faculties and their ways of functioning is, in itself, a miraculous human discovery. How do we, then, look at their creation and placement in man's body in such a way that is best suited to the nature of man's world. The degree of harmony achieved here reflects an overwhelming delicacy. Should only one of the many ratios that need to be met, in either man's nature or the nature of the universe, be disturbed, the whole relation no longer functions. Ears are not able to pick out sound, and eyes no longer see light. It is God's perfect design and limitless power that has achieved this perfect balance between human nature and the universe in which man lives. But man does not show gratitude to God for His favours: "*How seldom are you grateful.*" (Verse 78) Gratitude begins with a clear acknowledgement of the One who has given us all these favours and blessings, glorifying Him and recognizing His attributes, then addressing all worship to Him alone. His oneness is testified by His creation. Gratitude is further enhanced when we use our faculties and senses to enjoy life in the manner of a firm believer who looks up to God before every action and in every situation.

"*And He it is who caused you to multiply on earth.*" (Verse 79) He has placed you in charge of building human life on earth, after He gave you your hearing, eyesight and mind, as well as all the faculties and potentials that you need to fulfil the task assigned to you. "*And to Him you shall be gathered,*" when you will be accountable for all that you do in your lives on earth. You will be rewarded for all the good you do, and for following divine guidance. By contrast, you will reap the fruits of any evil or corruption of which you are guilty. Your lives on earth are not meant in vain, and you are not carelessly abandoned in your habitat. It is all for a definite purpose God has determined.

"*And He it is who grants life and causes death.*" (Verse 80) Both life and death occur at every moment, but it is God alone who causes them both to occur. Man, the highest of all creatures on earth, cannot give life to a single cell. Similarly, man is totally incapable of depriving any living being of its life in the full sense of the word. People may be the means of ending life, but they are not the ones who truly deprive a living entity of its life. It is God alone who grants life and causes death.

"*And to Him is due the alternation of night and day.*" (Verse 80) He is the One who has set this alternation in operation, just like He grants life and takes it away. Both sets of parallel situations are natural laws: one operates within the human being while the other operates in the world at large. When life is taken away from a particular body, it stops functioning and becomes motionless. Similarly, when light is taken away from the earth it darkens and becomes stagnant. But then life is brought back again and light is allowed to spread as the alternation takes place and the cycle continues uninterrupted, for as long as God wills. "*Will you not, then, use your reason?*" (Verse 80) Will you not draw the right conclusion and admit that it is all part of God's perfect design and elaborate planning. It is He alone who is in full control of life and the universe.

Questions with One Answer

The *sūrah* now stops its argument with the unbelievers, and reports their claims about resurrection and reckoning in the life to come. This discussion follows a long list of signs and pointers confirming God's oneness and His being the only Creator who causes life and death.

> *But they say like the people of old times used to say. They say: 'What! After we have died and become dust and bones, shall we be raised to life? This we have been promised before, we and our forefathers! This is nothing but fables of the ancients.'* (Verses 81–83)

Their claims sound exceptionally singular after the *sūrah* has enumerated many of the signs that testify to God's elaborate planning and His definite purpose of creation. It is He who has granted man his hearing, eyesight and mind, so that he is responsible for his deeds. He will thus earn a generous reward for his good actions or punishment for his bad ones. True reckoning and reward occur in full in the life to come. What we see in this life is that reward, whether good or bad, does not take place on earth. These are left until they fall due in the life to come.

God grants life and causes death. Hence, resurrection is by no means difficult. Life is breathed into beings at every moment, and it is only God who knows where it originates.

The point with these unbelievers is not that they fall short of appreciating God's wisdom and ability to resurrect life. They also ridicule the promises of resurrection and reward, saying that the same promise was given to their forefathers, but nothing of the sort has yet occurred. "*This we have been promised before, we and our forefathers! This is nothing but fables of the ancients.*" (Verse 83) Resurrection will certainly occur at the time and place God has set for it in His elaborate plan. It will be neither brought forward nor put back at anyone's request, or in response to the ridicule of anyone who is unable to see the truth.

The Arab idolaters of old were muddled in their faith. They did not deny God. Nor did they deny that He is the Creator of the heavens and earth or that He is always in full control of everything in the universe. But they, nevertheless, assigned to Him partners and claimed that they worshipped those partners so that they could bring them closer to God. They also claimed that He had daughters. Exalted is God above all such claims. Hence the *sūrah* puts to them the facts that they acknowledge in order to set the record straight and bring them back to the true faith based on God's absolute oneness. This is the logical conclusion to the premises they acknowledge. Indeed, they would have arrived at this conclusion themselves had they not deviated from their uncorrupted nature:

> *Say: 'To whom belongs the earth and all that lives therein? [Tell me] if you know.' They will reply: 'To God.' Say: 'Will you not, then,*

> *reflect?' Say: 'Who is the Lord of the seven heavens, and the Lord of the Supreme Throne?' They will reply: '[They all belong] to God.' Say: 'Will you not, then, fear Him?' Say: 'In whose hand rests the sovereignty of all things, protecting all, while against Him there is no protection? [Tell me] if you know.' They will reply: '[They all belong] to God.' Say: 'How, then, can you be so deluded?'* (Verses 84–89)

This shows the extent of the confusion that lacks sound reasoning. It tells us to what extent the beliefs of the idolaters had degenerated by the time Islam was revealed. The first question asks about the ownership of this earthly world: "*Say: To whom belongs the earth and all that lives therein? [Tell me] if you know.*" (Verse 84) They acknowledge that they all belong to God, but they overlook this true fact when they address their worship to deities other than Him. Hence the question the Prophet is told to put to them: "*Say: Will you not, then, reflect?*" (Verse 85)

"*Say: Who is the Lord of the seven heavens, and the Lord of the Supreme Throne?*" (Verse 86) This question is about absolute Lordship that controls the whole universe and God's Supreme Throne. The term 'seven heavens' may refer to seven celestial bodies, or solar systems, or seven clusters of stars, or seven galaxies, or any seven astronomical entities. When God's Throne is mentioned, it implies a reference to His might and control of the universe and all existence. Hence when they are asked about the Lordship over all these, they give the right answer, saying that they all belong to God. Yet they do not show any fear of the Lord of the Supreme Throne who controls all seven heavens and what lies beyond them. They associate with Him idols that cannot lift themselves when they are thrown on the ground. Hence, the question: "*Say: Will you not, then, fear Him?*" (Verse 87)

"*Say: In whose hand rests the sovereignty of all things, protecting all, while against Him there is no protection? [Tell me] if you know.*" (Verse 88) This question is about power and dominion, asking them about the One who has power over all things, and who gives protection to all of His creatures so that no one can harm them in any way, other than according to His will. At the same time, no one can protect anyone or anything else against God. If God wants to inflict harm or punishment on any of His creatures, nothing can prevent it. Again they acknowledge that such power belongs to God alone. Hence the question asking them about the cause of their delusion, which leaves them like people bewitched: "*Say: How, then, can you be so deluded?*" (Verse 89)

The True Concept of God

Having refuted all the idolaters' claims about God, taking to Himself a son or partners, the *sūrah* states in all clarity the true principle of God's oneness as explained by His Messenger, the Prophet Muḥammad (peace be upon him):

> *Nay, We have revealed to them the truth; and yet, they are certainly lying. Never did God take to Himself any offspring, nor has there ever been any deity alongside Him. Had there been any, each deity would surely have taken away his own creation, and they would surely have tried to establish superiority over one another. Limitless in His glory is God, far above all that which they attribute to Him. He knows all that is beyond the reach of human perception, and all that can be witnessed. Sublimely exalted is He above anything they associate as partner with Him.* (Verses 90–92)

Note how this statement employs different methods and styles. First, all argument with the idolaters is closed, and an emphatic assertion of their lying is given: "*Nay, We have revealed to them the truth; and yet, they are certainly lying.*" (Verse 90) Then follow some of the details of their lies: "*Never did God take to Himself any offspring, nor has there ever been any deity alongside Him.*" (Verse 91) Irrefutable proof is then stated rendering all their claims false and showing the absurdity of pagan beliefs based on associating partners with God: "*Had there been any each deity would surely have taken away his own creation.*" (Verse 91) Each deity would stress his independence and conduct the affairs of his creation according to his own law. Thus, every part of the universe, and every group of creatures would have a different basis and laws. There would be no common code applying to them all. Hence, those deities "*would surely have tried to establish superiority over one another.*" (Verse 91) Such superiority could take the form of a more sophisticated law operating in a particular part of the universe. However, the universe as a whole cannot function properly unless it is subject to a single law that applies to all its parts and all creatures living in it.

None of this multiplicity is found in the universe, where consistency of structure proves the oneness of its Creator, and inner harmony testifies to its being run by a single will. Indeed, we clearly see that all parts of the universe function in perfect harmony: "*Limitless in His glory is God, far above all that which they attribute to Him.*" (Verse 91)

"*He knows all that is beyond the reach of human perception, and all that can be witnessed.*" (Verse 92) None other than God has any authority over any part of His creation, knowing anything that is unknown to God. "*Sublimely exalted is He above anything they associate as a partner with Him.*" (Verse 92)

At this point, the *sūrah* stops addressing or speaking about them. It now turns its attention to God's Messenger, commanding him to appeal to God so that he is not placed with such people, if he ever witnesses the fulfilment of the warnings of suffering they have been given. He is further instructed to seek refuge with His Lord from the evil ones, satans, so as not to be irritated by or become fed up at what the unbelievers claim:

> *Say: 'My Lord! If it be Your will to show me that which they are warned against, then, my Lord, do not let me be one of those wrongdoing folk.' We are most certainly able to show you that which We promise them. Repel evil with that which is best. We are fully aware of all that they say. And say: 'My Lord! I seek refuge with You from the promptings of the evil ones; and I seek refuge with You, my Lord, lest they come near me.'* (Verses 93–98)

The Prophet is certainly not going to be with the wrongdoers when God inflicts on them a severe punishment in fulfilment of His warnings. But this prayer which he is instructed to repeat serves as a further precaution. It is also meant as a lesson to all believers so that they do not slacken. They should also be on their guard, attending to their duties, seeking refuge with God and praying to Him to bestow His grace on them.

God is certainly able to fulfil what He has warned the wrongdoers of, and to make it all happen during the lifetime of His Messenger: "*We are most certainly able to show you that which We promise them.*" (Verse 95) He certainly showed him some of it in the Battle of Badr and then when Makkah surrendered to Islam.

However, at the time of the revelation of this *sūrah*, the Prophet was still in Makkah enduring with his followers much persecution from the idolaters. The policy followed by the Muslim community then, in implementation of God's instructions, was to repel a bad thing with something better. Muslims also had to demonstrate their patience in the face of adversity, leaving their destiny entirely to God: "*Repel evil with that which is best. We are fully aware of all that they say.*" (Verse 96)

The Prophet was certainly immune to any promptings or persuasion by evil ones. However, here he is instructed to pray for protection against all this in an urgent appeal for further immunity against their evil. Being the perfect role model for all Muslims in all generations, his appeal provides a lead for them to follow. They should also seek refuge with God against all temptation put in their way by the evil ones. Indeed the Prophet is instructed to appeal to God for protection against such evil people coming near him in any way. "*I seek refuge with You, my Lord, lest they come near me.*" (Verse 98)

This may also be interpreted as an appeal lest they come near him at the time of his death. This sense is strengthened by the verse that follows: "*When death approaches any of them, he says: My Lord! Let me return [to life].*" (Verse 99) This follows the Qur'ānic method that ensures an easy flow from one point to another.

4

Justice and Grace

When death approaches any of them, he says: ‘My Lord! Let me return [to life], (99)

حَتَّىٰٓ إِذَا جَآءَ أَحَدَهُمُ ٱلۡمَوۡتُ قَالَ
رَبِّ ٱرۡجِعُونِ ٩٩

so that I may act righteously in whatever I have failed to do.’ By no means! It is but a word he says. Behind them there stands a barrier till the day when all will be raised from the dead. (100)

لَعَلِّيٓ أَعۡمَلُ صَٰلِحٗا فِيمَا تَرَكۡتُۚ كَلَّآۚ
إِنَّهَا كَلِمَةٌ هُوَ قَآئِلُهَاۖ وَمِن وَرَآئِهِم
بَرۡزَخٌ إِلَىٰ يَوۡمِ يُبۡعَثُونَ ١٠٠

Then, when the trumpet is sounded, there will be no ties of kinship between them on that day, nor will they ask about one another. (101)

فَإِذَا نُفِخَ فِي ٱلصُّورِ فَلَآ أَنسَابَ بَيۡنَهُمۡ
يَوۡمَئِذٖ وَلَا يَتَسَآءَلُونَ ١٠١

Those whose weight [of good deeds] is heavy in the scales will be successful; (102)

فَمَن ثَقُلَتۡ مَوَٰزِينُهُۥ فَأُوْلَٰٓئِكَ هُمُ
ٱلۡمُفۡلِحُونَ ١٠٢

but those whose weight is light will have lost their souls and will abide in hell. (103)

وَمَنۡ خَفَّتۡ مَوَٰزِينُهُۥ فَأُوْلَٰٓئِكَ
ٱلَّذِينَ خَسِرُوٓاْ أَنفُسَهُمۡ فِي جَهَنَّمَ
خَٰلِدُونَ ١٠٣

تَلْفَحُ وُجُوهَهُمُ ٱلنَّارُ وَهُمْ فِيهَا
كَـٰلِحُونَ ١٠٤

The fire will scorch their faces, and therein they will look gloomy. (104)

أَلَمْ تَكُنْ ءَايَـٰتِى تُتْلَىٰ عَلَيْكُمْ فَكُنتُم
بِهَا تُكَذِّبُونَ ١٠٥

'Were not My revelations read out to you, and did you not consider them as lies?' (105)

قَالُوا۟ رَبَّنَا غَلَبَتْ عَلَيْنَا شِقْوَتُنَا
وَكُنَّا قَوْمًا ضَآلِّينَ ١٠٦

They will reply: 'Our Lord! Our misfortune has overwhelmed us, and so we went astray. (106)

رَبَّنَآ أَخْرِجْنَا مِنْهَا فَإِنْ عُدْنَا فَإِنَّا
ظَـٰلِمُونَ ١٠٧

Our Lord! Bring us out of this [suffering]. If ever We relapse, then we shall be wrongdoers indeed.' (107)

قَالَ ٱخْسَـُٔوا۟ فِيهَا وَلَا تُكَلِّمُونِ ١٠٨

He will say: 'Away with you into this ignominy! And do not plead with Me. (108)

إِنَّهُۥ كَانَ فَرِيقٌ مِّنْ عِبَادِى يَقُولُونَ
رَبَّنَآ ءَامَنَّا فَٱغْفِرْ لَنَا وَٱرْحَمْنَا وَأَنتَ
خَيْرُ ٱلرَّٰحِمِينَ ١٠٩

Among My servants there were those who said: "Our Lord! We believe in You. Forgive us and have mercy on us; for You are the best of those who show mercy." (109)

فَٱتَّخَذْتُمُوهُمْ سِخْرِيًّا حَتَّىٰٓ أَنسَوْكُمْ ذِكْرِى
وَكُنتُم مِّنْهُمْ تَضْحَكُونَ ١١٠

But you made them the target of your derision to the point where it made you forget all remembrance of Me; and you went on laughing at them. (110)

Today I have rewarded them for their patience in adversity. Indeed it is they who have achieved triumph.' (111)

إِنِّي جَزَيۡتُهُمُ ٱلۡيَوۡمَ بِمَا صَبَرُوٓاْ أَنَّهُمۡ
هُمُ ٱلۡفَآئِزُونَ ١١١

And He will ask: 'How many years have you spent on earth?' (112)

قَٰلَ كَمۡ لَبِثۡتُمۡ فِي ٱلۡأَرۡضِ عَدَدَ
سِنِينَ ١١٢

They will answer: 'We have spent there a day, or part of a day; but ask those who keep count.' (113)

قَالُواْ لَبِثۡنَا يَوۡمًا أَوۡ بَعۡضَ يَوۡمٖ فَسۡـَٔلِ
ٱلۡعَآدِّينَ ١١٣

He will say: 'Brief indeed was your sojourn, if you but knew it. (114)

قَٰلَ إِن لَّبِثۡتُمۡ إِلَّا قَلِيلٗاۖ لَّوۡ أَنَّكُمۡ
كُنتُمۡ تَعۡلَمُونَ ١١٤

Did you think that We created you in mere idle play, and that to Us you would not have to return?' (115)

أَفَحَسِبۡتُمۡ أَنَّمَا خَلَقۡنَٰكُمۡ عَبَثٗا
وَأَنَّكُمۡ إِلَيۡنَا لَا تُرۡجَعُونَ ١١٥

Sublimely exalted is God, the Ultimate Sovereign, the Ultimate Truth. There is no deity other than Him, the Lord of the Glorious Throne. (116)

فَتَعَٰلَى ٱللَّهُ ٱلۡمَلِكُ ٱلۡحَقُّۖ لَآ إِلَٰهَ إِلَّا هُوَ
رَبُّ ٱلۡعَرۡشِ ٱلۡكَرِيمِ ١١٦

He that invokes besides God any other deity – a deity for whose existence he has no evidence – shall be brought to account before his Lord. Most certainly, the unbelievers shall never be successful. (117)

وَمَن يَدۡعُ مَعَ ٱللَّهِ إِلَٰهًا ءَاخَرَ لَا بُرۡهَٰنَ
لَهُۥ بِهِۦ فَإِنَّمَا حِسَابُهُۥ عِندَ رَبِّهِۦٓۚ إِنَّهُۥ
لَا يُفۡلِحُ ٱلۡكَٰفِرُونَ ١١٧

Say: 'My Lord! Forgive and have mercy. You are the best of those who show mercy.' (118)	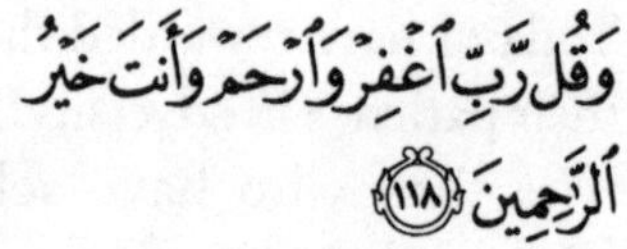

Overview

This last passage of the *sūrah* continues to discuss the fate of the idolaters, showing it in a complete scene of the Day of Resurrection. It starts with an image of approaching death ending this life, and moves on to show what happens after the Trumpet is blown and the dead are brought back to life. This is followed by an emphatic statement of God's oneness, coupled with a stern warning to those who associate partners with God, putting them on notice of what awaits them if they persist in their erring ways. The *sūrah* concludes with a directive given to the Prophet to seek God's forgiveness, and to pray for His grace. God is certainly the best of all who show mercy.

As Death Approaches

"*When death approaches any of them, he says: My Lord! Let me return [to life], so that I may act righteously in whatever I have failed to do.*" (Verses 99–100) This is the scene of approaching death, when the person is certain that he is about to die. At this moment, he appeals for a return to life so as to have a second chance to do what he should have done in the first place. He wants to set things right with regard to the family and assets he is leaving behind. This is shown as if it is happening at the present moment, witnessed by all. But the appeal is made too late. Hence, the answer is not given to the person concerned. It is declared for all to understand. "*By no means! It is but a word he says.*" (Verse 100)

It is only a word that carries little or no significance. It does not deserve to be considered. Indeed the speaker does not merit any attention. It does not express any sincerity; rather, it is prompted by the dawning awareness of the great difficulty ahead. It expresses the great stress the speaker finds himself under, but it has no basis in conviction.

Thus ends the image of the speaker at the point of death. Suddenly, barriers are raised between him and the rest of the world. The matter is settled, contacts are severed, doors closed and the curtain dropped: "*Behind them there stands a barrier till the day when all will be raised from the dead.*" (Verse 100) They neither belong to the people of this life, nor to those of the hereafter. They are in the stage in between, which will continue until all are resurrected.

The *sūrah* now speaks about that day, giving an image of what happens then and raising it for all to see. "*Then, when the Trumpet is sounded, there will be no ties of kinship between them on that day, nor will they ask about one another.*" (Verse 101) All bonds come to an end, and all values people observe in this life are no longer of any consequence. '*There will be no ties of kinship*' then. The awesome atmosphere makes them all silent, with no one uttering as much as a word, let alone enquiring about others.

The process of reckoning and weighing up deeds and actions is shown to proceed with speed: "*Those whose weight [of good deeds] is heavy in the scales will be successful; but those whose weight is light will have lost their souls and will abide in hell. The fire will scorch their faces, and therein they will look gloomy.*" (Verses 102–104) This process is shown in a material image, with action and movement taking place, in the standard pattern the Qur'ān employs. Hence we dread the scene of those idolaters being scorched by the fire, their faces changing colour, darkening and looking full of gloom. It is a terrible image that almost transmits pain.

Those with light weight have lost everything, including themselves. When a man loses himself, what else can he own? What is left for him? He has lost the very thing that makes his existence meaningful, or that gives him personality.

At this point the *sūrah* changes style. So far, it has employed a reporting format. Now it makes a direct address, speaking to the people themselves. This makes the physical punishment, terrible as it certainly is, much less painful than the humiliation that is now poured on them. This address is stated as if it were taking place at that very moment, starting a long dialogue: "*Were not My revelations read out to you, and did you not consider them as lies?*" (Verse 105) When they hear this question they imagine that they are allowed to speak and make a plea. They think that perhaps if they admit their guilt, their plea might be accepted: "*They will reply: Our Lord! Our misfortune has overwhelmed us, and so we went astray. Our Lord! Bring us out of this [suffering]. If ever We relapse, then we shall be wrongdoers indeed.*" (Verses 106–107)

Their admission of guilt tells of the bitter feelings they experience. They are indeed miserable. But they have exceeded the limits they are allowed. To go beyond these is to be impolite when they are addressed by none other than God. They are only permitted to answer the question put to them. Indeed the question is perhaps made only by way of rebuke, and it requires no answer. Hence they are strongly censured: "*He will say: Away with you into this ignominy! And do not plead with Me.*" (Verse 108) They are told to shut up and remain silent as only befits people held in ignominy.

Indeed they deserve all the punishment and the misery they are made to suffer.

> *Among My servants there were those who said: 'Our Lord! We believe in You. Forgive us and have mercy on us; for You are the best of those who show mercy.' But you made them the target of your derision to the point where it made you forget all remembrance of Me; and you went on laughing at them.* (Verses 109–110)

The crime they perpetrated was not merely that they disbelieved and made their rejection of the faith a personal matter, which is in itself a grave offence. They went much further by allowing their stupid impudence to go as far as ridiculing the believers who pray to God for mercy and forgiveness. They derided them so often that such derision became their main preoccupation, stopping them from remembering God and glorifying Him, and from reflecting on the numerous signs God has placed in the world pointing them in the direction of faith. They are now called upon to compare their own station with that of the people they ridiculed. "*Today I have rewarded them for their patience in adversity. Indeed it is they who have achieved triumph.*" (Verse 111)

A new phase of interrogation follows this stern, humiliating reply and the reasons that led to it: "*And He will ask: How many years have you spent on earth?*" (Verse 112) God certainly knows the answer, but the question is put to them to emphasize the triviality of life on earth and to stress the shortness of its duration. Yet they bartered the eternal life of the hereafter for their portion of life on earth. Now they feel that it was totally insignificant. In their despair they are impatient, and cannot bother about that life or its number of years: "*They will answer: We have spent there a day, or part of a day; but ask those who keep count.*" (Verse 113) Stress, grief and despair ooze from their reply.

They are given an answer that tells them that their life on earth is very short compared to what awaits them. They only need to have the right measure. "*He will say: Brief indeed was your sojourn, if you but knew it.*" (Verse 114) Again they are strongly rebuked for denying the life to come. This is coupled with an outline of the purpose behind resurrection. This purpose has been clearly stated ever since the first creation: "*Did you think that We created you in mere idle play, and that to Us you would not have to return?*" (Verse 115)

Indeed the purpose, or rather the wisdom behind resurrection is part of the wisdom behind creation. It is all well measured and accurately designed. Resurrection is no more than a stage that brings the cycle of creation to its fullness. Only those who remain blind, unwilling to reflect on God's purpose which is clearly evident everywhere in the universe around us, will not see it.

The Basic Issue of Faith

The final verses of the *sūrah* are dedicated to faith. They state its central tenet; namely, God's oneness. We have an announcement of the great loss suffered by those who associate partners with Him. This contrasts with the success declared at the beginning of the *sūrah* which is guaranteed to the believers. Coupled with this declaration is an instruction to turn to God, requesting His forgiveness and appealing for His mercy. He is certainly the most merciful of all those who are compassionate:

> *Sublimely exalted is God, the Ultimate Sovereign, the Ultimate Truth. There is no deity other than Him, the Lord of the Glorious Throne. He that invokes besides God any other deity – a deity for whose existence he has no evidence – shall be brought to account before his Lord. Most certainly, the unbelievers shall never be successful. Say: My Lord! Forgive and have mercy. You are the best of those who show mercy.* (Verses 116–118)

Coming as it does after a scene painting events taking place on the Day of Resurrection, and after a host of arguments, proofs and pointers outlined throughout the *sūrah*, the comment included in these final verses provides a logical conclusion to everything contained in the *sūrah*. This statement refutes all that the unbelievers say about God, declaring that He is the true Sovereign who controls the entire universe, and that He is the only deity who is in full command of all. He is indeed 'the Lord of the Glorious Throne'.

Any claim of partnership with God has absolutely no evidence to support it, neither from the universe and how it is run, nor from human logic or nature. Anyone who makes such a claim will have to face the reckoning in front of God, and the result is known in advance: "*Most certainly the unbelievers shall never be successful.*" (Verse 117) This is an unfailing rule that is bound to come true. Success, by contrast, is guaranteed for the believers.

All the favours and comforts that we see the unbelievers enjoying in this life, and all the power and resources they may sometimes have at their command does not mean success in reality. It is all given to them as a test, and it will end with their loss in this present life. However, if some of them escape punishment in this world, they will have to face the reckoning in the hereafter. There, in the life to come, is the final stage of this life cycle. It is not something separate or isolated. Indeed, it is an essential stage, clearly seen by those who have real vision.

The last verse in this *sūrah*, The Believers, gives the instruction to turn to God appealing for His mercy and forgiveness: "*Say: My Lord! Forgive and have mercy. You are the best of those who show mercy.*" (Verse 118)

Thus the opening of the *sūrah* and its end jointly emphasize success for the believers and utter failure and loss for the unbelievers. Both elements stress the basic qualities of believers. Thus, the beginning states that the believers humble themselves in prayer, while the end instructs them to humbly appeal to God for forgiveness and mercy. Both make the *sūrah* a complete, well designed unit.

SŪRAH 24

Al-Nūr

(Light)

Prologue

This *sūrah* is named *al-Nūr,* meaning The Light, and light is identified as an essential attribute of God: "*God is the light of the heavens and the earth.*" (Verse 35) It is also mentioned in respect of its effects on people's hearts and souls. Such effects are reflected in human morality and the manners of individuals, families and communities. They impart a brightness to human life that enlightens hearts and makes consciences transparent.

The *sūrah* begins with an emphatic declaration of the fact that it is bestowed from on high, and that it is decreed with all that it contains of directives, commandments and morality: "*A* sūrah *which We have bestowed from on high and which We have ordained; and in it have We revealed clear verses, so that you may keep them in mind.*" (Verse 1) This opening reflects the importance the Qur'ān attaches to the moral aspect of human life, and to its central position in the Islamic faith.

The central theme of the entire *sūrah* is the education of the Muslim community. At times, the methods employed by the *sūrah* increase in their stiffness so as to culminate in prescribing mandatory punishments. At other times the *sūrah* is softer and more gentle, filling our hearts with God's light and inviting us to reflect on the numerous signs He has placed throughout the entire universe. The aim of such contrasting approaches is one and the same: to cultivate people's consciences, enhance their sensitivity and refine their moral standards to the highest degree. The good manners of the individual, the family, the community and society's leadership are all intertwined as they all stem from the same source, which is belief in God, and shine with the same light received from Him. In essence, these manners combine light, transparency and brightness. Thus the education the *sūrah* aims to achieve derives all its aspects from the basic source of light in the heavens and earth; that is, God's light that dispels all darkness in the universe, as well as that in people's hearts and souls.

The *sūrah* may be divided into five parts, all tackling its basic theme. At the outset, the first delivers a decisive declaration outlining the status of this *sūrah*, followed by the details of the mandatory punishment for adultery. It denounces this crime in clear terms, making it clear that adulterers have no place in the Muslim community. It also explains the punishment for any false accusation of adultery, and the reasons for the severity of this mandatory punishment. Couples are exempted from this punishment when they take the prescribed oaths that end with their permanent separation. It then comments on the falsehood story. At the end it shows how men and women flock like with like: the good with the good and the evil with the evil.

The second part concerns itself with crime prevention, and the methods to reduce the temptation to sin. It begins with an outline of good manners when approaching others' homes and the need to seek permission before entry. It commands Muslims to lower their gaze and not to reveal women's charms and adornments to anyone other than their very close relatives whom they are not legally entitled to marry. There is also in this part a clear encouragement to facilitate the marriage of young women, and a stern warning against forcing slave girls into prostitution. All these are preventive measures that aim to promote purity and chastity in general. They aim to prevent what stirs up physical desire and to help people to maintain their chastity.

In the middle of this list of good manners as outlined in the *sūrah*, the third part provides a link between all such manners and God's light. Here the *sūrah* speaks of the people whose hearts are brightened with God's light and who always frequent mosques. By contrast, the unbelievers and their deeds are shown as though they are a mirage, or like layers of darkness. In this part we see different aspects of God's light throughout the universe: how all creatures glorify Him; how clouds are sent through the atmosphere; the succession of day and night; the creation of every walking creature out of water and how they acquire their different shapes, forms, types and roles. All these are there for people to look at and contemplate.

In the fourth part the hypocrites are seen to neglect the proper manners people should show when dealing with the Prophet. The most important of these are obedience to the Prophet and the implementation of any judgement he makes in disputes put to him for arbitration. By contrast, the believers are seen to maintain the appropriate standards in speaking to the Prophet and obeying him. In return, they are promised power, that they will establish and implement their faith and attain victory over the unbelievers.

The final part of the *sūrah* again examines the good manners of the Muslim community, highlighting the need to seek admission when visiting relatives and friends, of hospitality to guests, and the fine manners that make the whole Muslim community a single family, led by God's Messenger (peace be upon him).

The *sūrah* concludes with a declaration of God's ownership of all that is in the heavens and earth, His knowledge of people and what they harbour in their breasts, and their ultimate return to Him. They will have to face His reckoning on the basis of His knowledge of their deeds. Needless to say, His knowledge encompasses everything.

I

The Mandatory Punishment for Adultery

Al-Nūr (Light)

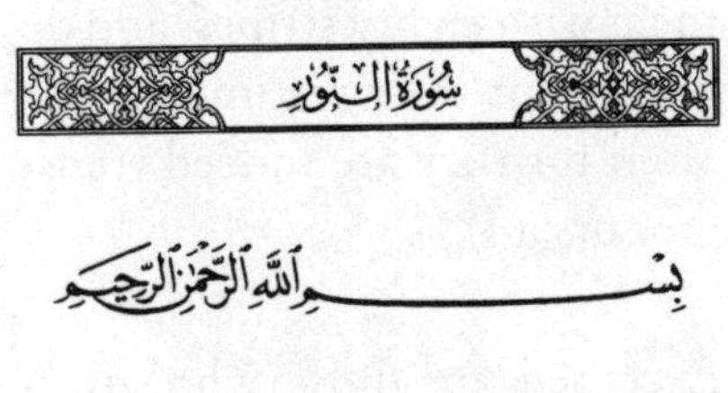

In the Name of God, the Merciful, the Beneficent

[This is] a *sūrah* which We have bestowed from on high and which We have ordained; and in it have We revealed clear verses, so that you may keep them in mind. (1)

سُورَةٌ أَنزَلْنَاهَا وَفَرَضْنَاهَا وَأَنزَلْنَا فِيهَا آيَاتٍ
بَيِّنَاتٍ لَّعَلَّكُمْ تَذَكَّرُونَ ١

As for the adulteress and the adulterer, flog each of them with a hundred stripes, and let not compassion for them keep you from [carrying out] this law of God, if you truly believe in God and the Last Day; and let a number of believers witness their punishment. (2)

الزَّانِيَةُ وَالزَّانِي فَاجْلِدُوا كُلَّ وَاحِدٍ مِّنْهُمَا مِائَةَ
جَلْدَةٍ ۖ وَلَا تَأْخُذْكُم بِهِمَا رَأْفَةٌ فِي دِينِ اللَّهِ
إِن كُنتُمْ تُؤْمِنُونَ بِاللَّهِ وَالْيَوْمِ
الْآخِرِ ۖ وَلْيَشْهَدْ عَذَابَهُمَا طَائِفَةٌ مِّنَ
الْمُؤْمِنِينَ ٢

The adulterer couples with none other than an adulteress or an idolatress; and with the adulteress couples none other than an adulterer or an idolater. This is forbidden to the believers. (3)

ٱلزَّانِى لَا يَنكِحُ إِلَّا زَانِيَةً أَوْ مُشْرِكَةً
وَٱلزَّانِيَةُ لَا يَنكِحُهَآ إِلَّا زَانٍ أَوْ مُشْرِكٌ ۚ
وَحُرِّمَ ذَٰلِكَ عَلَى ٱلْمُؤْمِنِينَ ﴿٣﴾

As for those who accuse chaste women [of adultery], and cannot produce four witnesses, flog them with eighty stripes; and do not accept their testimony ever after; for they are indeed transgressors. (4)

وَٱلَّذِينَ يَرْمُونَ ٱلْمُحْصَنَٰتِ ثُمَّ لَمْ يَأْتُوا۟
بِأَرْبَعَةِ شُهَدَآءَ فَٱجْلِدُوهُمْ ثَمَٰنِينَ جَلْدَةً
وَلَا تَقْبَلُوا۟ لَهُمْ شَهَٰدَةً أَبَدًا ۚ وَأُو۟لَٰٓئِكَ
هُمُ ٱلْفَٰسِقُونَ ﴿٤﴾

Excepted are those who afterwards repent and make amends; for God is Much-Forgiving, Merciful. (5)

إِلَّا ٱلَّذِينَ تَابُوا۟ مِنۢ بَعْدِ ذَٰلِكَ وَأَصْلَحُوا۟ فَإِنَّ
ٱللَّهَ غَفُورٌ رَّحِيمٌ ﴿٥﴾

And as for those who accuse their own wives [of adultery], but have no witnesses except themselves, let each of them call God four times to witness that he is indeed telling the truth; (6)

وَٱلَّذِينَ يَرْمُونَ أَزْوَٰجَهُمْ وَلَمْ يَكُن لَّهُمْ شُهَدَآءُ
إِلَّآ أَنفُسُهُمْ فَشَهَٰدَةُ أَحَدِهِمْ أَرْبَعُ شَهَٰدَٰتٍۭ
بِٱللَّهِ ۙ إِنَّهُۥ لَمِنَ ٱلصَّٰدِقِينَ ﴿٦﴾

and the fifth time, that God's curse be upon him if he is telling a lie. (7)

وَٱلْخَٰمِسَةُ أَنَّ لَعْنَتَ ٱللَّهِ عَلَيْهِ إِن كَانَ
مِنَ ٱلْكَٰذِبِينَ ﴿٧﴾

However, punishment is averted from her if she calls God four times to witness that he is indeed telling a lie; (8)

وَيَدْرَؤُا۟ عَنْهَا ٱلْعَذَابَ أَن تَشْهَدَ أَرْبَعَ
شَهَٰدَٰتٍۭ بِٱللَّهِ ۙ إِنَّهُۥ لَمِنَ ٱلْكَٰذِبِينَ ﴿٨﴾

and the fifth time, that God's wrath be upon her if he is telling the truth. (9)

وَٱلْخَٰمِسَةَ أَنَّ غَضَبَ ٱللَّهِ عَلَيْهَآ إِن كَانَ
مِنَ ٱلصَّٰدِقِينَ ﴿٩﴾

Were it not for God's favour upon you and His grace, and that God is the One who accepts repentance, the Wise…! (10)

وَلَوْلَا فَضْلُ ٱللَّهِ عَلَيْكُمْ وَرَحْمَتُهُۥ وَأَنَّ
ٱللَّهَ تَوَّابٌ حَكِيمٌ ﴿١٠﴾

Those who concocted the falsehood were a band from among you. Do not regard it as bad for you; indeed it is good for you. Each one of them shall bear what he has earned of sin; and awesome suffering awaits the one who took on himself the lead among them. (11)

إِنَّ ٱلَّذِينَ جَآءُو بِٱلْإِفْكِ عُصْبَةٌ مِّنكُمْ
لَا تَحْسَبُوهُ شَرًّا لَّكُم بَلْ هُوَ خَيْرٌ لَّكُمْ
لِكُلِّ ٱمْرِئٍ مِّنْهُم مَّا ٱكْتَسَبَ مِنَ
ٱلْإِثْمِ وَٱلَّذِى تَوَلَّىٰ كِبْرَهُۥ مِنْهُمْ لَهُۥ
عَذَابٌ عَظِيمٌ ﴿١١﴾

When you heard it, why did not the believers, men and women, think the best of themselves, and say: 'This is a blatant falsehood.' (12)

لَّوْلَآ إِذْ سَمِعْتُمُوهُ ظَنَّ ٱلْمُؤْمِنُونَ
وَٱلْمُؤْمِنَٰتُ بِأَنفُسِهِمْ خَيْرًا
وَقَالُوا۟ هَٰذَآ إِفْكٌ مُّبِينٌ ﴿١٢﴾

Why did they not produce four witnesses to prove it? Since they have not produced witnesses, then in the sight of God, they are certainly liars. (13)

لَّوْلَا جَآءُو عَلَيْهِ بِأَرْبَعَةِ شُهَدَآءَ فَإِذْ لَمْ
يَأْتُوا۟ بِٱلشُّهَدَآءِ فَأُو۟لَٰٓئِكَ عِندَ ٱللَّهِ
هُمُ ٱلْكَٰذِبُونَ ﴿١٣﴾

Were it not for God's favour upon you and His grace, in this world and in the life to come, awesome suffering would indeed have afflicted you on account of what you indulged in. (14)

وَلَوْلَا فَضْلُ ٱللَّهِ عَلَيْكُمْ وَرَحْمَتُهُۥ فِى
ٱلدُّنْيَا وَٱلْءَاخِرَةِ لَمَسَّكُمْ فِى مَآ أَفَضْتُمْ
فِيهِ عَذَابٌ عَظِيمٌ ﴿١٤﴾

You took it up with your tongues and uttered with your mouths something of which you have no knowledge, thinking it a light matter whereas in God's sight it is grave indeed. (15)

إِذْ تَلَقَّوْنَهُۥ بِأَلْسِنَتِكُمْ وَتَقُولُونَ
بِأَفْوَاهِكُم مَّا لَيْسَ لَكُم بِهِۦ عِلْمٌ
وَتَحْسَبُونَهُۥ هَيِّنًا وَهُوَ عِندَ ٱللَّهِ
عَظِيمٌ ﴿١٥﴾

If only when you heard it you said: 'It is not right for us to speak of this! All glory belongs to You. This is a monstrous slander.' (16)

وَلَوْلَآ إِذْ سَمِعْتُمُوهُ قُلْتُم مَّا يَكُونُ
لَنَآ أَن نَّتَكَلَّمَ بِهَٰذَا سُبْحَٰنَكَ هَٰذَا
بُهْتَٰنٌ عَظِيمٌ ﴿١٦﴾

God admonishes you lest you ever revert to the like of this, if you are truly believers. (17)

يَعِظُكُمُ ٱللَّهُ أَن تَعُودُوا۟ لِمِثْلِهِۦٓ أَبَدًا إِن
كُنتُم مُّؤْمِنِينَ ﴿١٧﴾

And God makes plain to you His revelations. God is All-Knowing, Wise. (18)

وَيُبَيِّنُ ٱللَّهُ لَكُمُ ٱلْءَايَٰتِ ۚ وَٱللَّهُ عَلِيمٌ
حَكِيمٌ ﴿١٨﴾

Those who love that gross indecency should spread among the believers shall be visited with grievous suffering both in this world and in the life to come. God knows, but you do not know. (19)

إِنَّ ٱلَّذِينَ يُحِبُّونَ أَن تَشِيعَ ٱلْفَٰحِشَةُ
فِى ٱلَّذِينَ ءَامَنُوا۟ لَهُمْ عَذَابٌ أَلِيمٌ فِى
ٱلدُّنْيَا وَٱلْءَاخِرَةِ ۚ وَٱللَّهُ يَعْلَمُ وَأَنتُمْ
لَا تَعْلَمُونَ ﴿١٩﴾

Were it not for God's favour upon you and His grace, and that God is Compassionate, Merciful …! (20)

وَلَوْلَا فَضْلُ ٱللَّهِ عَلَيْكُمْ وَرَحْمَتُهُۥ
وَأَنَّ ٱللَّهَ رَءُوفٌ رَّحِيمٌ ٢٠

Believers! Do not follow Satan's footsteps, for he who follows Satan's footsteps will only enjoin what is shameful and wrong. Were it not for God's favour upon you and His grace, none of you would have ever been pure. It is God who causes whomever He wills to grow in purity. God is All-Hearing, All-Knowing. (21)

يَٰٓأَيُّهَا ٱلَّذِينَ ءَامَنُوا۟ لَا تَتَّبِعُوا۟ خُطُوَٰتِ
ٱلشَّيْطَٰنِ ۚ وَمَن يَتَّبِعْ خُطُوَٰتِ ٱلشَّيْطَٰنِ
فَإِنَّهُۥ يَأْمُرُ بِٱلْفَحْشَآءِ وَٱلْمُنكَرِ ۚ وَلَوْلَا
فَضْلُ ٱللَّهِ عَلَيْكُمْ وَرَحْمَتُهُۥ مَا زَكَىٰ مِنكُم
مِّنْ أَحَدٍ أَبَدًا وَلَٰكِنَّ ٱللَّهَ يُزَكِّى مَن يَشَآءُ ۗ
وَٱللَّهُ سَمِيعٌ عَلِيمٌ ٢١

Let not those of you who have been graced with God's favour and ample means resolve by oath not to help those who are near of kin, the needy and those who have left their homes for the sake of God. But let them pardon and forbear. Do you not desire that God should forgive you your sins? God is indeed Much-Forgiving, Merciful. (22)

وَلَا يَأْتَلِ أُو۟لُوا۟ ٱلْفَضْلِ مِنكُمْ وَٱلسَّعَةِ
أَن يُؤْتُوٓا۟ أُو۟لِى ٱلْقُرْبَىٰ وَٱلْمَسَٰكِينَ
وَٱلْمُهَٰجِرِينَ فِى سَبِيلِ ٱللَّهِ ۖ وَلْيَعْفُوا۟
وَلْيَصْفَحُوٓا۟ ۗ أَلَا تُحِبُّونَ أَن يَغْفِرَ ٱللَّهُ
لَكُمْ ۗ وَٱللَّهُ غَفُورٌ رَّحِيمٌ ٢٢

Those who accuse chaste women who may have been unthinkingly careless but remained true believers, shall be rejected by God in this world as well as in the life to come. They shall endure awesome suffering; (23)

إِنَّ ٱلَّذِينَ يَرْمُونَ ٱلْمُحْصَنَٰتِ ٱلْغَٰفِلَٰتِ
ٱلْمُؤْمِنَٰتِ لُعِنُوا۟ فِى ٱلدُّنْيَا وَٱلْءَاخِرَةِ
وَلَهُمْ عَذَابٌ عَظِيمٌ ٢٣

on the day when their own tongues, hands and feet will testify to what they did. (24)

يَوْمَ تَشْهَدُ عَلَيْهِمْ أَلْسِنَتُهُمْ وَأَيْدِيهِمْ
وَأَرْجُلُهُم بِمَا كَانُوا۟ يَعْمَلُونَ ﴿٢٤﴾

On that day God will pay them in full their just due, and they will come to know that God alone is the Ultimate Truth, absolutely manifest. (25)

يَوْمَئِذٍ يُوَفِّيهِمُ ٱللَّهُ دِينَهُمُ ٱلْحَقَّ وَيَعْلَمُونَ
أَنَّ ٱللَّهَ هُوَ ٱلْحَقُّ ٱلْمُبِينُ ﴿٢٥﴾

Corrupt women are for corrupt men, and corrupt men for corrupt women, just as good women are for good men, and good men for good women. These are innocent of all that people may impute to them. Forgiveness and excellent sustenance are in store for them. (26)

ٱلْخَبِيثَٰتُ لِلْخَبِيثِينَ وَٱلْخَبِيثُونَ
لِلْخَبِيثَٰتِ وَٱلطَّيِّبَٰتُ لِلطَّيِّبِينَ
وَٱلطَّيِّبُونَ لِلطَّيِّبَٰتِ أُو۟لَٰٓئِكَ
مُبَرَّءُونَ مِمَّا يَقُولُونَ لَهُم مَّغْفِرَةٌ
وَرِزْقٌ كَرِيمٌ ﴿٢٦﴾

An Unusual Beginning

This *sūrah* has a unique opening that is not repeated anywhere else in the Qur'ān. What is special is the use of the clause '*We have ordained*'. We take this to imply an emphatic assertion that people must take everything that the *sūrah* includes in the same way. Social manners and morality are ordained in the same way as mandatory punishments. We need to remember here that such manners and morality are deeply rooted in human nature, but people tend to overlook them because of deviant social pressures and easy temptations. Hence, the divine revelations God has bestowed from on high place them back before people's eyes, explaining the clear logic of undistorted human nature.

This emphatic and clear opening is immediately followed with an explanation of the mandatory punishment for adultery, a ghastly crime that severs the ties between its perpetrator and the Muslim community.

As for the adulteress and the adulterer, flog each of them with a hundred stripes, and let not compassion for them keep you from [carrying out] this law of God, if you truly believe in God and the Last Day; and let a number of believers witness their punishment. The adulterer couples with none other than an adulteress or an idolatress; and with the adulteress couples none other than an adulterer or an idolater. This is forbidden to the believers. (Verses 2–3)

In the early days of Islam, the punishment prescribed for adulterers was that outlined in *Sūrah* 4, Women, which says: "*As for those of your women who are guilty of gross immoral conduct, call upon four from among you to bear witness against them. If they so testify, then confine the guilty women to their houses until death takes them or God opens another way for them.*" (4: 15) Thus the punishment for the guilty adulteress was confinement at home and verbal reprimand, while the adulterer was punished by verbal reprimand only. Sometime later, God revealed the new mandatory punishment specified in this *sūrah*. This is then the 'way' opened by God to which *Sūrah* 4 alluded.

Flogging is the punishment of male and female adulterers who have not been empowered through marriage. This punishment is enforced on any Muslim who is sane, of age and a free person whose guilt is established. As for a person who has had sexual relations within a proper marriage and then commits adultery even though he is sane, of age and free, his punishment is stoning.[1]

Such stoning is confirmed in the *Sunnah*, while flogging is established clearly in the Qur'ān. Since the Qur'ānic statement is phrased in general terms, and the Prophet inflicted stoning on a married man and a married woman who committed adultery, it is clear that the punishment of flogging applies only to adulterers who are unmarried.

---

1. One difference not mentioned by the author relates to whether stoning is mandatory or discretionary. The traditional view is that it is mandatory, but a number of eminent scholars have questioned this, classifying it as discretionary. A discretionary punishment is left to the judge looking into the case, or the ruler, to determine whether to apply it in full, reduce, or even withhold it. A mandatory punishment is stated by God and it must be applied as stated, when the offence is duly proven in accordance with the provision of Islamic law. – Editor's note.

There are several juristic differences in this area. For example, combining the two punishments of flogging and stoning for a married adulterer. Most scholars, however, agree that no such combination applies. Other points of difference include sending unmarried adulterers into exile in addition to the flogging, and the punishment for a slave adulterer. These juristic differences are very detailed, but we do not propose to speak about these here. Readers who are interested may refer to books on *Fiqh*. We instead will confine ourselves here to a discussion of the wisdom of this piece of legislation.

The first point to note is the difference in the punishment incurred by adulterers, depending on their marital status. A Muslim who is of age, free and sane and who has already experienced sex within marriage is fully aware of the clean and proper way to satisfy sexual desires. To abandon this and resort to adultery betrays a deviant and corrupt nature. Hence, punishment is increased in this case. A virgin on the other hand may feel the temptation so strongly when he is inexperienced. There is also a difference in the nature of the act itself. A married person is able to enjoy sex in a much better and more refined way than a virgin. Hence, he deserves increased punishment.

As has already been mentioned, the *sūrah* speaks here of the mandatory punishment for the unmarried adulterer only. It emphasizes the requirement to put it into effect, with no compassion shown to the perpetrator: "*As for the adulteress and the adulterer, flog each of them with a hundred stripes, and let not compassion for them keep you from [carrying out] this law of God, if you truly believe in God and the Last Day; and let a number of believers witness their punishment.*" (Verse 2) The Muslim community is required to implement this punishment showing no sympathy for the offenders. The punishment should be administered in public with a number of believers present. This makes it harder for the offenders and increases the deterrent effect for the beholders.

The crime is shown to be increasingly heinous. Hence, all ties between the perpetrators and the Muslim community are cut off: "*The adulterer couples with none other than an adulteress or an idolatress; and with the adulteress couples none other than an adulterer or an idolater. This is forbidden to the believers.*" (Verse 3)

This means that those who commit adultery do not do so while they are believers. They only commit it when they are in a state that is far removed from faith and the feelings it generates in people's hearts. A believer is not comfortable to enter into marital relations with someone who has abandoned faith through such a terrible offence. Indeed Imām Aḥmad is of the view that marriage is forbidden between an adulterer and a chaste woman, or between a chaste man and an adulteress. A prerequisite for such a marriage to be valid is for such offenders to genuinely repent. At any rate, the Qur'ānic verse makes it clear that by nature believing men and women feel that to be married to someone who commits adultery is strongly repugnant. Thus, it is very unlikely to happen, and this improbability is described here as a prohibition. Thus, ties between the Muslim community and individuals who commit adultery are non-existent.

A report giving the reason for the revelation of the second of these two verses mentions that Marthad, a man from the *Anṣār*, used to go to Makkah to free those who were imprisoned because of their belief in Islam. He would take those whom he managed to free to Madīnah. Before becoming a Muslim, he used to have a friend in Makkah called ʿAnāq who was a prostitute. On one of his visits, he arranged to smuggle out a prisoner held in Makkah. He said: "I stopped by the outside wall of a garden on a clear night with moonlight. ʿAnāq soon came and noticed a black shade against the wall. When she drew near, she recognized me and mentioned my name. I confirmed that it was I. She welcomed me and invited me to her place to stay the night. I said: 'ʿAnāq! God has forbidden adultery.' She gave me away, shouting to the people that I was smuggling their prisoners out. As I tried to disappear, eight of them followed me. I went into the garden and walked until I entered a cave. They followed me in and stood by my head, while I remained motionless. Some of them urinated over my head, but God helped me and they did not notice me. When they left, I returned to my man and helped him. He was very heavy, but I carried him for a distance, and then I untied him. I carried him on, but he helped me until we safely reached Madīnah. I then went to the Prophet and asked him if it was all right for me to marry ʿAnāq. I repeated my question twice, but he did not reply until this verse was revealed stating:

'*The adulterer couples with none other than an adulteress or an idolatress; and with the adulteress couples none other than an adulterer or an idolater. This is forbidden to the believers.*' The Prophet said to me: 'Marthad! An adulterer couples with none other than an adulteress or an idolatress. Do not marry her.'" [Related by Abū Dāwūd, al-Nasā'ī and al-Tirmidhī]

This verse, then, implies that a believer is forbidden to marry an adulteress unless she genuinely repents. The same applies to a female believer and an adulterer. This is the view Imām Aḥmad took, but other scholars had a different view. As a point of difference, it may be studied in *Fiqh* books. At any rate, this type of action alienates the perpetrator from the Muslim community, which in itself is a severe social punishment that is no less painful than flogging.

Is Hard Punishment Justified?

When enacting such severe punishments for this abominable offence, Islam does not overlook the natural desire behind it. Islam knows that human beings cannot and should not suppress such a natural desire. Nor does Islam wish that people should fight the physiological functions God has given them as part of their nature and part of the laws of life, ensuring the continuity of mankind. Islam only shuns an animal approach to this desire that treats one body the same as another, and which has no intention of building a home, life partnership or family. Islam wants sexual relations between a man and a woman to be based on fine human feelings that involve their hearts and souls in their physical union, so as to make it a union between two human beings sharing their lives, pains, hopes, and futures. In this way, any children will be reared by both parents building a future together.

This is the reason why Islam ordains such a severe punishment for adultery, considering it a setback that reduces man to an animal. It destroys all these fine feelings and goals. Adultery turns human beings into animal-like creatures that treat all men as males and all women as females, trying to satisfy a physical desire in a casual way. Its momentary ecstasy has neither a constructive aim nor a fine, durable love behind it. It is the continuity aspect that distinguishes such a fine feeling from a momentary and casual charge which many people describe as passion when it is in fact a physical desire momentarily taking the guise of fine feeling.

Islam neither suppresses natural feelings nor considers them dirty. It only regulates, purifies and elevates them above the physical level so that they become central to many psychological and social values. By contrast, adultery, and prostitution in particular, removes from such natural desires all the exquisite feelings, attractions and values that have been refined over the long history of human life. It leaves such desires naked, dirty and coarser than in animals. In many animal and bird species, couples live together in a regulated life. They do not have the sort of sexual chaos that adultery spreads in some human communities, particularly where prostitution is rife.

In order to spare man this type of setback, Islam prescribes such punishment for adultery. Needless to say, this offence causes numerous social ills that people often mention when they speak about this crime. These include false parenthood, undermining family life and causing hatred and grudges. Each one of these social ills justifies a very hard punishment for the offence causing it. But the primary reason for it is preserving the humanity of man, protecting the moral standards that have come to be associated with clean sex, furthering the aims of marital life that is intended to last. This is, in my view, the reason that serves all others.

Islam, then, prescribes a very heavy penalty for adultery, but it does not legislate such a penalty without first putting in place sufficient legislation to protect people from falling into such sin. It also ensures that the punishment is not enforced except in cases where there is certainty about the offence and its perpetrators. Islam is a complete code of living that is not based on punishment. Its basis is to provide all that promotes a clean and pure life. If some individuals then abandon this clean and easy life in order to deliberately submerge themselves in filth, they incur such heavy penalties.

When a crime takes place in spite of all these measures, Islam prevents the infliction of the penalty wherever possible. The Prophet says: "Spare Muslims the infliction of mandatory punishments wherever possible.

If there is any way out for the accused, let him go unpunished. It is better that the ruler errs on the side of pardon, rather than punishment." [Related by al-Tirmidhī] In the case of adultery, Islam requires four witnesses to testify that they have seen the offence, or else, a clear and confirmed confession.

It may be suggested, then, that the punishment is unreal and unenforceable, which renders it ineffective as a deterrent. As we have said, punishment is not the basis of the Islamic approach; its basis is prevention, education and cultivating people's finer feelings and consciences so that they refrain from even contemplating an offence. It only punishes those who are intent on committing the crime, paying little regard to society, so as to be seen by four witnesses. It also inflicts the punishment on those who wish to purify themselves of the effects of the offence after having committed it. In other words, the punishment is applied to those who confess to their offence. This is what happened to Māʿiz and his Ghāmidī consort when they went to the Prophet requesting him to inflict the punishment so as to purify them of their sin. Both were insistent, in spite of the Prophet turning away from them time after time. In fact, they confessed four times each, which left the Prophet no option but to inflict the punishment, for at this point the confession was no longer suspect. The Prophet said: "Spare yourselves mandatory punishments; for when I have established that a sin carrying such a punishment has been committed, the punishment must be done." [Related by Abū Dāwūd]

Thus, when certainty is established and the matter has been put to the ruler, or judge, the mandatory punishment must be applied, with no compassion shown to the offenders. Such compassion is misplaced, because it is in fact cruel to the community and human morality. God is much more compassionate to His creatures and He has chosen what He knows to serve their interests best. When God decides on a particular case, no believer, whether man or woman, can counter that choice. Nor is it right that anyone should speak out against such punishment, describing it as hard or savage. It is indeed much more compassionate than what awaits a community that allows adultery to spread.

Measures Against False Accusation

Prescribing a very hard punishment for adultery is not sufficient, on its own, to protect the Muslim community and ensure the purity of its atmosphere. Therefore, a supplementary order is given to isolate the adulterers from the rest of the Muslim community. Furthermore, heavy punishment is prescribed for those who accuse chaste women of adultery without providing firm evidence in support of their accusation:

> *As for those who accuse chaste women [of adultery], and cannot produce four witnesses, flog them with eighty stripes; and do not accept their testimony ever after; for they are indeed transgressors. Excepted are those who afterwards repent and make amends; for God is Much-Forgiving, Merciful.* (Verses 4–5)

Allowing people to accuse chaste women, whether married or not, without clear proof would mean that people could make such accusations without fear of repercussion. This in turn would stain the Muslim community's reputation. Every individual would feel threatened with false accusations. Every man would suspect his wife, and every wife her husband, and people would begin to doubt their legitimacy. In such an intolerable state of doubt and suspicion, every family would be undermined. Moreover, when such accusations are frequently made, those who steer themselves away from adultery might begin to think that such crime was common in society. They might then begin to see it in a different light, as less ghastly, as a result of such frequent mention. Furthermore, those who would not even have contemplated it at all might even begin to think of doing so, feeling that since many others do it, there is no harm in it.

Thus, in order to protect people's honour, and to prevent their suffering from suspicion as a result of uncorroborated accusations, the Qur'ān prescribes for false accusation a punishment that almost equals that of adultery. False accusers are to be flogged with 80 stripes each, and their future testimony in any case or situation rejected. Plus they are to be labelled as transgressors. The first part of this punishment is physical, while the second is moral. It is sufficient that the accuser is deprived of the right to testify, and considered an unreliable and unacceptable witness no matter what the case or situation. The third part is religious. The one guilty of false accusation follows a line that deviates from the straight path of faith. The only way out is that the accuser should provide four witnesses who have seen the offence being committed, or three alongside him if he himself has seen it. If the four give such testimony, the accusation is proved and the punishment for adultery is enforced on the perpetrator.

The point at issue here is that the Muslim community does not lose much by suppressing an accusation that cannot be proven. Conversely it loses much more by condoning accusations that cannot be proven. Indeed when such accusations become the subject of casual conversation, they serve to encourage people to do the same, while stopping any discussion of such matters, unless clearly proven, delivers a clear message that adultery, an abominable offence, is rare or even non-existent in society. Moreover, the false accusation of chaste women causes the latter much pain and mental suffering, in addition to its being a means of destroying families and relations.

The punishment meted out to the false accuser continues to hang over his head, even after its administration, unless he genuinely repents: "*Excepted are those who afterwards repent and make amends; for God is Much-Forgiving, Merciful.*" (Verse 5)

Scholars differ in their understanding of this exception: does it apply only to the last punishment, which means that the accuser is no longer considered a transgressor, but continues nevertheless to be unacceptable as a witness in any situation? Or would he be acceptable as a witness once he has declared his repentance? Mālik, Aḥmad and al-Shāfiʿī are of the view that once he has repented, he is no longer a transgressor. He is again acceptable as a witness. On the other hand, Abū Ḥanīfah maintains that repentance only stops him being considered a transgressor, but he remains unacceptable as a witness. Al-Shaʿbī and al-Ḍaḥḥāk, renowned scholars of the early Islamic period, say that despite his repentance, he is unacceptable as a witness unless he admits that his original accusation was false.

I personally prefer this last view, because it adds to the accuser's repentance a clear declaration by him that the accused is innocent. In this way, all effects of the accusation are removed. No one can then say that the punishment was inflicted on the accuser because of lack of sufficient supporting evidence. No one who heard the accusation can continue to entertain any thought that its substance was correct, and that it could have been proven if more witnesses were ready to come forward. Thus, the innocent would have their innocence confirmed both socially and legally. This leaves no reason to continue to punish the accuser by refusing his testimony, after he has repented his original action and declared that the accusation he made was false.

When a Husband Accuses His Wife

All the foregoing applies to accusing women of adultery. An exception is made, however, in the case of a husband accusing his wife. To require him to produce four witnesses is unreasonable. In normal situations, a man does not accuse his wife falsely, because the very accusation carries a negative reflection on his own honour and against his own children. Hence, this type of accusation carries a totally different ruling:

> *And as for those who accuse their own wives [of adultery], but have no witnesses except themselves, let each of them call God four times to witness that he is indeed telling the truth; and the fifth time, that God's curse be upon him if he is telling a lie. However, punishment is averted from her if she calls God four times to witness that he is indeed telling a lie; and the fifth time, that God's wrath be upon her if he is telling the truth. Were it not for God's favour upon you and His grace, and that God is the One who accepts repentance, the Wise…!* (Verses 6–10)

This ruling lightens the burden for married people in a way that takes their special circumstances into consideration. A man may find his wife in a compromising position but there be no one else as witness to the deed. In this case, he swears by God four times that he is telling the truth, and adds a fifth incurring God's curse on himself if he is telling a lie. These oaths are called testimonies, because he is the only witness. When he has done so, he pays her any portion of her dowry that may be outstanding, and she is immediately and finally divorced. She is also liable to the punishment for adultery. However, she can avert this punishment by swearing by God four times that her husband is telling lies, and adds a fifth incurring God's curse on herself if he is telling the truth. If she does, then no punishment is administered in this case, but the marriage is irrevocably terminated. If she is pregnant, the child is named after her, not after her husband. No one can attach any blame to the child. If anyone does make an accusation against the child, they are liable to punishment.

The *sūrah* comments on this delicate ruling by saying: "*Were it not for God's favour upon you and His grace, and that God is the One who accepts repentance, the Wise...!*" (Verse 10) It does not tell us what would have happened, had God not bestowed His favours and grace on us in this way, and extended His manifest grace by accepting our repentance. Instead, the statement leaves us with an impression that it is something very serious, and that people are much better off, avoiding it through God's grace.

Several reports explain the occasion when these verses were revealed. Imām Aḥmad reports on the authority of Ibn 'Abbās: "When the verse stating, '*As for those who accuse chaste women [of adultery], and cannot produce four witnesses, flog them with eighty stripes; and do not accept their testimony ever after,*' was revealed, Sa'd ibn 'Ubādah, the chief of the *Anṣār* said: 'Is that how it has been revealed, Messenger of God?' The Prophet said: 'People of the Anṣār! Do you hear what your chief is saying?' They said: 'Do not blame him, Messenger of God. He is a man with a keen sense of honour. He never married a woman unless she was a virgin. If he divorced a woman, none of us would dare to marry her, because we realize how he takes that.' Sa'd said: 'Messenger of God! I know it to be true and that it comes from God. I only wondered that if I would find a man on top of my wife, I could not disturb him until I have brought four witnesses. By the time I bring them, he would have finished his business.'

It was not long after that Hilāl ibn Umayyah went to the Prophet. He had been on his farm before going home at night. He found a man with his wife. He saw things with his own eyes, and he heard things with his ears. He did not fight with the man, but the next morning he said to the Prophet: 'Messenger of God! I went home last night and I found my wife with a man. I saw and heard things with my own eyes and ears.' The Prophet was very displeased when he heard this, and found it hard to deal with. The *Anṣār* said: 'What Sa'd ibn 'Ubādah foretold has come to pass. The Prophet must now subject Hilāl ibn Umayyah to punishment by flogging and declare him unacceptable as a witness.'

Hilāl said to his people: 'By God, I certainly hope that He will provide a way out for me.' Addressing the Prophet, he said: 'Messenger of God! I see that my story has been very difficult for you; but God knows that I am telling the truth.'

The Prophet was about to give orders that punishment should be inflicted on Hilāl when revelations were bestowed on him from on high. Those who were around him recognized this fact by the change in his face. These verses dealing with the situation were revealed. The Prophet's face regained its colour, and he said: 'Hilāl! Rejoice, for God has given you a way out.' Hilāl replied: 'I certainly hoped that God would grant me that.' The Prophet gave orders for the woman to be brought to him. When she came, the Prophet recited these verses to them both, reminding them both that punishment in the hereafter is far more severe than any punishment in this life. Hilāl said: 'Messenger of God! I have certainly said the truth when I accused her.' She said: 'He is lying.' The Prophet then said: 'Let them both say their oaths.'

Hilāl was first told to swear. He swore by God four times that what he said was the truth. Before saying his fifth oath, people said to him: 'Hilāl, fear God. This is the one that incurs punishment in the hereafter, while punishment in this world is that much less.' He said: 'By God! He will not punish me for this, just like He did not let me be flogged for it.' He made the fifth oath, invoking God's curse on himself if he were lying. The woman was then offered the chance to refute the charge. She swore by God four times that he was lying. When she was about to make her fifth oath, people said to her: 'Fear God, and remember that punishment in the hereafter is much more severe. This is the oath that incurs God's punishment for you.' She stopped for a while and thought about confessing. She then said: 'I will not bring a scandal on my people's heads.' She made her fifth oath, invoking God's curse on herself if her husband was telling the truth.

The Prophet ordered their marriage irrevocably terminated. He also judged that her child, should she be pregnant, would not be named after a father, and that the child would not be shamed. If anyone was to hurl an accusation at the child, then that person would be punished. His judgement also made it clear that she could not claim shelter in her husband's home, and she could not have any maintenance from him, as the marriage was dissolved without divorce or death. He also said: 'If her child, when born, has slightly reddish hair, a thin bottom and small legs, then he is Hilāl's child. If he is born dark, with strong features and curly hair, of large build, with large legs and a fat bottom, then he belongs to the man she has been accused of associating with.' When the child was born, he was of the second description. The Prophet said: 'If it was not for the oaths, I would have had something to sort out with her.'"

We see that this ruling was given to deal with a particular case that was not only hard for the husband concerned, but also the Muslim community and the Prophet. Indeed, the Prophet could not find a way out of it. According to al-Bukhārī's report, the Prophet said to Hilāl: 'You either bring the proof or lay your back for punishment.' Hilāl said to him: 'Messenger of God! If any of us finds a man on top of his wife, should he go and seek witnesses?'

Legislation is Given When Needed

As this case provides for a special situation which is exempted from the general rules of false accusation, it may be asked why God did not reveal this exception to the general rules in the first place? Why did God wait until a situation occurred, one which caused embarrassment and hardship?

God certainly knows all this, but in His infinite wisdom He bestowed from on high the revelation outlining the rules when the need for it was keenly felt. Thus, the rules were received with eagerness, and people immediately recognized the wisdom behind the legislation and the divine grace it ensured. Hence, the verses outlining the procedure conclude with the statement: "*Were it not for God's favour upon you and His grace, and that God is the One who accepts repentance, the Wise...!"* (Verse 10)

Let us pause a little here to reflect on the Islamic method of moulding the new Muslim community and how the Prophet re-educated his Companions by means of the Qur'ān. We should remember here that he was dealing with Arabs who were characteristically and strongly impulsive, particularly in cases of personal honour. They would rarely pause to consider options before rushing into action. Thus, when legislation was established outlining the punishment for accusing chaste women of adultery without providing the required proof, people found it difficult. Sa'd ibn 'Ubādah, the chief of the *Anṣār*, went as far as asking: "Is that how it has been revealed, Messenger of God?" He puts forward his question, knowing for certain that the verses were revealed in that way. His question, however, reflected the difficulty he felt in complying with that ruling in a particular situation he imagined. Hence, he explained: "Messenger of God! I know it to be true and that it comes from God. I only wondered that if I found a man on top of my wife, I could not disturb him until I had brought four witnesses. By the time I brought them, he would have finished his business."

Yet the situation that Sa'd found hard to imagine soon took place in reality. A man came forward, having found his wife with a stranger, seeing them with his own eyes, and hearing them with his own ears. Yet the Qur'ānic rules did not permit any measure to be taken against them. Therefore, he had to overcome his own feelings, traditions and the social environment that called for immediate action. Even harder than that, he had to restrain himself and wait for a ruling from God. Such restraint is especially difficult, but Islam re-moulded the Arabs to patiently bear such hardship so that there could be no rule other than God's. Only His rulings apply in all life situations.

How could this happen? Simply, those people felt that God was with them, and that He took care of them, without requiring them to put up with things they could not bear. They realized that God would never abandon them in a situation that went beyond their abilities and would never deal unjustly with them. They felt that they lived under God's care. Hence, they looked for His grace in the same way as children look to their parents' care.

Hilāl ibn Umayyah had come home to find his wife with a man, seeing and hearing them both. As he was alone, he could only complain of this to the Prophet who, in turn, felt that he must apply the ruling concerning an accusation not supported by four witnesses. Hence, he said to Hilāl: "You either bring the proof or lay your back for punishment." Hilāl, however, believed that God would not let him suffer a punishment when he only stated the truth. He knew that what he said about his wife was right. At this moment, God revealed new verses outlining an exception in the case of husbands accusing their wives. The Prophet gave the good news to Hilāl, who confidently said: "I certainly hoped that God would grant me that." He trusted to God's mercy, justice and care. Furthermore, he trusted that God was looking after that community of believers. It was faith that re-moulded the Arabs and made them submit fully to God's rulings, whatever they happened to be.

A False Accusation Against the Prophet's Wife

Having outlined the rules applicable in cases of accusing women of adultery, the *sūrah* mentions a case of false accusation that reflects the repugnance of this crime. This involved the Prophet's own household with its noble and chaste inhabitants. It reflected on the honour of the Prophet, the most beloved person by God, and the honour of his friend, Abū Bakr, the Prophet's closest Companion. It also involved the honour of a man, Ṣafwān ibn al-Mu'aṭṭal, who enjoyed the Prophet's own testimony that he never saw anything but good from him. It was a case that preoccupied the entire Muslim community in Madīnah for a whole month.

The Qur'ān refers to this whole episode, calling it The Falsehood, in a ten-verse passage that runs as follows:

> *Those who concocted the falsehood were a band from among you. Do not regard it as bad for you; indeed it is good for you. Each one of them shall bear what he has earned of sin; and awesome suffering awaits the one who took on himself the lead among them. When you heard it, why did not the believers, men and women, think the*

best of themselves, and say: 'This is a blatant falsehood.' Why did they not produce four witnesses to prove it? Since they have not produced witnesses, then in the sight of God, they are certainly liars. Were it not for God's favour upon you and His grace, in this world and in the life to come, awesome suffering would indeed have afflicted you on account of what you indulged in. You took it up with your tongues and uttered with your mouths something of which you have no knowledge, thinking it a light matter whereas in God's sight it is grave indeed. If only when you heard it you said: 'It is not right for us to speak of this! All glory belongs to You. This is a monstrous slander.' God admonishes you lest you ever revert to the like of this, if you are truly believers. And God makes plain to you His revelations. God is All-Knowing, Wise. Those who love that gross indecency should spread among the believers shall be visited with grievous suffering both in this world and in the life to come. God knows, but you do not know. Were it not for God's favour upon you and His grace, and that God is Compassionate, Merciful...! (Verses 11–20)

This false story caused the purest soul in human history much suffering, and made the Muslim community go through one of the hardest experiences in its long history. It left the hearts of the Prophet, his wife 'Ā'ishah, Abū Bakr and his wife, as well as Ṣafwān, for a whole month subject to doubt, worry and endless pain. Here are the details of the story as told by the pure and chaste lady at the centre of this painful episode.

> Every time the Prophet went abroad he made a toss among his wives to decide which of them should accompany him. At the time of the al-Muṣṭalaq expedition, the toss favoured me and I travelled with him. At the time, women did not eat much, which meant that they were slim and light. When my transport was prepared for me, I would sit in my howdah which would then be lifted onto the camel's back. When they had secured it, the camel driver would march with it.
>
> When the Prophet had completed his business on that expedition and was on his way back, he encamped one night at a

spot not very far from Madīnah. He stayed there only part of the night before the call to march was again made. People started to get ready and in the meantime I went out to relieve myself. I was wearing a necklace, and I did not feel it drop off me before I returned. Back in the camp I felt for my necklace and, realizing that it was gone, I looked for it there, but could not find it. People were just about to move. I therefore went quickly back to that particular spot and searched for my necklace until I found it.

In the meantime, the people who prepared my camel finished their task and took up the howdah, thinking that I was inside, and lifted it onto the camel's back and secured it. It did not occur to them that I was not inside. They, therefore, led the camel away. When I came back to where we had encamped, there was no one to be seen. The army had marched. I, therefore, tied my dress round my body and lay down. I realized that when I was missed, someone would come back for me. I soon fell asleep.

Ṣafwān ibn al-Mu'aṭṭal of the tribe of Sulaym was travelling behind the army. He was apparently delayed by some business and did not spend that night in the camp. When he noticed someone lying down, he came towards me. He recognized me since he used to see me before we were ordered to wear veils. He said: *Innā lillāhi wa innā ilayhi rāji'ūn*, "We all belong to God and to Him we shall return." I woke up when I heard him. I did not answer him when he asked me why I had been left behind. However, he made his camel sit down and asked me to ride it, which I did. He led the camel seeking to catch up with the army. Nobody missed me before they had stopped to rest. When everybody had sat down to relax, Ṣafwān appeared, leading his camel, on which I was riding. This prompted those people to invent the story of falsehood. The whole army was troubled with it, but I heard nothing.

It is worth noting here that when 'Abdullāh ibn Ubayy saw 'Ā'ishah approaching, he enquired who she was. When he was told that it was 'Ā'ishah, he said: "Your Prophet's wife has spent the whole night with a man, and now she turns up with him leading her camel!" This statement gave rise to the falsehood that was spread about ʿĀʾishah. ʿĀʾishah's narrative continues:

> Shortly after our arrival in Madīnah, I felt very ill. Nobody told me anything about what was going on. The Prophet and my parents heard the story, but they did not mention anything to me. However, I felt that the Prophet was not as kind to me during this illness of mine as he used to be. When he came in, he would ask my mother who was nursing me: "How is that woman of yours?" He said nothing else. I was distressed and requested his permission to be nursed in my parents' home. He agreed. I went there and heard nothing. I was ill for 20-odd nights before I began to get better.
>
> Unlike other people, we, the Arabs, did not have toilets in our homes. To us, they were disgusting. What we used to do was to go out at night, somewhere outside Madinah where we would relieve ourselves. Women went only at night. One night I went out with Umm Misṭaḥ [Abū Bakr's cousin]. While we were walking, she was tripped by her own dress and fell down. As she did so, she said: "Confound Misṭaḥ" to her own son.
>
> I said: "Improper indeed is what you have said about a man of the Muhājirīn who fought at Badr." She asked me: "Have you not heard the story then?" When I asked her what story, she recounted to me what the people of falsehood said about me. I swear I could not relieve myself that night. I went back and cried bitterly until I felt that crying would break me down. I said to my mother: "May God forgive you. People said what they said about me, and you mentioned nothing to me."
>
> My mother said: "Calm down, child. Any pretty woman married to a man who loves her will always be envied, especially if she shares him with other wives."
>
> I said: "Glory be to God. That people should repeat this sort of thing!" I cried bitterly throughout that night till morning, without a moment's sleep.
>
> The Prophet called ʿAlī ibn Abī Ṭālib and Usāmah ibn Zayd to consult them about divorcing me. Usāmah, who felt that I was

innocent, said: "Messenger of God, she is your wife and you have experienced nothing bad from her. This story is a blatant lie."

ʿAlī said: "Messenger of God, God imposed no restriction on you in matrimonial matters. There are many women besides her. If you would see fit to ask her maid, she would tell you the truth." The Prophet called in my maid, Barīrah, and asked her whether she had seen anything suspicious. Barīrah said: "By Him who sent you with the message of truth, there is nothing I take against her other than, being so young, she would doze off and let the hens eat the dough I had prepared for baking."

The Prophet addressed the Muslims in the mosque when I was still unaware of the whole matter. He said: "I have seen nothing evil from my wife. Those people are also involving a man from whom I have seen no evil. He never entered my wives' rooms except in my presence.

Saʿd ibn Muʿādh, the Aws leader, said: "Messenger of God, if these men belong to the Aws, our tribe, we will spare you their trouble. If, on the other hand, they belong to our brethren the Khazraj, you have only to give us your command."

Saʿd ibn ʿUbādah, the leader of the Khazraj, who enjoyed a good reputation, allowed his tribal feelings to get the better of him this time and said to Saʿd ibn Muʿādh: "By God, you shall not kill them. You are saying this only because you know that they are of the Khazraj."

Usayd ibn Ḥuḍayr, a cousin of Saʿd ibn Muʿādh, said to Saʿd ibn ʿUbādah: "You are no more than a hypocrite defending other hypocrites." People who belonged to both tribes were very angry and were about to fight. The Prophet was still on the pulpit and he tried hard to cool them down, until finally he succeeded.

I continued to cry for the rest of the day. I could not sleep. Next morning both my parents were with me – I had spent two nights and a day crying hard. My tears never stopped. Both of them felt that my crying would break my heart. While we were in that condition, a woman from the Anṣār came to me and started to cry with me.

Shortly afterwards the Prophet came and sat down. He had not sat in my room ever since the rumour started. For a whole month he received no revelations concerning me. When he sat down, he praised and glorified God before going on to say: 'Ā'ishah. People have been talking, as you are now well aware. If you are innocent, God will make your innocence known. If, however, you have committed a sin, then you should seek God's forgiveness and repent. If a servant of God admits her sin and repents, God will forgive her."

When the Prophet finished, my tears dried up completely and I turned to my father and said: "Answer the Prophet." He said: "By God, I do not know what to say to God's Messenger, peace be upon him."

I then said to my mother: "Answer the Prophet." She said: "I do not know what to say to God's Messenger, peace be upon him."

I was still a young girl, and I did not read much of the Qur'ān. However, I said: 'I know that you all have heard this story repeated again and again until you now believe it. If I tell you that I am innocent, and God knows that I am, you will not believe me. If, on the other hand, I admit something when God knows that I am innocent of it, you will believe me. I know no comparable situation to yours except that of Joseph's father [I tried to remember Jacob's name but I could not] when he said: "*Sweet patience! It is to God alone that I turn for support in this misfortune that you have described.*" (12: 18) I then turned round and lay on my bed. I knew that I was innocent and that God would make my innocence known. It did not occur to me for a moment, however, that God would reveal a passage of the Qur'ān concerning me. I felt myself too humble for God to include my case in His revelations. All I hoped for was that the Prophet should see something in his dream to prove my innocence. Before the Prophet left us, however, and before anyone left the house, God's revelations started. The Prophet was covered with his own robe, and a pillow was placed under his head. When I saw that, I felt no worry or fear. I was certain of my innocence, and I knew that

God, limitless as He is in His glory, would not be unjust to me. As for my parents – well, by Him who holds 'Ā'ishah's soul in His hand, while they waited for the Prophet to come back to himself, they could have died for fear that divine revelations might confirm what people said. Then it was all over. The Prophet sat up, with his sweat looking like pearls on a wet day. As he wiped his forehead, he said: " 'Ā'ishah, I have good news for you. God has declared your innocence." I said: "Praise be to God."

My mother said to me: 'Rise and go to God's Messenger, (peace be upon him).' I said: 'No. I am not rising, and I am not praising anyone other than God who has declared my innocence.' God revealed the passage starting with, '*Those who concocted the falsehood were a band from among you*,' in ten verses. When God thus declared my innocence, Abū Bakr, who used to support Misṭaḥ ibn Athāthah, considering that he was a poor relation of his, said: 'By God, I will never again give Misṭaḥ any assistance, after what he has said about 'Ā'ishah.' But God then revealed the verse that says: '*Let not those of you who have been graced with God's favour and ample means resolve by oath not to help those who are near of kin, the needy and those who have left their homes for the sake of God. But let them pardon and forbear. Do you not desire that God should forgive you your sins? God is indeed Much-Forgiving, Merciful.*' (Verse 22) Abū Bakr said: 'Yes, indeed. I do hope that God will forgive me my sins.' He then resumed his support of Misṭaḥ, saying: 'I will never stop my assistance to him.'

'Ā'ishah further mentions that the Prophet had asked another of his wives, Zaynab bint Jaḥsh, about her. She said: 'Messenger of God! I want to protect my hearing and sight. By God, I have seen from her nothing but good.' She was the one among the Prophet's wives who used to vie with me for a favourite position with the Prophet. God has thus protected her through her keen sense of piety. Her sister, Ḥamnah, however, continued to speak, as though to enhance her position. She was thus involved with those who circulated the false story. [Related by al-Bukhārī and Muslim]

As the Prophet Faces False Accusations

This account tells us how the Prophet and his household, Abū Bakr and his family, as well as Ṣafwān ibn al-Mu ʻaṭṭal, and the entire Muslim community lived in such a suffocating atmosphere, suffering much mental pain because of the false rumours circulating.

It is hard to imagine this particularly difficult period in the Prophet's life when his beloved wife, ʻĀ'ishah, young and sensitive as she was, endured such profound anguish. ʻĀ'ishah, pure, kind, innocent and entertaining only clear thoughts and with a clear conscience, faced an accusation about her most valued qualities. She, Abū Bakr's daughter who enjoyed the most noble and moral upbringing, was accused with regard to her honour; the wife of Muḥammad ibn ʻAbdullāh, who belonged to the noble clan of Hāshim, faced an accusation concerning her honesty; the wife enjoying the great love of her husband was charged with being unfaithful; the girl brought up according to Islamic values from a very early age was accused of being false to her faith. And ʻĀ'ishah was none other than the wife of God's Messenger, (peace be upon him)!

Such accusations were levelled at her when she was innocent, unaware, taking no precaution as she expected no harm. Hence, she had nothing to prove her innocence except hope for help from God Almighty. Her dearest wish was that the Prophet should have a dream revealing her innocence. But revelations slackened for a whole month, and this is for a definite purpose known to God alone. Hence, she continued to suffer.

Can we imagine her, much weakened by illness, when she received the shocking news from Misṭaḥ's mother? She suffered a recurrence of her fever. In her grief, she said to her mother: 'Glory be to God. That people should repeat this sort of thing!' A different version of the story quotes her saying to her mother: 'Does my father know of this?' Her mother told her that he did, and she went on: 'And God's Messenger?' Again her mother confirmed this.

Great indeed was her pain when she heard the Prophet in whom she believed saying to her: "People have been talking as you are now well aware. If you are innocent, God will make your innocence known. If, however, you have committed a sin, then you should seek God's forgiveness and repent. If a servant of God admits her sin and repents, God will forgive her." Hearing these words, she realized that he was uncertain of her innocence, and that he could not make a judgement about the accusation levelled at her. God had not yet told him the fact of which she herself was certain but had no means of proving, i.e. that she was absolutely innocent. She was aware that although she enjoyed a favourite position in his great heart, she now stood uncertain.

Consider the position of Abū Bakr, a man endowed with great sensitivity and a noble heart, feeling the painful sting of an accusation levelled at his daughter, married to his most intimate friend who was none other than the Prophet in whom he unhesitatingly believed. Strong and pain-enduring as he was, he let out an expression of the writhing thoughts troubling him: "We were never accused of such a thing in the days of ignorance! Are we to accept such a charge under Islam?" His sick and much tormented daughter said to him: "Answer the Prophet!" Dejected and forlorn, he said: "By God, I do not know what to say to God's Messenger, peace be upon him."

His wife, Umm Rawmān, tried to put a strong face on in front of her daughter who was rending her heart apart with crying. She said to her: "Calm down, child. Any pretty woman married to a man who loves her will always be envied, especially if she shares him with other wives." But her fortitude collapsed when her daughter said to her: "Answer the Prophet." Like her husband before her, she said: "By God, I do not know what to say to God's Messenger, peace be upon him."

And then, Ṣafwān ibn al-Mu'aṭṭal, a good believer who laid down his life to fight for God's cause, was accused of being unfaithful to the Prophet. Thus, the accusation touched his honour, honesty and faith. A God-fearing Companion of the Prophet was falsely accused of being untrue to everything the Prophet's Companions held dear. Yet he was certain of his innocence. When faced with this false accusation, he said: "All praise be to God! By God I have never taken a dress off a female's shoulder." When he heard that Ḥassān ibn Thābit was one of those who repeated the accusation, he hit him on the head with his sword, almost killing him. He knew that it was forbidden for him to hit a fellow Muslim, but the pain of this false accusation was unbearable.

Far worse, it was Muḥammad (peace be upon him), God's Messenger and the man at the pinnacle of the Hāshimite clan, the noblest in Arabia, who found himself subject to an accusation that involved none other than 'Ā'ishah, the woman who occupied a special place in his heart as his most beloved wife. This accusation meant that the most private place in his home, which was a source of purity, was not pure. The Prophet, who was very keen to guard every sanctity in his community, was faced with an accusation that violated the sanctity of his own household. God's Messenger, who was protected against all harm, was shown through this accusation to have no protection from God!

With this accusation levelled at 'Ā'ishah (may God be pleased with her), the Prophet encountered everything that ran against his personal honour and against everything that was held dear to an Arab, and to a Prophet. Yet the accusation had been made, and was the subject of conversation in Madīnah for a whole month, and he had no means to put an end to it. For a definite purpose of His own, God let this falsehood circulate for a whole month, revealing nothing to set the record straight and put the facts as they were. Meanwhile, Muḥammad, the man, suffered all that a human being experiences in such a hard situation. Shame and heart-felt pain were part of what he endured. But he also suffered the absence of the light that always illuminated his way, i.e. revelation. Doubt crept into his heart, despite the numerous indications that confirmed his wife's innocence. Yet he lacked clear certainty as the rumours continued to circulate in Madīnah. His loving heart was tormented by doubt which he could not clear because he was, after all, a human being who experienced all human feelings. He was a man who could not entertain the thought that his bed could be stained. Once the seed of doubt creeps into a man's heart, it is difficult to remove without clear and decisive evidence.

Alone, he found this whole burden too heavy. Therefore, he sent for Usāmah ibn Zayd, a young man who held a position close to his heart [as Usāmah was the son of the man the Prophet had adopted as his own son in pre-Islamic days]. He also sent for 'Alī ibn Abī Ṭālib, his trusted cousin. He consulted them both about this very private matter. 'Alī, the Prophet's close relative, was keenly aware of the difficulty of the situation and the pain, worry and doubt experienced by the Prophet, his cousin who had brought him up. Hence, he told him that God had not restricted him in matters of marriage. He also advised that the Prophet should ask the maid, so that he could get some reassurance. Usāmah, on the other hand, realized how compassionate the Prophet felt towards his wife, and how troubling to him was the thought of leaving her. He, therefore, stressed what he knew of her certain purity and the fact that those who circulated the rumour were indeed liars.

In his eagerness to establish the truth, and in his continued anxiety, Muḥammad, the man, derived some support from Usāmah's statement and the maid's report. He spoke to the people in the mosque, reproaching those who did not respect his honour, spoke ill of his wife and accused a man who was known to be virtuous and with no blemish on his character. This led to friction between the Aws and the Khazraj, culminating in mutual accusations and verbal abuse. All took place in the Prophet's presence, which gives us a picture of the atmosphere that prevailed in the Muslim community during that very strange period. It was a time when the sanctity of the Muslim leadership was breached. The Prophet was further hurt by the absence of the light which he always expected to illuminate his way. Therefore, he went to 'Ā'ishah, telling her of people's talk and asking her for a clear statement that could bring him relief.

At this point when the Prophet's pain was at its most acute, his Lord turned to him with compassion. Revelations were bestowed from on high, making 'Ā'ishah's innocence absolutely clear. Thus, the noble household of the Prophet was free of blame. The hypocrites who had circulated this falsehood were exposed. The proper way of dealing with such a serious matter was also outlined for the Muslim community.

Referring to this passage of the Qur'ān that was revealed to deal with her case, 'Ā'ishah said: "I knew that I was innocent and that God would make my innocence known. It did not occur to me for a moment, however, that God would reveal a passage of the Qur'ān concerning me. I felt myself too humble for God to include my case in His revelations. All I hoped for was that the Prophet should see something in his dream to prove my innocence."

But the question was not merely that of 'Ā'ishah and her personal status. It touched on the Prophet, his personality and his role in the Muslim community. It indeed touched on his relation with his Lord and his message. The falsehood story was not aimed at 'Ā'ishah as a person. Rather, it aimed to undermine the entire faith of Islam, by casting doubts about the Prophet sent by God to deliver this message. For this reason, a whole passage of the Qur'ān was revealed to provide a final verdict about this invented falsehood. Thus, the Qur'ān directed the Muslim camp in the raging battle, revealing the divine wisdom behind all developments.

How the False Story Was Circulated

"*Those who concocted the falsehood were a band from among you.*" (Verse 11) It was not merely one or a few individuals that circulated the story. On the contrary, they were a 'band' or a group working for a particular objective. 'Abdullāh ibn Ubayy was not the only one who fabricated the story. Rather, he was the one who took the lead and played the larger part in the affair. He simply represented the band of Jews or hypocrites who felt unable to fight Islam in open engagement. Therefore, they sought to hide behind the pretence that they were Muslims. They felt that this would enable them to scheme in secret against Islam. This false story was one of their worst schemes which was so successful that some Muslims were deceived and a few of them, like Ḥamnah bint Jaḥsh, Ḥassān ibn Thābit and Misṭaḥ ibn Athāthah repeated the story. The real culprits, however, were the band headed by 'Abdullāh ibn Ubayy, a canny schemer who operated behind the scene, saying nothing in public that might have incriminated him. He simply whispered into the ears of those whom he trusted never to testify against him. The plan was so subtle that the false rumours continued to circulate for a whole month in Madīnah, the purest society on earth at that time.

The Qur'ānic passage opens with stating this fact so as to make clear the enormity of the event and the fact that it was perpetrated by a group of people intent on wicked scheming against Islam. The *sūrah*, however, quickly reassures the Muslim community that the eventual outcome of the event will not harm them: "*Do not regard it as bad for you; indeed it is good for you.*" (Verse 11)

It was indeed good because it exposed those who schemed against Islam, targeting the Prophet and his family. It also showed the Muslim community the importance of prohibiting the accusation of adultery, and prescribing a severe punishment for such false accusations. The event also clearly showed the dangers that threatened the Muslim community if people were to casually accuse chaste female believers who might behave unwittingly. For once this begins, it never stops. Indeed, it can increase at such a scale that it eventually touches the most noble of leadership. The result is that the Muslim community loses all values that provide protection against such a state of affairs. Moreover, it is good for the Muslim community that God outlines how best to deal with such an affair.

As for the pain suffered by the Prophet, his household and the Muslim community in general, it is all part of the test they had to go through in order to learn through experience.

Those who were involved in circulating and repeating the false story will bear their fair share of sin, according to what they did or said: "*Each one of them shall bear what he has earned of sin.*" (Verse 11) Each will be taken to account by God for what they perpetrated. This is indeed vile because it is a sin that incurs punishment both in this world and in the life to come. Furthermore, "*awesome suffering awaits the one who took on himself the lead among them,*" to suite his role in this ghastly business. The one 'who took the lead' and masterminded the whole affair was 'Abdullāh ibn Ubayy ibn Salūl, the chief of the hypocrites who was consistently the worst schemer against Islam. He knew how to choose his moment which could have had devastating effects, had not God foiled all his schemes. In His grace, God preserved His faith, protected His Messenger and looked after the Muslim community. One report suggests that when Ṣafwān ibn al-Mu'aṭṭal, leading 'Ā'ishah's howdah, passed by him and a group of his people, 'Abdullāh ibn Ubayy asked: 'Who was that?' People said: ''Ā'ishah.' He said: 'By God! She has not been safe from him, nor was he safe from her.' He further exclaimed: 'Your Prophet's wife has passed the night with a man until the morning, then he comes leading her!'

This was a wicked remark which he repeated in various ways, circulating it through his band of hypocrites. They employed such wicked means that Madīnah was full of this incredible story for a whole month, despite all indications and evidence that confirmed its falsehood. Yet many were the Muslims who spoke about it in a casual manner when it should have been dismissed right away.

Two Steps for Proof

How could all this have happened in that particular community? Even today, we are surprised that such a flimsy fabrication could have circulated in that Muslim community, producing far-reaching effects and causing much pain to the noblest people on earth.

The whole episode was a battle fought by God's Messenger (peace be upon him), the Muslim community and Islam. It perhaps was the greatest battle fought by the Prophet. He emerged from it victorious, having controlled his great anguish, maintained his dignity and endured it all patiently. Not a word did he utter to indicate weakness or impatience. Yet he was experiencing the worst pain he ever endured in his life. He further recognized that the risks to which Islam was exposed as a result of this falsehood were among the worst it had to face at any time.

Yet had the Muslims then searched in their own hearts, they would have found the right answer. Had they applied simple natural logic, they would have been rightly guided. The Qur'ān directs all Muslims to follow this proper approach when they face such difficulties. It is the first step in arriving at the right conclusion: "*When you heard it, why did not the believers, men and women, think the best of themselves, and say: 'This is a blatant falsehood.'*" (Verse 12)

That would have been much better. Muslims should think well of themselves and realize that they are highly unlikely to sink so low. Their Prophet's pure wife and their brother who fought for Islam, laying down his life, belonged to them as a community. Hence, to think well of them was the better course of action. What is unbecoming of all Muslims is unbecoming of the Prophet's wife and of his Companion who was known as a good person. This is indeed what was done by Abū Ayyūb, Khālid ibn Zayd al-Anṣārī and his wife. According to Ibn Isḥāq, Abū Ayyūb was asked by his wife: "Have you heard what people are saying about 'Ā'ishah?" He replied: "Yes, I have, and it is all lies. Would you have done that, Umm Ayyūb?" She said: "No, by God! I would not." He said: "And by God, 'Ā'ishah is better than you." A different report is given by al-Zamakhsharī in his commentary on the Qur'ān, suggesting that it was Abū Ayyūb who asked his wife: "Have you heard what is being said?" In reply, she asked him: "Had you been in Ṣafwān's place, would you have thought ill of the Prophet's wife?" He said: "Certainly not." She said: "And if I were in 'Ā'ishah's place, I would never be unfaithful to the Prophet. Yet 'Ā'ishah is better than me, and Ṣafwān is better than you."

Both reports suggest that some Muslims at least searched their own hearts and ruled out the possibility that the false story suggested. They dismissed any notion that 'Ā'ishah or the Prophet's Companion could have committed such a grave sin and been unfaithful to the Prophet, and recognized how utterly flimsy the basis of the whole accusation was. This is the first step in the approach the Qur'ān outlines for dealing with such matters; it seeks evidence from within people's consciences. The second step is to produce material evidence: "*Why did they not produce four witnesses to prove it? Since they have not produced witnesses, then in the sight of God, they were certainly liars.*" (Verse 13)

This blatant fabrication targeted the highest position in the Muslim community and the purest people. Hence, it should not have been allowed to circulate casually without supporting evidence. Hence the requirement: "*Why did they not produce four witnesses to prove it?*" (Verse 13) They certainly did not produce any witnesses. Hence, they were, in God's judgement, liars. God never alters His verdict or modifies His decision. Thus, this description of those people as liars remains always true of them, and they cannot escape it in any situation.

Thus we have two steps in the Islamic approach: searching in our own hearts and basing our decision on firm and clear evidence. But the Muslim community at the time overlooked both steps, allowing the liars to speak ill of the Prophet and his honour. This was serious indeed and it could have landed the Muslim community in serious trouble, had it not been for God's grace. Hence, God warns the Muslims never to fall into such a trap again: "*Were it not for God's favour upon you and His grace, in this world and in the life to come, awesome suffering would indeed have afflicted you on account of what you indulged in.*" (Verse 14)

When Falsehood Circulates

God wanted this to be a very hard lesson for the fledgling Muslim community, but in His compassion He did not inflict any punishment on them. The offence itself merited stiff punishment because of the pain it caused the Prophet, his wife, close friend and his other Companion of whom he knew nothing but good. It also merited a punishment equal to the evil that circulated within the Muslim community, violating all its sacred values, and equal to the hypocrites' wickedness whose scheme aimed to undermine Islam by raising doubts about God, the Prophet and the Muslim community itself. This continued for a whole month which was a time of doubt, worry and confusion. But God's grace was forthcoming, and He bestowed His mercy on those who were in error after having learnt their bitter lesson.

The *sūrah* gives us a picture of the period, when standards and values were placed on the wrong footing, and the community lost sight of its principles: "*You took it up with your tongues and uttered with your mouths something of which you have no knowledge, thinking it a light matter whereas in God's sight it is grave indeed.*" (Verse 15) The picture painted here is one of recklessness and irresponsibility, showing little care for even the most serious of matters.

"*You took it up with your tongues.*" (Verse 15) One tongue picks it up from another paying little heed to what is being said. There was an utter lack of proper examination of the report, as though people repeated it without ever thinking of its significance. You "*uttered with your mouths something of which you have no knowledge.*" (Verse 15) It is just like that: a mouth utterance without thought or consideration. Mere idle talk uttered and circulated even before it is understood. They thought it a light matter, although it was an accusation against God's

Messenger's personal honour, causing him, his wife and household great pain. It was an accusation against Abū Bakr's family which suffered no similar trouble even in pre-Islamic days when moral values were of little importance. This false story also accused another Companion of the Prophet who laid his life down for the defence of Islam. It further had negative implications concerning the care God took of His Messenger. Yet, still they circulated the false rumour "*thinking it a light matter whereas in God's sight it is grave indeed.*" (Verse 15) Nothing could be described as grave in God's sight unless it is so serious that it shakes firm mountains and disturbs the heavens and earth.

A matter of such seriousness should have made people shudder just on hearing it. They should have been reluctant even to refer to it, and certainly been unwilling to accept it as a subject of conversation. They should have looked to God to protect His Messenger. Such falsehood should have been cast aside immediately: "*If only when you heard it you said: 'It is not right for us to speak of this. All glory belongs to You! This is a monstrous slander.'*" (Verse 16)

When the matter has thus been clarified, and those early Muslims were taken aback by the enormity of the affair and their role in it, they were given a very stern warning for the future: "*God admonishes you lest you ever revert to the like of this, if you are truly believers.*" (Verse 17)

The warning comes in the form of an admonition so as to be educative, choosing the time when the Muslim community is at its most receptive. But the admonition carries at the same time an implicit warning, and attaches their being believers to the heeding of this warning. Believers cannot retain their faith if they revert to the same type of action after they have been shown its enormity and after they have been given such a warning.

"*And God makes plain to you His revelations.*" (Verse 18) He has certainly shown the story to be plainly false, exposing the scheming behind it. He has also made plain the errors involved in this matter. "*God is All-Knowing, Wise.*" He knows motives, intentions, objectives, thoughts and feelings. His method of bringing out the best in people and providing proper restrictions and controls to set the community's life right testifies to His wisdom.

Further Warnings, More Grace

The *sūrah* further elaborates its comments on this falsehood and its effects, repeating its warning against anything that may be of a similar nature. It reminds the Muslims of God's grace and mercy, warning those who falsely accuse chaste women of committing indecency that they expose themselves to God's punishment in the life to come. It also purges people's hearts of the remaining effects of this confrontation, frees them of earthly restrictions and restores their purity. This is clearly reflected in Abū Bakr's attitude to Misṭaḥ ibn Athāthah, his relative who was involved in repeating the story.

"*Those who love that gross indecency should spread among the believers shall be visited with grievous suffering both in this world and in the life to come. God knows, but you do not know.*" (Verse 19) The ones who accused chaste women of adultery, particularly those who made their accusations against the Prophet's own family, really aimed to undermine the values of goodness, chastity and fidelity, so as to make it easier for people to commit adultery by implying that it was common practice. When people begin to think of it in this light, it will be practised more frequently.

This is the reason for describing the false accusers of chaste women as people who love to spread indecency among the believers. Hence they are warned against a very severe suffering both in this life and in the life to come.

It is an aspect of the Qur'ānic method of educating the Muslim community and a measure of prevention based on perfect knowledge of how people react and formulate their attitudes, feelings and lines of action. Hence, the comment at the end of the verse asserts: "*God knows, but you do not know.*" Who knows the human heart better than the One who created it? Who can provide humanity with a better code of living than the One who originated it? Who sees what is concealed as well as what is left in the open, and whose knowledge encompasses all things and situations?

Once again the *sūrah* reminds the believers of the grace God bestows on them: "*Were it not for God's favour upon you and His grace, and that God is Compassionate, Merciful...!*" (Verse 20)

The mistake committed was grave indeed, and its evil was about to engulf the whole Muslim community, but God's grace, mercy and care prevented this evil. Hence, God reminds them of this, time after time, as He aims this to be an edifying lesson. When they realized the extent of the matter that could have engulfed them all, had it not been for God's grace and mercy, they were told that what they did was indeed following in Satan's footsteps. They must not fall into this trap, since Satan is their avowed enemy, ever since the beginning of human life. Again they are warned against what this may entail in their life: "*Believers! Do not follow Satan's footsteps, for he who follows Satan's footsteps will only enjoin what is shameful and wrong. Were it not for God's favour upon you and His grace, none of you would have ever been pure. It is God who causes whomever He wills to grow in purity. God is All-Hearing, All-Knowing.*" (Verse 21)

Nothing but a terrible fate awaits the believers if they take just one step with Satan. They should steer away from him altogether and follow a different way. The very thought of following Satan is repugnant to believers. Hence, drawing it in this way and holding it in front of them should make them always alert. "*He who follows Satan's footsteps will only enjoin what is shameful and wrong.*" (Verse 21) This false story is a stark and gruesome example of how Satan leads believers to something evil.

Man is weak, susceptible to desires and whims which may leave him stained, unless he benefits by God's grace when he turns to Him and follows His guidance: "*Were it not for God's favour upon you and His grace, none of you would have ever been pure. It is God who causes whomever He wills to grow in purity.*" (Verse 21) When God's light shines in a believer's heart, it purifies it. It is only through God's favours and grace that people grow in purity. Since God knows all and hears all, He certainly knows the ones who deserve to be purified and who are genuinely good. It is these that He helps to grow in purity.

Attaining the Sublime

Within the context of purity, the *sūrah* calls on believers to forgive one another as they love to be forgiven their sins: "*Let not those of you who have been graced with God's favour and ample means resolve by oath not to help those who are near of kin, the needy and those who have left their homes for the sake of God. But let them pardon and forbear. Do you not desire that God should forgive you your sins? God is indeed Much-Forgiving, Merciful.*" (Verse 22)

This verse was revealed in connection with Abū Bakr after the Qur'ān had cleared his daughter, 'Ā'ishah the pure, of any misconduct. He realized that Misṭaḥ ibn Athāthah, his relative whom he supported because of his poverty, was among those involved in circulating the false rumour. Therefore, he vowed that he would never do Misṭaḥ a good turn in the future. This verse, however, reminds Abū Bakr and the believers that they also commit mistakes and hope for God's forgiveness. Hence, they should forgive one another their mistakes. They must not deprive those who need the support of their generosity, even though the latter might have committed a grave error.

Now we see how one of the souls touched by God's light grows in purity attaining a truly sublime standard. Abū Bakr, who was so deeply hurt by the false rumours targeting his daughter and attempting to disgrace his family, responded to the Qur'ānic call on the believers to forgive those who hurt them. He reflected on the inspiring question, "*Do you not desire that God should forgive you your sins?*" (Verse 22) And he rose above the pain and injury, and also above the logic that prevailed in his environment. He felt there could only be one answer to that question, and with certainty and contentment he said: "Yes, indeed. I love that God should forgive me." He reinstated the allowance he had been giving Misṭaḥ, and vowed anew that he would never stop it in future. His vow replaced his earlier one that he would not give him anything. With such a sublime standard of generosity, Abū Bakr's heart was cleansed of any hard feeling and retained its purity.

The forgiveness of which God reminds the believers is granted only to those who repent of their errors, accusing chaste women of adultery and spreading corruption in the Muslim community. On the other hand, those who, like Ibn Ubayy, deliberately, and out of malice, make such accusations, will have no pardon or forgiveness. Even though they may escape punishment in this world, because no witnesses will testify against them, they will inevitably endure the punishment in the hereafter when no witnesses will be required.

> *Those who accuse chaste women who may have been unthinkingly careless but remained true believers, shall be rejected by God in this world as well as in the life to come. They shall endure awesome suffering; on the day when their own tongues, hands and feet will testify to what they did. On that day God will pay them in full their just due, and they will come to know that God alone is the Ultimate Truth, absolutely manifest.* (Verses 23–25)

The *sūrah* paints their crime in stark colours so as to expose its odious nature. It is an accusation against chaste women believers who go about their lives, totally oblivious to any possibility of accusation. They behave naturally, not thinking that they will be accused of something, simply because they have done nothing wrong. To accuse them of immorality is thus seen to be very serious, betraying the contemptible and mean nature of their accusers. Hence, they are cursed now by God, and expelled from among those who receive His grace in this present life and in the life to come. The *sūrah* then shows us a fascinating scene: "*On the day when their own tongues, hands and feet will testify to what they did.*" (Verse 24) Thus we see them accusing one another, just as they used to accuse chaste believing women. The contrast is very clear, as is always the case in the Qur'ān.

"*On that day God will pay them in full their just due.*" (Verse 25) Their deeds will be accurately reckoned and they will be given all that they really deserve. At that time they will be certain of what they used to be in doubt about. "*They will come to know that God alone is the Ultimate Truth, absolutely manifest.*" (Verse 25)

The *sūrah* concludes its comments on this whole story of falsehood by highlighting God's justice in the way He has given man his nature so as to manifest itself in practice. This is why the corrupt will unite with their like and the good will associate with others of their type. This is how relations are consolidated between husband and wife. Hence, it is absolutely impossible that 'Ā'ishah could be like what her accusers said of her, because she was destined to be the wife of the best person that ever lived.

"*Corrupt women are for corrupt men, and corrupt men for corrupt women, just as good women are for good men, and good men for good women. These are innocent of all that people may impute to them. Forgiveness and excellent sustenance are in store for them.*" (Verse 26) The Prophet dearly loved 'Ā'ishah. It was inconceivable that God should let His Prophet love her so much unless she was innocent of all guilt, pure and deserving of such a great love.

Good men and women are, by their very nature, "*innocent of all that people may impute to them.*" (Verse 26) False accusations cannot stick to them. "*Forgiveness and excellent sustenance are in store for them.*" (Verse 26) They will be forgiven any mistake they may commit, and they have their reward with God, clearly indicating their high position with Him.

Thus the *sūrah* concludes its comments on this serious trial for the Muslim community because it aimed at undermining their trust that the Prophet's household was absolutely pure and that God would not allow anyone but the most pure to be a member of that household. God wanted this episode to be an edifying lesson for the Muslim community, elevating it to an even more sublime standard.

2

Measures to Preserve Decency

Believers, do not enter houses other than your own unless you have obtained permission and greeted their inmates. This is best for you, so that you may take heed. (27)

يَـٰٓأَيُّهَا ٱلَّذِينَ ءَامَنُوا۟ لَا تَدْخُلُوا۟ بُيُوتًا
غَيْرَ بُيُوتِكُمْ حَتَّىٰ تَسْتَأْنِسُوا۟
وَتُسَلِّمُوا۟ عَلَىٰٓ أَهْلِهَا ۚ ذَٰلِكُمْ خَيْرٌ لَّكُمْ
لَعَلَّكُمْ تَذَكَّرُونَ ٢٧

If you find no one in the house, do not enter it until you are given leave; and if you are told to go back, then go back, as it is most proper for you. God has full knowledge of all that you do. (28)

فَإِن لَّمْ تَجِدُوا۟ فِيهَآ أَحَدًا فَلَا تَدْخُلُوهَا
حَتَّىٰ يُؤْذَنَ لَكُمْ ۖ وَإِن قِيلَ لَكُمُ
ٱرْجِعُوا۟ فَٱرْجِعُوا۟ ۖ هُوَ أَزْكَىٰ لَكُمْ ۚ وَٱللَّهُ
بِمَا تَعْمَلُونَ عَلِيمٌ ٢٨

You will incur no sin if you enter uninhabited houses in which you have something of use. God knows all that you do openly, and all that you would conceal. (29)

لَّيْسَ عَلَيْكُمْ جُنَاحٌ أَن تَدْخُلُوا۟ بُيُوتًا غَيْرَ
مَسْكُونَةٍ فِيهَا مَتَـٰعٌ لَّكُمْ ۚ وَٱللَّهُ يَعْلَمُ
مَا تُبْدُونَ وَمَا تَكْتُمُونَ ٢٩

Tell believing men to lower their gaze and to be mindful of their chastity. This is most conducive to their purity. God is certainly aware of all that they do. (30)

قُل لِّلْمُؤْمِنِينَ يَغُضُّوا۟ مِنْ أَبْصَـٰرِهِمْ
وَيَحْفَظُوا۟ فُرُوجَهُمْ ۚ ذَٰلِكَ أَزْكَىٰ لَهُمْ ۗ إِنَّ
ٱللَّهَ خَبِيرٌۢ بِمَا يَصْنَعُونَ ٣٠

And tell believing women to lower their gaze and to be mindful of their chastity, and not to display their charms except what may ordinarily appear thereof. Let them draw their head-coverings over their bosoms and not display their charms to any but their husbands, or their fathers, or their husbands' fathers, or their sons, or their husbands' sons, or their brothers, or their brothers' sons, or their sisters' sons, or their womenfolk, or those whom they rightfully possess, or such male attendants as are free of physical desire, or children that are as yet unaware of women's nakedness. Let them not swing their legs in walking so as to draw attention to their hidden charms. Believers, turn to God in repentance, so that you may achieve success. (31)

وَقُل لِّلْمُؤْمِنَٰتِ يَغْضُضْنَ مِنْ
أَبْصَٰرِهِنَّ وَيَحْفَظْنَ فُرُوجَهُنَّ
وَلَا يُبْدِينَ زِينَتَهُنَّ إِلَّا مَا ظَهَرَ
مِنْهَا ۖ وَلْيَضْرِبْنَ بِخُمُرِهِنَّ عَلَىٰ
جُيُوبِهِنَّ ۖ وَلَا يُبْدِينَ زِينَتَهُنَّ
إِلَّا لِبُعُولَتِهِنَّ أَوْ ءَابَآئِهِنَّ
أَوْ ءَابَآءِ بُعُولَتِهِنَّ أَوْ أَبْنَآئِهِنَّ
أَوْ أَبْنَآءِ بُعُولَتِهِنَّ أَوْ إِخْوَٰنِهِنَّ
أَوْ بَنِىٓ إِخْوَٰنِهِنَّ أَوْ بَنِىٓ أَخَوَٰتِهِنَّ
أَوْ نِسَآئِهِنَّ أَوْ مَا مَلَكَتْ أَيْمَٰنُهُنَّ
أَوِ ٱلتَّٰبِعِينَ غَيْرِ أُو۟لِى ٱلْإِرْبَةِ
مِنَ ٱلرِّجَالِ أَوِ ٱلطِّفْلِ ٱلَّذِينَ
لَمْ يَظْهَرُوا۟ عَلَىٰ عَوْرَٰتِ ٱلنِّسَآءِ ۖ
وَلَا يَضْرِبْنَ بِأَرْجُلِهِنَّ لِيُعْلَمَ
مَا يُخْفِينَ مِن زِينَتِهِنَّ ۚ وَتُوبُوٓا۟
إِلَى ٱللَّهِ جَمِيعًا أَيُّهَ ٱلْمُؤْمِنُونَ
لَعَلَّكُمْ تُفْلِحُونَ ﴿٣١﴾

Marry the single from among you as well as such of your male and female slaves as are virtuous. If they are poor, God will grant them sufficiency out of His bounty. God is Munificent, All-Knowing. (32)

وَأَنكِحُوا۟ ٱلْأَيَٰمَىٰ مِنكُمْ وَٱلصَّٰلِحِينَ
مِنْ عِبَادِكُمْ وَإِمَآئِكُمْ ۚ إِن يَكُونُوا۟
فُقَرَآءَ يُغْنِهِمُ ٱللَّهُ مِن فَضْلِهِۦ ۗ وَٱللَّهُ
وَٰسِعٌ عَلِيمٌ ﴿٣٢﴾

As for those who are unable to marry, let them live in continence until God grants them sufficiency out of His bounty. And if any of your slaves desire to obtain a deed of freedom, write it out for them if you are aware of any good in them; and give them something of the wealth God has given you. Do not force your maids to prostitution when they desire to preserve their chastity, in order to make some worldly gain. If anyone should force them, then after they have been compelled, God will be much forgiving, merciful [to them]. (33)

وَلْيَسْتَعْفِفِ ٱلَّذِينَ لَا يَجِدُونَ نِكَاحًا
حَتَّىٰ يُغْنِيَهُمُ ٱللَّهُ مِن فَضْلِهِۦ ۗ وَٱلَّذِينَ
يَبْتَغُونَ ٱلْكِتَٰبَ مِمَّا مَلَكَتْ
أَيْمَٰنُكُمْ فَكَاتِبُوهُمْ إِنْ عَلِمْتُمْ
فِيهِمْ خَيْرًا ۖ وَءَاتُوهُم مِّن مَّالِ
ٱللَّهِ ٱلَّذِىٓ ءَاتَىٰكُمْ ۚ وَلَا تُكْرِهُوا۟
فَتَيَٰتِكُمْ عَلَى ٱلْبِغَآءِ إِنْ أَرَدْنَ تَحَصُّنًا
لِّتَبْتَغُوا۟ عَرَضَ ٱلْحَيَوٰةِ ٱلدُّنْيَا ۚ وَمَن
يُكْرِههُّنَّ فَإِنَّ ٱللَّهَ مِنۢ بَعْدِ
إِكْرَٰهِهِنَّ غَفُورٌ رَّحِيمٌ ﴿٣٣﴾

We have bestowed upon you from on high revelations clearly showing the truth, and lessons from [the stories of] those who have passed away before you, and admonition for the God-fearing. (34)

وَلَقَدْ أَنزَلْنَآ إِلَيْكُمْ ءَايَٰتٍ مُّبَيِّنَٰتٍ
وَمَثَلًا مِّنَ ٱلَّذِينَ خَلَوْا۟ مِن قَبْلِكُمْ
وَمَوْعِظَةً لِّلْمُتَّقِينَ ﴿٣٤﴾

Overview

We mentioned previously that in the clean and healthy society it establishes, Islam does not rely on punishment; rather its main line of defence is prevention. It does not suppress natural desires. It regulates them within a clean atmosphere that is free of deliberate stimulation. The main element in the Islamic method of educating its followers is to reduce the chances of error, eliminate temptation, and remove all impediments that prevent the satisfaction of natural desires in a perfectly natural and clean way.

It is in this light that we should look at the way Islam accords a certain sanctity for homes. When they are at home, people should not be surprised by strangers coming in without first asking leave to enter. Otherwise, people's privacy would be invaded when they least expect it. In addition, Islam requires both men and women to lower their gaze and not expose what may arouse sexual desire.

From the same perspective, Islam facilitates marriage for poor men and women, because marriage is the best guarantee against adultery. It prohibits sending slaves into prostitution, because prostitution encourages people to indulge in prohibited sex. Let us now consider these points in more detail.

Before Entering a House

> *Believers, do not enter houses other than your own unless you have obtained permission and greeted their inmates. This is best for you, so that you may take heed. If you find no one in the house, do not enter it until you are given leave; and if you are told to go back, then go back, as it is most proper for you. God has full knowledge of all that you do. You will incur no sin if you enter uninhabited houses in which you have something of use. God knows all that you do openly, and all that you would conceal.* (Verses 27–29)

God has made homes places of comfort where people may relax and enjoy privacy and reassurance. At home, they do not feel the need to be cautious or on the alert. Thus, they may relax and take things easy. But homes cannot be so unless their privacy is strictly respected. No one may enter a home without its occupier's knowledge and permission, at the time they choose, and in the manner they prefer.

Should we be able to go into other people's homes without first seeking permission, we may see them in situations they want to keep private, or we may see what arouses desire and opens the way to error. This could come about through a chance meeting, or a casual glance. When these are repeated, they become deliberate, motivated by the desires aroused by the casual glance in the first place. It may even develop into a sinful relation or cause a suppressed desire leading to a psychological problem.

In pre-Islamic days in Arabia, visitors used to enter a home and then announce themselves. It could be that inside a man may be with his wife in a position they did not want anyone to see; or that the man or woman were undressed. All this used to hurt people, and deprived them of a sense of security at home. Furthermore, when visitors saw charm and beauty, temptation might be strong or even irresistible.

For all such reasons, God laid down the requirement to observe fine manners, making it necessary for a Muslim to announce himself and greet the people inside before entering. This establishes a friendly atmosphere right from the first moment.

"*Believers, do not enter houses other than your own unless you have obtained permission and greeted their inmates.*" (Verse 27) Seeking permission is expressed in the Arabic original in an unusual way, *tasta'nisū*, which implies friendliness. Thus we may say that we should not enter other people's houses until we have obtained friendly and cordial permission. This implies that the visitor should be gentle in his approach so as to be welcomed by the people inside. Such refinement is characteristic of Islamic manners.

When permission is sought, it follows that the house is either empty or people are inside. If there is no one in, then the caller cannot enter, because entry follows permission. "*If you find no one in the house, do not enter it until you are given leave.*" (Verse 28) But if there is someone in, seeking permission is not enough for entry. It is merely a request, and if the request is not granted, entry is prohibited. It is better to leave without delay: "*If you are told to go back, then go back, as it is most proper for you.*" (Verse 28) The person who is told to go back should do so without feeling upset or offended. People have their secrets and they may have good reason for not receiving a visitor at a particular time. It is up to them to determine their own situation.

"*God has full knowledge of all that you do.*" (Verse 28) He knows people's secrets and motives.

Visiting People When They Are Not Ready

Places that are more or less public, like hotels, guest houses and reception halls which are separate from the main house are treated differently. We may enter such places without first seeking permission, because the very reason for seeking permission before entry does not apply to them. Requiring permission first may be inconvenient in such places.

"*You will incur no sin if you enter uninhabited houses in which you have something of use. God knows all that you do openly, and all that you would conceal.*" (Verse 29) The point here is that of God's knowledge of all our situations and what we do in public or private. The feeling that God watches us in all situations should make people more obedient and willing to observe the refined manners which He has outlined in His book that lays down a code of living for all humanity.

As a complete code for human life, the Qur'ān emphasizes this point of detail in social life because it aims to regulate life in all its aspects, bringing its details in line with its fundamental issues. Thus, seeking permission before entering other people's homes respects the sanctity which makes the home a place of relaxation. It spares its people the embarrassment of being taken by surprise, or being seen in a situation that they prefer not to be seen in. We are not talking here only about the parts of the human body which should be covered. At home people may be in a situation which they simply do not like others to see. It could relate to their personal appearance, the way they dress or lay their furniture, or anything else. It could also relate to feelings and emotions. Who of us would like to be seen in a situation of weakness, crying or angry or in pain or distress?

The Qur'ānic code of manners attends to all these details through the requirement of seeking permission before entering someone else's home. It also seeks to reduce chances of casual meetings or sightings that could arouse desire and develop into unacceptable relations that Satan may stealthily encourage. The first Muslim community to be addressed by the Qur'ān clearly understood such directives and their purpose. The Prophet himself was the first to implement them.

The Prophet visited Sa'd ibn 'Ubādah, the chief of the *Anṣār*, at home and sought permission, saying: "*Assalāmu 'alaykum wa raḥmatullāh*", meaning, peace and God's mercy be bestowed on you. Sa'd replied in a low voice. His son, Qays, asked him: "Are you not letting God's Messenger in?" Sa'd said: "Let him wish us peace more." Again the Prophet repeated his greeting and Sa'd replied in a low voice twice more. Therefore, the Prophet departed, but Sa'd ran after him and explained what happened, saying: "Messenger of God, I certainly heard your greetings and replied quietly hoping that you would wish us peace more and more." The Prophet went in with him. Sa'd ordered water to be brought for the Prophet to wash. Then he gave him a small blanket dyed with saffron to cover himself. The Prophet then raised his hands, praying: "My Lord, shower Your blessings and grace on Sa'd ibn 'Ubādah's family." [Related by Abū Dāwūd and al-Nasā'ī]

The Prophet taught his Companions how to approach someone else's home, saying: "If you come towards a home, do not face the door straight, but stand to the right or to the left, and say: *Assalāmu 'alaykum! Assalāmu 'alaykum!"* At that time, there were no screens on doors. [Related by Abū Dāwūd]

Sa'd ibn Abī Waqqāṣ came to the Prophet and stood facing the door, seeking permission. The Prophet said to him: "Move this way or that way, because permission is sought before a person looks in." [Related by Abū Dāwūd]

An authentic *ḥadīth* quotes the Prophet as saying: "If a person overlooks you without having obtained permission, and you hit him with a small stone, and cause him a severe injury in his eye, you have nothing to answer for." [Related by al-Bukhārī and Muslim]

Rib'ī, a Companion of the Prophet, reports: "A man from the 'Āmir clan sought permission to enter the Prophet's home, saying: 'Can I enter?' The Prophet said to his servant: 'Go to this man and teach him how to seek permission. Tell him to say: '*Assalāmu 'alaykum.* May I come in?' The man overheard the Prophet and said exactly that. The Prophet gave him permission and he entered." [Related by Abū Dāwūd]

'Abdullāh ibn 'Umar was walking, troubled by the heat, and he urgently needed to relieve himself. He approached a Qurayshi woman's place, and said: "*Assalāmu 'alaykum*. May I come in?" She said: "Enter with peace." He repeated what he said, and she repeated her reply. He was unable to stand still. He told her to say: "Come in", if she wanted to give him permission and she did so. He then entered.

'Aṭā' ibn Rabāḥ, a scholar who studied under 'Abdullāh ibn 'Abbās, the Prophet's cousin whose scholarly knowledge was recognized as highly authoritative, reported: "I asked Ibn 'Abbās: 'Should I seek permission before entering when only my orphan sisters are at home considering that I look after them and they live with me in the same home?' He said: 'Yes.' I asked him again so that he might give me a concession, but he refused. Instead, he asked me: 'Do you like to see your sister undressed?' I answered in the negative. He said: 'Then seek permission before entry.' I repeated the question once more, but he asked me: 'Do you love to obey God?' I said: 'Yes.' He said: 'Then seek permission.'"

An authentic *ḥadīth* makes it clear that the Prophet prohibited a man from entering his own home unannounced so surprising his wife. In another version the prohibition is attached to such a surprise being made at night, implying that his family might be doing something unacceptable.

Another *ḥadīth* mentions that the Prophet arrived with his Companions at Madīnah during the day. So, he encamped at the outskirts, explaining his purpose: "Wait until the end of the day, so that a woman has a chance to attend to her uncombed hair, or remove unwanted hair on her body."

Good Manners and High Morals

Such refined manners were characteristic of the Prophet and his Companions after God had taught them the Islamic way. Today, however, we find that such fine considerations are largely meaningless despite our being Muslims. A man may just turn up at his brother's door at any time of the day or night, knocking hard and caring little for disturbing the people inside, until the door is opened. The people may have a telephone which provides an excellent way of seeking permission to visit before starting out.[2] He could thus easily find out a time suitable to his hosts. Nevertheless, people simply do not take such steps. A man may arrive at someone's home without a prior appointment or permission. What is worse, our social tradition makes it imperative that a visitor who has come unannounced be received, even though his visit might be extremely inconvenient.

We are certainly Muslims, but we surprise our friends at any moment, even at meal times. If we are not invited to a meal, we may feel aggrieved. We may even surprise them late at night, and if they do not invite us to stay the night, we are offended. We allow our hosts no excuses either way.

All this takes place simply because we neglect Islamic manners. We do not bring our own preferences in line with what has been taught by God's Messenger. We insist on following a mistaken social tradition that has no divine authority.

We look at other, non-Muslim communities and find that their social traditions are closer to the values and manners Islam wants us to adopt. Sometimes we admire these, but at other times we may even ridicule them, without even trying to look into what Islam wants us to do.

Proper Control of a Natural Desire

Having dealt with the proper manners of entering homes after taking permission, the *sūrah* moves on to prevent desire from running loose. It simply prevents looking at what is bound to excite desire, and it prohibits action that encourages sin.

> *Tell believing men to lower their gaze and to be mindful of their chastity. This is most conducive to their purity. God is certainly aware of all that they do. And tell believing women to lower their gaze and to be mindful of their chastity, and not to display their charms except what may ordinarily appear thereof. Let them draw their*

---

2. At the time this was written telephones were largely uncommon in people's houses in Egypt. – Editor's note.

head-coverings over their bosoms and not display their charms to any but their husbands, or their fathers, or their husbands' fathers, or their sons, or their husbands' sons, or their brothers, or their brothers' sons, or their sisters' sons, or their womenfolk, or those whom they rightfully possess, or such male attendants as are free of physical desire, or children that are as yet unaware of women's nakedness. Let them not swing their legs in walking so as to draw attention to their hidden charms. Believers, turn to God in repentance, so that you may achieve success. (Verses 30–31)

Islam wants to establish a clean society where desire is not aroused at every moment, and erotic scenes are not displayed everywhere. Continual excitement of the sexual urge leads to an insatiable desire that may become unstoppable. A stealthy look, a seductive move, flagrant make-up and thinly-dressed bodies are meant only to add to such insatiable and uncontrolled excitement. Thus, prudence and self control are heavily taxed. Hence, there remains one of two alternatives: either total permissiveness that disregards all checks and values, or psychological problems and disorders that result from having to suppress a desire that has been strongly aroused. This borders on unmitigated torture.

One way Islam uses for achieving its goal of establishing a clean human society is to prevent such uncontrollable excitement of the sexual urge. It wants the natural sexual urge, of both men and women, to remain healthy, maintaining its natural strength and to satisfy it in the proper, clean manner.

At some point in time, the idea was promoted that easy mixing between the two sexes, playful conversation and revealing physical attractions help to provide a relaxed social atmosphere, with no rigid inhibitions. It was said that this is necessary as a preventive measure against arbitrary suppression of natural desires and psychological complexes and disorders. It reduces the pressure of the sexual urge and prevents an uncontrollable explosion, etc.

Such ideas were promoted as a result of the advancement of theories that aimed to deprive man of his distinctive characteristics that separate the human race from animals, and which put man at the same level as animals. The most important of these theories was Freud's. But all this was no more than theoretical assumptions. I have seen with my own eyes, in a permissive society that abandoned all social, moral and religious restrictions, solid evidence to undermine its very foundation.[3] I have seen in a country that does not place a single restriction on exposing the human body or on sexual relations, in all forms and types, that such freedom in no way refines or controls the sexual urge. On the contrary, it led to an insatiable quest for sexual pleasure. I also saw much of the psychological problems and disorders which were claimed to be triggered only by deprivation and isolation from the other sex. They were on the increase, as were all types of sexual perversion. And all this was a direct result of free, unrestrained mixing between the two sexes, total permissiveness, exposure of much of the human body in the street, seductive gestures, suggestive glances, etc. This is not the place for recording such scenes in detail, but I only have to say that all this indicates the need to revise those theories, which are contradicted by what prevails in society.

Attraction to the other sex is both natural and profound, because God has made it the means by which human life continues and by which man can fulfil his task on earth. It is a permanent attraction that subsides for a while and then regains strength. To stir it at all times will undoubtedly keep it on the boil. Thus, it requires physical satisfaction. If this does not take place, tension will rise and man finds himself in a sort of permanent torture. Excitement takes place through a look, a move, a smile, a joke and even the tone in one's speech. The best safeguard is to reduce such excitement so that the mutual attraction between man and woman remains within its natural limits, and finds its satisfaction in the proper and natural way. This is the line Islam prefers.

The two verses we are now discussing give us some examples of how Islam helps to reduce the chances of excitement and sin: "*Tell believing men to lower their gaze and to be mindful of their chastity. This is most conducive to their purity. God is certainly aware of all that they do.*" (Verse 30)

---

3. The author is referring here to his stay in the USA in 1949–1951. – Editor's note.

Lowering their gaze is an act of refining men's manners. It represents an attempt to rise above the desire to look at women's physical charms. As such, it is a practical step to ensure that the first window of temptation is shut. Minding their chastity is the natural result of lowering their gaze. It is indeed the second step that comes after strengthening one's will and rising above the natural urge right at the beginning. Hence, the two are stated in the same verse as a cause and effect, or as two consecutive steps both in personal conscience and in reality.

"*This is most conducive to their purity.*" (Verse 30) It ensures that their feelings remain pure, unaffected by licentious desire and promiscuous action. Thus, feelings retain their noble human standards, and do not sink to animal levels. This protects honour, integrity and sanctities within the community. Besides, it is God who lays down such preventive measures, fully aware as He certainly is of people's psychology, natural instincts thoughts and motives: "*God is certainly aware of all that they do.*"

"*And tell believing women to lower their gaze and to be mindful of their chastity.*" (Verse 31) They must not cast hungry or seductive looks at men to arouse their desire. Nor are they permitted any sexual behaviour other than what is lawful and clean. Thus, children that are born as a result will have nothing to be ashamed of when they have to face society and play their roles in it.

"*And not to display their charms except what may ordinarily appear thereof.*" (Verse 31) The Arabic term *zīnah*, translated here as 'charms', has wider connotations than natural beauty. It includes adornments women add to look more attractive. Such adornments are lawful for women to use, because they satisfy a natural female tendency that makes women always want to look beautiful and attractive. Such adornments differ from one time to another, but whatever form they take, they are meant to satisfy the same natural motive of appearing more beautiful and displaying charms before men.

Since this is a natural tendency, Islam does not suppress it; it brings it under control so that a woman displays her charms before one man, who is her spouse who sees her as no one else does. In addition, her close relatives who may not be married to her may see some of her charms as well, because their desires are not excited as a result, considering their close relation. However, the charms or adornments that appear on a woman's face and hands are permissible to see. The Prophet said to Asmā' bint Abī Bakr, his sister-in-law: "Asmā'! When a woman attains puberty, nothing should be seen of her except this [and he pointed to face and hands]." [Related by Abū Dāwūd][4]

Prompt Compliance with Divine Orders

A further instruction is given to women with regard to their public appearance: "*Let them draw their head-coverings over their bosoms.*" (Verse 31) We have a translation problem here because the Qur'ānic verse uses the term *jayb*, which does not mean 'bosom'. *Jayb* instead means the top opening of a dress which is bound to reveal a part of a woman's bosom. Hence, women are ordered to bring their head coverings down so as to cover this opening, thus covering their heads, necks and chests. In this way, they cover their charms so as not to be displayed before hungry eyes, not even in a sudden encounter between man and woman. A God-fearing man will always try not to make such a look last long, or repeat it. Yet, it may have a lasting effect if charms and adornments are seen suddenly. Hence, the instruction to keep them covered. What is important to realize here is that God wants to spare people this type of test.

Despite their natural desire to want to appear beautiful, the Muslim women who received this instruction did not slacken to put it into effect because their hearts were resplendent with God's light. In pre-Islamic ignorant days, women used to go out in public revealing their bosoms, just like women do today in non-Islamic societies. Yet when the order was revealed requiring women to cover themselves and reveal only what appears naturally of their charms, their response was as 'Ā'ishah describes: "May God bestow His grace on the early Muslim women: when God revealed His order, 'Let them draw their head-coverings over their bosoms,' they tore their dresses and used them to cover their heads." [Related by al-Bukhārī]

4. This *ḥadīth* is classified as *mursal*, which means that it is poor in authenticity.

Ṣafiyyah bint Shaybah reports: "We were at 'Ā'ishah's place when some women spoke about Qurayshi women and their virtues. 'Ā'ishah said: There is no doubt that Qurayshi women have their virtues, but I have seen none like the Anṣār women in their ardent belief in God's book and undoubted faith in divine revelations. When the verse was revealed in *Sūrah al-Nūr* stating, 'Let them draw their head-coverings over their bosoms,' their men went home and read to them what God had revealed. A man would read this to his wife, daughter, sister and other relatives. Every single woman of them took out her printed dress and wrapped it over her head, in obedience to what God had revealed in confirmation of its application to them. In the morning they prayed behind God's Messenger, wearing their head coverings as though they were carrying crows on their heads." [Related by Abū Dāwūd]

Islam has refined the tastes of Islamic society and its sense of beauty for it no longer seeks the lewd and licentious. Exposing bodily charms attracts a man's physical instinct. Modesty, on the other hand, shows a clean type of beauty that refines man's sense. It is the type of beauty worthy of man, because it imparts a sense of purity and chastity.

Today, Islam produces the same effect among women believers, despite the fact that the general taste in society has sunk so low as to encourage the revealing of physical charms and the exposure of other parts of the human body. Nevertheless, women believers voluntarily cover themselves as God requires them to do, while other women around them try to attract men by their physical presence.

Maintaining such modesty in appearance is another preventive measure Islam puts in place to protect both the individual and society. Hence, it is not required in situations where temptation is inconceivable. Thus, close relatives who are barred from inter-marriage are excluded. Normally there is no sexual attraction between such relatives who include fathers, sons, fathers-in-law, stepsons, brothers and nephews. Also excepted are Muslim women, as the verse makes clear: "*or their womenfolk*." Women generally are not included in this exception, because they may describe Muslim women and their charms to their husbands, brothers and other men. An authentic *ḥadīth* quotes the

Prophet as saying: "No woman should describe another woman to her husband as though he is seeing her." [Related by al-Bukhārī and Muslim] Muslim women, on the other hand, are reliable. Their faith prevents them from describing the physical charms of a Muslim woman to their husbands.

Another exception applies to slaves: "*or those whom they rightfully possess.*" Some scholars say that this applies to women slaves only, while others include male slaves too because a slave does not look up to his mistress in a carnal way. But the first view is more logical because a slave is a man with all the desire any other man has, even though he is placed in a special or unfavourable situation. Also excepted are "*such male attendants as are free of physical desire,*" who may not be attracted to women for one reason or another, such as being impotent or feeble minded. In this case, a woman's physical beauty causes no temptation. Similarly excepted are "*children that are as yet unaware of women's nakedness.*" These are children who do not yet feel any sexual desire because they are too young. When they are older and become sexually aware and attracted to women, even though they might not have attained their puberty, nonetheless the original rules apply to them.

All these – with the exception of husbands – may see a woman uncovered, except for the area between her waistline and knees, because the cause that prevents such looks does not apply in their case. A husband, on the other hand, may see his wife without restriction.

Since this is a preventive measure, the Qur'ānic verse goes on to prohibit the movements a woman may make in order to attract attention to her adornments or charms that are not readily visible. Such movements may be exciting even though the adornments themselves may remain invisible.

"*Let them not swing their legs in walking so as to draw attention to their hidden charms.*" (Verse 31) This order results from profound knowledge of human psychology. Sometimes, the human imagination may be a more powerful trigger for desire. Many are the men who, on seeing a woman's shoes, dress or jewellery, are more excited than by seeing her body. Many are the ones that are sexually excited by the mental image they draw of a woman than by seeing her in person. Psychiatrists have identified such cases which may need treatment. The tinkle of jewellery or the smell of perfume may excite some people and kindle their sexual desire. With some, this could become irresistible. The Qur'ān takes effective and appropriate action against all this, because its message is sent by God the Creator who knows His creation and who is kind to, and fully aware of, them all.

The verse concludes with turning people's hearts to God, opening the door of repentance and forgiveness for all that was done before its revelation. "*Believers, turn to God in repentance, so that you may achieve success.*" (Verse 31) Thus, it enhances their feelings that God watches over them, and that He is kind to them, taking care of them. He helps them overcome their weakness in respect of sexual desire. Yet nothing can bring this under proper control more effectively than faith and fearing God.

Promoting Easy Marriage

Up to this point, the measures the Qur'ān speaks about are preventive. Yet sexual attraction is very real and needs practical steps to ensure its proper control. The most important solution is marriage and the taking of positive steps to encourage it, together with making other ways of sexual response far more difficult or even totally unavailable.

> *Marry the single from among you as well as such of your male and female slaves as are virtuous. If they are poor, God will grant them sufficiency out of His bounty. God is Munificent, All-Knowing. As for those who are unable to marry, let them live in continence until God grants them sufficiency out of His bounty. And if any of your slaves desire to obtain a deed of freedom, write it out for them if you are aware of any good in them; and give them something of the wealth God has given you. Do not force your maids to prostitution when they desire to preserve their chastity, in order to make some worldly gain. If anyone should force them, then after they have been compelled, God will be much forgiving, merciful [to them].* (Verses 32–33)

Marriage is the proper way to satisfy natural sexual desires. Hence, all impediments that make marriage difficult should be removed so that human life can progress in this natural and simple way. Money is the primary impediment facing those who wish to establish families and protect themselves against sin. Hence, Islam puts in place an integrated system that does not make a requirement without providing its tools or the conditions that are conducive to its fulfilment. As it requires people to maintain their chastity, it makes marriage easy for all people. Hence only the one who deliberately turns away from the clean and pure way indulges in sin. Therefore, Islam requires the Muslim community to provide financial assistance for those who lack the wherewithal to get married: "*Marry the single from among you as well as such of your male and female slaves as are virtuous. If they are poor, God will grant them sufficiency out of His bounty.*" (Verse 32)

The order includes all those who are single, men and women, although only free people are meant here initially. Those who are in bondage are specifically mentioned later: "*as well as such of your male and female slaves as are virtuous.*" They all need money for this purpose, as it is clearly understood from the rest of the verse: "*If they are poor, God will grant them sufficiency out of His bounty.*"

This order is given to the Muslim community to enable single people to marry. The majority of scholars are of the view that this order is meant as a recommendation because there were single people during the time of the Prophet and they were not made to marry. Had this order been meant as an obligation, the Prophet would have ensured they all married. In our view, this order states an obligation, but it does not mean that a Muslim ruler is required to compel those who are single to get married. What it means instead is that the Muslim community must help single people who wish to get married, thus enabling them to guard their chastity. Islam considers this to be a practical measure of protection so that the Muslim community remains free of adultery, as it is duty bound to remain so. Providing the means to fulfil an obligation is also obligatory.

We should remember though that Islam is a fully integrated system. Hence, it provides adequate measures to set the economy of the Muslim community on the right footing. Thus, it provides good job opportunities for those who are able to work, so that they do not need assistance from the treasury. However, in exceptional situations, the public treasury is required to provide such assistance. This means that in the Islamic economic system, everyone has an income to meet their needs. The provision of jobs giving adequate income is a duty of the Muslim state and a right owing to individual citizens. Giving financial assistance by the public treasury is the exception, not the rule.

Financial Help for Marriage

When, despite all this, there remain in the community single men and women who are poor, unable to meet the expenses of marriage, the Muslim community must help them marry. The same applies to slaves, of both sexes. However, this duty applies in the first place to their masters, if they can meet such expenses. Poverty should never be an impediment preventing marriage when single men or women are suitable for marriage and are willing. It is God who provides for all. He has made it clear that He will give them enough when they choose the clean and healthy way, guarding their chastity through marriage. "*If they are poor, God will grant them sufficiency out of His bounty.*" (Verse 32) The Prophet says: "Three categories of people have the right to help provided by God: a person striving for God's cause, and a slave who has arranged to buy his own freedom and wants to fulfil his commitment, and one who wants to marry in order to guard his own chastity." [Related by al-Tirmidhī and al-Nasā'ī]

Until the Muslim community provides the necessary help to enable them to get married, single people are instructed to guard their chastity. "*As for those who are unable to marry, let them live in continence until God grants them sufficiency out of His bounty.*" (Verse 33) This He certainly does, because "*God is Munificent, All-Knowing.*" (Verse 33) He does not stint the means of a person who wants to stick to the way of purity and chastity as He is fully aware of people's intentions.

We see how Islam provides a practical solution to a real problem. Every individual who is fit to marry should be able to do so, even though he or she may lack the necessary financial ability. In most cases, money, or the lack of it, is the most difficult barrier that prevents people from getting married.

It is recognized that the presence of slaves within the community allows moral standards to fall, encouraging loose moral attitudes because, generally speaking, slaves have a weaker sense of human dignity. At the same time slavery was inevitable at the advent of Islam, considering the need to apply the same rules to captives of war taken by Muslims as Muslim captives received at the hands of their non-Muslim captors. Yet Islam took a unilateral initiative to free slaves whenever possible, until a new world order allowed for the total abolition of slavery. It is in this vein that Islam required that a slave who wished to buy his own freedom should be freed in return for an agreed sum of money which he paid to his master. "*And if any of your slaves desire to obtain a deed of freedom, write it out for them if you are aware of any good in them.*" (Verse 33)

Scholars have different views on whether this is obligatory, but we believe it to be so because it fits well with the line Islam adopts on freedom and human dignity. When a slave signs a deed of freedom, the money he earns through his own work belongs to him so that he can fulfil his commitment under the deed of freedom. What is more is that he can rightfully claim to be helped from *zakāt* funds: "*And give them something of the wealth God has given you.*" (Verse 33) The only condition that applies in such situations is that the master should be aware that the slave is a good person. The goodness that the verse refers to is that the slave should be a Muslim in the first place, and that he or she should be able to earn their living through their work. A freed slave should not become a liability to society, or forced to resort to degrading practices in order to survive. Islam lays down a system of social security which is very practical. It does not raise empty slogans nor does it try to meet them without looking at the realities that follow. It does not merely seek to free slaves without giving that freedom real meaning. Slaves will not achieve a real standard of freedom unless they are able to earn their living so that they neither beg nor resort to some dirty practices to survive. Some such practices are far worse than slavery.

Islam frees slaves in order to cleanse society, and so avoid it becoming more contaminated with vice.

By the grace of God, slavery has been abolished after the signing of international treaties and conventions that prohibit the enslavement of captives of war. Under Islam, slavery was allowed only provisionally, on the basis of measure-for-measure in the treatment of enemy captives of war.

Fair Treatment for the Least Privileged

What is worse than the presence of slaves in the community is that some slaves might be put to prostitution. In pre-Islamic days, a master might make his female slaves prostitutes, taking some or all of their wages. This form of prostitution continues to be practised today. As Islam wants the Islamic social environment to be pure, it forbids all adultery, particularly this form of prostitution. "*Do not force your maids to prostitution when they desire to preserve their chastity, in order to make some worldly gain. If anyone should force them, then after they have been compelled, God will be much forgiving, merciful [to them].*" (Verse 33) This verse warns those who force their maids into prostitution, and rebukes them for seeking to enrich themselves in this highly immoral way. It also promises those who are forced to it forgiveness and mercy.

Al-Suddī mentions that this verse points directly to 'Abdullāh ibn Ubayy, the chief hypocrite in Madīnah. He had a slave maid named Mu'ādhah. When he received a guest, he would give him this maid to sleep with, hoping to gain financial reward or some other favour from him. The maid complained of this to Abū Bakr, and Abū Bakr reported it to the Prophet who ordered 'Abdullāh ibn Ubayy to refrain from such deeds. 'Abdullāh complained: "Who will restore justice to us against Muḥammad? He interferes on behalf of our maid!" This verse was then revealed.

The prohibition of compelling girls, who wish to maintain their chastity, into prostitution for financial gain was part of the Qur'ānic method of cleansing the Islamic social environment and of blocking all dirty methods of satisfying sexual desires. When prostitution is condoned in society, it tempts many people because it is so easy. When such avenues are not available, people have to seek the clean way of marriage to satisfy their natural desires.

There is no validity in the argument that prostitution works as a safety device to protect families, or that it is the only way to satisfy a natural need when marriage is difficult, or that unless such an easy way is found, people assault honourable women. This is indeed a twisted argument that confuses causes and results. Sexual desire must remain clean, pure and directed to serve the purpose of procreation, so that new generations can grow up in a clean environment. Communities must reform their economic systems so that everyone can have a reasonable standard of living which enables him or her to marry. Should there remain exceptional cases, these would be properly considered and appropriate treatment found for them. This leaves no need for prostitution, or filthy brothels where those who want to ease the pressure of their natural sexual desire can throw aside their burden, in the same way as garbage is publicly thrown over a dunghill. It is the economic system that should be reformed so as to prevent such filth from existing. The inadequacy of economic systems should never be the basis of an argument for brothels where humanity is exceedingly humiliated.

This is exactly the method Islam adopts, providing an integrated system that maintains purity and helps people preserve their chastity. It is a system that provides a bridge linking this world with heaven, and elevates humanity to a sublime level that is enlightened with God's guidance.

The whole passage concludes with a verse that provides suitable comments on its subject matter: "*We have bestowed upon you from on high revelations clearly showing the truth, and lessons from [the stories of] those who have passed away before you, and admonition for the God-fearing.*" (Verse 34) Its verses are clear. They show the truth, leaving no room for ambiguity or distortion. It portrays the fate of earlier communities that deviated from the divine method and the punishment meted out to them. The Qur'ān also provides an admonition for the

God-fearing who realize that God watches all that we do. Thus, they stand in awe of God and they follow the right path. All the rules and the rulings outlined in this passage fit well with this comment which emphasizes the bond between people's hearts with God Almighty who bestowed this Qur'ān from on high.

3

The Light of Heaven and Earth

God is the light of the heavens and the earth. His light may be compared to a niche containing a lamp; the lamp within a glass, the glass like a radiant star; lit from a blessed tree – an olive tree that is neither of the east nor of the west. Its very oil would almost give light even though no fire had touched it. Light upon light! God guides to His light him that wills [to be guided]. God propounds parables for all people, since God alone has full knowledge of all things. (35)

ٱللَّهُ نُورُ ٱلسَّمَٰوَٰتِ وَٱلْأَرْضِ ۚ مَثَلُ نُورِهِۦ
كَمِشْكَوٰةٍ فِيهَا مِصْبَاحٌ ۖ ٱلْمِصْبَاحُ فِى
زُجَاجَةٍ ۖ ٱلزُّجَاجَةُ كَأَنَّهَا كَوْكَبٌ دُرِّىٌّ يُوقَدُ
مِن شَجَرَةٍ مُّبَٰرَكَةٍ زَيْتُونَةٍ لَّا شَرْقِيَّةٍ
وَلَا غَرْبِيَّةٍ يَكَادُ زَيْتُهَا يُضِىٓءُ وَلَوْ لَمْ
تَمْسَسْهُ نَارٌ ۚ نُّورٌ عَلَىٰ نُورٍ ۗ يَهْدِى ٱللَّهُ
لِنُورِهِۦ مَن يَشَآءُ ۚ وَيَضْرِبُ ٱللَّهُ ٱلْأَمْثَٰلَ
لِلنَّاسِ ۗ وَٱللَّهُ بِكُلِّ شَىْءٍ عَلِيمٌ ﴿٣٥﴾

In houses which God has sanctioned to be raised so that His name be remembered in them, there are [such as] extol His limitless glory, morning and evening (36)

فِى بُيُوتٍ أَذِنَ ٱللَّهُ أَن تُرْفَعَ وَيُذْكَرَ
فِيهَا ٱسْمُهُۥ يُسَبِّحُ لَهُۥ فِيهَا بِٱلْغُدُوِّ
وَٱلْءَاصَالِ ﴿٣٦﴾

رِجَالٌ لَّا تُلْهِيهِمْ تِجَٰرَةٌ وَلَا بَيْعٌ عَن
ذِكْرِ ٱللَّهِ وَإِقَامِ ٱلصَّلَوٰةِ وَإِيتَآءِ ٱلزَّكَوٰةِ
يَخَافُونَ يَوْمًا تَتَقَلَّبُ فِيهِ ٱلْقُلُوبُ
وَٱلْأَبْصَٰرُ ﴿٣٧﴾

– people whom neither commerce nor profit can divert from the remembrance of God, and from attending regularly to prayer, and from charity; who are filled with fear of the day when all hearts and eyes will be convulsed; (37)

لِيَجْزِيَهُمُ ٱللَّهُ أَحْسَنَ مَا عَمِلُوا۟ وَيَزِيدَهُم
مِّن فَضْلِهِۦ ۗ وَٱللَّهُ يَرْزُقُ مَن يَشَآءُ بِغَيْرِ
حِسَابٍ ﴿٣٨﴾

who [only hope] that God may reward them in accordance with the best that they ever did, and lavish His grace upon them. God gives to whom He wills beyond all reckoning. (38)

وَٱلَّذِينَ كَفَرُوٓا۟ أَعْمَٰلُهُمْ كَسَرَابٍۭ بِقِيعَةٍ
يَحْسَبُهُ ٱلظَّمْـَٔانُ مَآءً حَتَّىٰٓ إِذَا جَآءَهُۥ لَمْ
يَجِدْهُ شَيْـًٔا وَوَجَدَ ٱللَّهَ عِندَهُۥ فَوَفَّىٰهُ
حِسَابَهُۥ ۗ وَٱللَّهُ سَرِيعُ ٱلْحِسَابِ ﴿٣٩﴾

As for the unbelievers, their deeds are like a mirage in the desert, which the thirsty traveller supposes to be water, but when he comes near to it, he finds that it is nothing. But he finds that God [has always been present] with him, and that He will pay him his account in full; for God is swift in reckoning. (39)

أَوْ كَظُلُمَٰتٍ فِى بَحْرٍ لُّجِّىٍّ يَغْشَىٰهُ مَوْجٌ
مِّن فَوْقِهِۦ مَوْجٌ مِّن فَوْقِهِۦ سَحَابٌ ۚ
ظُلُمَٰتٌۢ بَعْضُهَا فَوْقَ بَعْضٍ إِذَآ أَخْرَجَ
يَدَهُۥ لَمْ يَكَدْ يَرَىٰهَا ۗ وَمَن لَّمْ يَجْعَلِ ٱللَّهُ لَهُۥ
نُورًا فَمَا لَهُۥ مِن نُّورٍ ﴿٤٠﴾

Or else, like the depths of darkness in a vast deep ocean, covered by waves above which are waves, with clouds above it all: depths of darkness, layer upon layer, [so that] when one holds up his hand, he can hardly see it. Indeed the one from whom God withholds light shall find no light at all. (40)

Are you not aware that it is God whose limitless glory all creatures that are in the heavens and earth extol, even the birds as they spread out their wings? Each of them knows how to pray to Him and to glorify Him; and God has full knowledge of all that they do. (41)

أَلَمۡ تَرَ أَنَّ ٱللَّهَ يُسَبِّحُ لَهُۥ مَن فِي
ٱلسَّمَٰوَٰتِ وَٱلۡأَرۡضِ وَٱلطَّيۡرُ صَٰٓفَّٰتٖۖ
كُلّٞ قَدۡ عَلِمَ صَلَاتَهُۥ وَتَسۡبِيحَهُۥۗ وَٱللَّهُ
عَلِيمُۢ بِمَا يَفۡعَلُونَ ﴿٤١﴾

To God belongs the dominion over the heavens and the earth, and to God shall all return. (42)

وَلِلَّهِ مُلۡكُ ٱلسَّمَٰوَٰتِ وَٱلۡأَرۡضِۖ وَإِلَى
ٱللَّهِ ٱلۡمَصِيرُ ﴿٤٢﴾

Are you not aware that it is God who causes the clouds to move onwards, then joins them together, then piles them up in masses, until you can see rain come forth from their midst. He it is who sends down from the skies mountainous masses charged with hail, striking with it whom He wills and averting it from whom He wills. The flash of His lightning well-nigh deprives people of their sight. (43)

أَلَمۡ تَرَ أَنَّ ٱللَّهَ يُزۡجِي سَحَابٗا ثُمَّ يُؤَلِّفُ بَيۡنَهُۥ
ثُمَّ يَجۡعَلُهُۥ رُكَامٗا فَتَرَى ٱلۡوَدۡقَ يَخۡرُجُ
مِنۡ خِلَٰلِهِۦ وَيُنَزِّلُ مِنَ ٱلسَّمَآءِ مِن جِبَالٖ
فِيهَا مِنۢ بَرَدٖ فَيُصِيبُ بِهِۦ مَن يَشَآءُ وَيَصۡرِفُهُۥ
عَن مَّن يَشَآءُۖ يَكَادُ سَنَا بَرۡقِهِۦ يَذۡهَبُ
بِٱلۡأَبۡصَٰرِ ﴿٤٣﴾

It is God who causes night and day to alternate. In this too there is surely a lesson for all who have eyes to see. (44)

يُقَلِّبُ ٱللَّهُ ٱلَّيۡلَ وَٱلنَّهَارَۚ إِنَّ فِي ذَٰلِكَ
لَعِبۡرَةٗ لِّأُوْلِي ٱلۡأَبۡصَٰرِ ﴿٤٤﴾

God has created every animal from water; and among them are such as creep on their bellies, and such as walk on two legs, and others yet on four. God creates what He wills. Surely God has power over all things. (45)

وَٱللَّهُ خَلَقَ كُلَّ دَآبَّةٍ مِّن مَّآءٍ ۖ فَمِنْهُم مَّن يَمْشِى عَلَىٰ بَطْنِهِۦ وَمِنْهُم مَّن يَمْشِى عَلَىٰ رِجْلَيْنِ وَمِنْهُم مَّن يَمْشِى عَلَىٰٓ أَرْبَعٍ ۚ يَخْلُقُ ٱللَّهُ مَا يَشَآءُ ۚ إِنَّ ٱللَّهَ عَلَىٰ كُلِّ شَىْءٍ قَدِيرٌ ﴿٤٥﴾

Overview

So far the *sūrah* has dealt with the most crude aspects of the human constitution in order to purify and refine them. It has dealt with sexual desire, including its different appeals, as well as the inclination to spread rumours and level accusations at people causing anger and distress. It has also dealt with indecency fermenting within people's hearts, finding verbal expression and then spreading into actual life itself. In all these it laid down very stern punishments for adultery and for false accusation of committing it. It portrayed a horrid example of false accusations levelled at chaste women who are unaware of what is being said about them. It also provided prevention measures, such as seeking permission before entering other people's homes, lowering one's gaze when meeting others, and covering personal charms and adornments. It further warned against unnecessary sexual excitement, encouraged marriage and the freedom of slaves and prohibited prostitution. All these measures, varied as they are, help to control the physical impulse and strengthen the motives to maintain one's chastity and aspire to higher standards of purity.

At the conclusion of its comments on the false story about 'Ā'ishah the *sūrah* dealt with the lingering effects of that incident: in particular the distress, anger, distortion of values and anxiety. Thus we find the Prophet (peace be upon him) calm and reassured, 'Ā'ishah herself well satisfied and happy, her father Abū Bakr kind and forgiving, and Ṣafwān ibn al-Mu'aṭṭal pleased with God's declaration of his innocence, and the whole Muslim community turning back to God after realizing how they were lost in confusion. Now they are back on track, recognizing God's favours and grace, and following His guidance.

With such directives, education and refinement the *sūrah* now deals with the human soul, how it suddenly lights up, aspiring to the great light that fills the heavens and earth. Muslims are now ready to receive the enlightenment that they need in a world full of light.

God's Radiant Light

"*God is the light of the heavens and the earth.*" (Verse 35) No sooner does this remarkable statement impart its meaning than a bright light spreads over the whole universe and lightens up feelings and emotions, filling hearts and minds. The entire universe swims in a radiant light. Screens and curtains are removed, hearts radiate, spirits fly high, and everything is purified in a sea of light. All shed their burdens and join together in an atmosphere of pure happiness and delight. Indeed, the universe and all it contains break their fetters so as to let the heavens and earth meet, the distant and the near come together, as do the animate and the inanimate. What is hidden joins with what is apparent, as do people's hearts and senses.

"*God is the light of the heavens and the earth.*" He is the light from which they derive their essence as well as their perfect system. He is the One who gives them their existence and the law that governs such existence. Man has recently been able to discover, through scientific achievements, a part of this great truth when what they used to call 'matter' was transformed, through nuclear fusion, into radiation that has no form or substance other than light. Thus, man discovered that an atom contains electrons that produce radiation. By contrast, the human heart was able to comprehend this great truth many centuries before science made its discoveries. Every time the human heart attained a high level of purity, aspiring to the sublime light, it was able to understand this truth. It was fully comprehended by Muḥammad, God's Messenger, as he started his journey back from Ṭā'if, when he gave up on people and sought refuge with his Lord. Appealing to God Almighty, he said: "I seek refuge in the light of Your face by which all darkness is dispelled and both this life and the life to come are put on their right courses." His heart shined with this sublime light on his night journey which took him from Makkah to Jerusalem and then to heaven. When later 'Ā'ishah, his wife, asked him whether he saw his Lord, he answered: "It is all light. How could I see Him?"

An Example Portraying God's Light

The human heart cannot take such abundant light for long; nor can it aspire to that great horizon for long. Hence, after this statement that opens up this endless scope, the *sūrah* begins to bring it closer so as to make it better understood. The example is at once tangible and practical:

> *His light may be compared to a niche containing a lamp; the lamp within a glass, the glass like a radiant star; lit from a blessed tree – an olive tree that is neither of the east nor of the west. Its very oil would almost give light even though no fire had touched it. Light upon light!* (Verse 35)

This comparison seeks to put the infinite right before a mind that has finite ability. It simply portrays a miniscule picture to present it to man who cannot contemplate its great reality. It seeks to show the nature of light when the human imagination cannot entertain its endless spread.

The verse begins by stating the fact that "*God is the light of the heavens and the earth,*" but then it brings us fast from this great expanse to a niche, a small artificial wall recess in which a lamp is placed so as to focus its light and make it shine. "*His light may be compared to a niche containing a lamp.*" It adds one element of strength and concentration after another: "*The lamp within a glass,*" which protects it from the wind and purifies its light to make it stronger and more radiant: "*The glass like a radiant star.*" We see the glass painted here as bright, transparent, almost shining. At this point the verse links the example and the reality, the likeness and the original, the small glass and the radiant star. Thus we do not concentrate our reflection on the miniscule picture which is presented only to help us understand the great reality.

The *sūrah* immediately reverts to the small example of the lamp, which is "*lit from a blessed tree – an olive tree...*" The purest light known to the first people addressed by the Qur'ān was that of olive oil. But this is not the only reason for choosing this example. It is an example that has connotations of sacredness associated with the blessed tree. These connotations recall the image of the sacred valley, the nearest place to Arabia in which olive trees grow in abundance. The Qur'ān refers to this tree and gives it special significance: "*We bring forth... a tree that grows on Mount Sinai yielding oil and relish for all to eat.*" (23: 19–20) It is a tree that lives for ages, and it brings endless benefits to man through its oil, wood, leaves and fruit. Once again the text turns from the little example to remind us of the great reality. This tree is not a particular one, and it does not belong to a particular place or direction. It is merely an example given to make the reality easier to understand. Hence, it is described as "*neither of the east nor of the west.*" Moreover, its oil is not the one we see and know. It is different and far more remarkable: "*Its very oil would almost give light even though no fire had touched it.*" It is so transparent and bright that it almost gives light without burning. The example concludes with another remarkable statement: "*Light upon light.*" Thus, we are back with the original light that bears no comparison.

It is God's light that dispels all darkness in the heavens and the earth. It is a light whose nature and scope are beyond our comprehension. The aim here is to make our hearts aspire to see this light: "*God guides to His light him that wills [to be guided].*" (Verse 35) Those who open their hearts to the light will see it because it spreads far and wide in the heavens and the earth. It is permanent, unending, unscreened, and it never fades. Whenever the human heart looks for it, it is sure to find it. In the midst of his confusion, man can always find it providing guidance and establishing a bond between him and his Lord.

This comparison is given by God so as to make our minds able to comprehend the nature of His light. He alone knows the full extent of our ability: "*God propounds parables for all people, since God alone has full knowledge of all things.*" (Verse 35)

This light which spreads in abundance in the heavens and earth is best seen in perfect clarity in the houses of God where people's hearts look up to Him, remember Him, stand in awe of Him and dedicate themselves to Him in preference to all else:

> *In houses which God has sanctioned to be raised so that His name be remembered in them, there are [such as] extol His limitless glory, morning and evening – people whom neither commerce nor profit can divert from the remembrance of God, and from attending regularly to prayer, and from charity; who are filled with fear of the day when all hearts and eyes will be convulsed; who [only hope] that God may reward them in accordance with the best that they ever did, and lavish His grace upon them. God gives to whom He wills beyond all reckoning.* (Verses 36–38)

There is a close affinity between the scene of the niche in the first verse and the following scene of God's houses. This is perfectly in line with the Qur'ānic method of putting together images that have close parallels. Likewise, there is close affinity between the lamp shining with light in the niche and hearts shining with the light of glorifying God in His houses.

When God sanctions something, it takes place just as He has approved. Since He has sanctioned the raising of these houses, they are there, functioning, purified and respected. The view showing them standing tall is in harmony with God's light that radiates throughout the heavens and the earth. These houses are naturally noble which again fits perfectly with the brilliant light described earlier. Their special, venerated position makes them fit for the remembrance of God's name: "*In houses which God has sanctioned to be raised so that His name be remembered in them.*" (Verse 36) They are also in harmony with the radiant hearts of the believers who stand up in prayer, glorify God and extol His praises. They are "*people whom neither commerce nor profit can divert from the remembrance of God, and from attending regularly to prayer, and from charity.*" (Verse 37) Needless to say, trade and commerce aim to make a profit. Yet although these believers are engaged in such enterprises, they are not diverted from their obligation towards God or their fellow human beings. Hence they attend regularly and properly to their prayers and pay their *zakāt* and charity. These people "*are filled with fear of the day when all hearts and eyes will be convulsed.*" (Verse 37) On that day, people's hearts and eyes will be in turmoil, unsteady. It is a day of utter fear and distress. Hence, they fear what may happen to them then. In order to spare themselves, they are never diverted by their immediate concerns of business and profit from attending to their duties towards their Lord.

Yet despite their fear, they have high hopes "*that God may reward them in accordance with the best that they ever did, and lavish His grace upon them.*" (Verse 38) Their hopes will never be frustrated; for, "*God gives to whom He wills beyond all reckoning.*" (Verse 38) There are no limits to God's favours and no restrictions on what He may wish to bestow on His devoted servants.

Deeds That Come to Nothing

In contrast to this radiant light that shines throughout the heavens and the earth, focusing on the houses dedicated to God and enlightening the hearts of the faithful, the *sūrah* shows a different situation where no light can penetrate and no one is safe; a situation devoid of all goodness. That is the situation in which the unbelievers find themselves:

> *As for the unbelievers, their deeds are like a mirage in the desert, which the thirsty traveller supposes to be water, but when he comes near to it, he finds that it is nothing. But he finds that God [has always been present] with him, and that He will pay him his account in full; for God is swift in reckoning.* (Verse 39)

This is the first of two remarkable scenes the *sūrah* paints of the unbelievers and their destiny. Both are full of life and movement. In this scene their actions are shown like a mirage in an open space. It gives a false shine which attracts the thirsty traveller who moves towards it. He is totally unaware of what he might find there, other than the prospect of quenching his thirst. Suddenly, the whole scene moves swiftly, and we see the thirsty traveller arriving at this place but finding no water to drink. Instead, he is in for a great surprise, one which he could never have imagined. It is awesome, striking fear into his heart and leaving him utterly bewildered. What he finds is the realization that God has always been present with him. He had denied God's existence, turned his back on Him and adopted a hostile attitude to faith. In his state of total oblivion to anything other than the water he needs, should he find there a human adversary, he would be startled and confused. But he finds no human opponent. He finds God Almighty who takes him to account.

And then what happens? "*God will pay him his account in full.*" All this occurs very quickly, in line with the initial and sudden shock. The final comment on this scene is "*God is swift in reckoning.*" Again the comment perfectly suits the rapidity of the scene.

In the second scene layers of darkness gather on top of each other, to contrast with the false brightness of the mirage. Great fear is transmitted by the bottomless ocean engulfed in darkness, and waves upon waves moving in a never-ending motion. Above all this, dark clouds gather. Thus, layers of darkness amass, to the extent that if someone were to hold out their hand, they would fail to see it in the engulfing darkness. Hence it is a darkness that spreads an air of fear and panic.

This is all a description of unbelief, which is shown as darkness totally isolated from the divine light that radiates throughout the universe. It is a deep error which prevents people from seeing even the nearest sign of guidance, a fear that leaves no trace of security. For, "*indeed the one from whom God withholds light shall find no light at all.*" (Verse 40) God's light is guidance planted in people's hearts, giving them an informed insight, and a bond between human nature and the laws that operate in the universe at large. It is the only true enlightenment. A person who is cut off from this light remains in a darkness that cannot be removed, in a fear without security, and in error without return. At the end he finds all his actions to be a mirage leading him to ruin. No action is valid unless it is based on faith. There is no guidance without faith, and no light unless it is God's light.

All Glorify God

This is an extraordinary scene of unbelief, error and darkness in human life. Yet it is followed by one of faith, guidance and light in the great universe. This is a scene showing the entire universe with all that lives in it, human and *jinn*, planets and stars, and all beings, whether animate or inanimate, sharing in God's glorification. We feel how awesome the scene is as we hear the glorification echoed everywhere in the heavens and the earth:

> *Are you not aware that it is God whose limitless glory all creatures that are in the heavens and earth extol, even the birds as they spread out their wings? Each of them knows how to pray to Him and to glorify Him; and God has full knowledge of all that they do.* (Verse 41)

Man does not live alone in this universe. All around him, to his right and to his left, above him and beneath him, and in the expanse beyond, whether reached by his imagination or not, there are beings God has created with different natures, forms and shapes. All share in their belief in God, turn to Him and extol His praises. He "*has full knowledge of all that they do.*"

The Qur'ān directs man to look around him: all is of God's making and all living things everywhere in the heavens and the earth are His creatures, glorifying Him and singing His praises. The Qur'ān also directs our full attention to something we see every day without stirring any feeling in us because of its familiarity: it is the scene of birds lifting up their legs and spreading out their wings as they fly. They also glorify God. "*Each of them knows how to pray to Him and to glorify Him.*" (Verse 41) Only man neglects to glorify his Lord when he is the one who should be most aware of the importance of believing in God and glorifying Him.

In this scene, the whole universe appears full of humility as it turns to its Creator, singing His praises, addressing its prayers to Him. This it does by nature. Its obedience to God is represented in its laws which operate by God's will. When man refines his senses, he sees this scene as reality, as though he hears the rhythm of God's glorification echoed throughout the universe. He shares with all creatures their prayers and appeals to God. Such was Muḥammad, God's Messenger, (peace be upon him). When he walked, he heard the gravel under his feet singing God's praises. Such was David too for when he chanted his Psalms, the mountains and birds chanted with him.

"*To God belongs the dominion over the heavens and the earth, and to God shall all return.*" (Verse 42) No one should turn anywhere other than to Him, and no refuge is to be sought except with Him. Meeting Him is inevitable. His punishment, if deserved, cannot be averted except through His grace. To Him all shall return.

Snatching Eyesight

Next the *sūrah* portrays yet another scene which people pass by paying little attention to it. It is very pleasant to the eye, carrying a message to the heart and inviting the mind to reflect on God's creation as well as the pointers to faith available everywhere in the universe. It provides an area to contemplate the only source of real light, right guidance and true faith.

> *Are you not aware that it is God who causes the clouds to move onwards, then joins them together, then piles them up in masses, until you can see rain come forth from their midst. He it is who sends down from the skies mountainous masses charged with hail, striking with it whom He wills and averting it from whom He wills. The flash of His lightning well-nigh deprives people of their sight.* (Verse 43)

The scene is portrayed at leisure, slowly, with its component parts being raised up for reflection before they combine panoramically. All this is done deliberately, so that the very sight of these details touches people's hearts and awakens their minds to reflection on God's perfect design.

It is God's design that drives the clouds from one place to another, before allowing these clouds to come together and pile up into a great mass. When this becomes heavy, it bears water that begins to ooze out and then pour down in heavy rain. When piled up, the clouds look like great mountains, producing small pieces of hail. No one sees the clouds look like mountains better than a passenger in a plane that flies higher than the clouds, or moves through them. The scene at this elevation shows the clouds just like mountains, their huge sizes, steep cliffs, as well as high and low peaks. It is a scene that shows a reality people could not have seen before they were able to fly.

These mountains are subservient to God's orders, functioning in accordance with His law that governs the universe. It is in accordance with this law that God lets rain drop over any community He wants and diverts it from others as He wills. The scene is completed with this final statement: "*The flash of His lightning well-nigh deprives people of their sight.*" (Verse 43) It thus provides an element of harmony with the great light that fills the whole universe.

And yet there is another universal scene, showing the night and day: "*It is God who causes night and day to alternate. In this too there is surely a lesson for all who have eyes to see.*" (Verse 44)

When we reflect on the alternation of the night and day, in a perfect system that never fails or slackens, our senses are sharpened and we can better appreciate the perfection of God's work and His law that governs the universe. The Qur'ān alerts our hearts to such scenes which we normally overlook because of their familiarity. Yet they contain a clear message. Hence the Qur'ān helps our hearts to always face the universe with sharpened sensitivity and fresh reaction. Many a heart has wondered at the alternation of night and day. Yet it is always the same, losing nothing of its striking beauty. It is only our hearts that have lost their interaction with this great phenomenon. Much indeed do we lose of the beauty of this universe when we look at such phenomena paying little attention to them only because they have become familiar.

The Qur'ān reinvigorates our blunted sensitivity, touches our cold hearts and awakens our tired minds so that we can look at the universe as though we see it for the first time. We thus stop at every phenomenon reflecting on how it works and enquiring about its secrets. We see God's hand doing its work in everything around us, and we reflect on His wisdom and the signs pointing to Him.

Limitless is God in His glory. He wants to give us more of His favours. He wants to gift us the whole universe every time we contemplate one of its phenomena in a way that we appreciate it as though we are seeing it for the first time. Thus, we are alert to the universe and its message a countless number of times. We then enjoy it anew every time we look at it.

This universe is beautiful, awesome and has a nature that is harmonious with our own nature. Both are derived from the same source, subject to the same law. Thus when we relate to the universe we feel greater reassurance, and we experience the sort of happiness that we feel when we meet someone dear who has been absent for a long time. Besides, in the universe we see God's light, for "*God is the light of the heavens and the earth.*" (Verse 35) We experience this light in the great expanse of the universe, as well as within ourselves, at the same moment at which we look at the universe with an open heart that wants to understand the secret of God's elaborate planning.

Therefore, the Qur'ān reawakens us time and again, drawing our hearts and souls to a variety of great universal scenes, so that we do not pass by them with closed eyes and sealed hearts. If we do, we end our life journey with very little gain to show for our efforts.

The *sūrah* continues to portray scenes of the universe arousing our interest in them. It shows how all life, with its rich variety, originates from the same source, and has the same nature: "*God has created every animal from water; and among them are such as creep on their bellies, and such as walk on two legs, and others yet on four. God creates what He wills. Surely God has power over all things.*" (Verse 45)

Here the Qur'ān states in a very simple way a great fact that confirms that the origin of all creatures is water. This could mean that water is the basic component of all living species. It could also mean what contemporary scientists have been trying to prove, namely that life started in the sea, making water its first origin. Later, numerous species came into existence.

We, however, do not like to link any fact stated in the Qur'ān with scientific theory, because such theories admit change, modification, or abrogation. Hence, we take this statement at its face value, confirming its truth which makes clear that God has created all living things from water. This means that having the same origin, they present, as we clearly see with our eyes, a wide and rich variety: crawlers creep on their bellies, while man and birds walk on two legs, but most animals use all four limbs when they walk. All this takes place in accordance with the laws of nature God has set in operation. Nothing occurs by chance or coincidence. "*God creates what He wills,*" unrestricted by form or shape. The laws that operate in the universe have been established by God's will: "*Surely God has power over all things.*" (Verse 45)

With the great variety that we see in all creatures, an almost endless range of shapes, sizes, colours and characteristics is set before us. Yet they all originate from the same source. This suggests that it is all intended as such, reflecting the elaborate planning in the universe at large. It portrays as false the notion that life started by mere coincidence. What coincidence could give birth to such planning or such great variety? It is all the work of God who, in His wisdom, has given every living soul its shape and form and guided it to what suits it best in this life.

4

Guidance to the Straight Path

We have sent down revelations that make things manifest; and God guides onto a straight way him who wills [to be guided]. (46)

لَّقَدْ أَنزَلْنَآ ءَايَٰتٍ مُّبَيِّنَٰتٍ ۚ وَٱللَّهُ يَهْدِى
مَن يَشَآءُ إِلَىٰ صِرَٰطٍ مُّسْتَقِيمٍ ﴿٤٦﴾

They say: 'We believe in God and in the Messenger, and we obey.' But then some of them turn away after this [assertion]. Surely these are not believers. (47)

وَيَقُولُونَ ءَامَنَّا بِٱللَّهِ وَبِٱلرَّسُولِ وَأَطَعْنَا
ثُمَّ يَتَوَلَّىٰ فَرِيقٌ مِّنْهُم مِّنۢ بَعْدِ ذَٰلِكَ ۚ
وَمَآ أُو۟لَٰٓئِكَ بِٱلْمُؤْمِنِينَ ﴿٤٧﴾

Whenever they are summoned to God and His Messenger in order that he might judge between them, some of them turn away; (48)

وَإِذَا دُعُوٓا۟ إِلَى ٱللَّهِ وَرَسُولِهِۦ لِيَحْكُمَ بَيْنَهُمْ
إِذَا فَرِيقٌ مِّنْهُم مُّعْرِضُونَ ﴿٤٨﴾

but if the right is on their side, they come to him with all submission. (49)

وَإِن يَكُن لَّهُمُ ٱلْحَقُّ يَأْتُوٓا۟ إِلَيْهِ
مُذْعِنِينَ ﴿٤٩﴾

Is there disease in their hearts? Or are they full of doubt? Or do they fear that God and His Messenger might deal unjustly with them? Nay, it is they who are the wrongdoers. (50)

أَفِي قُلُوبِهِم مَّرَضٌ أَمِ ٱرْتَابُوٓا۟ أَمْ يَخَافُونَ أَن
يَحِيفَ ٱللَّهُ عَلَيْهِمْ وَرَسُولُهُۥ ۚ بَلْ أُو۟لَٰٓئِكَ
هُمُ ٱلظَّٰلِمُونَ ﴿٥٠﴾

The response of believers, whenever they are summoned to God and His Messenger in order that he may judge between them, is none other than, 'We have heard, and we obey.' It is they that shall be successful. (51)

إِنَّمَا كَانَ قَوْلَ ٱلْمُؤْمِنِينَ إِذَا دُعُوٓا۟ إِلَى ٱللَّهِ
وَرَسُولِهِۦ لِيَحْكُمَ بَيْنَهُمْ أَن يَقُولُوا۟ سَمِعْنَا
وَأَطَعْنَا ۚ وَأُو۟لَٰٓئِكَ هُمُ ٱلْمُفْلِحُونَ ﴿٥١﴾

Those who obey God and His Messenger, stand in awe of God and remain truly God-fearing are the ones who shall certainly triumph. (52)

وَمَن يُطِعِ ٱللَّهَ وَرَسُولَهُۥ وَيَخْشَ ٱللَّهَ
وَيَتَّقْهِ فَأُو۟لَٰٓئِكَ هُمُ ٱلْفَآئِزُونَ ﴿٥٢﴾

They swear their most solemn oaths by God that if you [God's Messenger] should ever bid them to do so, they would most certainly march forth. Say: 'Do not swear. Your [sort of] obedience is well known. God is certainly well aware of all that you do.' (53)

وَأَقْسَمُوا۟ بِٱللَّهِ جَهْدَ أَيْمَٰنِهِمْ لَئِنْ أَمَرْتَهُمْ
لَيَخْرُجُنَّ ۖ قُل لَّا تُقْسِمُوا۟ ۖ طَاعَةٌ مَّعْرُوفَةٌ ۚ
إِنَّ ٱللَّهَ خَبِيرٌۢ بِمَا تَعْمَلُونَ ﴿٥٣﴾

Say: 'Obey God, and obey the Messenger.' But if you turn away, he will have to answer only for whatever he has been charged with, and you, for what you have been charged with. If you obey him, you shall be rightly guided. The Messenger is not bound to do more than clearly deliver his message. (54)

قُلْ أَطِيعُوا۟ ٱللَّهَ وَأَطِيعُوا۟ ٱلرَّسُولَ ۖ فَإِن
تَوَلَّوْا۟ فَإِنَّمَا عَلَيْهِ مَا حُمِّلَ وَعَلَيْكُم
مَّا حُمِّلْتُمْ ۖ وَإِن تُطِيعُوهُ تَهْتَدُوا۟ ۚ
وَمَا عَلَى ٱلرَّسُولِ إِلَّا ٱلْبَلَٰغُ ٱلْمُبِينُ ﴿٥٤﴾

God has promised those of you who believe and do good deeds that, of a certainty, He will cause them to accede to power on earth, in the same way as He caused those who lived before them to accede to it; and that, of a certainty, He will firmly establish for them the religion which He has chosen for them; and that, of a certainty, He will cause their erstwhile state of fear to be replaced by a state of security. They will thus worship Me alone and associate with Me no partners whatsoever. Those who, after this, choose to disbelieve are indeed wicked. (55)

وَعَدَ ٱللَّهُ ٱلَّذِينَ ءَامَنُوا۟ مِنكُمْ وَعَمِلُوا۟
ٱلصَّٰلِحَٰتِ لَيَسْتَخْلِفَنَّهُمْ فِى
ٱلْأَرْضِ كَمَا ٱسْتَخْلَفَ ٱلَّذِينَ
مِن قَبْلِهِمْ وَلَيُمَكِّنَنَّ لَهُمْ دِينَهُمُ
ٱلَّذِى ٱرْتَضَىٰ لَهُمْ وَلَيُبَدِّلَنَّهُم مِّنۢ بَعْدِ
خَوْفِهِمْ أَمْنًا ۚ يَعْبُدُونَنِى لَا يُشْرِكُونَ
بِى شَيْـًٔا ۚ وَمَن كَفَرَ بَعْدَ ذَٰلِكَ
فَأُو۟لَٰٓئِكَ هُمُ ٱلْفَٰسِقُونَ ﴿٥٥﴾

Attend regularly to your prayers and pay your *zakāt*, and obey the Messenger, so that you might be graced with God's mercy. (56)

وَأَقِيمُوا۟ ٱلصَّلَوٰةَ وَءَاتُوا۟ ٱلزَّكَوٰةَ وَأَطِيعُوا۟
ٱلرَّسُولَ لَعَلَّكُمْ تُرْحَمُونَ ﴿٥٦﴾

Do not think that the unbelievers can frustrate [God's plan] on earth. The fire is their abode, and vile indeed is such a journey's end. (57)

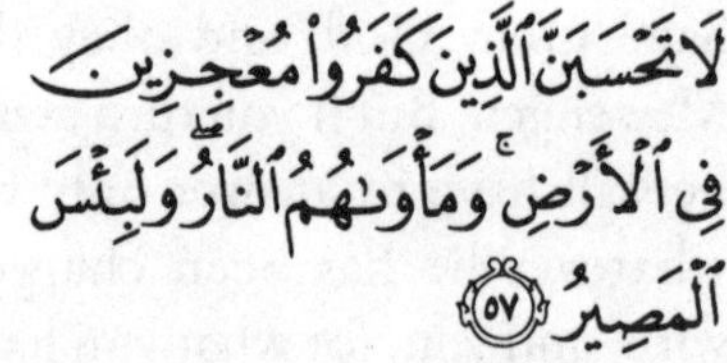

Overview

Having thus taken us on a broad round of inspiring universal scenes, the *sūrah* brings us back to its main theme, namely good manners and moral values the Qur'ān aims to establish in the Muslim community. Once more we see that the Qur'ān wants hearts to be purified so as to be bright, reflecting the great light God has placed in the heavens and the earth.

Earlier in the *sūrah* mention was made of people who are not distracted by their business or commercial dealings from their duties of remembering God, attending regularly to prayers and paying their *zakāt*. It also highlighted the situation of the unbelievers, their deeds, the layers of darkness in which they live and their eventual destiny. Now the *sūrah* speaks of the hypocrites who benefit nothing by the clear signs God has placed all around them, or by His revelations that set all things most clearly. These turn their backs on divine guidance. Even though they profess to be believers, their attitude is markedly different from that of believers who obey God's Messenger and are happy with his judgement in their affairs and disputes. In marked contrast to their arrogance, the believers' behaviour confirms what they profess. And it is the believers that God has promised to establish in the land where they will be able to practise their faith and conduct their lives in line with His teachings. This is their reward for adopting the right attitude towards God and His Messenger, obeying them in all situations, despite the fact that the unbelievers stand in opposition to them for so doing. The *sūrah* confirms once again that the unbelievers cannot defy God. They will receive their fair punishment in hell, the worst abode for anyone.

Contrasting Attitudes

"*We have sent down revelations that make things manifest; and God guides onto a straight way him who wills [to be guided].*" (Verse 46) God's revelations provide clarity, allowing God's resplendent light to be seen. They point to the sources of His guidance, making clear what is good and what is evil. They set out the Islamic way of life without ambiguity or equivocation. They define the divine rules which must be implemented in human life on earth. When people implement them in their lives and resort to them for judgement in their disputes, they implement a code that is clearly set out, providing all guarantees that ensure equity and justice for all, and which allow no confusion between true and false or permissible and forbidden.

"*God guides onto a straight way him who wills [to be guided].*" (Verse 46) The Arabic statement could also be read as "God guides whom He wills onto a straight way." This is indeed the translation adopted by most translators. If we read it in this way then the statement makes clear that God's will is free from all restriction. However, God has established a way to ensure guidance. Any human being who moves towards that way will definitely receive God's light and guidance. By God's will, their path will be made smooth until they reach their destination. Those who turn away from it will lose their guiding light and become hardened in error. Such is God's will with regard to providing guidance to mankind.

The *sūrah* points out that despite the revelations and the signs God had placed in the universe, there is a special type of people who are hypocrites, claiming to be Muslims, but showing no respect for Islamic values:

> *They say: 'We believe in God and in the Messenger, and we obey.' But then some of them turn away after this [assertion]. Surely these are not believers. Whenever they are summoned to God and His Messenger in order that he might judge between them, some of them turn away; but if the right is on their side, they come to him with all submission. Is there disease in their hearts? Or are they full of doubt? Or do they fear that God and His Messenger might deal unjustly with them? Nay, it is they who are the wrongdoers.* (Verses 47–50)

When faith is genuinely established in a person's heart, it is reflected in that person's behaviour. Islam is a proactive faith that cannot remain idle. When it is genuinely accepted as a personal belief, it moves on to show its influence in practice. It must be translated into action. The Islamic method of educating its followers always seeks to transform the mental acceptance of faith into a practical approach that soon becomes a habit or a rule. At the same time, it seeks to provide the mental motivation to make belief and action mutually complementary.

The hypocrites used to claim that they believed in God and His Messenger and that they were keen to obey them, but theirs was a hollow, verbal claim that lacked practical credence. They simply turned away, making their actions belie their claims. "*Surely these are not believers,*" because believers confirm with their actions what they claim to be their faith. Faith is not a toy which a person uses for amusement before discarding it. It is something that settles in a person's heart, reshaping his feelings and influencing his actions. Moreover, when it is firmly established in someone's mind and heart, there is no going back on it.

Those who claimed to be believers did not hesitate to contradict that claim when they were summoned to put their disputes to God's Messenger for judgement on the basis of His law: "*Whenever they are summoned to God and His Messenger in order that he might judge between them, some of them turn away; but if the right is on their side, they come to him with all submission.*" (Verses 48–49) They were well aware that a judgement made by God and His Messenger could only seek to establish what is right and ensure justice. It would never be influenced by personal likings. But such hypocrites did not care for justice and right. Hence, they were not prepared to seek the Prophet's judgement. Indeed, they refused to put their disputes to him, except when they were sure that justice was on their side. In such a situation, they did not hesitate to go to him, declaring their prior acceptance of his judgement, because they were certain that it would be in their favour. It would be a judgement on the basis of God's law that gave everyone their due.

Such people provide a typical example of hypocrites at all times: they dare not declare their disbelief; so they pretend to be Muslim. Yet they do not submit to God's law. When they are called upon to put their cases to God and His Messenger for judgement they refuse, seeking any excuse. They are described as unbelievers, because a genuine believer will never reject God's judgement. To accept such judgement is the practical evidence of belief. It is the attitude that confirms strong belief and due respect to God and His Messenger. Only a person whose heart has not been enlightened by faith and who has not adopted Islamic manners rejects God's Messenger's judgement.

Hence, their attitude is the subject of questions that confirm the fact that their hearts are diseased and wonders at their doubts: "*Is there disease in their hearts? Or are they full of doubt? Or do they fear that God and His Messenger might deal unjustly with them?*" (Verse 50)

The first question requires no confirmation, for heart disease is sure to bring about such an effect. No one with a sound human nature could deviate so badly from the truth. It is heart disease, a disease that makes someone imbalanced, unable to appreciate true faith and its moral code.

The second question wonders at them doubting God's judgement when they claim to believe in Him. Do they doubt that it comes from God, or that it is the judgement that administers justice? Whatever the case, their attitude differs from that of believers.

The third question combines wonder with denunciation. Do they fear that God and His Messenger might be unfair to them? It is most singular for anyone to entertain such a fear. God is the Creator of all people: it is inconceivable that He would favour some of His creatures at the expense of others. "*Nay, it is they who are the wrongdoers.*" (Verse 50)

God's judgement is the only judgement that is free of all prejudice, because God is fair to all and does not deal unjustly with anyone. All of His creation are to Him in the same position. Hence, He does not favour any of them at the expense of another. Any judgement other than God's may be susceptible to unfairness. When people legislate, they cannot entirely free themselves of leaning towards what serves their interests. This applies to all human beings; be they individuals, a class or government.

When an individual legislates, he is bound to look for what ensures his own protection and serves his own interests. The same applies when a class, country or a block of countries legislates for another. But when God legislates, no personal security, protection or interest comes into play. His legislation aims to ensure absolute justice which cannot be achieved under any law other than divine law. Hence, those who reject God's judgement, and that of His Messenger, are indeed unjust and wrongdoers. They do not want justice to be administered or right to be supreme. In fact, deep at heart they know that they do not doubt that God's judgement only seeks to ensure justice. The point is that "*it is they who are the wrongdoers.*" (Verse 50)

The Road to True Success

True believers have a different attitude that reflects their complete respect for God's judgement. When they are summoned so that God's Messenger can arbitrate in their disputes, their reaction reflects the profound enlightenment of their hearts: "*The response of believers, whenever they are summoned to God and His Messenger in order that he may judge between them, is none other than, 'We have heard, and we obey.' It is they that shall be successful.*" (Verse 51)

This is an attitude of complete obedience. There is no hesitation, argument or dispute, because it is an obedience based on complete trust that God's judgement is right and just, and whatever differs with it is based on personal prejudice. Such obedience testifies to complete submission to God, who gives life and conducts it as He wills. It demonstrates full trust that what God chooses for people is infinitely better than what they choose for themselves. God, the Creator, knows His creation better than they know themselves.

"*It is they that shall be successful.*" (Verse 51) Since God conducts their affairs, organizes their relations and judges between them on the basis of His knowledge and justice, they must be in a far better position than those who rely, in all such matters, on other human beings who are similarly short of knowledge. Besides, the believers are successful because they follow a single straight path that allows no deviation. They are confident of the soundness of their code of living, follow it without hesitation, which means that their energy, talents and skills work in coherence. They suffer no internal division based on conflicting desires. They follow their own path, charted for them by God.

"*Those who obey God and His Messenger, stand in awe of God and remain truly God-fearing are the ones who shall certainly triumph.*" (Verse 52) The previous verse spoke of obedience and submission when judgement is made. This verse speaks of complete obedience in all matters, implementing every order or prohibition. Such obedience must be coupled with God consciousness and standing in awe of Him. The latter is more pervasive because it entails watching God and feeling His presence at every turn. This makes a person very uneasy about committing anything that God has forbidden, for they are ashamed and fear His punishment.

"*Those who obey God and His Messenger, stand in awe of God and remain truly God-fearing are the ones who shall certainly triumph.*" (Verse 52) They save themselves in this life and in the life to come. This is what God has promised, and God is always true to His promise. They deserve to triumph, as they have practically taken the necessary measures to ensure such a triumph. Obedience to God and His Messenger requires diligent following of the right way God in His wisdom has defined for mankind. Following this way automatically ensures success in this life and in the life to come. Moreover, standing in awe of God and fearing Him ensure continuity in one's conduct, helping one to ignore all temptations that lure believers away from their straight path.

Obeying God and His Messenger, coupled with fearing God, provide a high standard of propriety that reflects a person's enlightenment and strong bond with God. It also reflects the dignity of believers. Obedience to anyone or any authority means humiliation unless it is based on obeying God and His Messenger. No honourable believer will accept such humiliation, for a true believer will never bow his head before anyone other than God Almighty.

Having so contrasted the attitudes of believers and hypocrites, the *sūrah* now resumes its discussion of the latter's behaviour, making it clear that only one sort of attitude can be adopted by believers. It then moves on to outline God's promise to the believers.

> *They swear their most solemn oaths by God that if you [God's Messenger] should ever bid them to do so, they would most certainly march forth. Say: 'Do not swear. Your [sort of] obedience is well known. God is certainly well aware of all that you do.' Say: 'Obey God, and obey the Messenger.' But if you turn away, he will have to answer only for whatever he has been charged with, and you, for what you have been charged with. If you obey him, you shall be rightly guided. The Messenger is not bound to do more than clearly deliver his message.* (Verses 53–54)

The hypocrites used to solemnly swear in front of the Prophet that he needed only to give them his orders and they would readily join him on any expedition against his enemies. They would not hesitate to fight for Islam under his banner. But God was fully aware that they were lying. Hence, He decries their assertions and looks at their oaths with sarcasm: "*Do not swear. Your obedience is well known.*" (Verse 53) This means that there is no need for their oaths, because their obedience is too well known to need any assertion or oath. It is as if we say to a person whom we know to be a habitual liar that he need not assert to us that he is saying the truth, because we know him to be always truthful.

This sarcastic reply is followed by the assertion: "*God is certainly well aware of all that you do.*" (Verse 53) He is certainly in no need of their oaths. He knows that they would not obey any order to go to war, and that they would not join the Prophet when he went on such an expedition.

Therefore, a fresh order is given to them to show true obedience to God and His Messenger, not the sort they are known to show, because that is false. "*Say: Obey God, and obey the Messenger.*" (Verse 54)

"*But if you turn away,*" resorting to your habitual hypocrisy, then "*he will have to answer only for whatever he has been charged with.*" (Verse 54) His only task for which he is answerable is to deliver God's message, as he has surely done. "*And you, for what you have been charged with.*" (Verse 54) Your task is to obey him most sincerely. But so far, you have not done so. However, "*if you obey him, you shall be rightly guided.*" (Versc 54) You will be following the right path that leads you to success in both this life and the life to come. "*The Messenger is not bound to do more than clearly deliver his message.*" (Verse 54) He is not responsible for your acceptance or rejection of the faith. If you turn away, he will not be deemed to have fallen short of fulfilling his task. You are the ones who will have to account for that, and you are the ones who run the risk of being punished for your disobedience of the orders given to you by God and His Messenger.

God's True Promise

Once the attitude of the hypocrites has been discussed and settled, the *sūrah* leaves them aside and speaks about obedient believers. It outlines the reward of sincere obedience and proactive faith. The first instalment of such reward is given in this life, before human beings are held to account on the Day of Resurrection.

> *God has promised those of you who believe and do good deeds that, of a certainty, He will cause them to accede to power on earth, in the same way as He caused those who lived before them to accede to it; and that, of a certainty, He will firmly establish for them the religion which He has chosen for them; and that, of a certainty, He will cause their erstwhile state of fear to be replaced by a state of security. They will thus worship Me alone and associate with Me no partners whatsoever. Those who, after this, choose to disbelieve are indeed wicked.* (Verse 55)

Such is God's promise to the believers who do good deeds and follow the Prophet Muḥammad's guidance. They will be given power and will be established on earth. Their state of fear will be replaced by a state of reassurance and security. God's promise will always come true. It is, then, pertinent to ask about the nature of faith and the practical fulfilment of this promise by God.

True faith, which ensures that God's promise comes true, is great indeed. It influences all human activity and defines its direction. Once faith is well established in a person's heart, it begins to manifest itself in the form of positive and constructive action undertaken for God's sake and addressed to Him. It means full compliance with His orders in all matters, major and minor. It transforms a believer's desires and inclinations so as to make them all in line with the Prophet's guidance, because such guidance has been given to him by God.

It is the sort of faith that fills people's whole entity, their feelings, aspirations, natural inclinations, actions, movements, as well as their behaviour at home, in society and with their Lord. All these must be addressed or dedicated to God alone. This is specifically mentioned in the *sūrah* as justification for giving believers power and establishing them on earth: "*They will thus worship Me alone and associate no partners with Me whatsoever.*" (Verse 55) Idolatry can take different shapes and forms, and can creep into a person's mind through a variety of ways and means. The *sūrah* makes it clear however that to address any action or feeling to anyone other than God is a manifestation of idolatry.

Belief in God is a complete way of life. It incorporates all divine orders including the provision of all means, taking all precautions and ensuring all that is necessary to fulfil the great trust of being in charge of the earth and building human life on it. So what does this involve in reality?

It does not just entail being in power and forming a government. Rather it involves all this with the proviso that it is used for promoting sound human life and the implementation of the way of life God has chosen for mankind. It is only through such implementation that humanity can achieve the level of perfection that befits the species God has honoured.

The trust given to man on earth is an ability to build and promote goodness, not to corrupt and destroy. It involves ensuring justice and happiness for all, not injustice or suppression. It leads to the elevation of humanity and human life, and not letting them sink to the level of animals.

It is such power and such trust that God has promised the believers who do good deeds. He promised to give them power on earth, just as He gave it to earlier communities of believers, so that they would put into practice the constitution He chose for mankind, establish justice and enable humanity to attain sublimity. People who spread corruption and injustice, and promote carnal desires are not in the position of trustees. They are subjected to a test or are the means to test others. All this is done to fulfil God's purpose.

To further demonstrate this aspect of giving power to the believers is the fact that this promise is followed in the same verse by a further one: "*of a certainty, He will firmly establish for them the religion which He has chosen for them.*" (Verse 55) The firm establishment of His religion means that this will take a firm hold on people's hearts on the one hand, and form the basis on which all life affairs are conducted on the other. God has promised the believers who do righteous deeds to grant them power on earth and to make their faith govern human life. Their faith bids them to do well, establish justice, shun worldly desires, and build a happy human life making good use of all the resources God has placed on earth. It also bids the believers to dedicate all this to God alone.

Furthermore, God's promise to the believers stipulates "*that, of a certainty, He will cause their erstwhile state of fear to be replaced by a state of security.*" The Prophet's Companions were for a long period of time in a state of fear. They could not put down their arms, even after the Prophet and his Companions had migrated to Madīnah, the city that served as the first base for Islam in history.

Al-Rabīʿ ibn Anas quotes Abū al-ʿĀliyah's comments on this verse: "The Prophet and his Companions remained in Makkah for around ten years calling on people to believe in God and to worship Him alone, associating no partners with Him. But they did so in secret, as they were in a state of fear and were prevented from fighting. When they later migrated to Madīnah, God bid them to fight for their cause. This meant that they were again in a state of fear, wearing their body armour day and night. They persevered for as long as God willed. One of his Companions asked the Prophet: 'Are we to remain in fear for the rest of time? Will there come a time when we can put our armaments aside?' The Prophet said: 'It will not be long before any one of you can sit among a huge crowd without anyone carrying arms.' Soon afterwards, God revealed this verse. The Prophet was able to establish his authority over the whole of Arabia and his followers were in a state of security. They put down their arms. Sometime later, the Prophet passed away, and the Muslims remained in security during the reigns of Abū Bakr, 'Umar and 'Uthmān. Then friction occurred between them and God allowed fear to creep into their midst. They had to employ guards. When they changed their overall stance, their conditions also changed."

Not Included in God's Promise

"*Those who, after this, choose to disbelieve are indeed wicked.*" (Verse 55) They are the ones who do not meet God's conditions, and, therefore, God's promise does not apply to them.

God's promise was fulfilled once, and remained effective for as long as the Muslims continued to meet His conditions: "*They will thus worship Me alone and associate with Me no partners whatsoever.*" (Verse 55) This includes any partners, whether in the form of deities to which worship is addressed or desires and ambitions. They must believe and do righteous deeds. God's promise applies to anyone who meets these conditions, and it remains in force till the end of human life. However, victory, power and security may be slow in coming, but this will only be the result of a failure by the believers to meet some aspects of the conditions outlined, or their failure to attend to a particular duty involved. But when the Muslim community has benefited by the trials they have to endure and passed the test God sets for them; when they have endured fear and sought security; when they yearn for dignity after having suffered humiliation; when they aspire to having power after being weak; God's promise will be fulfilled to them in spite of any opposing power. One proviso applies, however: in their perseverance through tests and trials, and in their aspiration to the fulfilment of God's promise, the believers must always resort to the means God has outlined and fulfil the conditions He has made clear.

Therefore, the promise is followed with an order to attend to Islamic duties, such as prayer, *zakāt* and obeying the Prophet. Moreover, the Prophet and his followers must never give any weight to the power of unbelievers who fight them on account of their faith.

> *Attend regularly to your prayers and pay your* zakāt, *and obey the Messenger, so that you might be graced with God's mercy. Do not think that the unbelievers can frustrate [God's plan] on earth. The fire is their abode, and vile indeed is such a journey's end.* (Verses 56–57)

Believers must maintain their bond with God, keep their minds and hearts on the right path through prayer, resist stinginess, purify themselves as individuals and as a community through the payment of *zakāt*, obey the Prophet and accept his judgement, implement God's law in all matters, great or small, so as to set human life on the path He has chosen. Believers must do all this so that they "*might be graced with God's mercy.*" (Verse 56) In this life, God's mercy removes corruption, fear, worry and error, and in the hereafter, it removes His punishment.

Addressing them directly, God says to the believers: if you remain steadfast, following My path, then you need not worry about the might of the unbelievers. They cannot frustrate God's purpose on earth. The power they apparently wield will not stand in your way. You are far stronger when equipped with your faith, implement your system and raise whatever power you can muster. In material power, you may not be a match for them, but believers who strive for the truth can work miracles.

Islam is a great truth which must be carefully examined by anyone who wishes to see the fulfilment of God's promise outlined in the above verses. Such a person must also look at how it came true in human history, understand the true meaning of its conditions before entertaining any doubt about it or worry about the slowness of its fulfilment.

Never did the Muslim community follow God's way, implementing the constitution He has laid down, allowing it to operate in all spheres of life, without reaping the reward of God's promise to grant it power and security. Whenever it abandoned this course, it went to the end of the line, suffered humiliation, lived in fear and misery and saw its faith retreat from guiding human life.

Nevertheless, God's promise remains in force, and His conditions are well defined. Whoever wants to see the promise fulfilled, must do their task and fulfil its conditions. No one is ever more true to his promises than God.

5
Perfect Manners

يَـٰٓأَيُّهَا ٱلَّذِينَ ءَامَنُوا۟ لِيَسْتَـْٔذِنكُمُ
ٱلَّذِينَ مَلَكَتْ أَيْمَـٰنُكُمْ وَٱلَّذِينَ لَمْ يَبْلُغُوا۟
ٱلْحُلُمَ مِنكُمْ ثَلَـٰثَ مَرَّٰتٍ ۚ مِّن قَبْلِ صَلَوٰةِ
ٱلْفَجْرِ وَحِينَ تَضَعُونَ ثِيَابَكُم مِّنَ
ٱلظَّهِيرَةِ وَمِنۢ بَعْدِ صَلَوٰةِ ٱلْعِشَآءِ ۚ
ثَلَـٰثُ عَوْرَٰتٍ لَّكُمْ ۚ لَيْسَ عَلَيْكُمْ
وَلَا عَلَيْهِمْ جُنَاحٌۢ بَعْدَهُنَّ ۚ طَوَّٰفُونَ
عَلَيْكُم بَعْضُكُمْ عَلَىٰ بَعْضٍ ۚ كَذَٰلِكَ
يُبَيِّنُ ٱللَّهُ لَكُمُ ٱلْـَٔايَـٰتِ ۗ وَٱللَّهُ عَلِيمٌ
حَكِيمٌ ٥٨

Believers! Let those whom you rightfully possess, and those of you who have not yet attained to puberty, ask leave of you at three times of day: before the prayer of daybreak, and whenever you lay aside your garments in the middle of the day, and after the prayer of nightfall. These are three occasions on which you may happen to be undressed. Beyond these occasions, neither you nor they will incur any sin if they move freely about you, attending to one another. Thus God makes clear to you His revelations. God is All-Knowing, Wise. (58)

وَإِذَا بَلَغَ ٱلْأَطْفَـٰلُ مِنكُمُ ٱلْحُلُمَ
فَلْيَسْتَـْٔذِنُوا۟ كَمَا ٱسْتَـْٔذَنَ ٱلَّذِينَ
مِن قَبْلِهِمْ ۚ كَذَٰلِكَ يُبَيِّنُ ٱللَّهُ لَكُمْ
ءَايَـٰتِهِۦ ۗ وَٱللَّهُ عَلِيمٌ حَكِيمٌ ٥٩

Yet when your children attain to puberty, let them ask leave of you, as do those senior to them [in age]. Thus does God make revelations clear to you. God is All-Knowing, Wise. (59)

Such elderly women as are past the prospect of marriage incur no sin if they lay aside their [outer] garments, provided they do not make a showy display of their charms. But it is better for them to be modest. God hears all and knows all. (60)

وَٱلۡقَوَٰعِدُ مِنَ ٱلنِّسَآءِ ٱلَّٰتِي لَا يَرۡجُونَ
نِكَاحٗا فَلَيۡسَ عَلَيۡهِنَّ جُنَاحٌ أَن
يَضَعۡنَ ثِيَابَهُنَّ غَيۡرَ مُتَبَرِّجَٰتِۭ
بِزِينَةٖۖ وَأَن يَسۡتَعۡفِفۡنَ خَيۡرٞ لَّهُنَّۗ
وَٱللَّهُ سَمِيعٌ عَلِيمٞ ٦٠

No blame attaches to the blind, nor does blame attach to the lame, nor does blame attach to the sick; and neither to yourselves for eating from your houses, or your fathers' houses, or your mothers' houses, or your brothers' houses, or your sisters' houses, or your paternal uncles' houses, or your paternal aunts' houses, or your maternal uncles' houses, or your maternal aunts' houses, or in houses of which the keys are in your possession, or in the houses of your friends. You will incur no sin by eating in company or separately. But when you enter houses, greet one another with a blessed, goodly greeting, as enjoined by God. Thus does God make His revelations clear to you, so that you may use your reason. (61)

لَّيۡسَ عَلَى ٱلۡأَعۡمَىٰ حَرَجٞ وَلَا عَلَى ٱلۡأَعۡرَجِ
حَرَجٞ وَلَا عَلَى ٱلۡمَرِيضِ حَرَجٞ وَلَا عَلَىٰٓ
أَنفُسِكُمۡ أَن تَأۡكُلُواْ مِنۢ بُيُوتِكُمۡ
أَوۡ بُيُوتِ ءَابَآئِكُمۡ أَوۡ بُيُوتِ أُمَّهَٰتِكُمۡ
أَوۡ بُيُوتِ إِخۡوَٰنِكُمۡ أَوۡ بُيُوتِ أَخَوَٰتِكُمۡ
أَوۡ بُيُوتِ أَعۡمَٰمِكُمۡ أَوۡ بُيُوتِ عَمَّٰتِكُمۡ
أَوۡ بُيُوتِ أَخۡوَٰلِكُمۡ أَوۡ بُيُوتِ
خَٰلَٰتِكُمۡ أَوۡ مَا مَلَكۡتُم مَّفَاتِحَهُۥٓ
أَوۡ صَدِيقِكُمۡۚ لَيۡسَ عَلَيۡكُمۡ
جُنَاحٌ أَن تَأۡكُلُواْ جَمِيعًا أَوۡ
أَشۡتَاتٗاۚ فَإِذَا دَخَلۡتُم بُيُوتٗا فَسَلِّمُواْ عَلَىٰٓ
أَنفُسِكُمۡ تَحِيَّةٗ مِّنۡ عِندِ ٱللَّهِ مُبَٰرَكَةٗ
طَيِّبَةٗۚ كَذَٰلِكَ يُبَيِّنُ ٱللَّهُ لَكُمُ
ٱلۡأٓيَٰتِ لَعَلَّكُمۡ تَعۡقِلُونَ ٦١

They only are true believers who believe in God and His Messenger, and who, whenever they are with him upon a matter requiring collective action, do not depart unless they have obtained his leave. Those who ask leave of you are indeed the ones who believe in God and His Messenger. Hence, when they ask your leave to attend to some business of theirs, grant you this leave to whomever of them you choose, and pray to God to forgive them. God is indeed Much-Forgiving, Merciful. (62)

إِنَّمَا الْمُؤْمِنُونَ الَّذِينَ آمَنُوا بِاللَّهِ
وَرَسُولِهِ وَإِذَا كَانُوا مَعَهُ عَلَىٰ أَمْرٍ
جَامِعٍ لَّمْ يَذْهَبُوا حَتَّىٰ يَسْتَأْذِنُوهُ إِنَّ
الَّذِينَ يَسْتَأْذِنُونَكَ أُولَٰئِكَ
الَّذِينَ يُؤْمِنُونَ بِاللَّهِ وَرَسُولِهِ فَإِذَا
اسْتَأْذَنُوكَ لِبَعْضِ شَأْنِهِمْ فَأْذَن
لِّمَن شِئْتَ مِنْهُمْ وَاسْتَغْفِرْ لَهُمُ
اللَّهَ إِنَّ اللَّهَ غَفُورٌ رَّحِيمٌ ﴿٦٢﴾

Do not address God's Messenger in the manner you address one another. God certainly knows those of you who would slip away surreptitiously. So, let those who would go against His bidding beware, lest some affliction or grievous suffering befall them. (63)

لَّا تَجْعَلُوا دُعَاءَ الرَّسُولِ بَيْنَكُمْ
كَدُعَاءِ بَعْضِكُم بَعْضًا قَدْ يَعْلَمُ
اللَّهُ الَّذِينَ يَتَسَلَّلُونَ مِنكُمْ لِوَاذًا
فَلْيَحْذَرِ الَّذِينَ يُخَالِفُونَ عَنْ أَمْرِهِ أَن
تُصِيبَهُمْ فِتْنَةٌ أَوْ يُصِيبَهُمْ عَذَابٌ
أَلِيمٌ ﴿٦٣﴾

To God belongs all that is in the heavens and on earth. Well does He know what you are intent upon. One day, all will be brought back to Him, and then He will tell them all that they have done. God has full knowledge of everything. (64)

أَلَا إِنَّ لِلَّهِ مَا فِي السَّمَاوَاتِ وَالْأَرْضِ
قَدْ يَعْلَمُ مَا أَنتُمْ عَلَيْهِ وَيَوْمَ يُرْجَعُونَ
إِلَيْهِ فَيُنَبِّئُهُم بِمَا عَمِلُوا وَاللَّهُ بِكُلِّ
شَيْءٍ عَلِيمٌ ﴿٦٤﴾

Overview

Islam is a complete way of life, setting a code that organizes human life in all situations. It lays down values that govern all human relations and social actions. Islam establishes values that are relevant to points of detail in daily situations and behaviour, in the same way as it lays down values and principles that govern serious and momentous matters. It ensures harmony between the two and makes acceptance by God and earning His pleasure the goal of all human activities.

The present *sūrah* provides an example of such harmony. It specifies certain mandatory punishments for serious offences, and it speaks of seeking permission before entering others' homes. Alongside the two it portrays spectacular scenes from the universe. The *sūrah* then speaks of the Muslims' proper attitude as they submit to the rule of God and His Messenger, contrasting this with the hypocrites' insolence. Alongside this comes God's true promise to the believers that they will be established on earth and live in peace and security. In this last passage, the *sūrah* again speaks of proper manners within the home, and when inmates need to seek permission before entering rooms, so as not to intrude on others' privacy. It also makes clear the requirement of seeking permission before leaving the Prophet. It also outlines the proper manner of visiting relatives and friends where one may partake of food. Alongside this, it outlines the proper way of addressing the Prophet. All these form part of the Islamic manners that every Muslim community should adopt, realizing that the Qur'ān provides guidance in all life situations, even though they may not be of a serious nature.

Good Manners at Home

Believers! Let those whom you rightfully possess, and those of you who have not yet attained to puberty, ask leave of you at three times of day: before the prayer of daybreak, and whenever you lay aside your garments in the middle of the day, and after the prayer of nightfall. These are three occasions on which you may happen to be undressed. Beyond these occasions, neither you nor they will incur any sin if they move freely about you, attending to one another. Thus God makes clear to you His revelations. God is All-Knowing, Wise. (Verse 58)

Earlier in the *sūrah* the proper manner of seeking permission before entering a house is outlined. Now the *sūrah* speaks of the need to seek permission within the home. Servants, who were slaves, and children who are not so young but have not yet attained puberty enter rooms without knocking to seek permission, except during three times of the day. These are periods of relaxation when adults may be undressed. These three occasions are: 1) shortly before the daybreak prayer, i.e. *fajr*, when people normally still wear their night garments, or they may be putting on their day clothes in readiness to go out; 2) about midday when people take a nap after changing into more comfortable garments for relaxation; and 3) after they have offered their nightfall prayer, i.e. *'ishā'*. At this time, people put on their night clothes for more comfort.

During these three periods, servants and children below the age of puberty must knock before entering rooms in the house so that they do not see their relatives undressed. Many people do not observe such manners at home, thinking little of the psychological and moral effects of their laxity. Or they may think that servants do not stare at their masters' nakedness, or that children below the age of puberty do not take notice. With the progress achieved today in the field of human psychology, experts emphasize that people are often influenced for life by what they see or experience in childhood, and that such experience may cause them psychological problems that are not easy to cure. God, who knows everything, including the finest and most subtle feelings, outlines these manners which He wants the Muslim community to observe, so that it remains a community with sound hearts and minds, free from psychological problems.

These three occasions are specified because it is more likely that people will be undressed. Children and servants are not required to knock before entry all the time, because this would be difficult to observe, considering that these two groups frequently enter their elders' rooms: either because servants are going about their tasks or because children cannot stay away from their parents for long. Hence the description: "*Beyond these occasions, neither you nor they will incur any sin if they move freely about you, attending to one another.*" We see how the divine instruction strikes a balance between the need to ensure that people do not show their nakedness in front of others, even though they may be young or servants, and the practical need for easy access. Hence, the instruction does not order seeking permission to enter on all occasions.

When children attain to puberty, the same rules of entry apply to them as to those who are not related to the family. This means that they must seek permission before entering a room at any time, in accordance with the general rules outlined earlier in the *sūrah*: "*Yet when your children attain to puberty, let them ask leave of you, as do those senior to them [in age]. Thus does God make revelations clear to you. God is All-Knowing, Wise.*" (Verse 59)

We note that the final comment in these verses stresses God's knowledge and wisdom, because the instructions given are based on His knowledge of our inner feelings and the manners that are most likely to refine such feelings. In His wisdom, God lays down the teachings that set minds and hearts on the right course.

Rules Relaxed

Earlier in the *sūrah* orders were given requiring women to cover their charms and adornments so that there is little room for temptation or exciting desire. An exception is made here in the case of older women who no longer have the desire to consort with men, and who no longer excite men's desires:

> *Such elderly women as are past the prospect of marriage incur no sin if they lay aside their [outer] garments, provided they do not make a showy display of their charms. But it is better for them to be modest. God hears all and knows all.* (Verse 60)

Such elder women may, if they choose, put aside their cloaks and outer garments, provided that this does not expose their nakedness, and that they do not make a show, displaying their charms or adornments. It is better for them that they should not do so, continuing to wear their outer, loose garments. In describing such modesty the *sūrah* uses the word *yasta'fifna*, which is derived from the Arabic root *'iffah*, meaning chastity. Thus, this attitude is described as aiming to maintain chastity because of the close link between chastity and covering women's charms, while exposing such charms is closely linked to temptation. This instruction is in line with the general Islamic view that the best method of guarding people's chastity is to reduce the chances for temptation.

"*God hears all and knows all.*" He is aware of all things, including what is uttered and what is entertained in one's thoughts. The question here is one of intention and conscience.

The *sūrah* then tackles another aspect of relations with friends and relatives:

> *No blame attaches to the blind, nor does blame attach to the lame, nor does blame attach to the sick; and neither to yourselves for eating from your houses, or your fathers' houses, or your mothers' houses, or your brothers' houses, or your sisters' houses, or your paternal uncles' houses, or your paternal aunts' houses, or your maternal uncles' houses, or your maternal aunts' houses, or in houses of which the keys are in your possession, or in the houses of your friends. You will incur no sin by eating in company or separately. But when you enter houses, greet one another with a blessed, goodly greeting, as enjoined by God. Thus does God make His revelations clear to you, so that you may use your reason.* (Verse 61)

Reports suggest that in the early days of Islam, Muslims used to eat in such houses mentioned in this verse without asking the owners' permission. They also took with them poor people who were blind, lame or ill. Then when a verse was revealed stating: "*Do not devour one another's property wrongfully,*" (2: 188) they felt very uneasy about eating in relatives' homes. Furthermore, such poor people as were blind, lame or ill felt uneasy about joining them, unless they were specifically invited by the owner. This reflects the keen sensitivity of the early Muslims, and their desire to avoid anything that was even remotely connected with what God prohibited. Hence, this present verse was revealed, making it perfectly permissible for relatives to eat in the homes of such relatives mentioned in the verse, and to bring with them such needy people as the verse describes. All this is understood to be contingent on the clear understanding that the home owner is not averse to this, and their eating in his home does not cause him any harm. Adding such a proviso is based on general rules like those outlined in the following two *ḥadīths*: "There shall be no infliction of harm on oneself or others," and "It is not permissible to take the property of a Muslim except with his consent." [Related by al-Shāfi'ī]

Since this verse lays down certain legislation we note how it is phrased, choosing its wording very carefully so as not to leave any room for doubt or confusion. We also note how relatives are mentioned in a specific order. It starts with a reference to the homes of one's own children and spouses without even mentioning these relatives. The verse includes these in the general reference to "your houses", because the house of one's son, daughter, wife or husband is like one's own. Then other homes are mentioned, starting with those belonging to a father, mother, paternal uncle and aunt, maternal uncle and aunt. Added to these is a person who is entrusted with looking after one's property, having the keys to it. Such a person may eat from that house in accordance with what is reasonable, not taking more than what he needs for his own food. Also added are friends' homes so as to make the relation with them similar to that with one's own relatives. Indeed, friends may be very happy for friends to eat at their homes without the need for any permission. But all this is conditional on causing no harm to the home owner.

Having mentioned the homes in which one may eat without seeking prior permission, the verse continues to explain the manner in which such eating may take place: "You will incur no sin by eating in company or separately." In pre-Islamic days some Arabs disliked eating alone. If such a person did not find someone to eat with, he would not touch the food. God lifted this restriction, because it causes unnatural complications. He left the matter simple to cater for all situations. Hence people may eat alone or in company.

The verse adds an instruction on manners to be observed when entering such homes where people are allowed to eat: "*When you enter houses, greet one another with a blessed, goodly greeting, as enjoined by God.*" (Verse 61) The phraseology of this instruction in the Arabic original employs a fine touch as it says: *sallimū 'alā anfusikum* 'greet yourselves' to express the meaning given in translation as 'greet one another'. This is an indication of the strength of the relationship between those mentioned in this verse. A person who greets his relative or friend is actually greeting himself, and the greeting offered is enjoined by God, as though coming from Him. It is thus blessed, full of goodness. As such it establishes a bond between them that is never severed.

These instructions emphasize that the believers feel their bond with God in all matters and appreciate the wisdom behind divine legislation: "*Thus does God make His revelations clear to you, so that you may use your reason.*" (Verse 61)

Good Manners with the Prophet

The *sūrah* then moves on to organizing relations within the larger family of the Muslim community and its leader, the Prophet, and how Muslims should behave in his presence:

> *They only are true believers who believe in God and His Messenger, and who, whenever they are with him upon a matter requiring collective action, do not depart unless they have obtained his leave. Those who ask leave of you are indeed the ones who believe in God and His Messenger. Hence, when they ask your leave to attend to some business of theirs, grant you this leave to whomever of them you choose, and pray to God to forgive them. God is indeed Much-Forgiving, Merciful. Do not address God's Messenger in the manner you address one another. God certainly knows those of you who would slip away surreptitiously. So, let those who would go against His bidding beware, lest some affliction or grievous suffering befall them. To God belongs all that is in the heavens and on earth. Well does He know what you are intent upon. One day, all will be brought back to Him, and then He will tell them all that they have done. God has full knowledge of everything.* (Verses 62–64)

Ibn Isḥāq mentions the occasion when these verses were revealed. He says that when the Quraysh and the confederate tribes marched towards Madinah, pledging to annihilate the Muslims, the Prophet ordered the digging of a moat around the entrance to Madīnah. He himself took part in the digging work so as to encourage those who were also taking part. All Muslims were working hard, except for a number of hypocrites. They tried to hide their lack of commitment by doing a little work before sneaking away, without the Prophet's knowledge or permission. On the other hand, the true Muslims continued to work hard. If any of them needed to leave for some important business, he mentioned this to the Prophet, requesting permission before so leaving. The Prophet granted him permission, and he returned as soon as he had attended to the business in hand. They all felt that taking part in this work would earn them reward from God. God described those true believers in the verse: "*They only are true believers...*" In reference to the hypocrites who sneaked away without permission, God says: "*Do not address God's Messenger in the manner you address one another...*"

Whatever was the background behind the revelation of these verses, they include important rules for the Muslim community which should be observed between the leader and the members of that community. These rules should be so ingrained as to become part of the traditions, feelings and regulations within the community. Otherwise, the community will fall into total chaos. Thus, "*They only are true believers who believe in God and His Messenger,*" and not the ones who verbally declare themselves believers but show no practical evidence of their obedience. "*And who, whenever they are with him upon a matter requiring collective action, do not depart unless they have obtained his leave.*" (Verse 62) This applies to serious matters that require collective action, such as a decision on going to war, or a matter that concerns the whole community. When such a grave matter is being considered or acted upon, believers do not absent themselves without first obtaining their leader's permission. Thus, no room is left for disorder.

People with faith do not seek permission to leave unless they are in real need to do so. Their faith and discipline ensure that they are not away when a serious collective matter is at hand. The Qur'ān, however, gives the Prophet, who is the leader of the Muslim community, the right to grant or withhold such permission: "*When they ask your leave to attend to some business of theirs, grant you this leave to whomever of them you choose.*" (Verse 62) This means that there is no harm in withholding permission, should the situation require this. The leader of the Muslim community thus exercises his authority in determining whether or not to allow an individual to leave, depending on how he sees the interests of the community being best served.

Nevertheless, the *sūrah* makes clear that it is better for the individual to try to overcome personal needs, so as to stay with the Prophet. Receiving permission to depart for a while means falling short on fulfilling one's duty. Hence, it needs for the Prophet to pray to God to forgive those who needed to be absent for a time: "*When they ask your leave to attend to some business of theirs, grant you this leave to whomever of them you choose, and pray to God to forgive them. God is indeed Much-Forgiving, Merciful.*" (Verse 62) This puts a check on the believer through his own conscience, ensuring that he does not seek a leave of absence in such situations unless he has very compelling reasons.

A Stern Warning to the Disobedient

The *sūrah* then alerts the Muslims to the need to address the Prophet with respect when they seek his permission, and indeed in all situations. They should not call him by his name or nickname, as they call each other. He is to be addressed as the man God has honoured by making him His Messenger: "*Do not address God's Messenger in the manner you address one another.*" (Verse 63) Indeed people must be full of respect for him as God's Messenger, so that they pay due heed to every word he says and every directive he gives. Teachers and leaders should be held in high esteem and addressed with respect. The fact that the Prophet was very modest in his approach, and easy to deal with, did not mean that it was appropriate for his Companions to forget that he was their leader who educated them and refined their manners, addressing him as they would address one another. Deep in their hearts, those who are being educated should hold their educator in high regard so that they are ashamed if they happen to overstep the requirements of respect when dealing with him.

The hypocrites who sneaked away, covering for one another, are given a stern warning. If the Prophet could not see them, God was certainly watching them: "*God certainly knows those of you who would slip away surreptitiously.*" (Verse 63) The Arabic wording, *yatasallalūn... liwādhā,* practically shows their stealthy movements, as they left stealthily, like despicable cowards.

"*So, let those who would go against His bidding beware, lest some affliction or grievous suffering befall them.*" (Verse 63) The warning here is very stern. Those who disobey the Prophet's orders, seeking a way different from his, sneaking away in pursuit of personal gain or to avoid potential risk, should beware. They may find themselves in the midst of a situation where values and standards are blurred, where the true and false are not easily distinguished and the community finds itself in disarray. In such a situation no one is sure of his own safety, as people do not abide by the law and good may not be easily distinguished from evil. Such a situation is miserable for everyone: "*Lest some affliction or grievous suffering befall them.*" Such grievous suffering could befall people in this life or in the life to come, in retribution for disobeying God's orders and rejecting the way of life He has laid down.

The *sūrah* concludes with a verse that balances the warning with a statement making it clear to both believers and unbelievers that God sees them all, and knows their actions and the intentions behind each action:

> *To God belongs all that is in the heavens and on earth. Well does He know what you are intent upon. One day, all will be brought back to Him, and then He will tell them all that they have done. God has full knowledge of everything.* (Verse 64)

Thus, the conclusion aims to remind people to remain God-fearing. Being so provides the ultimate guarantee for the fulfilment of His orders, abiding by the rules He has set, observing the manners He has outlined. We have seen many of these clearly stated in this *sūrah*, relating to different aspects of life, but all treated on an equal footing.

SŪRAH 25

Al-Furqān

(The Criterion)

Prologue

This *sūrah*, a Makkan revelation, appears to aim at comforting the Prophet and giving him solace, reassurance and support as he faced the stubborn rejection, maltreatment, haughty argument and open hostility of the Quraysh idolaters. In one aspect, it shows the divine kindness bestowed by God on His Messenger, dispelling his pain, comforting his heart so that it overflowed with reassurance and showing him an abundance of care and compassion. In another aspect, it portrays the fierce battle against arrogant mortals who stubbornly oppose God's Messenger, combining falsehood with arrogance, and hostility with a wilful rebuffal of divine guidance.

It is ordinary people who insult this glorious Qur'ān, with such boasting as: "*This [Qur'ān] is nothing but a lie which he has devised with the help of other people.*" (Verse 4) Or they describe it as: "*Fables of ancient times which he has caused to be written down, so that they might be read out to him morning and evening.*" (Verse 5) Furthermore people are ready with their abuse of the Prophet, saying: "*The man you follow is certainly bewitched.*" (Verse 8) Or they may say in ridicule: "*Is this the one whom God has sent as His emissary?*" (Verse 41) As if all this rejection is not enough, such people are often ready to direct their arrogant remarks at God Himself: "*Yet when they are told,*

'Prostrate yourselves before the Most Merciful,' they ask, 'What is the Most Merciful? Are we to prostrate ourselves before whatever you bid us?' And they grow more rebellious." (Verse 60) Or they may say: "*Why have no angels been sent down to us? – or, Why do we not see our Lord?"* (Verse 21)

Ever since Noah's time unbelievers held the same attitude as the Quraysh idolaters towards Muḥammad, God's final Messenger. They all objected to the fact that God's Messenger was mortal, an ordinary man like them, saying: "*What sort of messenger is this, who eats food and goes about in the market-places? Why has not an angel been sent down to him to give warning alongside him?*" (Verse 7) They also objected to his limited wealth, saying: "*Why has not a treasure been granted to him?*" (Verse 8) They further objected to the method of revelation: "*The unbelievers ask: Why has not the Qur'ān been revealed to him all at once?"* (Verse 32) Such voiced objections came on top of their blatant rejection of faith, as also their ridicule and aggression.

The Prophet Muḥammad, (peace be upon him), confronted all this alone, having neither physical power nor wealth. He stood within his appropriate limits, suggesting nothing to his Lord, doing nothing other than turning to his Lord seeking His pleasure, caring for nothing else. He prayed: "My Lord! If You are not displeased with me, I do not care what I face… To You I submit until I earn Your pleasure."

Here, in this *sūrah*, we see the Prophet enjoying his Lord's compassion, who gives him comfort and solace, and provides him with support against all the difficulties placed in his way, including the ridicule of others. After all, they are often impolite with their Lord who creates them and gives them all that they have. The Prophet then should not be much troubled if he receives a little of such ridicule and ill treatment. "*Yet people worship, instead of God, things that can neither benefit nor harm them. An unbeliever always gives support against his Lord.*" (Verse 55) "*Yet, some choose to worship, instead of Him, deities that cannot create anything but are themselves created, and have it not in their power to avert harm from, or bring benefit to, themselves, and have no power over death, life or resurrection.*" (Verse 3) "*Yet when they are told, 'Prostrate yourselves before the Most Merciful,' they ask, 'What is the Most Merciful?'"* (Verse 60)

God redresses the ridicule the Prophet suffers by portraying the very low level into which the unbelievers have sunk: "*Have you considered the one who makes his desires his deity? Could you, then, be held responsible for him? Or do you think that most of them listen and use their reason? They are but like cattle. Nay, they are even far worse astray.*" (Verses 43–44) God promises him support in any dispute or argument he may have with them: "*Whenever they come to you with an argument, We shall reveal to you the truth and the best explanation.*" (Verse 33)

When the battle is over, God shows His Messenger scenes of the destruction of earlier communities which rejected His messages, such as the people of Noah, the 'Ād, Thamūd and the people of al-Rass, as well as others. The way they met their dismal end is shown in a series of images from the Day of Resurrection: "*Those who will be gathered to hell on their faces – they will be worst in station and still farther away from the [right] path.*" (Verse 34) "*Nay! It is the Last Hour that they deny. For those who deny the Last Hour We have prepared a blazing fire. When it sees them from a far-off place, they will hear its fury and its raging sigh. And when, chained together, they are flung into a tight space within, they will pray for extinction there and then. [But they will be told]: 'Do not pray today for one single extinction, but pray for many extinctions!'*" (Verses 11–13) "*On that day the wrongdoer will bite his hands and say: 'Would that I had followed the path shown to me by the Messenger. Oh, woe is me! Would that I had never taken so-and-so for a friend!'*" (Verses 27–28)

God further comforts him by the fact that he faces the same difficulties earlier messengers faced: "*Even before you, We never sent messengers other than [men] who indeed ate food and went about in the market-places.*" (Verse 20) "*Thus against every prophet We have set up enemies from among those who are guilty. Sufficient is your Lord to provide guidance and support.*" (Verse 31)

God also makes clear to him that his task is to remain patient against all adversity, standing up to the unbelievers and striving hard against them using the Qur'ān to make his argument clear, well founded and overpowering. "*Do not obey the unbelievers, but strive most vigorously against them with this Qur'ān.*" (Verse 52) The Prophet is clearly told that his best support in his striving for God's cause is to place his trust in God alone: "*Hence, place your trust in the Living One who does not die, and extol His limitless glory and praise. Sufficient is it that He is well aware of his servants' sins.*" (Verse 58)

The *sūrah* continues along the same lines: one aspect of it overflows with solace and reassurance given by God to His Messenger, and the other portrays the intransigence of the unbelievers and the difficulties they put up against him. It threatens them with punishment and destruction that will be visited upon them by God Almighty. It thus moves on until it approaches its end when it spreads an air of ease, comfort, peace and reassurance. It portrays a detailed image of 'the servants of God the Most Merciful'. These are the people "*who walk gently on earth, and who, whenever the ignorant address them, say: Peace.*" (Verse 63) They are seen here as if they are the final product of the long *Jihād*, or tough striving against people who stubbornly refuse to abandon their erroneous ways and follow divine guidance, or the sweet fruit of the human tree, despite its thorny branches. The *sūrah* ends with a picture of how little value humanity has in God's sight, except for those believers who turn to Him and address their prayers to Him alone: "*Say: No weight or value would my Lord attach to you were it not for you calling out [to Him]. You have indeed denied [His message], and in time this [sin] will cleave unto you.*" (Verse 77)

Such is the general atmosphere of the *sūrah* and such is its subject matter. It is a single unit that is hard to divide into sections, but we can distinguish four parts in its treatment of themes.

The first part begins with extolling God's limitless glory and praising Him for the revelation of the Qur'ān which serves as a warner to mankind. It emphasizes in clear, unequivocal terms God's oneness and sovereignty over the heavens and the earth. It affirms that He alone controls the universe and conducts its affairs in His absolute wisdom, making it clear that He has neither offspring nor partner. It then mentions that the unbelievers nevertheless ascribe divinity to alleged deities that can create nothing, but are themselves created. All this is stated before referring to their hurtful statements about God's Messenger, denying his message and alleging that it is fabrication of his own making, or the fables of ancient communities. It also comes before any reference to their objection to Muḥammad, God's

Messenger, being a human being who eats food and walks in the streets and market places. Also later come their other statements suggesting that he should be supported by an angel, or that he should have a treasure or a garden providing him with all his food. Furthermore, the *sūrah* reports their insults claiming that he is bewitched. It appears that the *sūrah* begins by quoting their denials of their Lord so as to comfort the Prophet as he hears their abusive remarks about him and his message.

The *sūrah* then declares that they have gone far astray as they deny the Last Hour. It warns them against the punishment God has prepared for them in hell, where they are to be thrown in a narrow space, chained one to the other. It contrasts this with an image of the believers in heaven where they abide forever, enjoying whatever they wish. It further shows their fate on the Day of Judgement when they are made to face their alleged deities which will confront them with the falsity of their beliefs. This first line in the *sūrah* ends with further consolation to the Prophet, making it clear to him that all earlier messengers God sent were mortals like him who ate food and walked about the streets and market places.

The second part begins with the arrogant statements of those who deny their inevitable meeting with God. They impudently say: "*Why have no angels been sent down to us? – or, Why do we not see our Lord?*" (Verse 21) They are then quickly brought face to face with a scene of the day when they will see the angels: "*It will be a day of dire distress for the unbelievers. On that day the wrongdoer will bite his hands and say: 'Would that I had followed the path shown to me by the Messenger.'*" (Verses 26–27) This is meant to give reassurance to the Prophet as he complains to his Lord about his people's disregard of the Qur'ān. It quotes their objections to the way the Qur'ān is revealed as they ask: "*Why has not the Qur'ān been revealed to him all at once?*" (Verse 32) The answer to this objection is a scene showing them being gathered to hell on their faces on the Day of Judgement, the day they now deny. Further comment is given in an outline of the fate of past communities that similarly rejected the faith, such as the peoples of Noah, Moses, and the 'Ād, Thamūd, al-Rass and many other generations in between. It wonders at their attitude as they pass by the destroyed towns of the people of Lot taking no heed. All this is meant to comfort the Prophet as he hears their ridicule when they refer to him saying: "*Is this the one whom God has sent as His emissary?*" (Verse 41) The *sūrah* comments on their ridicule, putting them in their rightful place: "*They are but like cattle. Nay, they are even far worse astray.*" (Verse 44)

The third part of the *sūrah* is made up of a number of scenes from the universe, starting with a description of the shadow and moving to the scene of the succession of day and night, before showing the wind as a herald of revitalizing rain and the creation of man from water. Despite all this, the unbelievers continue to worship deities that have no power to bring them benefit or cause them harm. They even go further, by aiding one another against their Lord who has created them. When they are called upon to address their worship to the only true Lord of the universe, they revert to arrogance: "*Yet when they are told, 'Prostrate yourselves before the Most Merciful,' they ask: What is the Most Merciful?*" (Verse 60) The *sūrah* explains that God is "*He who has set up in the skies great constellations, and has placed among them a lamp and a light-giving moon. And He it is who causes the night and the day to succeed one another; [a clear sign] for him who would take heed or would show gratitude.*" (Verses 61–62)

The fourth and final part of the *sūrah* paints a detailed picture of the 'servants of the Most Merciful', showing them as they prostrate themselves before Him in total devotion, recording their statements that earn them their noble positions as His servants. It opens the door of repentance to anyone who wishes to join this group, describing their reward for their perseverance and patience in the face of adversity, and their fulfilment of the requirements of faith: "*These will be rewarded for all their patient endurance [in life] with a high station in heaven, and will be met there with a greeting of welcome and peace.*" (Verse 75)

The *sūrah* concludes with a statement to the effect that all mankind would have been discarded by God, had it not been for those of His servants who obey Him and do His bidding, recognizing His authority and His right to be obeyed. By putting erring humanity in its place, the Qur'ān also shows that the harassment the Prophet is subjected to should be seen as trivial, for that is what it really is.

I

To Distinguish Right from False

Al-Furqān (The Criterion)

In the Name of God, the Merciful, the Beneficent

Blessed is He who from on high bestowed upon His servant the standard to discern the true from the false, so that it might be a warning to all the worlds: (1)

تَبَارَكَ ٱلَّذِى نَزَّلَ ٱلْفُرْقَانَ عَلَىٰ عَبْدِهِۦ
لِيَكُونَ لِلْعَـٰلَمِينَ نَذِيرًا ١

He to whom belongs the dominion over the heavens and the earth, and who begets no offspring, and has no partner in His dominion. It is He who has created all things and ordained them in due proportions. (2)

ٱلَّذِى لَهُۥ مُلْكُ ٱلسَّمَـٰوَٰتِ وَٱلْأَرْضِ وَلَمْ
يَتَّخِذْ وَلَدًا وَلَمْ يَكُن لَّهُۥ شَرِيكٌ فِى
ٱلْمُلْكِ وَخَلَقَ كُلَّ شَىْءٍ فَقَدَّرَهُۥ تَقْدِيرًا ٢

Yet, some choose to worship, instead of Him, deities that cannot create anything but are themselves created, and have it not in their power to avert harm from, or bring benefit to, themselves, and have no power over death, life or resurrection. (3)

وَاتَّخَذُوا مِن دُونِهِۦٓ ءَالِهَةً لَّا يَخْلُقُونَ
شَيْـًٔا وَهُمْ يُخْلَقُونَ وَلَا يَمْلِكُونَ
لِأَنفُسِهِمْ ضَرًّا وَلَا نَفْعًا وَلَا يَمْلِكُونَ
مَوْتًا وَلَا حَيَوٰةً وَلَا نُشُورًا ﴿٣﴾

The unbelievers say: 'This [Qur'ān] is nothing but a lie which he has devised with the help of other people.' In truth, it is they who have perpetrated an inequity and a falsehood. (4)

وَقَالَ الَّذِينَ كَفَرُوٓا إِنْ هَٰذَآ إِلَّآ إِفْكٌ
افْتَرَىٰهُ وَأَعَانَهُۥ عَلَيْهِ قَوْمٌ ءَاخَرُونَ
فَقَدْ جَآءُو ظُلْمًا وَزُورًا ﴿٤﴾

And they say: 'Fables of ancient times which he has caused to be written down, so that they might be read out to him morning and evening.' (5)

وَقَالُوٓا أَسَٰطِيرُ الْأَوَّلِينَ اكْتَتَبَهَا
فَهِيَ تُمْلَىٰ عَلَيْهِ بُكْرَةً وَأَصِيلًا ﴿٥﴾

Say: 'This [Qur'ān] is bestowed from on high by Him who knows the secrets of the heavens and the earth. He is indeed Much-Forgiving, Merciful.' (6)

قُلْ أَنزَلَهُ الَّذِي يَعْلَمُ السِّرَّ فِي السَّمَٰوَٰتِ
وَالْأَرْضِ إِنَّهُۥ كَانَ غَفُورًا رَّحِيمًا ﴿٦﴾

They also say: 'What sort of messenger is this, who eats food and goes about in the market-places? Why has not an angel been sent down to him to give warning alongside him? (7)

وَقَالُوا مَالِ هَٰذَا الرَّسُولِ يَأْكُلُ الطَّعَامَ
وَيَمْشِي فِي الْأَسْوَاقِ لَوْلَآ أُنزِلَ إِلَيْهِ
مَلَكٌ فَيَكُونَ مَعَهُۥ نَذِيرًا ﴿٧﴾

أَوْ يُلْقَىٰٓ إِلَيْهِ كَنزٌ أَوْ تَكُونُ لَهُۥ جَنَّةٌ
يَأْكُلُ مِنْهَا ۚ وَقَالَ ٱلظَّـٰلِمُونَ
إِن تَتَّبِعُونَ إِلَّا رَجُلًا مَّسْحُورًا ﴿٨﴾

Or why has not a treasure been granted to him? Or he should have a garden to provide his sustenance.' The wrongdoers say: 'The man you follow is certainly bewitched.' (8)

ٱنظُرْ كَيْفَ ضَرَبُوا۟ لَكَ ٱلْأَمْثَـٰلَ
فَضَلُّوا۟ فَلَا يَسْتَطِيعُونَ سَبِيلًا ﴿٩﴾

See to what they liken you. They have certainly gone astray and are unable to find a way back [to the truth]. (9)

تَبَارَكَ ٱلَّذِىٓ إِن شَآءَ جَعَلَ لَكَ خَيْرًا مِّن
ذَٰلِكَ جَنَّـٰتٍ تَجْرِى مِن تَحْتِهَا ٱلْأَنْهَـٰرُ
وَيَجْعَل لَّكَ قُصُورًۢا ﴿١٠﴾

Blessed is He who, if it be His will, shall give you better things than these; gardens through which running waters flow, and shall give you palaces too. (10)

بَلْ كَذَّبُوا۟ بِٱلسَّاعَةِ ۖ وَأَعْتَدْنَا لِمَن
كَذَّبَ بِٱلسَّاعَةِ سَعِيرًا ﴿١١﴾

Nay! It is the Last Hour that they deny. For those who deny the Last Hour We have prepared a blazing fire. (11)

إِذَا رَأَتْهُم مِّن مَّكَانٍۭ بَعِيدٍ سَمِعُوا۟ لَهَا
تَغَيُّظًا وَزَفِيرًا ﴿١٢﴾

When it sees them from a far-off place, they will hear its fury and its raging sigh. (12)

وَإِذَآ أُلْقُوا۟ مِنْهَا مَكَانًا ضَيِّقًا مُّقَرَّنِينَ
دَعَوْا۟ هُنَالِكَ ثُبُورًا ﴿١٣﴾

And when, chained together, they are flung into a tight space within, they will pray for extinction there and then. (13)

لَّا تَدْعُوا۟ ٱلْيَوْمَ ثُبُورًا وَٰحِدًا وَٱدْعُوا۟
ثُبُورًا كَثِيرًا ﴿١٤﴾

[But they will be told]: 'Do not pray today for one single extinction, but pray for many extinctions!' (14)

قُلْ أَذَٰلِكَ خَيْرٌ أَمْ جَنَّةُ ٱلْخُلْدِ
ٱلَّتِى وُعِدَ ٱلْمُتَّقُونَ كَانَتْ لَهُمْ
جَزَآءً وَمَصِيرًا ﴿١٥﴾

Say: 'Which is better: that, or the paradise of eternity which the God-fearing have been promised as their reward and their ultimate abode?' (15)

لَّهُمْ فِيهَا مَا يَشَآءُونَ خَٰلِدِينَ كَانَ
عَلَىٰ رَبِّكَ وَعْدًا مَّسْـُٔولًا ﴿١٦﴾

There they will have all they wish for, abiding there forever. It is a promise given by your Lord, always to be prayed for. (16)

وَيَوْمَ يَحْشُرُهُمْ وَمَا يَعْبُدُونَ مِن
دُونِ ٱللَّهِ فَيَقُولُ ءَأَنتُمْ أَضْلَلْتُمْ عِبَادِى
هَٰٓؤُلَآءِ أَمْ هُمْ ضَلُّوا۟ ٱلسَّبِيلَ ﴿١٧﴾

On the day He gathers them with all those they worship instead of God, He will ask: 'Was it you who led these My servants astray, or did they by themselves stray from the right path?' (17)

قَالُوا۟ سُبْحَٰنَكَ مَا كَانَ يَنۢبَغِى لَنَآ أَن نَّتَّخِذَ
مِن دُونِكَ مِنْ أَوْلِيَآءَ وَلَٰكِن مَّتَّعْتَهُمْ
وَءَابَآءَهُمْ حَتَّىٰ نَسُوا۟ ٱلذِّكْرَ وَكَانُوا۟
قَوْمًۢا بُورًا ﴿١٨﴾

They will say: 'Limitless are You in Your glory! It was never proper for us to take for our masters anyone but Yourself. But You allowed them and their fathers to enjoy [the pleasures of] life, until they forgot the Reminder. For they were people devoid of all good.' (18)

فَقَدْ كَذَّبُوكُم بِمَا تَقُولُونَ
فَمَا تَسْتَطِيعُونَ صَرْفًا وَلَا نَصْرًا
وَمَن يَظْلِم مِّنكُمْ نُذِقْهُ عَذَابًا
كَبِيرًا ﴿١٩﴾

[Then God will say]: 'Now have they denied all your assertions, and you can neither avert [your punishment] nor obtain help. Whoever of you does wrong, him shall We cause to taste grievous suffering.' (19)

Even before you, We never sent messengers other than [men] who indeed ate food and went about in the market-places. We have made some of you a means of testing others. Are you able to endure with patience? Surely your Lord sees all. (20)

وَمَآ أَرْسَلْنَا قَبْلَكَ مِنَ ٱلْمُرْسَلِينَ
إِلَّآ إِنَّهُمْ لَيَأْكُلُونَ ٱلطَّعَامَ وَيَمْشُونَ
فِى ٱلْأَسْوَاقِ ۗ وَجَعَلْنَا بَعْضَكُمْ
لِبَعْضٍ فِتْنَةً أَتَصْبِرُونَ ۗ وَكَانَ
رَبُّكَ بَصِيرًا ٢٠

The Purpose of Qur'ānic Revelations

This opening gives a clear indication of the main themes of the *sūrah*, namely the revelation of the Qur'ān by God, the addressing of its message to all mankind, God's absolute oneness that admits no partner or offspring, and His sovereignty over the whole universe which He, in His wisdom, controls. Yet despite all this, the unbelievers continue to associate partners with Him and the fabricators persevere in their falsehood. Moreover, baseless arguments and arrogant statements are made.

"*Blessed is He who from on high bestowed upon His servant the standard to discern the true from the false, so that it might be a warning to all the worlds.*" (Verse 1) The Arabic word, *tabārak*, translated here as 'blessed' is a derivative of the root word, *barakah*, denoting blessing but adds a further dimension of increase and growth so as to signify the continuous increase of praise and God's blessings. God is not mentioned in the verse by name. Rather, a relative noun is used, "*He who from on high bestowed... the standard.*" This is useful in highlighting His action of sending a message to mankind, because the essential argument of the *sūrah* is the truth of the revelation of the Qur'ān and its message.

The Qur'ān is named here as '*al-Furqān*', which is also the title of the *sūrah*. The name indicates distinction and separation between the truth and falsehood, divine guidance and erroneous beliefs. Furthermore, the Qur'ān makes a clear distinction between two different ways of life and two epochs in human life. It outlines a clear way of life as it is conceived in human conscience and in practice. This way of life is distinct from anything humanity has ever known. It ushers in a new era for humanity, unlike anything it ever witnessed. Thus it is a criterion in this broad sense, separating the stage of human childhood that has just ended from the stage of maturity about to begin. The age of physical miracles is thus ended to start that of rational miracles. Moreover, local and provisional messages come to an end with the revelation of the Qur'ān, God's final and universal message to all mankind: "*so that it might be a warning to all the worlds.*" (Verse 1)

Special honour for God's Messenger is shown at this point, describing him as 'God's servant'. The same description is given to him when the Prophet's night journey is highlighted. "*Limitless in His glory is He who transported His servant by night from the Sacred Mosque [in Makkah] to the Aqṣā Mosque [in Jerusalem].*" (17: 1) Also in the context of prayer and supplication, the Prophet is given the same description: "*When His servant stood up praying to Him...*" (72: 19) Another instance of using this description is the opening of *Sūrah* 18 which also speaks of the revelation of the Qur'ān: "*All praise is due to God who has bestowed this Book from on high on His servant, and has ensured that it remains free of distortion.*" (18: 1) Describing man as God's servant in these contexts indicates the highest and most honourable status to which any human being can aspire. It also serves as an implicit reminder that when man achieves his highest status, he is no more than God's servant, while the position of majesty belongs to Him alone, with absolutely no hint or suggestion of there being anyone who bears any resemblance to Him or is His partner. It was situations like the Prophet's night journey to Jerusalem and from there to heaven, or direct supplication to God and speaking to Him, or receiving His directives and revelations that tempted some of the followers of earlier messengers to weave legends speaking about a son of God or a relationship other than that of Godhead and servitude to Him. Hence, the Qur'ān emphasizes the status of man's servitude to God as the highest position to which a chosen human being can aspire.

The *sūrah* defines God's purpose of the revelation of the Qur'ān to His servant, "*so that it might be a warning to all the worlds.*" (Verse 1)

As a Makkan revelation, this Qur'ānic statement is important as it proves the universal character of the Islamic message right from its early days. This is contrary to the claims made by some non-Muslim 'historians' suggesting that the Islamic message initially had only local aspirations, but became more ambitious and outward looking as it secured a number of military victories. The truth is that this message was addressed from the start to all mankind. By its very nature, and the means it employed, it was clearly a universal message aiming to take all mankind into a new era, where a new code and style of life are implemented. It defined its universal nature when the Prophet was still in Makkah, facing determined and unrelenting opposition. It sought to achieve all this through the Qur'ān, the criterion God revealed to His Messenger to serve as a warning to all the worlds.

The One who revealed to His Messenger this standard is "*He to whom belongs the dominion over the heavens and the earth, and who begets no offspring, and has no partner in His dominion. It is He who has created all things and ordained them in due proportions.*" (Verse 2)

Once more God is not mentioned here by name, but a relative pronoun is used instead to emphasize certain suitable attributes of His: "*He to whom belongs the dominion over the heavens and the earth.*" He has absolute dominion over the heavens and the earth: a dominion that signifies ownership, control and ability to change and transform.

"*Who begets no offspring.*" Procreation is one of the natural laws God has set in operation to ensure the continuity of life, but God is Eternal and able to accomplish His purpose, whatever that may be.

He "*has no partner in His dominion.*" Everything in the heavens and the earth testifies to the unity of design, nature, law and control.

"*It is He who has created all things and ordained them in due proportions.*" He determines the size, shape, function, time and place of everything as well as all their interactions and harmonization.

The nature of the universe, its make up and constitution fill us with wonder. It makes nonsense of any suggestion that the universe came into being by chance. It demonstrates the meticulous and detailed proportioning of creation, which human knowledge can hardly manage to fathom even in one area of the vast universe. With every scientific progress made, more aspects of the harmony and balance in the universe and its natural laws are discovered. Consequently, we can better appreciate the meaning of this wonderful statement: "*It is He who has created all things and ordained them in due proportions.*"

It is useful to mention here some scientific facts that emphasize the fine proportions observed in the creation of our world. A.C. Morrison writes:

> It is at least extraordinary that in this adjustment of nature there should have been such exquisite nicety. For, had the crust of the earth been ten feet thicker, there would be no oxygen, without which animal life is impossible; and had the ocean been a few feet deeper, carbon dioxide and oxygen would have been absorbed and vegetable life on the surface of the land could not exist... If the atmosphere had been much thinner, some of the meteors which are now burned in the outer atmosphere by the millions every day would strike all parts of the earth. They travel from six to forty miles a second and would set fire to every burnable object. If they travelled as slowly as a bullet, they would all hit the earth and the consequences would be dire. As for man, the impact of a tiny meteor travelling ninety times as fast as a bullet would tear him in pieces by the heat of its passage. The atmosphere is just thick enough to let in the actinic rays needed for vegetation and to kill bacteria, produce vitamins, and not harm man unless he exposes himself too long. In spite of all the gaseous emanations from the earth of all the ages, most of them poisonous, the atmosphere remains practically uncontaminated and unchanging in its balanced relationship necessary to man's very existence.
>
> The great balance wheel is that vast mass of water, the sea, from which have come life, food, rain, temperate climate, plants, animals, and ultimately man himself.[1]
>
> If, for instance, instead of 21 per cent oxygen were 50 per cent or more of the atmosphere, all combustible substances in the

1. A.C. Morrison, *Man Does Not Stand Alone*, Morrison and Gibb Ltd., London, 1962, pp. 27–28.

world would become inflammable to such an extent that the first stroke of lightning to hit a tree would ignite the forest, which would almost explode. If it were reduced to 10 per cent or less, life might through the ages have adjusted itself to it, but few of the elements of civilization now so familiar to man, such as fire, would be available.[2]

How strange is the system of checks and balances which has prevented any animal, no matter how ferocious, how large, or subtle, from dominating the earth since the age of trilobites and probably not then. Man only has upset this balance of nature by moving plants and animals from place to place, and he has immediately paid a severe penalty in the development of animal, insect, and plant pests.

A striking illustration which will point out specifically the importance of recognizing these checks in connection with the existence of man is the following fact. Many years ago a species of cactus was planted in Australia as a protective fence. The cactus had no insect enemies in Australia and soon began a prodigious growth. The march of the cactus persisted until it had covered an area approximately as great as England, crowded the inhabitants out of towns and villages, and destroyed their farms, making cultivation impossible. No device which the people discovered could stop its spread. Australia was in danger of being overwhelmed by a silent, uncontrollable, advancing army of vegetation. The entomologists scoured the world and finally found an insect which lived exclusively on cactus, would eat nothing else, would breed freely, and which had no enemies in Australia. Here the animal conquered the vegetation and today the cactus pest has retreated, and with it all but a small protective residue of the insects, enough to hold the cactus in check forever.

The checks and balances have been provided, and have been persistently effective. Why has not the malarial mosquito so dominated the earth that our ancestors through the ages have not

2. Ibid., p. 30.

> either died or become immune? The same may be said of the yellow fever mosquito, which lived one season as far north as New York. Mosquitoes are plentiful in the Arctic. Why has not the tsetse fly evolved so that he would live in other than his tropical surroundings and wipe out the human race? One has but to mention the plagues and the deadly germs against which man has had no protection until yesterday, and his total lack of knowledge of sanitation as an animal, to understand how wonderful has been his preservation…

The insects have no lungs such as man possesses, but breathe through tubes. When insects grow large the tubes cannot grow in relation to the increasing size of the body of the insect. Hence there never has been an insect more than inches long and a little longer wing spread. Because of the mechanism of their structure and their method of breathing, there never could be an insect of great size. This limit in their growth held all insects in check and prevented them from dominating the world. If this physical check had not been provided, man could not exist. Imagine a primitive man meeting a hornet as big as a lion or a spider equally large.

Little has been said regarding the many other marvellous adjustments in the physiology of animals, without which no animal, or indeed vegetable, could continue to exist.[3]

Thus, day by day, human knowledge uncovers more and more of the elaborate system that gives every creature their measure, proportion and balance. With such increased knowledge we appreciate even better the significance of the Qur'ānic statement: "*It is He who has created all things and ordained them in due proportions.*" (Verse 2)

The unbelievers at the time of the Prophet did not understand any of this. Hence they persisted with their unbelief. "*Yet, some choose to worship, instead of Him, deities that cannot create anything but are themselves created, and have it not in their power to avert harm from, or bring benefit to, themselves, and have no power over death, life or resurrection.*" (Verse 3)

3. Ibid., pp. 92–94.

Their false deities are deprived of the most essential characteristics of Godhead. Thus, they "*cannot create anything,*" while God has created everything, and false deities "*are themselves created.*" Their servants create them in the sense that they make them, if they are statues or idols, while if they are angels, devils, humans or some other object of God's making, then God creates them, in the sense of bringing them into existence. Furthermore, they "*have it not in their power to avert harm from, or bring benefit to, themselves,*" let alone doing so to others. Someone who might not be able to bring himself benefit may still be able to cause harm, but even this is out of the hands of such false deities. Hence, this is mentioned first as the easiest thing to do, then it is followed by other qualities that only God can have: they "*have no power over death, life or resurrection.*" If these deities cannot cause a living thing to die, or bring to life anything dead, or bring someone to life after death, what characteristic of Godhead could they have? How could these idolaters ascribe divinity to such beings?

It is a case of straying so far from the truth that it is not surprising that they make singular claims against the Prophet. Their claims against God are even more singular and more impudent. Could there be anything worse than that a human being should claim that God has partners when it is God who has created him as well as everything else in the universe? The Prophet was asked: "Which is the most cardinal sin?" His reply was: "That you should claim that God has equals, when it is He who has created you." [Related by al-Bukhārī and Muslim]

Accusations without Basis

Having shown how they fabricate such allegations against God, who is limitless in His glory, the *sūrah* refers to their impudent claims against God's Messenger, replying to them in a way that shows how false and absurd it all is.

> *The unbelievers say: 'This [Qur'ān] is nothing but a lie which he has devised with the help of other people.' In truth, it is they who have perpetrated an inequity and a falsehood. And they say: 'Fables of*

ancient times which he has caused to be written down, so that they might be read out to him morning and evening.' Say: 'This [Qur'ān] is bestowed from on high by Him who knows the secrets of the heavens and the earth. He is indeed Much-Forgiving, Merciful.' (Verses 4–6)

It was a most blatant lie that the unbelievers of the Quraysh said when they knew deep at heart that it had absolutely no basis. Their elders who instructed them to circulate these lies were fully aware that the Qur'ān which Muḥammad recited could not have been authored by a human being. They actually knew this given their appreciation of fine poetry. Furthermore, they could not stop themselves from being influenced by the Qur'ān. Moreover, they knew Muḥammad long before his prophethood, and they were aware that he was exemplary in his honesty: he never told a lie, broke a promise, or breached a trust. How could he, then, invent a lie against God, attributing to Him words which He did not say?

But they were stubborn, motivated by fear for their social status that relied on religious position. Hence, they resorted to such tactics, making false allegations that could be accepted by ordinary people who might not have similar literary talent. They claimed that the Qur'ān was "*nothing but a lie which he has devised with the help of other people.*" (Verse 4) It is said that those other people were three foreign slaves, or even more. This is such an absurd allegation. If a man could, with the help of others, devise this Qur'ān, or invent it, what would stop them from producing, with the help of others, a similar Qur'ān to refute Muḥammad's argument? He repeatedly challenged them to do so and they failed to take up the challenge.

Hence why the *sūrah* does not employ any argument to refute their absurd allegations. Instead, it gives its clear judgement on their statements: "*They have perpetrated an inequity and a falsehood.*" (Verse 4) It is an act of injustice against the truth, Muḥammad and themselves. Moreover, it is a blatant falsehood.

The *sūrah* gives other examples of their false accusations against the Prophet and the Qur'ān: "*And they say: Fables of ancient times which he has caused to be written down, so that they might be read out to him morning and evening.*" (Verse 5) The Qur'ān gives accounts of the history of past communities for the dual purpose of serving as lessons and admonition for people, and providing guidance for them. The unbelievers, however, label such true accounts of history as '*fables of ancient times*', alleging that the Prophet sought such fables to be written down so that they could be read out to him, because he was unlettered, unable to read. When they were read to him every morning and evening, he would then recite them to people claiming that they were revealed to him by God. Such unfounded allegations do not stand up to any examination. We need only look at the logical sequence of the historical accounts given in the Qur'ān, the relevance of each story to the context in which it is placed, and the perfect balance and harmony between the objectives of each story and the *sūrah* in which it occurs. All this confirms the deliberate choice and meticulous presentation of Qur'ānic historical accounts. Nothing of this is found in legends and fables that are related for entertainment. They hardly ever serve a basic theme or support a particular idea.

Their allegation that these accounts were fables of ancient communities indicates that they were accounts of events that took place much earlier. This means that Muḥammad (peace be upon him) could not have known them without being taught by some of those who circulated such fables, generation after generation. Hence, the *sūrah* replies that the One who revealed them to Muḥammad was the One whose knowledge is absolute. It is He who knows all secrets everywhere in the universe. Indeed, no situation, past present or future, is unknown to Him: "*Say: This [Qur'ān] is bestowed from on high by Him who knows the secrets of the heavens and the earth.*" (Verse 6) How could the knowledge of legend reciters be compared with God's perfect knowledge? How could legends and fables be compared to the secrets of the heavens and the earth, which are perfectly known to God? This is no more than comparing a drop of water to an endless ocean.

When they make such absurd allegations against the Prophet they commit a gross error, which is added to their persistent associating of partners with God, their Creator. Nevertheless, the door to repentance remains open, if they wish to desist from their sinful ways. God, who is fully aware of their fabrications and schemes, will extend mercy and forgiveness to them: "*He is indeed Much-Forgiving, Merciful.*" (Verse 6)

The *sūrah* then examines their false accusations against the Prophet, their absurd objections to his being human, and their unreasonable suggestions about his message:

> *They also say: 'What sort of messenger is this, who eats food and goes about in the market-places? Why has not an angel been sent down to him to give warning alongside him? Or why has not a treasure been granted to him? Or he should have a garden to provide his sustenance.' The wrongdoers say: 'The man you follow is certainly bewitched.' See to what they liken you. They have certainly gone astray and are unable to find a way back. Blessed is He who, if it be His will, shall give you better things than these; gardens through which running waters flow, and shall give you palaces too.* (Verses 7–10)

The first point they make concerns Muḥammad's status: they wonder why he eats food and goes about the streets and market places. Why is he an ordinary human being, doing what other humans do? This is an objection all communities made against every messenger God sent. How could such a person, raised by such a family, living with them and behaving like them in all respects, be a messenger from God, receiving revelations from on high? How could he have contact with another world, receiving knowledge that is unavailable to them when he is just one of them, while they receive no such revelations and know nothing about this other world?

Honouring Mankind

From this angle, the whole idea seems unlikely. However, taken from another angle, it seems perfectly natural. God has breathed of His own spirit in man, and with this breath man has become distinguished among all God's creation, and placed in charge of the earth. Yet human knowledge, experience, and abilities remain limited and inadequate. God would not leave man without support and guidance to show him the way to fulfil his trust. Hence, He gave him the potential to be in contact with Him through the breath of the divine spirit that distinguishes him. It is no wonder that God should choose a human being who has the spiritual potential to receive His message and so impart to him what guides him and humanity along the right way.

This is an aspect of the grace God bestows on man, which appears amazing in one way and perfectly natural in another. But those who do not know the value of this creature and the true nature of the honour God has bestowed on him deny that a human being should be in contact with God through divine revelation. They refuse to acknowledge that such a person should be chosen by God as His Messenger. They think that angels are better placed to carry out such a role: "*Why has not an angel been sent down to him to give warning alongside him?*" (Verse 7) But God had ordered the angels to prostrate themselves before man as He granted him superior qualities associated with the breathing of His spirit in him.

It is divine wisdom that determines the sending of a human messenger to a human community. Such a messenger shares their feelings, experiences, hopes and sorrows. He knows their aspirations, needs and limitations. Thus, he understands their weaknesses, taps their strengths, and leads them along the way, step by step, knowing their motivations and reactions. After all, he is one of them, guiding them towards God's pleasure, supported by His revelation and guidance.

For their part they find in God's human Messenger an easy example to follow. He is one of them who takes them gradually along the road to a sublime standard. He lives among them implementing the moral standards, the actions and the duties God requires them to observe and fulfil. Thus, he personally serves as the practical implementation of the faith he preaches. Everything in his life and behaviour are presented to them so that they can look at every detail and aspire to follow his example, knowing that it is within man's capability. Had God's Messenger been an angel, they would not think about his actions and behaviour, and would not even attempt to follow his suit. They would feel that since he has a different nature, they could not aspire to his standard or follow his example.

We see how God's infinite wisdom, which ordains all things in due proportion, has determined that His Messenger should be a human being so that he fulfils the role of leading mankind along the way He has laid down for them. To object to this choice is to betray ignorance of such wisdom and the honour God has granted mankind.

Another absurd objection focused on God's Messenger walking about the market-place earning his living. His position as Messenger would have been recognized had he been granted great wealth to save him the trouble of so working for his living: "*Or why has not a treasure been granted to him? Or he should have a garden to provide his sustenance.*" (Verse 8)

But God willed that His Messenger should not have treasure or garden, because He wanted him to be a perfect example to be followed by his community. He was to fulfil the great task of delivering his message while he worked, earning a living at the same time. Thus, none of his followers could argue that the Prophet was freed from the responsibility of work, and thus was able to devote all his time to his message. None would take this as an excuse for not fulfilling his duty towards the divine message. We see clearly that the Prophet worked for his living while he also worked for his message. It is right, then, that everyone of his followers should do the same, so as to fulfil his own task towards the divine faith.

Wealth was later given in abundance to the Prophet so as the first experience should be completed and the example he provided be perfected. He did not allow such wealth to become his preoccupation, preventing him from the fulfilment of his task. Indeed, his generosity was so superior that it was likened by his Companions to unrestrained wind. He provided a perfect example in resisting the lure of wealth so as to enable his followers to look at affluence in the proper perspective. Thus, no one could say that Muḥammad was able to fulfil the duties of his message because he was poor, having no preoccupations of wealth, free from the task of looking after it. Instead, he fulfilled his duties in both situations of poverty and affluence.

Besides, what value is wealth, treasures and gardens when compared with contact between man, a weak mortal, and God the Eternal? What significance has this earth and all that it contains, or indeed this whole universe, when compared to contact with God the Creator who grants everyone all that they have? But unbelievers appreciate nothing of this.

The *sūrah* then refers to another false accusation the unbelievers repeated time after time against the Prophet. The Qur'ān mentions this blatant lie here as well as in *Sūrah* 17, The Night Journey. In both *sūrahs* the Qur'ān gives the exact same reply to this accusation quoting it in exactly the same words in both *sūrahs*. "*The wrongdoers say: 'The man you follow is certainly bewitched.' See to what they liken you. They have certainly gone astray and are unable to find a way back [to the truth].*" (Verses 8–9)

Both *sūrahs* deal with more or less the same subject, tackling it in similar fashion. Needless to say, the unbelievers employ such a personal attack against the Prophet aiming to detract from his social standing. They liken him to a man who is bewitched, saying things that normal people do not say. Yet at the same time their accusation implies recognition that what he says is unusual or unfamiliar in the sense that it is above human standards. The reply the *sūrah* gives wonders at their attitude: "*See to what they liken you.*" They liken him to bewitched people at one time, accuse him of false fabrication at another, and even compare him at times to those who relate legends. All this is far beyond the truth. They have missed every road that leads to the truth and are left in error: "*They have certainly gone astray and are unable to find a way back [to the truth].*" (Verse 9)

This argument ends on a note that shows the stupidity of their suggestions. They propose that the Prophet should be given some luxuries, thinking that a true messenger of God should have plenty of such worldly comforts as a treasure store or a garden providing him with his food requirements. Had God so willed, he would have given him much more than everything they suggest: "*Blessed is He who, if it be His will, shall give you better things than these; gardens through which running waters flow, and shall give you palaces too.*" (Verse 10) But God has willed to give His Messenger what is much better and more valuable than gardens and palaces. He has given him a direct relation with the One who gives all such luxuries, bestowing on him His care and guidance. He enjoys this relationship which is far superior to any worldly comfort or luxury, great as it may be.

Denying Resurrection

At this point in its discussion of their wrongful statements about God and His Messenger, the *sūrah* reveals another dimension of their disbelief. They deny the Last Hour. Hence, they have no qualms about making baseless accusations or fabrications. They do not fear that they will face God who will hold them to account for their lies and fabrications. We see them here as they stand on the Day of Judgement when hardened hearts are shaken to their core. They are made to see what awaits them there in comparison with the happiness that is prepared for the believers:

> *Nay! It is the Last Hour that they deny. For those who deny the Last Hour We have prepared a blazing fire. When it sees them from a far-off place, they will hear its fury and its raging sigh. And when, chained together, they are flung into a tight space within, they will pray for extinction there and then. [But they will be told]: 'Do not pray today for one single extinction, but pray for many extinctions!' Say: 'Which is better: that, or the paradise of eternity which the God-fearing have been promised as their reward and their ultimate abode?' There they will have all they wish for, abiding there forever. It is a promise given by your Lord, always to be prayed for.* (Verses 11–16)

They have indeed denied the Last Hour going to great extents in their disbelief. The Qur'ānic expression implies this as it puts aside all that was said earlier in order to magnify the extent: "*Nay! It is the Last Hour that they deny.*" It then paints the destiny that awaits those who are guilty of such a terrible thing. It is a blazing fire made ready to receive them: "*For those who deny the Last Hour We have prepared a blazing fire.*" (Verse 11)

Personification, or the representation of inanimate objects or states as having life of their own, is a special artistic feature the Qur'ān employs to such perfection that it defies imitation. It makes such objects so alive that we take them as such.

Here we are in front of the blazing fire which is now granted life. It looks and sees at a distance those who have denied the Last Hour. It is angry, furious with them, raging to engulf them. As they proceed towards it, it wants to take them all at once. It is a fearful scene that leaves even the most courageous badly shaken.

Then we see them having arrived there. They are not just left to face such a raging fire, but are thrown in it, their hands and feet chained together. The tightness of the area increases their misery and makes it impossible for them to free themselves from their chains. Then we see them, having despaired of breaking loose, realizing that their stress is endless. Therefore, they pray for their own destruction as a way out of this endless misery: "*When, chained together, they are flung into a tight space within, they will pray for extinction there and then.*" (Verse 13) Their own destruction seems to them the best that they can hope for as a way of escaping this unbearable torment. But they soon hear the answer to their prayers. It is a sarcastic response that fills them with bitterness: "*Do not pray today for one single extinction, but pray for many extinctions!*" (Verse 14) To be destroyed and made extinct once is not sufficient to redeem them. Hence, the sarcastic suggestion.

In contrast to such fearful prospects, the *sūrah* portrays what is prepared in the hereafter for the God-fearing who are eager to meet their Lord and who believe in the Last Hour. Again, sarcasm is fully employed to leave its telling effect on the unbelievers:

> *Say: Which is better: that, or the paradise of eternity which the God-fearing have been promised as their reward and their ultimate abode? There they will have all they wish for, abiding there forever. It is a promise given by your Lord, always to be prayed for.* (Verses 15–16)

Which is better: the end of the unbelievers already described in the *sūrah* or the paradise God has promised to the believers. He has indeed given them leave to ask Him about it, requesting the fulfilment of His promise, which is always honoured. They are free to request there whatever they wish for. Can the two be compared? The question is put sarcastically by way of reply to their own sarcasm levelled at the Prophet (peace be upon him).

The *sūrah* goes on to portray another scene of the Day of Judgement which is denied by the unbelievers. Now we see them gathered together with their alleged deities, and they all stand before God for interrogation:

> *On the day He gathers them with all those they worship instead of God, He will ask: 'Was it you who led these My servants astray, or did they by themselves stray from the right path?' They will say: 'Limitless are You in Your glory! It was never proper for us to take for our masters anyone but Yourself. But You allowed them and their fathers to enjoy [the pleasures of] life, until they forgot the Reminder. For they were people devoid of all good.' [Then God will say]: 'Now have they denied all your assertions, and you can neither avert [your punishment] nor obtain help. Whoever of you does wrong, him shall We cause to taste grievous suffering.'* (Verses 17–19)

The ones who were worshipped may be idols, angels or *jinn*, and indeed everyone and everything that has ever been worshipped instead of God or alongside Him. God certainly knows all the answers, but the interrogation carried out when all creatures are gathered together, standing there in the open, means reproach and publicity. As such the very interrogation is a means of fearful suffering. The answer comes from those who were worshipped. They declare their own submission to God Almighty, and that He is free of all that the unbelievers allege. They disclaim not merely any aspiration to Godhead, but also any thought on their part of taking for themselves any masters other than Him. They also ridicule the ignorant who associated partners with God and denied the Last Hour: "*They will say: Limitless are You in Your glory! It was never proper for us to take for our masters anyone but Yourself. But You allowed them and their fathers to enjoy [the pleasures of] life, until they forgot the Reminder. For they were people devoid of all good.*" (Verse 18)

The enjoyment that people are allowed for a long time, inheriting it generation after generation, without acknowledgement of the One who gives such blessings or expression of thanks and gratitude to Him, has been their main preoccupation. They forgot to turn to the One who gives us everything we have, and thus their hearts became devoid of all goodness, barren, like a land without fruit, vegetation or life.

At this point, the address is directed to those who worshipped such beings, emphasizing their humiliation: "*Now have they denied all your assertions, and you can neither avert [your punishment] nor obtain help.*" (Verse 19) You cannot do anything for yourselves, neither avoiding your well deserved punishment, nor gaining support from anyone or any quarter.

All this is shown as a scene of the Day of Judgement which is held before our eyes. Suddenly, the address is made to those unbelievers in their present condition here on earth: "*Whoever of you does wrong, him shall We cause to taste grievous suffering.*" (Verse 19) Such is the Qur'ānic method of addressing people's hearts at the moment when they are ready to respond, influenced as they may be by the fearful scene already portrayed.

Entrusting God's Message to Man

Thus they are shown to have witnessed the end of all false fabrication concerning faith and ridicule of God's Messenger. Now the *sūrah* addresses the Prophet consoling and reassuring him, telling him that his was not a special case among God's messengers. They all shared the same essential attributes:

> *Even before you, We never sent messengers other than [men] who indeed ate food and went about in the market-places. We have made some of you a means of testing others. Are you able to endure with patience? Surely your Lord sees all.* (Verse 20)

If the unbelievers voice objections, these are not made against the Prophet in person; rather, they are objections to a law God has put in place for a definite purpose: "*We have made some of you a means of testing others.*" Thus, those who do not appreciate God's wisdom and plans will object, while those who have full trust in His wisdom and support will persevere and remain reassured. The divine message will continue the struggle using human means and methods, so that those who have faith will demonstrate their patience in adversity: "*Are you able to endure with patience?*"

"*Surely your Lord sees all.*" He sees human nature, and what is in people's inner thoughts. He sees to what end each one is driving. We note here the use of the possessive pronoun, 'your Lord', to give the Prophet a feeling of comfort and reassurance. God knows what best affects people's hearts and feelings.

2

Below Animal Level

Those who entertain no hope of meeting Us say: 'Why have no angels been sent down to us?' – or, 'Why do we not see our Lord?' Indeed, they are far too proud of themselves and they have been insolently overbearing. (21)

وَقَالَ ٱلَّذِينَ لَا يَرْجُونَ لِقَآءَنَا لَوْلَآ أُنزِلَ
عَلَيْنَا ٱلْمَلَـٰٓئِكَةُ أَوْ نَرَىٰ رَبَّنَا ۗ لَقَدِ
ٱسْتَكْبَرُوا۟ فِىٓ أَنفُسِهِمْ وَعَتَوْ عُتُوًّا
كَبِيرًا ﴿٢١﴾

On the day when they shall see the angels, the sinners will receive no happy news then, and they will say: 'a forbidding ban!' (22)

يَوْمَ يَرَوْنَ ٱلْمَلَـٰٓئِكَةَ لَا بُشْرَىٰ يَوْمَئِذٍ
لِّلْمُجْرِمِينَ وَيَقُولُونَ حِجْرًا مَّحْجُورًا ﴿٢٢﴾

We shall turn to whatever deeds they have done, and We shall transform it all into scattered dust. (23)

وَقَدِمْنَآ إِلَىٰ مَا عَمِلُوا۟ مِنْ عَمَلٍ فَجَعَلْنَـٰهُ
هَبَآءً مَّنثُورًا ﴿٢٣﴾

On that day, those destined for paradise will be graced with the best of abodes and the fairest place of repose. (24)

أَصْحَـٰبُ ٱلْجَنَّةِ يَوْمَئِذٍ خَيْرٌ مُّسْتَقَرًّا
وَأَحْسَنُ مَقِيلًا ﴿٢٤﴾

وَيَوْمَ تَشَقَّقُ ٱلسَّمَآءُ بِٱلْغَمَٰمِ وَنُزِّلَ ٱلْمَلَٰٓئِكَةُ
تَنزِيلًا ﴿٢٥﴾

On the day when the skies shall be rent asunder with clouds, and the angels shall be sent down [in ranks]. (25)

ٱلْمُلْكُ يَوْمَئِذٍ ٱلْحَقُّ لِلرَّحْمَٰنِ ۚ وَكَانَ
يَوْمًا عَلَى ٱلْكَٰفِرِينَ عَسِيرًا ﴿٢٦﴾

On that day, true sovereignty belongs to the Most Merciful [alone]. It will be a day of dire distress for the unbelievers. (26)

وَيَوْمَ يَعَضُّ ٱلظَّالِمُ عَلَىٰ يَدَيْهِ يَقُولُ
يَٰلَيْتَنِى ٱتَّخَذْتُ مَعَ ٱلرَّسُولِ سَبِيلًا ﴿٢٧﴾

On that day the wrongdoer will bite his hands and say: 'Would that I had followed the path shown to me by the Messenger. (27)

يَٰوَيْلَتَىٰ لَيْتَنِى لَمْ أَتَّخِذْ فُلَانًا خَلِيلًا ﴿٢٨﴾

Oh, woe is me! Would that I had never taken so-and-so for a friend! (28)

لَّقَدْ أَضَلَّنِى عَنِ ٱلذِّكْرِ بَعْدَ إِذْ جَآءَنِى ۗ
وَكَانَ ٱلشَّيْطَٰنُ لِلْإِنسَٰنِ خَذُولًا ﴿٢٩﴾

He surely led me astray from the Reminder after it had come to me!' Satan is ever treacherous to man. (29)

وَقَالَ ٱلرَّسُولُ يَٰرَبِّ إِنَّ قَوْمِى ٱتَّخَذُوا۟
هَٰذَا ٱلْقُرْءَانَ مَهْجُورًا ﴿٣٠﴾

And the Messenger will say: 'My Lord! My people have regarded this Qur'ān as something to be discarded!' (30)

وَكَذَٰلِكَ جَعَلْنَا لِكُلِّ نَبِىٍّ عَدُوًّا مِّنَ
ٱلْمُجْرِمِينَ ۗ وَكَفَىٰ بِرَبِّكَ هَادِيًا
وَنَصِيرًا ﴿٣١﴾

Thus against every prophet We have set up enemies from among those who are guilty. Sufficient is your Lord to provide guidance and support. (31)

The unbelievers ask: 'Why has not the Qur'ān been revealed to him all at once?' Thus [it has been revealed] so that We might strengthen your heart with it, and We have imparted it to you by gradual revelation. (32)

وَقَالَ ٱلَّذِينَ كَفَرُوا۟ لَوْلَا نُزِّلَ عَلَيْهِ ٱلْقُرْءَانُ
جُمْلَةً وَٰحِدَةً ۚ كَذَٰلِكَ لِنُثَبِّتَ بِهِۦ
فُؤَادَكَ ۖ وَرَتَّلْنَٰهُ تَرْتِيلًا ﴿٣٢﴾

Whenever they come to you with an argument, We shall reveal to you the truth and the best explanation. (33)

وَلَا يَأْتُونَكَ بِمَثَلٍ إِلَّا جِئْنَٰكَ بِٱلْحَقِّ
وَأَحْسَنَ تَفْسِيرًا ﴿٣٣﴾

Those who will be gathered to hell on their faces – they will be worst in station and still farther away from the [right] path. (34)

ٱلَّذِينَ يُحْشَرُونَ عَلَىٰ وُجُوهِهِمْ إِلَىٰ جَهَنَّمَ
أُو۟لَٰٓئِكَ شَرٌّ مَّكَانًا وَأَضَلُّ سَبِيلًا ﴿٣٤﴾

Indeed, We gave the book to Moses, and appointed his brother Aaron to help him to bear his burden. (35)

وَلَقَدْ ءَاتَيْنَا مُوسَى ٱلْكِتَٰبَ وَجَعَلْنَا
مَعَهُۥٓ أَخَاهُ هَٰرُونَ وَزِيرًا ﴿٣٥﴾

And We said: 'Go you both to the people who denied Our signs,' and then We utterly destroyed those people. (36)

فَقُلْنَا ٱذْهَبَآ إِلَى ٱلْقَوْمِ ٱلَّذِينَ كَذَّبُوا۟
بِـَٔايَٰتِنَا فَدَمَّرْنَٰهُمْ تَدْمِيرًا ﴿٣٦﴾

When the people of Noah rejected their messengers, We caused them to drown, and made of them an example for mankind. For the wrongdoers We have prepared grievous suffering. (37)

وَقَوْمَ نُوحٍ لَّمَّا كَذَّبُوا۟ ٱلرُّسُلَ
أَغْرَقْنَٰهُمْ وَجَعَلْنَٰهُمْ لِلنَّاسِ
ءَايَةً ۖ وَأَعْتَدْنَا لِلظَّٰلِمِينَ عَذَابًا
أَلِيمًا ﴿٣٧﴾

وَعَادًا وَثَمُودَا۟ وَأَصْحَـٰبَ ٱلرَّسِّ وَقُرُونًۢا بَيْنَ
ذَٰلِكَ كَثِيرًا ﴿٣٨﴾

And also the 'Ād and Thamūd, and the people of al-Rass, and many generations in between. (38)

وَكُلًّا ضَرَبْنَا لَهُ ٱلْأَمْثَـٰلَ ۖ وَكُلًّا
تَبَّرْنَا تَتْبِيرًا ﴿٣٩﴾

To each of them did We proffer lessons, and each of them did We utterly annihilate. (39)

وَلَقَدْ أَتَوْا۟ عَلَى ٱلْقَرْيَةِ ٱلَّتِىٓ أُمْطِرَتْ مَطَرَ
ٱلسَّوْءِ ۚ أَفَلَمْ يَكُونُوا۟ يَرَوْنَهَا ۚ بَلْ
كَانُوا۟ لَا يَرْجُونَ نُشُورًا ﴿٤٠﴾

They must have surely passed by the town which was rained upon with a shower of evil. Have they, then, never seen it? But nay, they would not believe in resurrection. (40)

وَإِذَا رَأَوْكَ إِن يَتَّخِذُونَكَ إِلَّا هُزُوًا
أَهَـٰذَا ٱلَّذِى بَعَثَ ٱللَّهُ رَسُولًا ﴿٤١﴾

When they see you, they make you a target of their mockery, [saying]: 'Is this the one whom God has sent as His emissary? (41)

إِن كَادَ لَيُضِلُّنَا عَنْ ءَالِهَتِنَا لَوْلَآ أَن
صَبَرْنَا عَلَيْهَا ۚ وَسَوْفَ يَعْلَمُونَ حِينَ
يَرَوْنَ ٱلْعَذَابَ مَنْ أَضَلُّ سَبِيلًا ﴿٤٢﴾

He could almost have led us astray from our deities, had we not been steadfastly attached to them!' But in time, when they see the suffering, they will come to know who it was that went farthest astray. (42)

أَرَءَيْتَ مَنِ ٱتَّخَذَ إِلَـٰهَهُۥ هَوَىٰهُ أَفَأَنتَ
تَكُونُ عَلَيْهِ وَكِيلًا ﴿٤٣﴾

Have you considered the one who makes his desires his deity? Could you, then, be held responsible for him? (43)

Or do you think that most of them listen and use their reason? They are but like cattle. Nay, they are even far worse astray. (44)	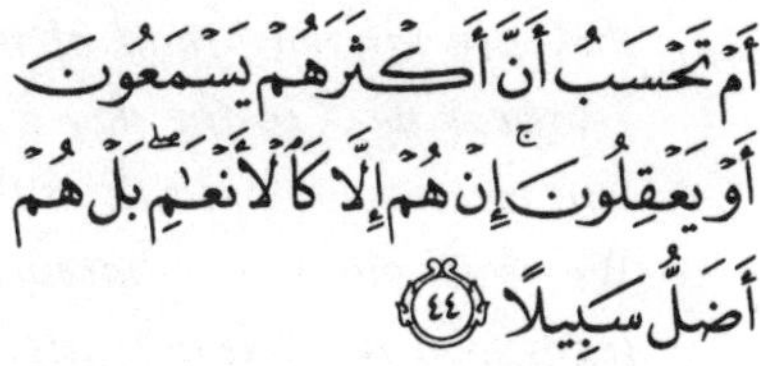

Overview

This second passage of the *sūrah*, like the first, starts with the allegations, suggestions and objections made by the unbelievers as a prelude to their statements about the Prophet himself. All this is given here with the aim of comforting the Prophet. In this passage, however, we have an early account of the punishment in store for their arrogance, one which is posited in a series of images of the hereafter. All this is given in reply to their question: "*Why have no angels been sent down to us?' – or, 'Why do we not see our Lord?*" (Verse 21)

The *sūrah* then quotes their objection to the revelation of the Qur'ān over a long period, and explains the purpose behind this, reassuring the Prophet that God's help is ready at hand whenever the unbelievers challenge him: "*Whenever they come to you with an argument, We shall reveal to you the truth and the best explanation.*" (Verse 33)

The *sūrah* describes to the Prophet and the unbelievers the fate suffered by earlier communities which denied God's messages, reminding them in particular of the destruction suffered by Lot's people. This has a greater effect, because they pass by that township, with its remains telling its terrible story. Yet they are hardened to it, and its sight does not inspire them to take steps in order to avoid a similar fate.

All this is given by way of introduction to the unbelievers' ridicule of the Prophet and their offensive remarks about him. The *sūrah* immediately delivers a strong comment on this portraying them in a very contemptible light: "*They are but like cattle. Nay, they are even far worse astray.*" (Verse 44)

Ominous Prospects for the Unbelievers

Those who entertain no hope of meeting Us say: 'Why have no angels been sent down to us?' – or, 'Why do we not see our Lord?' Indeed,

> *they are far too proud of themselves and they have been insolently overbearing. On the day when they shall see the angels, the sinners will receive no happy news then, and they will say: 'a forbidding ban!' We shall turn to whatever deeds they have done, and We shall transform it all into scattered dust. On that day, those destined for paradise will be graced with the best of abodes and the fairest place of repose. On the day when the skies shall be rent asunder with clouds, and the angels shall be sent down [in ranks]. On that day, true sovereignty belongs to the Most Merciful [alone]. It will be a day of dire distress for the unbelievers. On that day the wrongdoer will bite his hands and say: 'Would that I had followed the path shown to me by the Messenger. Oh, woe is me! Would that I had never taken so-and-so for a friend! He surely led me astray from the Reminder after it had come to me!' Satan is ever treacherous to man.* (Verses 21–29)

The unbelievers do not hope to meet God. This means that they do not expect such a meeting and do not take it into account so as to determine their prior behaviour. In their hearts they do not feel any awe of God. Hence, they are ready to make utterances that no one who expects to meet God would entertain. "*Those who entertain no hope of meeting Us say: Why have no angels been sent down to us? – or, Why do we not see our Lord?*" (Verse 21)

They considered it unreasonable that God's Messenger should be a man. They demanded that angels be sent to them testifying to the truth of the message in order for them to believe in it. An alternative demand they made was that they should see God, so as to believe in Him. Such an overbearing attitude betrays the sort of ignorance associated with denying God and His attributes, having no proper esteem for Him. Who are they to make such overbearing demands? What are they in comparison with God Almighty? In God's dominion, they are no more than a particle floating aimlessly in the air, unless they establish a bond between them and God through believing in Him, deriving their strength from Him. Hence, the reply given them in the same verse shows the source of their overbearing attitude: "*Indeed, they are far too proud of themselves and they have been insolently overbearing.*" (Verse 21)

They have given themselves airs and graces, become conceited, proud and haughty. All of which has led them to great transgression. Their pride is their main preoccupation, which means that they no longer give proper estimation to other things and values. They think themselves too great, or masters of the universe who deserve that God should appear before them in person so that they can believe in Him.

A truly sarcastic reply is given to them as they are informed of the terrible eventuality awaiting them when they see the angels, which is the less overbearing of their demands. For they will only see the angels on a very hard and difficult day on which they will be destined to receive unbearable and inescapable suffering. That is the Day of Reckoning when evil deeds are punished. "*On the day when they shall see the angels, the sinners will receive no happy news then, and they will say: 'a forbidding ban!'*" (Verse 22)

This is the day when their suggestion is granted, "*On the day when they shall see the angels*". No good news is given to the sinners on that day, for their punishment awaits them. How terrible is the fulfilment of their request! This is when they say, '*a forbidding ban!*' This phrase used to be said by the Arabs to avert evil and enemies. It is a sort of appeal which hopes to drive enemies away and avoid any harm that might ensue. They utter it on that day by force of habit, because the whole thing comes as a surprise. But what will their words avail them of on that day?

"*We shall turn to whatever deeds they have done, and We shall transform it all into scattered dust.*" (Verse 23) It all happens in a brief moment. Our imagination follows the motion described in detail, with actions being raised and thrown up in the air. In no time, all good works they did in this present life are left like scattered dust, because they were not based on faith. Faith establishes a bond between people's hearts and God, and makes good works a way of life, chosen on purpose with due reflection, not in response to a fleeting whim or sudden impulse. With believers, good works are never reduced to the sort of single action that does not reflect a well defined method and clear objective.

According to Islam, man's life and action are closely related to the universe and the law that governs its existence and binds it all to God, including man and all his activities in life. When man's life is separated from its central access that relates it to the universe, he finds himself lost, without influence and with no value attached to his work. Indeed his actions become non-existent. It is faith that binds man to his Lord, adding value to his actions and giving them credit in the overall system of the universe.

Hence, the works of the unbelievers are thus made to die, and their death is shown in a highly tangible image: "*We shall turn to whatever deeds they have done, and We shall transform it all into scattered dust.*" (Verse 23)

On the other side we find the believers, who dwell in heaven, in a perfectly contrasting image: "*On that day, those destined for paradise will be graced with the best of abodes and the fairest place of repose.*" (Verse 24) They are well settled, enjoying their comfort. This feeling of settlement contrasts with the scattered dust in the opposite image, and the reassurance felt by the believers contrasts with the fear of the unbelievers that obliges them to make a worried prayer.

The unbelievers also used to suggest that God and the angels should appear before them on the tops of clouds. Such suggestions perhaps show the influence of Jewish legends speaking of God revealing Himself over a cloud or a column of fire. Therefore, the Qur'ān shows another image of the day when their request to see angels is granted: "*On the day when the skies shall be rent asunder with clouds, and the angels shall be sent down [in ranks]. On that day, true sovereignty belongs to the Most Merciful [alone].*" (Verses 25–26)

This verse, and many others in the Qur'ān, make it clear that that day will witness far-reaching celestial events indicating a complete collapse of the system that controls all parts of the universe, including all celestial bodies. Such an upheaval indicates the end of this world. This upheaval is not limited to the earth, but includes planets, stars, solar systems and galaxies. It is useful to look at some aspects of this upheaval as described in different *sūrahs*: "*When the sun is darkened, when the stars fall and disperse, when the mountains are made to move away… when the seas are set alight.*" (81: 1–3 and 6) "*When the sky is cleft asunder, when the stars are scattered, when the oceans are made to explode, when the graves are hurled about.*" (82: 1–4) "*When the sky is rent asunder, obeying her Lord in true submission; when the earth is stretched out and casts forth all that is within her and becomes empty, obeying her Lord in true submission!*" (84: 1–5) "*When the sky is rent asunder and becomes red like burning oil.*" (55: 37) "*When the earth is severely shaken, and when the mountains crumble away, so as to become like scattered dust.*" (56: 4–6) "*When the trumpet is blown with a single blast, and the earth and the mountains are lifted up and crushed with a single stroke! Then that which must come to pass will on that day have come to pass; and the sky will be rent asunder – for, frail will it have become on that day.*" (69: 13–16) "*On a day when the sky will be like molten lead, and the mountains will be like tufts of wool.*" (70: 8–9) "*When the earth is rocked by her [final] earthquake, when the earth shakes off her burdens.*" (99: 1–2) "*The day when people will be like scattered moths, and the mountains like tufts of carded wool.*" (101: 4–5) "*Wait, then, for the day when the skies shall bring forth a pall of smoke which will make obvious [the approach of the Last Hour], enveloping all mankind. 'Grievous is this suffering!'*" (44: 10–11) "*On the day when the earth and the mountains will be convulsed, and the mountains will become like a sand-dune on the move.*" (73: 14) "*On that day, the skies shall be rent asunder.*" (73: 18) "*When the earth is systematically levelled down.*" (89: 21) "*When every eye is dazzled, and the moon darkens, and the sun and the moon are brought together.*" (75: 7–9) "*When the stars are effaced, and when the sky is rent asunder, and when the mountains are scattered like dust.*" (77: 8–10) "*They ask you about the mountains. Say: 'My Lord will scatter them far and wide, and leave the earth level and bare, with no curves or ruggedness to be seen.'*" (20: 105–107) "*You will see the mountains, which you deem so firm, pass away as clouds pass away.*" (27: 88) "*One day We shall cause the mountains to move and you will see the earth void and bare.*" (18: 47) "*On the day when the earth shall be changed into another earth, as shall be the heavens.*" (14: 48) "*On that Day We shall roll up the heavens like a scroll of parchment.*" (21: 104)

All these verses indicate that our world will come to a fearful end characterized by a violent shake-up of the earth, while the mountains will be scattered like dust. The seas will be set alight, or made to explode, either by being overfull as a result of the upheaval taking place or its molecules will explode and turn into fire. The stars will be darkened, the sky rent asunder and the planets scattered. Distances will be confused as the sun and the moon will be brought together.

The sky will look like smoke at one time and alight and red at another. It is a fearful event that leaves nothing in place.

What Use is Regret?

In this *sūrah* God threatens the unbelievers with the sky being rent asunder by clouds. This may be a reference to clouds formed out of the vapours produced by the great explosions. On that day, the angels will go to the unbelievers, as the latter suggested, but their task will not be to confirm the Prophet's message, but rather to administer punishment to the unbelievers as God will have ordered: "*It will be a day of dire distress for the unbelievers.*" (Verse 26) So why do they want the angels to go to them when their arrival signals so much distress?

The *sūrah* then portrays an image showing the regret and remorse felt by the unbelievers. It is portrayed at length, in detail, giving the impression that it is unending, where every wrongdoer bites his own hand in a gesture of regret:

> *On that day the wrongdoer will bite his hands and say: 'Would that I had followed the path shown to me by the Messenger. Oh, woe is me! Would that I had never taken so-and-so for a friend! He surely led me astray from the Reminder after it had come to me!' Satan is ever treacherous to man.* (Verses 27–29)

Everything around the wrongdoing unbeliever is still, while he sends out expressions of regret, with sorrow marking his voice. The rhythm here is deliberately long to add to the sound effects. As we read or hear these verses, we also seem to participate in the expression of regret. "*On that day the wrongdoer will bite his hands.*" (Verse 27) One hand is not enough. He bites both, alternating from one to the other, because his sorrow and regret are so keen. The movement itself is very common, expressing what the person making it feels. Hence, it is shown in full clarity.

The wrongdoer will also say: "*Would that I had followed the path shown to me by the Messenger!*" (Verse 27) Would that I followed his way and had not moved a single step away from it! He says this about

God's Messenger despite the fact that he had denied the very possibility that God might have entrusted him with a message.

"*Oh, woe is me! Would that I had never taken so-and-so for a friend!*" (Verse 28) No name is mentioned here, but the friend is described as 'so and so' to include every bad friend who encouraged him to turn away from the path of God's Messenger and follow the wrong way. "*He surely led me astray from the Reminder after it had come to me!*" (Verse 29) He was indeed Satan's aide, or was himself just another Satan. "*Satan is ever treacherous to man,*" leading him into situations of error and letting him down when he most needs help.

We see how the Qur'ān shakes their hearts, painting these fearful scenes of their fate as though this is already happening before their eyes. Yet still they deny God and speak of Him in a way that shows no respect. Indeed they make careless suggestions when what awaits them is certain to fill them with regret.

Perhaps we should add that some reports mention that these verses were revealed to the Prophet by way of comment on an incident involving 'Uqbah ibn Abī Mu'ayt, who frequently visited and sat with the Prophet. One day he invited the Prophet for a meal. The Prophet said that he would not eat 'Uqbah's food unless 'Uqbah uttered the declaration, 'I bear witness that there is no deity other than God, and that Muḥammad is God's Messenger.' 'Uqbah did so. His friend, Ubayy ibn Khalaf, however later remonstrated with him, saying: 'You have abandoned your religion.' 'Uqbah said: 'No, by God! It was only that he refused to eat my food when he was in my home, and I felt embarrassed, so I granted his wish.' Ubayy said: 'I will not be satisfied unless you go and step over him and spit in his face.' 'Uqbah looked for the Prophet until he found him in prostration near Dar al-Nadwah, and he did just that. The Prophet said to him: 'Should I ever meet you outside Makkah, I will hit your head with my sword.' 'Uqbah was taken prisoner in the Battle of Badr, and the Prophet ordered 'Alī to execute him.

A Complaint by God's Messenger

After these scenes of the Day of Judgement the *sūrah* brings us back to this world with a discussion of the unbelievers' attitude towards the

Prophet and their objections to the method of revealing the Qur'ān from on high. This part of the *sūrah* again ends with a scene of what happens to the unbelievers on the Day of Judgement.

> *And the Messenger will say: 'My Lord! My people have regarded this Qur'ān as something to be discarded!' Thus against every prophet We have set up enemies from among those who are guilty. Sufficient is your Lord to provide guidance and support. The unbelievers ask: 'Why has not the Qur'ān been revealed to him all at once?' Thus [it has been revealed] so that We might strengthen your heart with it, and We have imparted it to you by gradual revelation. Whenever they come to you with an argument, We shall reveal to you the truth and the best explanation. Those who will be gathered to hell on their faces – they will be worst in station and still farther away from the [right] path.* (Verses 30–34)

They have abandoned the Qur'ān, which God revealed to His Messenger to warn and explain to them what lies ahead for mankind. They refused to listen to it because they feared they would be attracted to its message. Stubbornly, they refused to consider its message which would have guided them to the truth and given them light. Although God revealed it as a constitution for human life, guiding it to all that is best, they shut their minds to it. "*And the Messenger will say: My Lord! My people have regarded this Qur'ān as something to be discarded!*" (Verse 30) His Lord certainly knew this, but God's Messenger made his complaint, humbly stating that he had exerted his best efforts, but still his people adamantly refused to listen to the Qur'ān and consider its message.

God comforts His Messenger, telling him that the same was the case with all earlier messengers. Every prophet has had enemies who discard divine guidance and deliberately turn people away from faith. But God is certain to guide His messengers to the way that ensures their victory over foul and wicked enemies. "*Thus against every prophet We have set up enemies from among those who are guilty. Sufficient is your Lord to provide guidance and support.*" (Verse 31)

Divine wisdom is perfect indeed. The fact that wicked people wage war against prophets and their messages is certain to strengthen these messages, giving them the sort of seriousness that fits their nature. The struggle of advocates of divine faith against those who fight it may be hard, involving much sacrifice, but it is such struggle that eventually distinguishes true and sincere advocates from false ones, strengthening the former and expelling the latter. Thus, only those who are true to their faith, dedicated to its cause, aspiring to no personal or easy gain remain, dedicating their efforts to God alone.

Had advocacy of the divine faith been comfortable and easy, moving along a smooth way adorned with flowers, and without opposition, everyone would have become an advocate. Indeed true causes would have been muddled with false ones, and much confusion would have resulted. When a message or a cause faces determined opposition, the struggle for it becomes inevitable and sacrifice necessary. Only serious believers are ready to endure pain and make sacrifices for their causes, because such believers consider their faith to be more important than this whole world and the comforts it offers. Indeed, to them, faith is more important than life itself. Only the strongest in faith and most enduring among them can carry this fight to its end, because these are the ones who aspire most to what God has in store for them.

It is those who render sacrifices and remain steadfast that are eventually entrusted with the implementation of the divine message, because they are the ones who, having paid the heavy price of victory, are able to shoulder its continued burden. Their experience teaches them how to overcome the many hazards that lie along their way. The hardship they endure sharpens their abilities and talents, increases their strength and knowledge. All these will stand them in good stead as they continue to advocate the divine faith in all situations.

What happens in most cases is that the majority of people stand aside while the struggle between the wicked and advocates of the divine faith rages on. The sacrifices of these advocates will inevitably mount, but their steadfastness, despite the great pain they have to endure, remains strong and they are not shaken in any way. As a result, the multitude standing by begin to feel that the message these believers advocate is more precious than all their sacrifices. They start to examine it in order to see what makes such a message dearer to its advocates than life. What happens then is that these people, who have long stood by, begin to embrace the faith in large numbers.

For this reason God has willed that every prophet has to face enemies. Such wicked people stand in the face of the divine message, which is the message of truth. Its advocates then resist its enemies and bear whatever sacrifices they are called on to give. The end is predetermined, and those who place their trust in God are certain of it. It is the provision of divine guidance that leads to the ultimate victory: "*Sufficient is your Lord to provide guidance and support.*" (Verse 31)

That the wicked should stand against prophets is only natural. The prophets advocate the message of the truth which is given at the appropriate time to rectify corruption that creeps into community life or into human life in general. This is a corruption that affects hearts, systems and life itself. Such corruption is initiated, promoted and exploited by the wicked. They are the ones whose interests and values are served through the promotion of such corruption. Their opposition to the prophets aims to defend themselves and their interests. They want to retain the corrupt atmosphere in which they thrive. Some insects are stifled by the fine smell of flowers because they can only survive on dump heaps. Some worms survive only in dirty stagnating water, and perish in clean, running water. Such are the wicked. Hence their hostility to the message of truth. They fight it tooth and nail. But it is only natural that it will emerge triumphant, because it promotes life and looks up to the sublime horizon which binds it to God. "*Sufficient is your Lord to provide guidance and support.*" (Verse 31)

The Time Span of Qur'ānic Revelations

The *sūrah* goes on examining the arguments of the wicked who stand in opposition to the Qur'ān:

> *The unbelievers ask: 'Why has not the Qur'ān been revealed to him all at once?' Thus [it has been revealed] so that We might strengthen your heart with it, and We have imparted it to you by gradual revelation.* (Verse 32)

The purpose of revealing the Qur'ān is to re-educate a community and establish a new social order. Such a task requires time. In a process of proper education it is not enough to understand the words being said, rather one must interact with them as also with the ideas expressed. This interaction should then be brought into the practical world. Human nature does not go through a total transformation overnight, as a result of reading a book which provides a complete new way of life. It is more likely to be influenced day by day, and by one aspect after another. This gives human nature the chance to gradually, but thoroughly understand it, and to get used to it bit by bit, bearing the responsibilities it requires. Thus, people are not scared off as they might be were it presented in full, surrounded by difficulties. This gradual approach is like serving a fresh nourishing meal every day, from which the recipient becomes stronger and better able to benefit by the next meal, enjoying it even more.

The Qur'ān provides a comprehensive way of life, as well as a system of education that suits human nature. For it is revealed by God, the Creator of human nature who knows it thoroughly. For this reason, it was revealed in parts, to suit the real needs of the Muslim community as it came into existence and began to grow. It is not meant to be a theoretical book which is read for enjoyment or increasing one's knowledge. It is meant to be implemented in full, with every task accomplished and every detailed order carried out. Indeed its verses are 'orders of the day' which Muslims receive and start to implement immediately, just like military personnel receive their daily orders on the battlefield. They must understand these orders properly, interact with, and implement them.

For all this, the Qur'ān was revealed in small parts, explaining things first to the Prophet and strengthening his resolve to fulfil his task. Its revelation progressed, one passage or *sūrah* after another, as suited the different stages along the road the Muslim community travelled. "*Thus [it has been revealed] so that We might strengthen your heart with it, and We have imparted it to you by gradual revelation.*" (Verse 32) The Arabic term *tartīl*, translated here as 'gradual revelation', indicates successive steps according to God's knowledge of what suited the Muslims at the time and their readiness to receive more.

This method accomplished miracles in transforming the community which so received it, interacting with it day after day and absorbing its message part after part. When the Muslims ignored this method, viewing the Qur'ān as a book for theoretical knowledge and recitation in worship only, they no longer benefited by it. They simply abandoned its method which aimed to reshape their way of thinking and their everyday lives.

The *sūrah* continues to reassure the Prophet that he will be given the ultimate argument and the final evidence whenever the unbelievers come up with a new suggestion or objection. "*Whenever they come to you with an argument, We shall reveal to you the truth and the best explanation.*" (Verse 33)

Their argument is false, and God refutes it with the truth. Indeed the Qur'ān aims to establish the truth in full clarity. It does not aim to win an argument or to be applauded in a debate. It has no time for such pursuits.

God, limitless is He in His glory, promises to help His Messenger in any argument he may have with his people. He follows the truth, and God empowers him with the truth that overcomes all falsehood. How can the unbelievers' argument stand up to God's ultimate proof? How can the falsehood they advocate resist the overpowering truth revealed by God?

This passage ends with an image showing the unbelievers' resurrection and how they are gathered in hell, as a punishment for their rejection of the truth and for their upholding twisted logic and values: "*Those who will be gathered to hell on their faces – they will be worst in station and still farther away from the [right] path.*" (Verse 34) This picture of them gathering on their faces in hell is a very humiliating one. It contrasts with their arrogance and turning away from the truth. This image is placed before the Prophet to strengthen him against the opposition he faced from them. It is also placed before them as a warning against what awaits them. The portrait as a whole is meant to undermine their arrogance and show how weak their position is. Yet despite such strong warnings, they stubbornly held on to their rejection of the truth.

The Fate of Earlier Unbelievers

The *sūrah* then makes some quick and brief references to earlier communities who rejected God's message, as given to them through His messengers. First we are told about Moses who was granted the support of his brother Aaron. Aaron was to share the task assigned to Moses. They were ordered to confront the people who '*denied Our signs*', for Pharaoh and his people denied God's signs even before Moses and Aaron were sent to them with God's message. Such signs are available all the time, giving clear evidence. God's messengers simply remind people of their negligence of such signs. Before the second verse speaking about them is completed, a quick picture of their fate is shown: "*We utterly destroyed these people.*" (Verse 36)

This is followed by a reference to Noah's people who '*rejected their messengers*' and in consequence, God '*caused them to drown*'. It should be explained here that Noah's people denied only Noah's message and their rejection applied only to him, but we have to remember that Noah only preached the faith advocated by all God's messengers. Hence, when they rejected what he told them, it was as though they rejected all messengers, most of whom lived after their own time. God states that He '*made of them an example for mankind.*' (Verse 37) The great floods could not be forgotten despite the passage of time. Anyone who looks carefully at the result of that flood will understand its lesson, provided he approaches it with an open mind. "*For the wrongdoers We have prepared grievous suffering.*" (Verse 37) It is now ready, requiring no further waiting. We note that the wrongdoers are mentioned by their attribute, rather than by the use of a pronoun, which would have been perfectly correct from the point of view of style, but mentioning this quality explains the reason behind their punishment.

The next verse groups together the 'Ād, Thamūd and the people of al-Rass, as well as many generations in between. Al-Rass refers to a ground well which was not properly built. Its people, who lived in a village in Yamāmah, killed the Prophet sent to them. Al-Ṭabarī, however, says that they are the ones mentioned in *Sūrah* 85, The Constellations, as having lit a fire in a great pit to burn all the believers. Whatever the truth of this, the fact remains that all these communities faced the same fate after they were given a clear message, proffering clear lessons. None heeded what they were told and none averted the terrible fate against which they were warned.

All these peoples, as well as Lot's township which suffered a shower of evil rained upon it, followed the same line and shared the same fate: "*To each of them did We proffer lessons*" so that they may take heed. But this was not to be. Hence, the outcome of their stubborn rejection of God's message was that "*each of them did We utterly annihilate.*" (Verse 39)

The *sūrah* makes this very quick reference to all these communities, ending by mentioning the fate of Lot's people, whose township, Sodom, the Arabs passed by on their summer trade journey to Syria. Sodom was destroyed with a volcanic rain that brought on them gases and stones, destroying the town completely. The *sūrah* states that they did not take heed because they did not believe in resurrection and did not hope to meet God. Hence, their hearts remained hardened. This gave rise to their objections to, and ridicule of their messengers.

Ridiculing God's Messenger

After this quick reference to earlier communities, the *sūrah* mentions the ridicule faced by the Prophet Muḥammad (peace be upon him) from his people. This follows upon the earlier mention of their arrogance and objection to the method of revelation of the Qur'ān. The *sūrah* also earlier described what will happen to them on the Day of Resurrection, and also the fate suffered by earlier unbelievers. All this is given by way of solace to the Prophet before mentioning the ridicule they direct at him. They are warned that they will be placed in a position lower than that of animals: "*When they see you, they make you a target of their mockery, [saying]: 'Is this the one whom God has sent as His emissary?"* (Verse 41)

Prior to his choice as God's Messenger, Muḥammad was highly respected among his people, being the descendant of a leading family and tribe. His honesty and morality enhanced his position, as he was nicknamed *al-amīn*, which meant 'the trustworthy'. When the community faced a serious dispute over which tribe should replace the

Black Stone, they accepted him as arbiter. When he gathered them to give them the first news of his mission, he asked them whether they would believe him if he were to tell them that armed people were moving behind the hills, preparing to attack them, they said: "Yes, because you enjoy our full trust."

Yet when he told them of his mission and recited to them this great book of divine revelations, they ridiculed him, saying: '*Is this the one whom God has sent as His emissary?*' This is cruel ridicule. Yet, were they so convinced that he deserved such ridicule, or that the message he preached also deserved it? Not at all! For it was all a scheme devised by the Quraysh elders to detract from his great personality and to counter the irresistible influence of the Qur'ān. They felt that the new message constituted a threat to their social and economic positions. Hence, they resorted to every conceivable means to counter it.

They convened meetings and conferences to devise plots and strategies, and to agree on what accusations they should level at Muḥammad, knowing full well that they were only fabricating blatant lies.

Ibn Isḥāq reports that one year as the pilgrimage season approached, a group of the Quraysh attended al-Walīd ibn al-Mughīrah, who was a high-ranking elderly figure. He said to them: "Now that the pilgrimage season is approaching, people will start arriving from all over the place. They must have heard about your friend (meaning the Prophet). So you had better agree what to say when you are asked about him. We must guard against having too many opinions, particularly if they are mutually contradictory."

When his audience asked his advice as to what they should say, he preferred to listen to their suggestions first. Someone suggested that they should describe Muḥammad as a fortune-teller. Al-Walīd said: "It is clearly recognized that he is not. We have seen fortune-tellers and what he says is nothing like the incomprehensible rhyming phrases they use." Another suggestion was to say that he was a madman, but al-Walīd rejected this too, saying: "We have seen madness and its effect on people. His is nothing like a madman's seizure, convulsion or hallucination." A third suggestion was to say that he was nothing more than a poet, but al-Walīd again told them that it would not do. "We have learnt poetry in all its forms and metres, and what Muḥammad says is nothing like poetry." Someone suggested that they should say that Muḥammad was a magician. Al-Walīd said: "He is not a magician. We have seen such people and their gestures as they blow and contract. He is totally unlike them."

Giving up, they said: "What shall we say, then?" Al-Walīd said: "What Muḥammad says is certainly beautiful. It is like a date tree with solid roots and rich fruit. Every one of these suggestions you have made is bound to be recognized as false. The least disputable one is to claim that he is a magician who repeats magic words which make a man fall out with his father, mother, wife and clan." They all approved of al-Walīd's suggestion and set about preparing their propaganda campaign. They made sure to meet pilgrims as they arrived in Makkah so as to warn them about the Prophet.

This is but one example of the plots they devised. It also shows how they were at a loss concerning the accusations they could level at the Prophet. Yet it also shows that they were well aware of how truthful he was. Indeed their mockery as they said: '*Is this the one whom God has sent as His emissary?*' was merely one of the forms they used in their propaganda against Islam and its advocates. In arriving at such claims, the elders of the Quraysh did not express their true feelings about the truth of Islam. It was simply a device aiming to lower the Prophet's esteem in the public eye. For they were keen that the masses should continue to look up to them in matters of religion, as this would ensure that they continued to enjoy their social and economic privileges. In all this, the Quraysh were no different from other forces that are hostile to the truth and its advocates in all places and generations.

Although they were keen to project an attitude of ridicule towards the Prophet, their words reflected the great anxiety they felt, their knowledge of his strong argument and the powerful message the Qur'ān embodied. They said: "*He could almost have led us astray from our deities, had we not been steadfastly attached to them!*" (Verse 42)

They admitted that they were greatly shaken to the extent that, keen as they were to stick to their religion which gave them numerous privileges, they were about to abandon their deities and idol worship altogether. They maintained this only through a great deal of resistance.

Steadfastness, which they speak about, is only required to resist what is powerfully appealing. They also described the right guidance the Prophet gave as '*leading astray*', which shows how wrong they were in their evaluation of the situation. Despite the appearances they put on of mocking the Prophet, they could not conceal the tremor they felt in their hearts as Muḥammad advocated his message, reciting the Qur'ān. Hence, a quick and general warning is given which struck fear in their hearts: "*But in time, when they see the suffering, they will come to know who it was that went farthest astray.*" (Verse 42) They will know then whether Muḥammad brought them a message of truth or one of error. But their newly acquired knowledge would then be of little use to them, because suffering would be staring them in the face. This is true whether the suffering is of the type that is inflicted in this present life, like the Quraysh suffered at the Battle of Badr, or in the hereafter.

When Desire is Worshipped

The *sūrah* then addresses the Prophet consoling and comforting him. He did not fail to deliver his message or to employ strong arguments in advocating it. He certainly deserved nothing of the mockery and ridicule they levelled at him. It is they that are wicked. They make their own desires an idol which they worship. They have no argument for the stand they adopted. How could such a person formulate even the semblance of an argument?

"*Have you considered the one who makes his desires his deity? Could you, then, be held responsible for him?*" (Verse 43) This verse is carefully phrased to paint a picture showing the psychological condition of a person who pays no heed to accepted standards or values. Instead, they only submit to their own desires and worship none but their own pleasure. They apply no standard, recognize no value, acknowledge no logic. Once their desire moves clearly in a particular direction, they follow like slaves submitting to a powerful master.

God, who is limitless in His glory, addresses His servant and Messenger in a kindly and compassionate manner, referring to this type of person. He asks him: "*Have you considered...*" He follows this by drawing a picture of a man who pays no regard to truth, logic or sound argument. He comforts the Prophet so that he does not feel too disappointed at having failed to guide someone who has no propensity to follow guidance. Hence, the Prophet need not concern himself with such people: "*Could you, then, be held responsible for him?*" (Verse 43)

The *sūrah* hurls further ridicule on those who submit to their lust and worship their desire, turning a blind eye to the truth. It puts them on the same level as animals which are devoid of hearing or logic. This is followed by yet more ridicule which shows such people as even inferior to animals: "*Or do you think that most of them listen and use their reason? They are but like cattle. Nay, they are even far worse astray.*" (Verse 44)

This very clear statement that maintains accuracy applies, as the *sūrah* says, to 'most of them', because only a minority of unbelievers showed any inclination to accept guidance, or reflect on what they heard. The majority, who took their desires as their gods which they blindly obeyed, ignored all the signs they heard and saw, and were indeed like cattle. Indeed man is distinguished from animals by his propensity to reflect and understand, as well as by his ability to mould his life in accordance with the truth he accepts upon consideration and reflection. His great human quality is that he is able to change course on being convinced by sound argument. When man deliberately abandons such qualities, he puts himself in a position worse than that of animals. An animal is guided to what suits it by the abilities and susceptibilities God has placed within it. Thus, it fulfils its role without deviation. Man, on the other hand, often disregards the qualities God has given him, making little use of them. In this he is worse than an animal who does not neglect any inclination given to it.

"*They are but like cattle. Nay, they are even far worse astray.*" (Verse 44) This comment expels those who ridicule the Prophet from the ranks of mankind. They are to be looked down upon, never to command respect.

3

Raising Support Against God

Do you not see how your Lord causes the shadow to lengthen when, had He so willed, He could have indeed made it stand still? But then We have made the sun its guide. (45)

أَلَمْ تَرَ إِلَىٰ رَبِّكَ كَيْفَ مَدَّ ٱلظِّلَّ وَلَوْ شَآءَ
لَجَعَلَهُۥ سَاكِنًا ثُمَّ جَعَلْنَا ٱلشَّمْسَ عَلَيْهِ
دَلِيلًا ﴿٤٥﴾

And then, little by little, We draw it in towards Ourselves. (46)

ثُمَّ قَبَضْنَٰهُ إِلَيْنَا قَبْضًا يَسِيرًا ﴿٤٦﴾

He it is who makes the night a garment for you, and sleep a repose. He makes every day a resurrection. (47)

وَهُوَ ٱلَّذِى جَعَلَ لَكُمُ ٱلَّيْلَ لِبَاسًا وَٱلنَّوْمَ
سُبَاتًا وَجَعَلَ ٱلنَّهَارَ نُشُورًا ﴿٤٧﴾

And He it is who sends forth the winds as heralds of His coming grace. And We cause pure water to descend from the skies, (48)

وَهُوَ ٱلَّذِىٓ أَرْسَلَ ٱلرِّيَٰحَ بُشْرًۢا بَيْنَ
يَدَىْ رَحْمَتِهِۦ ۚ وَأَنزَلْنَا مِنَ ٱلسَّمَآءِ
مَآءً طَهُورًا ﴿٤٨﴾

so that with it We may bring dead land to life and give drink to a countless number of Our creation, beasts as well as human. (49)

لِّنُحْۦِىَ بِهِۦ بَلْدَةً مَّيْتًا وَنُسْقِيَهُۥ مِمَّا خَلَقْنَآ
أَنْعَٰمًا وَأَنَاسِىَّ كَثِيرًا ﴿٤٩﴾

Many times have We explained this [in the] Qur'ān to them, so that they may take it to heart, but most people refuse to be anything but unbelievers. (50)

وَلَقَدْ صَرَّفْنَٰهُ بَيْنَهُمْ لِيَذَّكَّرُوا۟ فَأَبَىٰٓ أَكْثَرُ
ٱلنَّاسِ إِلَّا كُفُورًا (٥٠)

Had We so willed, We could have sent a warner to every city. (51)

وَلَوْ شِئْنَا لَبَعَثْنَا فِى كُلِّ قَرْيَةٍ نَّذِيرًا (٥١)

Do not obey the unbelievers, but strive most vigorously against them with this Qur'ān. (52)

فَلَا تُطِعِ ٱلْكَٰفِرِينَ وَجَٰهِدْهُم بِهِۦ
جِهَادًا كَبِيرًا (٥٢)

He it is who has brought the two bodies of water to meet; the one sweet and thirst-quenching, and the other salty and bitter. Yet between them He has made a barrier and a forbidding ban. (53)

وَهُوَ ٱلَّذِى مَرَجَ ٱلْبَحْرَيْنِ هَٰذَا عَذْبٌ
فُرَاتٌ وَهَٰذَا مِلْحٌ أُجَاجٌ وَجَعَلَ بَيْنَهُمَا
بَرْزَخًا وَحِجْرًا مَّحْجُورًا (٥٣)

And He it is who has created man from water and established for him bonds of lineage and marriage. All-Powerful is your Lord. (54)

وَهُوَ ٱلَّذِى خَلَقَ مِنَ ٱلْمَآءِ بَشَرًا فَجَعَلَهُۥ
نَسَبًا وَصِهْرًا ۗ وَكَانَ رَبُّكَ قَدِيرًا (٥٤)

Yet people worship, instead of God, things that can neither benefit nor harm them. An unbeliever always gives support against his Lord. (55)

وَيَعْبُدُونَ مِن دُونِ ٱللَّهِ مَا لَا يَنفَعُهُمْ
وَلَا يَضُرُّهُمْ ۗ وَكَانَ ٱلْكَافِرُ عَلَىٰ رَبِّهِۦ
ظَهِيرًا (٥٥)

We have sent you only as a herald of good news and a warner. (56)

وَمَآ أَرْسَلْنَٰكَ إِلَّا مُبَشِّرًا وَنَذِيرًا (٥٦)

Say: 'No reward do I ask of you for this. All I ask is that he who so wills may find a way leading to his Lord.' (57)

قُلْ مَآ أَسْـَٔلُكُمْ عَلَيْهِ مِنْ أَجْرٍ إِلَّا مَن
شَآءَ أَن يَتَّخِذَ إِلَىٰ رَبِّهِۦ سَبِيلًا ٥٧

Hence, place your trust in the Living One who does not die, and extol His limitless glory and praise. Sufficient is it that He is well aware of his servants' sins. (58)

وَتَوَكَّلْ عَلَى ٱلْحَىِّ ٱلَّذِى لَا يَمُوتُ
وَسَبِّحْ بِحَمْدِهِۦ ۚ وَكَفَىٰ بِهِۦ بِذُنُوبِ
عِبَادِهِۦ خَبِيرًا ٥٨

He it is who has created the heavens and the earth and all that is between them in six days, and is established on the throne of His Almightiness, the Most Merciful. Ask, then, about Him, the One who knows everything. (59)

ٱلَّذِى خَلَقَ ٱلسَّمَٰوَٰتِ وَٱلْأَرْضَ وَمَا بَيْنَهُمَا
فِى سِتَّةِ أَيَّامٍ ثُمَّ ٱسْتَوَىٰ عَلَى ٱلْعَرْشِ ۚ
ٱلرَّحْمَٰنُ فَسْـَٔلْ بِهِۦ خَبِيرًا ٥٩

Yet when they are told, 'Prostrate yourselves before the Most Merciful,' they ask, 'What is the Most Merciful? Are we to prostrate ourselves before whatever you bid us?' And they grow more rebellious. (60)

وَإِذَا قِيلَ لَهُمُ ٱسْجُدُوا۟ لِلرَّحْمَٰنِ قَالُوا۟
وَمَا ٱلرَّحْمَٰنُ أَنَسْجُدُ لِمَا تَأْمُرُنَا وَزَادَهُمْ
نُفُورًا ۩ ٦٠

Blessed is He who has set up in the skies great constellations, and has placed among them a lamp and a light-giving moon. (61)

تَبَارَكَ ٱلَّذِى جَعَلَ فِى ٱلسَّمَآءِ بُرُوجًا
وَجَعَلَ فِيهَا سِرَٰجًا وَقَمَرًا مُّنِيرًا ٦١

And He it is who causes the night and the day to succeed one another; [a clear sign] for him who would take heed or would show gratitude. (62)

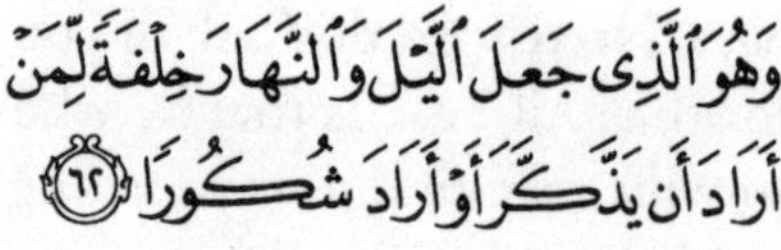

Overview

This passage concentrates on some of the great wonders in the universe that testify to God's existence and the unique system He has put in place to control and conduct everything that happens. It directs the Prophet to look carefully at these signs and interact with them. Such interaction, particularly when it is done with an open heart and mind, is sufficient to redress any lingering effects of the hardship caused by the unbelievers. He will be looking at the great horizons against which the unbelievers' schemes and hostilities are reduced to insignificance.

The Qur'ān always directs people's hearts and minds to reflect on, and interact with, what they see in the universe. They will then recognize the work of God's hand in all that they see, hear and feel. They will have much to reflect upon which will strengthen their bond with God through His work.

When man lives in the universe with an open heart and mind, and an alert soul, his life rises above the petty concerns of this world. His sense of life is heightened as he feels, at every moment, that the universe around him is much larger and greater than his own world, while all that he sees and feels comes into being through one and the same will, are subject to the same law, and submit to One Creator. He will realize that he is but one of countless creatures that submit to God, and that God's hand is visible in all that he sees, hears and feels.

To fear only God will be mixed in anyone's consciousness with parallel feelings of friendliness and trust. These feelings will fill his soul and his whole world, imparting a mixture of love and reassurance that will accompany him on his life journey and remain with him until he meets God. He cannot fail to experience such feelings when everything around him is made by God, according to His fine and elaborate system of creation.

We see in this passage how the *sūrah* paints a scene of shadows extending then gently contracting, before we move to a picture of a quiet night of deep slumber and a bustling day of tireless activity. We then see the winds as heralds of God's mercy, followed by water pouring down from the skies to quicken barren land. We see the salty sea and the sweet river water, and the barrier between them preventing them from mixing. Then we look at a different type of fluid, the semen that gives rise to human life. We contemplate how the heavens and the earth were created in six days, and look at the star constellations in the sky, with the sun as a lamp lightening the world for us, and the moon doing the same at night. We also contemplate the unfailing succession of night and day.

As it paints these images, the *sūrah* directs our hearts and minds to reflect that they are all of God's creation, reminding us of His power and fine planning. It shows how singular the unbelievers' attitude is when they associate partners with God and worship alongside Him entities that can cause them neither benefit nor harm. The unbelievers are so ignorant that they speak impudently about God and support one another in denying Him. This is very strange, particularly when seen against the multitude of universal signs demonstrating God's creation. It is all a great display that the Creator raises before our eyes for us to contemplate.

Moving Shadows, Still Night

> *Do you not see how your Lord causes the shadow to lengthen when, had He so willed, He could have indeed made it stand still? But then We have made the sun its guide. And then, little by little, We draw it in towards Ourselves.* (Verses 45–46)

This image of shadow and shade imparts to a troubled and tired soul a feeling of comfort, relaxation and security, as if it is a gentle, compassionate hand that wipes away pain and worry, giving comfort and energy. Is this God's purpose as He directs the Prophet, who has suffered the unbelievers' ridicule and opposition, to contemplate the shadow? In the tough battle the Prophet went through in Makkah, facing determined opposition and wicked scheming, his soul must have felt the burden too heavy, with only a small number of believers supporting him against the overwhelming majority of unbelievers. Not only so, but he was not then even allowed to retaliate against physical aggression or repel hostile ridicule. In this troubled atmosphere passages of the Qur'ān were revealed to Muḥammad (peace be upon him) to serve as a healing balsam, a relaxing shade and kind blessing. It provided him with support in the midst of determined denial and opposition. Shade, particularly when considered against a hot desert background, gives an image that is in complete harmony with the whole atmosphere of the *sūrah* that is full of compassion and blessings.

The *sūrah* shows the shadow as being gently stretched by God's hand before it then contracts: "*Do you not see how your Lord causes the shadow to lengthen?*" (Verse 45) Some time later, "*little by little, We draw it in towards Ourselves.*" (Verse 46) The shadow is a faint darkness made by the sun's rebounding rays. It moves along with the movement of the earth in relation to the sun, changing its position, length and shape. The sun points it with its light and heat, determining its area and length. When we follow how the shadow changes shape and extent, we experience a feeling of comfort and are gently alerted to the fact that it is an aspect of God's work.

When the sun starts its decline, we see the shadows lengthen and further lengthen. Suddenly all shadows disappear as the sun sets. Where have all the shadows gone? God's unseen hand has collected them all as the deep darkness of the night gathers and spreads over our world. This is all the work of God's able hand which humans fail to see, but which continues without fail.

"*Had He so willed, He could have indeed made it stand still?*" (Verse 45) The way the visible universe and solar system are made makes the shadow move in the gentle way it does. Had the system been even slightly different, this would have had a different effect on the shadow. Had the earth been motionless, the shadow cast over it would have stood still, neither extending nor shrinking. On the other hand, if the earth's movement had been faster or slower, the extension and shrinking of the shadow would have been proportionately slower or faster. It is the way the universe is made, with its operative laws, that gives the shadow its specific features.

The highlighting of this phenomenon, which we see every day without paying much attention to it, is part of the Qur'ānic method of making our consciousness interact with the universe so as to respond to aspects that we tend to ignore because of their familiarity. We only need to contemplate the countless marvels around us for our thoughts to move in the right direction.

Moving on, the *sūrah* highlights an image of the night, its stillness and peaceful slumber, contrasted with the day and its bustling movement. "*He it is who makes the night a garment for you, and sleep a repose. He makes every day a resurrection.*" (Verse 47)

The night spreads its cover over animate and inanimate objects so as to make the world appear as though it wears the blackness of the night. Hence, the night is described as a garment. At night, movement stops and footsteps cease to allow people and most animals, birds and insects to sleep. Sleep is a cessation of sensation, consciousness and feeling, which is why it is described as 'repose'. Then the dawn starts to breathe and movement begins. Life is thus resumed. Hence, the day is a new 'resurrection' after a short mini-death. The two alternate with every daily cycle of the earth. Again this phenomenon is ignored by human beings, but it is indicative of the great design of the universe made by God, who never sleeps or overlooks anything.

The *sūrah* highlights another universal phenomenon that is closely related to life:

> *And He it is who sends forth the winds as heralds of His coming grace. And We cause pure water to descend from the skies, so that with it We may bring dead land to life and give drink to a countless number of Our creation, beasts as well as human.* (Verses 48–49)

All life on earth depends on rain water, either directly, or through the rivers and other water courses, springs, wells and underground reservoirs it supplies. Only those who directly depend on rain for their living properly appreciate God's grace as He sends rain. They look forward to rain, full of hope, realizing that it brings them life. They look for wind, which they know to drive the clouds. Hence, they realize that the wind is an early indicator, announcing the forthcoming act of God's grace, provided that they believe in God.

It is important to look at the last two verses very carefully: "*We cause pure water to descend from the skies.*" (Verse 48) We note how the concept of purity and purification points to the life brought about by rain: "*so that with it We may bring dead land to life and give drink to a countless number of Our creation, beasts as well as human.*" (Verse 49) Thus, life is given an added aspect of purity, because God wants human life, and indeed all life on earth, to be pure of evil. Thus, He washes the face of the earth with pure water that brings life to an otherwise dead land, and which also serves as a pure drink for all creatures.

Jihād by Means of the Qur'ān

At this point the *sūrah* refers to the Qur'ān which, like pure rain water, descends from on high to purify people's hearts and souls. It wonders how man warms to rain, which is essential for physical life, but does not warm to the Qur'ān which gives life to hearts and souls.

> *Many times have We explained this [in the] Qur'ān to them, so that they may take it to heart, but most people refuse to be anything but unbelievers. Had We so willed, We could have sent a warner to every city. Do not obey the unbelievers, but strive most vigorously against them with this Qur'ān.* (Verses 50–52)

We have put it to them in a great variety of forms, styles and presentations, addressing it to their minds, hearts, souls and feelings. We sought to awaken their consciences to its import in numerous ways, employing different means to ensure that they interact with it. All it needs from them is that they should '*take it to heart.*' The point is that the Qur'ān aims to remind people of a truth that is well established in their nature, even though they often forget it. What makes them heedless of it is the fact that they submit to their desires: "*but most people refuse to be anything but unbelievers.*" (Verse 50)

This means that the mission entrusted to God's Messenger is a very tough one. He faces the whole of mankind when the great majority of them choose to follow their desires, insisting on unbelief, being ingrate, despite the presence of numerous signs pointing to the truth of faith.

"*Had We so willed, We could have sent a warner to every city.*" (Verse 51) Such a course would have divided the task and made it easier to carry out. God, however, chose one of His servants, the last of His messengers, and required him to address all mankind, so as to give them the same message which remains free from local variations. God also gave His Messenger the Qur'ān, so as to make it the address he drove home to them: "*Do not obey the unbelievers, but strive most vigorously against them with this Qur'ān.*" (Verse 52)

This Qur'ān has great power and influence. It is irresistible. When God's Messenger addressed the Arabs with it, it shook their hearts and consciences. They tried hard to counter its effects, employing every means at their disposal, but all their efforts were useless. The Quraysh elders used to say to their people: "*Do not listen to this Qur'ān, but rather talk frivolously about it, so that you might gain the upper hand.*" (41: 26) This betrayed their profound fear that the Qur'ān would touch their own hearts and the hearts of their followers and that they would embrace Islam. They were aware that it took only the reading of a couple of verses, or perhaps a *sūrah* or two, by Muḥammad, and listeners were so affected they accepted his message. To them, it seemed like the Qur'ān had a magic effect on people.

The elders of the Quraysh were themselves touched by the power of the Qur'ān. It was only because they were keenly aware of this profound effect that they resorted to such tactics, warning their people against listening to it and encouraging them to take it frivolously. Indeed, their statement is indicative of how worried they were about the effect of the Qur'ān.

Ibn Isḥāq reports that three of the Quraysh elders, Abū Jahl, Abū Sufyān and al-Akhnas ibn Sharīq went out one night to listen to the Qur'ān being recited by the Prophet as he prayed in his home during the night. Each of them was on his own, thinking that no one would know about what he did. As the day began to break, they went back. However, the three of them inevitably met. There was no need for them to ask each other what they were doing. Therefore, they remonstrated with one another and concluded that their action was inadvisable: "Should some of your followers see you," one of them said, "you would stir doubts in their minds."

The following night they did the same, and once again they met at the break of day. Again they counselled each other against such 'irresponsible' action. Nevertheless, the third night each of them went to sit outside the Prophet's home and listen to the Qur'ān. When they met in the morning, they were ashamed of themselves. One of them suggested that they should give each other their word of honour not to listen to the Qur'ān again. They did so before going home.

Later that morning al-Akhnas ibn Sharīq went to see Abū Sufyān at his home. He asked him what he thought about what he heard Muḥammad reciting. Abū Sufyān said: "I heard things which I know and recognize to be true, but I also heard things whose nature I cannot understand." Al-Akhnas said that he felt the same. He then left and went to Abū Jahl's home to put the same question to him.

Abū Jahl's answer was totally different. For once, he was candid and honest with himself and his interlocutor: "I will tell you about what I heard! We have competed with the clan of 'Abd Manāf (the Prophet's clan) for honours: they fed the poor, and we did the same; they provided generous support to those who needed it and we did the same. When we were together on the same level, like two racehorses running neck and neck, they said that one of their number was a Prophet receiving revelations from on high! When can we attain such an honour? By God, we shall never believe in him."

This is just an example of how strongly attracted they were to the Qur'ān. They felt that it was too powerful for them. Hence, they needed to pledge their word of honour that they would not listen to it again. What they feared most was that some of their subordinates might see them so taken by the Qur'ān that they too would be unable to resist it.

Indeed, the Qur'ān embodies simple and natural facts which link hearts directly to the truth that issues forth with irresistible power. It includes scenes and images of the Day of Judgement, and others derived from the universe around us, historical accounts, scenes of the fate of past communities, and powerful arguments, all of which strike basic cords in our hearts. Indeed, we often find that a single *sūrah* affects us so powerfully as to take hold of our whole being. Indeed, the Qur'ān is often described as more powerful than great armies. It is no wonder, therefore, that God ordered His Messenger not to obey the unbelievers, and not to budge from fulfilling his task. The divine order also required the Prophet to vigorously strive against unbelievers by means of the Qur'ān. Having been given the Qur'ān, the Prophet was equipped with something much more forceful and compelling than any human logic.

Separating Types of Water

The *sūrah* again portrays images from the world around us. Having spoken about winds heralding rain and its pure water, now it speaks of the great bodies of water, some of which are sweet and some salty, and how they do not mix.

> *He it is who has brought the two bodies of water to meet; the one sweet and thirst-quenching, and the other salty and bitter. Yet between them He has made a barrier and a forbidding ban.* (Verse 53)

It is God who created both types and left them to run their courses, meeting at certain points. Nevertheless, their waters do not mix because they have a natural barrier keeping them apart. In most cases, rivers run at a level higher than the sea, which means that at the meeting point, it is the river with its sweet water that runs into the salty sea. It is very rare that a river runs below sea level. Hence, the sea with its much greater body of water does not overpower the river whose water gives life to plants, animals and man. The fact that this is the natural order in practically all cases where a river meets the sea means that it is certainly not coincidental. It happens by the will of the Creator who made the universe in such a way as to fulfil His purpose and remain subject to His laws of nature.

Indeed the natural laws God has set in operation ensure that the salty waters of sea and ocean do not overrun dry land or overpower rivers. This remains so even during high tides caused by the moon's gravity as it affects the earth's surface water.

It is useful to cite here some scientific observations that stress the facts mentioned in the Qur'ān:

> The moon is 240,000 miles away, and the tides twice a day are usually a gentle reminder of its presence. Tides of the ocean run as high as sixty feet in some places, and even the crust of the earth is twice a day bent outward several inches by the moon's attraction. All seems so regular that we do not grasp to any degree the vast power that lifts the whole area of the sea several feet and bends the crust of the earth, seemingly so solid. Mars has a moon – a little one – only six thousand miles away from it. If our moon was, say, fifty thousand miles away instead of its present respectable distance, our tides would be so enormous that twice a day all the lowland of all the continents would be submerged by a rush of water so enormous that even the mountains would soon be eroded away, and probably no continent could have risen from the depths fast enough to exist today. The earth would crack with the turmoil and tides in the air would create daily hurricanes. If the continents were washed away, the average depth of water over the whole earth would be about a mile and a half and life could not exist except perhaps in the abysmal depth of the ocean, where it would feed upon itself till extinct.[4]

But the hand that manages this universe has let the two bodies of water free, placing between them a barrier that prevents either from encroaching on the other. This barrier is erected between them through their very nature and the nature of the universe which demonstrates such balances that testify to the wisdom of its Maker.

As the *sūrah* proceeds, it refers to a fluid that is totally different from the water pouring down from the skies, or moving along in seas and rivers. It mentions the sperm that gives rise to human life: "*And*

4. A.C. Morrison, *Man Does Not Stand Alone*, Morrison and Gibb Ltd., London, 1962, pp. 22–23.

He it is who has created man from water and established for him bonds of lineage and marriage. All-Powerful is your Lord." (Verse 54) It is from this particular fluid that a fetus takes form and becomes a male child related to its ancestors by lineage, or a female one that enables the marriage relationship to take place.

The human life that comes into existence through this fluid is far greater and more wonderful than life caused by rain. Just one cell, out of a countless number comprised in one drop of man's semen, fertilizes the woman's egg to initiate the formation of the greatly sophisticated creature, man, the most remarkable of all living creatures.

It is from practically identical sperms and female eggs that boys and girls come into existence, in a remarkable process that human knowledge has not yet fathomed. None of the many thousands of sperms shows any clear signs that makes it able to produce a male or a female. Similarly, no female egg shows such signs. Nevertheless, one eventually produces a man, while another produces a woman. "*All powerful is your Lord.*" This amazing phenomenon shows just one aspect of His power.

The Great Miracle of Life

If we were to look minutely into this fluid, we would be overawed as we look for a complete set of human characteristics in exceedingly minute components that carry the hereditary aspects of the human race, as also the parents and their immediate families, which are then transferred to the fetus, male or female, in accordance with God's will. Here we quote from the chapter on genes in A.C. Morrison's *Man Does Not Stand Alone*:

> In every cell, male and female, are chromosomes and genes. Chromosomes form the darkened nucleus which contains the genes. The genes are the main deciding factor as to what every living thing or a human being shall be. The cytoplasm is the extraordinary chemical combinations which surround them both. The genes are so infinitesimal that if all of them which are responsible for all the human beings on earth today, with their

> individuality, psychology, colour, and race, could be collected and put in one place, there would be less than a thimbleful. These ultra-microscopic genes are the absolute keys to all human, animal, and vegetable characteristics. A thimble is a small place in which to put all the individual characteristics of two billions of human beings. However, the facts are beyond question… The embryo recapitulating in its progressive development from protoplasm to racial identity indicates recorded history retained and expressed by atomic arrangement in the genes and cytoplasm…[5]
>
> We have found that genes are recognized to be submicroscopic arrangements of the atoms in the sex cells of all things that have life. They hold the design, ancestral record and characteristics of each living thing. They control in detail root, trunk, leaf, flower and fruit of every plant as exactly as they determine the shape, scales, hair, wings of every animal, including man.[6]

Such a glimpse into the marvels of life is sufficient as a pointer to the wise Creator's great hand: "*All powerful is your Lord.*" (Verse 54)

In League Against God

In this atmosphere of careful planning of creation, and in the light of life that is produced by rain water and human sperm, the very thought of worshipping anyone other than God is incompatible with nature, as also singular and absurd. Hence, the *sūrah* refers to the unbelievers' worship and puts it in perspective: "*Yet people worship, instead of God, things that can neither benefit nor harm them. An unbeliever always gives support against his Lord.*" (Verse 55)

Every single unbeliever, including the idolaters who opposed Islam in Makkah, joins the fight against their Lord who has created them and given them shape and form. How can this be when the unbeliever is so insignificant as to stand in opposition to God? In fact unbelievers oppose God's faith and the code of living He has laid down for human

5. Ibid., pp. 78–79.
6. Ibid., p. 86.

life. In order to show the enormity of their offence, the *sūrah* describes them as opponents of God, their Lord and Master.

When someone stands in opposition to God's Messenger and his message, he is actually fighting against God. The Prophet need not worry about this person, because his opponent is God, who will certainly ensure that he cannot do the Prophet any harm.

God then reassures His Messenger, lightening his burden. He assures him that once he has discharged his duty, delivering his message, with what it brings to people of good news and warnings, striving hard against the unbelievers through the Qur'ān, then there is no reason for him to be troubled at the unbelievers' stubborn rejection of his message. God will take over the fight against those who oppose him. All he needs to do is to place his trust in God and leave matters to Him.

> *We have sent you only as a herald of good news and a warner. Say: 'No reward do I ask of you for this. All I ask is that he who so wills may find a way leading to his Lord. Hence, place your trust in the Living One who does not die, and extol His limitless glory and praise. Sufficient is it that He is well aware of his servants' sins.* (Verses 56–58)

Thus the task of God's Messenger is defined: it is to give happy news and issue a warning. At the time this *sūrah* was revealed, the Prophet was still in Makkah and had not yet received orders to take up arms against the idolaters to ensure the freedom of expression and advocacy of his message. That order was given to him later, after his immigration to Madīnah. There was certainly a definite purpose behind withholding such an order at the time, and this is best known to God Himself. However, we think that at the time the Prophet was still inculcating the new faith in the minds and hearts of his followers. He wanted it to sink deep so as to impart its distinctive character to them and for it to become manifest in their lives and actions. Thus, they would become the nucleus of the Muslim society which moulds itself on the basis of its Islamic faith. Moreover, the order to refrain from fighting during the Makkan period avoided bloody hostilities and vengeance killing which could have shut the door firmly between the Quraysh and Islam. God certainly knew that eventually they would all embrace Islam, with some of them doing so before the Prophet's immigration to Madīnah and the rest after the Muslims' re-entry into Makkah. They would form the solid base of the new faith.

Nevertheless, the core of the Islamic message remained the same in Madīnah: giving happy news and issuing serious warnings. Fighting was permitted only to remove physical barriers erected by the unbelievers to deprive God's message of free expression, and to protect the believers against religious oppression. This means that the Qur'ānic statement was applicable both in Makkah and Madīnah: "*We have sent you only as a herald of good news and a warner.*" (Verse 56)

In Whom to Trust

"*Say: 'No reward do I ask of you for this. All I ask is that he who so wills may find a way leading to his Lord.'*" (Verse 57) God's Messenger does not entertain any thought of making any worldly gain or profit as a result of people's acceptance of Islam. None will have to pay any fee or make any offering as he embraces the Islamic faith. All that he needs to do is to say certain words verbally, provided that he believes in them with his heart. This is the distinctive feature of Islam which has no room for any priesthood of any kind, which would charge fees for services rendered. There is no 'joining fee', and no price has to be paid to reveal a mystery or bestow a blessing or organize entry. Islam is free of all that may deter anyone from faith. It allows no room for anyone to stand as an intermediary between people and their Lord. God's Messenger receives only one reward for all his troubles in advocating God's faith, and this reward is nothing other than the fact that someone answers the divine call and receives God's guidance: "*that he who so wills may find a way leading to his Lord.*" (Verse 57) Such are his only wages. When the Prophet sees someone accepting divine guidance and seeking to earn God's pleasure, then his compassionate heart finds comfort, and his noble conscience is set at ease.

"*Hence, place your trust in the Living One who does not die, and extol His limitless glory and praise.*" (Verse 58) Everyone other than God is dead, because life comes to an end with death. The only one that remains is God, the Living One who does not die. If we rely on someone whose life comes to an end after a short or long time, then we are only putting our weight against a wall that will eventually collapse, or seeking shade that will inevitably fade away. To be truly assured one must rely only on the One who never dies, and place one's trust solely in Him. "*Extol His limitless glory and praise.*" (Verse 58) The only one worthy of praise is God who grants all favours and blessings. Hence the Prophet is instructed to leave alone those unbelievers who heed no warning and care for no happy news. He should give them up to Him since He knows their sins. Nothing is hidden from Him: "*Sufficient is it that He is well aware of his servants' sins.*" (Verse 58)

Within the same context of God's limitless knowledge and His power to grant reward and inflict punishment, the *sūrah* mentions the facts that He is the One who has created the heavens and the earth, and established Himself on the Throne:

> *He it is who has created the heavens and the earth and all that is between them in six days, and is established on the throne of His Almightiness, the Most Merciful. Ask, then, about Him, the One who knows everything.* (Verse 59)

The days in which God created the heavens and the earth are certainly different from our earth days. For our days are only a product of the solar system, measuring a celestial cycle that came into existence after the creation of the heavens and the earth. Our days are equivalent to the time the earth rotates in its position relevant to the sun. Besides, creation does not require more than God should will something to exist. This is given the verbal symbol 'Be', and whatever is intended comes into existence. Perhaps these six days, whose measure is known only to God, refer to long stages that brought the heavens and the earth to their present status.

That God is '*established on the throne*' refers to His being the Almighty who controls everything in the universe. The Arabic text uses the conjunctive word, *thumma,* which means 'then', after it mentions the creation of the heavens and the earth and before it refers to God being on the throne. However, this does not signify a chronological order. It only indicates the superiority of this lofty status.

Together with God's greatness, control and might comes His all-encompassing mercy, and with it is joined His absolute knowledge: *"The Most Merciful. Ask, then, about Him, the One who knows everything."* (Verse 59) Thus, when you put your request to God, you are putting it to the One whose knowledge includes everything anywhere in the universe.

Setting the Universe to Order

Yet those impudent, shameless people behave discourteously when they are called upon to believe in God, the Most Merciful, and worship Him:

> *Yet when they are told, 'Prostrate yourselves before the Most Merciful,' they ask, 'What is the Most Merciful? Are we to prostrate ourselves before whatever you bid us?' And they grow more rebellious.* (Verse 60)

This is a particularly distasteful picture of impudence, mentioned here to comfort the Prophet who was at the receiving end of their insolence and disrespect. These people have no respect for their Lord. They speak in such an impudent way about God Almighty. Is it surprising, then, that they should say whatever they do about His Messenger? They even dislike God's name, and say that they do not know His attribute, the Most Merciful. Hence, they ask the Prophet about Him, using the interrogative word 'what', thus adding insult to injury. Their rudeness was at its worst when they said that the only Raḥmān, which is the Arabic word for the Most Merciful, they knew was the one in Yamāmah, referring to Musaylamah, the liar who claimed that he was a prophet.

Their shameless impertinence is answered by stressing that all glory belongs to God, highlighting His greatness and the great signs He has placed in the universe:

> *Blessed is He who has set up in the skies great constellations, and has placed among them a lamp and a light-giving moon. And He it is who causes the night and the day to succeed one another; [a clear sign] for him who would take heed or would show gratitude.* (Verses 61–62)

Most probably the term 'constellations', as mentioned here, refers to the positions of the planets and their great orbits. Their mention contrasts with the mockery sensed in the unbelievers' question: 'What is the Most Merciful?' These constellations, in their real and perceived greatness, are only one aspect of His creation. In these the sun takes its position, and the sun is called here 'a lamp' as it sends light to our planet as well as to other planets. And among them there is a light-giving moon, which spreads a gentle air of calm.

The *sūrah* also refers to the succession of day and night, which are two of God's great signs that people always overlook, although reflection on them is enough for anyone '*who would take heed or would show gratitude.*' Had it not been for the fact that God made the day and night to succeed each other in this fashion, no vegetal, animal or human life could have emerged on this planet. Indeed, life would not be possible if the length of the day and night cycle were changed. Scientists tell us:

> The earth rotates on its axis in twenty-four hours or at the rate of one thousand miles an hour. Suppose it turned at the rate of a hundred miles an hour. Why not? Our days and nights would then be ten times as long as now. The hot sun of summer would then burn up our vegetation each long day and every sprout would freeze in such a night.[7]

---

7. Ibid., p. 20.

Blessed, then, is the One who created the heavens and the earth, and created everything according to a definite measure. Blessed is the One who "*Set up in the skies great constellations, and has placed among them a lamp and a light-giving moon. And He it is who causes the night and the day to succeed one another; [a clear sign] for him who would take heed or would show gratitude.*" (Verses 61–62)

4
God's True Servants

The true servants of the Most Merciful are those who walk gently on earth, and who, whenever the ignorant address them, say: 'Peace'; (63)

وَعِبَادُ ٱلرَّحْمَٰنِ ٱلَّذِينَ يَمْشُونَ عَلَى ٱلْأَرْضِ
هَوْنًا وَإِذَا خَاطَبَهُمُ ٱلْجَٰهِلُونَ قَالُوا۟
سَلَٰمًا ﴿٦٣﴾

who stay up far into the night in adoration of their Lord, prostrating themselves and standing; (64)

وَٱلَّذِينَ يَبِيتُونَ لِرَبِّهِمْ سُجَّدًا
وَقِيَٰمًا ﴿٦٤﴾

who pray: 'Our Lord, avert from us the suffering of hell, for the suffering it causes is indeed a dire torment; (65)

وَٱلَّذِينَ يَقُولُونَ رَبَّنَا ٱصْرِفْ عَنَّا عَذَابَ
جَهَنَّمَ إِنَّ عَذَابَهَا كَانَ غَرَامًا ﴿٦٥﴾

it is indeed an evil abode and a terrible station; (66)

إِنَّهَا سَآءَتْ مُسْتَقَرًّا وَمُقَامًا ﴿٦٦﴾

and who, whenever they put their money to use, are neither wasteful nor niggardly, but always maintain a just mean between the two; (67)

وَٱلَّذِينَ إِذَآ أَنفَقُوا۟ لَمْ يُسْرِفُوا۟ وَلَمْ يَقْتُرُوا۟
وَكَانَ بَيْنَ ذَٰلِكَ قَوَامًا ﴿٦٧﴾

and who never invoke any deity side by side with God, and do not take any human being's life – [the life] which God has willed to be sacred – except for a just cause, and do not commit adultery. Whoever does any of this will face punishment, (68)

وَٱلَّذِينَ لَا يَدۡعُونَ مَعَ ٱللَّهِ إِلَٰهًا ءَاخَرَ
وَلَا يَقۡتُلُونَ ٱلنَّفۡسَ ٱلَّتِي حَرَّمَ ٱللَّهُ
إِلَّا بِٱلۡحَقِّ وَلَا يَزۡنُونَۚ وَمَن يَفۡعَلۡ ذَٰلِكَ
يَلۡقَ أَثَامٗا ﴿٦٨﴾

and on the Day of Resurrection his suffering will be doubled, and he will abide therein in ignominy. (69)

يُضَٰعَفۡ لَهُ ٱلۡعَذَابُ يَوۡمَ ٱلۡقِيَٰمَةِ
وَيَخۡلُدۡ فِيهِۦ مُهَانًا ﴿٦٩﴾

Excepted, however, shall be they who repent, attain to faith and do righteous deeds, for God will transform their bad deeds into good ones. God is indeed Much-Forgiving, Merciful. (70)

إِلَّا مَن تَابَ وَءَامَنَ وَعَمِلَ عَمَلٗا
صَٰلِحٗا فَأُوْلَٰٓئِكَ يُبَدِّلُ ٱللَّهُ سَيِّـَٔاتِهِمۡ
حَسَنَٰتٖۗ وَكَانَ ٱللَّهُ غَفُورٗا رَّحِيمٗا ﴿٧٠﴾

Whoever repents and does what is right has truly turned to God by [his act of] repentance. (71)

وَمَن تَابَ وَعَمِلَ صَٰلِحٗا فَإِنَّهُۥ يَتُوبُ
إِلَى ٱللَّهِ مَتَابٗا ﴿٧١﴾

[And the true servants of God are] those who never bear witness to what is false, and whenever they pass by [people engaged in] frivolity, pass on with dignity; (72)

وَٱلَّذِينَ لَا يَشۡهَدُونَ ٱلزُّورَ وَإِذَا مَرُّواْ
بِٱللَّغۡوِ مَرُّواْ كِرَامٗا ﴿٧٢﴾

and who, whenever they are reminded of their Lord's signs, do not fall deaf and blind to them; (73)

وَٱلَّذِينَ إِذَا ذُكِّرُواْ بِـَٔايَٰتِ رَبِّهِمۡ
لَمۡ يَخِرُّواْ عَلَيۡهَا صُمّٗا وَعُمۡيَانٗا ﴿٧٣﴾

and who pray: 'Our Lord! Grant us spouses and offspring who will be a joy to our eyes, and cause us to be foremost among the God-fearing.' (74)

وَالَّذِينَ يَقُولُونَ رَبَّنَا هَبْ لَنَا مِنْ
أَزْوَاجِنَا وَذُرِّيَّاتِنَا قُرَّةَ أَعْيُنٍ
وَاجْعَلْنَا لِلْمُتَّقِينَ إِمَامًا ﴿٧٤﴾

These will be rewarded for all their patient endurance [in life] with a high station in heaven, and will be met there with a greeting of welcome and peace, (75)

أُولَٰئِكَ يُجْزَوْنَ الْغُرْفَةَ بِمَا صَبَرُوا
وَيُلَقَّوْنَ فِيهَا تَحِيَّةً وَسَلَامًا ﴿٧٥﴾

and there they shall abide; how goodly an abode and how high a station; (76)

خَالِدِينَ فِيهَا ۚ حَسُنَتْ مُسْتَقَرًّا
وَمُقَامًا ﴿٧٦﴾

Say: 'No weight or value would my Lord attach to you were it not for you calling out [to Him]. You have indeed denied [His message], and in time this [sin] will cleave unto you.' (77)

قُلْ مَا يَعْبَأُ بِكُمْ رَبِّي لَوْلَا دُعَاؤُكُمْ ۖ فَقَدْ
كَذَّبْتُمْ فَسَوْفَ يَكُونُ لِزَامًا ﴿٧٧﴾

Overview

This final passage of the *sūrah* portrays the distinctive features of the true servants of God, the Most Merciful. They appear to be the highest model of humanity that remains after the end of the long battle between true guidance and error, between those who impertinently deny the truth and God's messengers who bring His guidance for humanity. They seem to be the fruit ripening after such a long struggle. They are the ones who bring comfort to the bearers of divine guidance, after they had been met with denial and rejection.

The previous passage recounted the unbelievers' impertinent remark when they said that they did not know the name *Raḥmān*, or the Most Merciful, as belonging to God. In this passage we have a full description of 'the true servants of the Most Merciful' who know Him well and deserve to be described as belonging to Him. The *sūrah* shows their distinctive features as reflected in their behaviour and the way they conduct their lives. They provide a living example of the Muslim community which Islam aims to build, and the type of person it moulds through the implementation of its perfect system. These are the ones who deserve God's care. Mankind generally are too unimportant for God to care about, except for the presence of God's true servants who always turn to Him, praying for His support.

The Distinctive Features of Faith

> *The true servants of the Most Merciful are those who walk gently on earth, and who, whenever the ignorant address them, say: 'Peace.'* (Verse 63)

The true servants' first feature is that they walk gently, with no affectation, pretension, or display of arrogance. Like every movement man makes, walking delivers an expression of one's personality and feelings. A serious, reassured and sound personality demonstrates itself through its gait. A person of this type walks with an air of seriousness and reassurance, reflecting clarity of purpose and strength. To '*walk gently on earth*' does not mean that believers hang their heads down, affecting weakness and lack of support, as understood by some of those who think that by so doing they show themselves to be God-fearing! God's Messenger used to bend forward when he walked. He was the fastest and best walker, with an air of serenity. Abū Hurayrah reports: "I have never seen anyone more handsome than God's Messenger: he looked as if the sun was reflected in his face. And I have never seen anyone who walked faster than God's Messenger. It was as though the earth would shrink for him. [As we walked with him] we would put in our best effort, but he was most relaxed." 'Alī ibn Abī Ṭālib describes:

"When the Prophet walked he bent forward, as though he was walking quickly downhill."

In their serious and dignified approach, and in their attention to serious concerns, God's true servants do not bother themselves with other people's absurdities and stupidities. They do not waste their time or energy in futile arguments with such people. They recognize that engaging in an argument with people who argue for argument's sake is fruitless. Hence, "*whenever the ignorant address them, [they] say: Peace.*" (Verse 63) But this is by no means a sign of weakness or lack of ability. It is simply a dignified approach which does not permit them to waste time and energy over what is unbecoming of the honourable.

Such is their conduct in daytime when they are with other people. At night they reflect their God-fearing nature, as they stand in awe of God and fear His punishment.

> *Who stay up far into the night in adoration of their Lord, prostrating themselves and standing; who pray: 'Our Lord, avert from us the suffering of hell, for the suffering it causes is indeed a dire torment; it is indeed an evil abode and a terrible station.* (Verses 64–66)

The *sūrah* highlights here the two main movements Muslims perform in prayer, namely prostration and standing up. Thus it reflects their action in the depth of the night, when others are fast asleep. Such true servants of God stay up prostrating themselves and standing before their Lord, addressing themselves completely to Him. They are not concerned about not being in bed, because they have something that they enjoy, giving them far more comfort, energy and happiness than sleep can ever give. They are preoccupied with being close to their Lord, addressing Him with all their being. Hence, people go to sleep while they pray standing and prostrating themselves. Other people are concerned with their position on earth while these true servants of God look up to the throne of the Most Merciful.

In their prayers, with all its movements, and all their inner feelings, they are fully conscious of their Lord, fearing to incur His displeasure and so His punishment. Thus they appeal to Him: "*Our Lord, avert from us the suffering of hell, for the suffering it causes is indeed a dire torment; it is indeed an evil abode and a terrible station.*" (Verses 65–66) They have not seen hell or its suffering, but they believe in it. They also visualize it according to its descriptions in the Qur'ān and in the Prophet's statements. Thus their genuine fear of it is the fruit of true faith.

Humbly and most seriously they pray to their Lord to avert their suffering in hell. They do not feel safe simply because they spend part of the night in worship, prostrating themselves and standing in prayer. Their God-fearing sense makes them think little of what they do, feeling always that they fall short of what is needed. Hence, they pray for God's grace and forgiveness so that He spares them the punishment of hell.

This description implies that hell tries to engulf every human being, with its gates open and hands outstretched trying to grab them. God's true servants who stay up far into the night in their devotion fear it and appeal most sincerely to their Lord to spare them from such punishment. As they address their prayer, they shiver with fear: "*for the suffering it causes is indeed a dire torment.*" (Verse 65) It engulfs its victim, not allowing them any room for escape. This is what makes it dire indeed. Moreover, "*it is indeed an evil abode and a terrible station.*" (Verse 66) Could there be a worse station than hell as a place of abode and settlement? How can anyone settle within the fire? How can there be an abode in a place of continuous burning?

Steering Away from Sin

God's true servants lead a balanced life that is exemplary in its seriousness and moderation: "*Whenever they put their money to use, they are neither wasteful nor niggardly, but always maintain a just mean between the two.*" (Verse 67) Balance is the distinctive feature that Islam establishes in the life of the individual and the community. Its achievement is what Islam aims for through educating its followers and through its legal system. Its whole structure is based on balance and moderation.

Although Islam approves private ownership, a Muslim is not free to spend his money without restriction, as is the case in the capitalist system and in communities which do not conduct their lives in accordance with divine law. A Muslim is required to strike a balance between extravagance and miserliness. Both attitudes are bad for the individual, society and for money itself. Indeed, a miser not only deprives himself of the benefits of his money, but also deprives the community of the benefits of keeping money in circulation. Indeed money is meant to provide services for the community. Both extremes of overspending and withholding money produce social and economic imbalance, leading to crises, in addition to their unhealthy effect on people's hearts and ethics.

As Islam regulates this aspect of human life, it begins with the individual, making the adoption of a balanced approach in life a feature of faith. Thus, whenever true servants of God, the Most Merciful, put their money to use, they "*are neither wasteful nor niggardly, but always maintain a just mean between the two.*" (Verse 67)

The next important quality of God's true servants is that they "*never invoke any deity side by side with God, and do not take any human being's life – [the life] which God has willed to be sacred – except for a just cause, and do not commit adultery. Whoever does any of this will face punishment, and on the Day of Resurrection his suffering will be doubled, and he will abide therein in ignominy.*" (Verses 68–69)

To believe in God's oneness is the cornerstone of the Islamic faith. It is the point where clarity, straightforwardness and simplicity of beliefs is separated from ambiguity, confusion and complexity. Needless to say, no proper system of life can be based on the latter.

Similarly, prevention of killing anyone, except for a legitimate reason, is central to the achievement of security in society so that human life is given its rightful value and due respect. Otherwise, life would become like a jungle where no one was safe or able to do constructive work.

Likewise, preventing adultery is basic to the establishment of a clean social life where man rises above naked physical desires, and where he feels that the union of the two sexes has a nobler purpose than the mere satisfaction of desire. Otherwise, life sinks low and men and women become preoccupied with the satisfaction of unrestrained physical desire.

These three qualities distinguish the sound and clean life that is worthy of man from the life of cheap pleasures that reduces man to the rank of an animal. Hence, God mentions these qualities as belonging to His true servants who are the most honourable in His sight. Their outline is followed with a stern warning: "*Whoever does any of this will face punishment.*" (Verse 68) This punishment is outlined in the next verse: "*On the Day of Resurrection his suffering will be doubled, and he will abide therein in ignominy.*" (Verse 69) Thus, it is not merely a double measure of punishment, but ignominy too, which is even worse.

Erasing Sin Through Repentance

But the door remains open for anyone who wishes to save himself from such a fate. This requires repentance, firm belief and good action: "*Excepted, however, shall be they who repent, attain to faith and do righteous deeds.*" (Verse 70) Those who fulfil these three conditions are promised that whatever sin they did prior to their repentance will be changed into good deeds which will be added to their newly earned good actions: "*for God will transform their bad deeds into good ones.*" (Verse 70) This is an aspect of God's bounty that is granted without the person concerned having to do anything to deserve it other than turn away from error and seek refuge with Him: "*God is indeed Much-Forgiving, Merciful.*" (Verse 70)

The door of repentance is always open to admit anyone whose conscience is reawakened and wants to return to the fold. No one is ever turned away from it, no matter who he might be or what sins he might have committed in the past. A *ḥadīth* related by al-Ṭabarānī mentions that Abū Farwah asked the Prophet: "If a man has done all kinds of sin, leaving out nothing, will his repentance be accepted?" The Prophet asked him: "Are you a Muslim?" When he answered in the affirmative, the Prophet said: "Then do what is good and abandon what is evil, and God will change all your past misdeeds into good ones." The man asked: "And even my worst, treacherous ones?" The Prophet said: "Yes." The man glorified God and continued to do so as he went away.

There is a rule for repentance and a condition for its acceptance, which are clearly spelled out: "*Whoever repents and does what is right has truly turned to God by [his act of] repentance.*" (Verse 71) Repentance begins with genuine regret and desisting from bad deeds and is made complete through doing good deeds that prove that it is a serious and genuine repentance. At the same time, good deeds produce a positive sense that favourably compensates for abandoning sin. Sin is an action which, when withdrawn, leaves a vacuum that must be filled with an action in the opposite direction. Otherwise, the feeling of emptiness makes one miss one's old sinful ways. Hence we see here a remarkable feature of the Qur'ānic method of cultivating goodness within the community of believers. It is based on profound knowledge of human nature. Who can know this better than the Creator?

Further Qualities of True Believers

Having completed this interposition of the conditions of repentance, the *sūrah* resumes its outline of the qualities of the true servants of the Most Merciful: "*Those who never bear witness to what is false, and whenever they pass by [people engaged in] frivolity, pass on with dignity.*" (Verse 72) This may be taken literally which means that they never give false testimony, since such an action leads to usurping people's rights and helps injustice. It may also be taken to mean that they do not attend any place or stay with any group where falsehood is said or done. They steer away from such places or company so as not to be party to anything that happens there. This is a more powerful meaning. They also steer away from all frivolity and idle talk: "*Whenever they pass by people engaged in frivolity, pass on with dignity.*" (Verse 72) They remove themselves from participation in any such practice. A believer has more serious preoccupations that leave no time for frivolous and idle pursuits. His mind is full with what his faith requires of him so as to ensure that God's message is delivered to mankind. This is sufficient preoccupation for anyone.

Another of their qualities is that they are quick to remember when a reminder is given to them. Their hearts are open to the understanding of God's signs and revelations: "*And who, whenever they are reminded of their Lord's signs, do not fall deaf and blind to them.*" (Verse 73) The picture drawn here is critical of the idolaters who approach their deities and false beliefs like the deaf and blind, deprived of guidance and light. It shows them in a state of blind fanaticism, while God's true servants are fully aware of the truth in their faith, and in God's signs and revelations. Hence, they accept the faith with open eyes, hearts and minds. They are free of fanaticism. When they show enthusiasm for their faith, it is an enthusiasm based on true knowledge and profound insight.

Finally, these true servants of God are not content with staying up far into the night offering their voluntary worship, prostrating themselves to God, and allowing their other fine qualities to shine. They want something more. What they hope for is that they should have spouses of their type and children who follow in their footsteps, thus bringing them great joy. Not only so, but in this way, those who are classified as God's servants will multiply. They also pray that God will make of them a good example for those who are God-fearing: "And who pray: *Our Lord! Grant us spouses and offspring who will be a joy to our eyes, and cause us to be foremost among the God-fearing.*" (Verse 74)

This is a natural feeling based on a profound sense of faith. It expresses a strong desire to increase the numbers of people who follow divine guidance, and that the first in such increased numbers should be their own offspring and spouses who are the closest to them. Indeed, these are a man's first responsibility. Added to this natural feeling is the believers' hope that they will provide examples of goodness to be followed by those who are keen to earn God's pleasure. There is no element of selfishness or arrogance in such a wish, because all the God-fearing are on the way that God defines.

Destined for the Finest Abode

What reward do God's true servants receive? This outline of their qualities concludes with what they earn:

These will be rewarded for all their patient endurance [in life] with a high station in heaven, and will be met there with a greeting of welcome and peace, and there they shall abide; how goodly an abode and how high a station. (Verses 75–76)

The Arabic text uses the term *al-ghurfah*, which is translated here as 'a high station in heaven'. The term may be taken to mean in this context either heaven, or a special place in heaven. Linguistically speaking it means, 'the room', which is a more honourable place than the reception room where Arabs normally received their guests. True servants are received in this high position with a warm welcome, on account of their patient endurance of whatever they had to put up with in order to maintain their sound qualities. What is implied here is recognition of the strong will-power needed to restrain desire and resist temptation. This is not easy to do without a good degree of endurance that can only be shown by someone who is deservedly mentioned by God in His book, the Qur'ān.

In contrast to hell from which they pray to God to save them, God rewards them with heaven where "*they shall abide; how goodly an abode and how high a station.*" (Verse 76) There they are in the best state, enjoying God's favours and blessings.

With the picture of God's true servants fully drawn, showing them as the cream of humanity, the *sūrah* concludes by stating that mankind are worth very little in God's sight, except for the fact that some of them turn to Him in prayer. As for those who deny Him and His messages, they will be punished. "*Say: No weight or value would my Lord attach to you were it not for you calling out [to Him]. You have indeed denied [His message], and in time this [sin] will cleave unto you.*" (Verse 77)

It is a fitting final statement which is intended to give comfort and reassurance to the Prophet, consoling him for the stiff resistance and impudent remarks he received from his people who persisted with their opposition in order to maintain their false beliefs. What value would they and humanity have, if it had not been for the small group of believers who prayed and appealed to God, as do His true servants? What significance do they have when the earth on which all mankind live is no more than a tiny particle in the great universal expanse? Moreover, man is no more than one of the numerous species that live on earth. Any nation is but one of many that live on earth, and a single generation of one nation is no more than a single page of a great book the number of whose pages is known only to God Almighty.

Despite all this man continues to give himself airs, thinking himself to be of real value. He is so lost in his arrogance that he speaks impertinently about his Creator. In truth, man is weak, powerless and insignificant, except when he establishes his links with God and derives from Him strength and guidance. Only then does he acquire weight on God's scales, to the extent that this becomes greater than that of angels. This is indeed a blessing God bestows on man whom He has honoured and before whom He ordered His angels to bow. The purpose of all this was that man should know his Lord and worship Him alone, for only then does he maintain his qualities for which the angels bow. Otherwise, he is insignificant and valueless.

"*Say: No weight or value would my Lord attach to you were it not for you calling out [to Him].*" (Verse 77) The phraseology here is meant to give support and honour to the Prophet who speaks of his Lord who grants him His protection. What are the unbelievers if they continue to refuse to join God's true servants? They are no more than fuel for hell: "*You have indeed denied [His message], and in time this [sin] will cleave unto you.*" (Verse 77)

Index